# The Thinking Christian

# The Thinking Christian

Twenty-Three Pathways of Awareness

Gene Wesley Marshall

WIPF & STOCK · Eugene, Oregon

THE THINKING CHRISTIAN
Twenty-Three Pathways of Awareness

Wipf & Stock
An Imprint of Wipf and Stock Publishers
199 W. 8th Ave., Suite 3
Eugene, OR 97401

www.wipfandstock.com

PAPERBACK ISBN: 978-1-5326-9522-3
HARDCOVER ISBN: 978-1-5326-9523-0
EBOOK ISBN: 978-1-5326-9524-7

Manufactured in the U.S.A.                                03/19/20

Our ultimate question in this existential situation of dependent freedom is not whether we will choose in accordance with reason or by faith, but whether we will choose with reasoning faithlessness or reasoning faith.

—H. RICHARD NIEBUHR, *CHRIST AND CULTURE*

# Contents

# Acknowledgements

PERHAPS A HUNDRED WRITERS and activists have made significant contributions to this book. I will be mentioning many of their names along the way. Four people, however, I want to mention by name for their direct contributions to this manuscript. Alan Jay Richard, my fellow faculty member of Realistic Living, has read and discussed with me every chapter. These discussions have alerted me not only to mistakes and omissions, but inspired me to further thoughts on most of these topics. Marie Sharp has focused her eagle eye and theological mind on every sentence—found numerous typos, misuses, better wording, and needless paragraphs. Jeffrey W. Robbins has given helpful feedback to many of these chapters. Joyce Marshall, my wife of forty-three years, has sought out, studied, explored, and lived out with me all of these topics. She has indeed led our research on many of these topics. Even if she may not agree totally with all of my conclusions, she has contributed to them. And she has supported me and assisted me with the preparation of this manuscript.

# Introductory Comments

THE THINKING CHRISTIAN IS a big-vision book for Christian clergy and ex-clergy, for Christian laity and ex-laity, and anyone else who might consider being a leader in envisioning and organizing a viable and vital future for Christian practice. It takes poetry to link us to our profound humanity. Here is one of my poems on that matter.

**A Taste of Eternity**

We camp now
in some partial
consciousness.

Tomorrow,
or the next day
or next year
we may move,
if we are fortunate,
into another
more inclusive
partiality.

The everlasting,
the eternal
the final,
the endless,
is not coming.

Our hunger
to see,
to know,
to realize
the whole of allness
will have to chew on this:

more never becomes all,
next never becomes last.

The taste of eternity
allowed our species
is this:
to die to what we have been,
then rise from death
into what we have
never been
before.

Christianity is one, but only one, of the religions that have capti-vated more than a billion people. All religions are part of my story in this book. We live in an interreligious era, but this need not mean that we need to blend all religions into one practice. The vast variety of religious practices, like the vast variety of human languages, is a natural feature. What we need to decrease is our intolerance of practices other than our own. Inflexible, narrow thinking prevents us from learning from others and from improving our own religious practices.

Part One of this book is a brief summary of my philosophy of reli-gion after sixty-eight years of engaging, thinking, and writing about these topics. It includes an overview of these five basic questions:

What is mind?

What is consciousness?

What is truth?

What is profound consciousness?

What is religion?

The key aim of Part One is to share my thinking about why we have religion as a basic part of our social and personal practice, occurring in every age of human history. I do not deny that my thinking about religion is an ongoing quest that will never reach a completion point. Neverthe-less, my thoughtfulness about religion summarized in these five chapters is foundational for my theologizing and organizing a next Christianity that is relevant for this period of time.

Part Two is an overview of Christian theologizing, beginning with the death of classical God-talk and moving toward seeing resurrection as a happening to real humans in every century and in every place. I deal with these questions:

What do we now do with the word "God" and its devotional equivalents?

What is theologizing in a Christian sense?

What is the core problem and the help that Christianity has to offer?

How do we reinterpret for our times the Christian vocabulary and its scriptures?

How do we distinguish the essence of Christianity from its many forms?

My aim in Part Two is to share what theologizing means as an ongoing communal project of thinking within and for the life of Christian practitioners, as well as a gift to the history of the world at large.

Part Three is about the ongoing task of creating a next communal Christian practice that includes both our life together and our ethical activism for the planet and humanity in the twenty-first century. I deal with these questions:

How do we rescue Christianity from its classical cultural containers of patriarchy, hierarchy, imperialism, and ecological neglect?

How might we imagine some fresh, relevant, and useful sociological forms for the practice of a next Christian religion?

How might the Christian "revelation" be best communicated to persons of this century?

How does the Christian "revelation" contribute to the social transformations called for and being met by the ongoing justice movements of this century?

How might the patterns of organization for a next Christian practice look locally, regionally, and globally?

My aim in Part Three is to envision sociological forms and religious practices for a Christianity set lose from its worn-out religious containers—new wineskins for some very old yet still ever new wine.

## THE OTHER IN THE MIDST OF THE THIS

A mentor who has inspired my living and religious thinking is an obscure, but remarkably creative person, Joseph Wesley Mathews. He died in 1977. He probably impacted less than half a million people, but the waves of his impact have continued among the tens of thousands whom he impacted deeply.

Mathews inspired four charts entitled "The Other World in the Midst of This World." Each of these charts consists of sixteen "treks" of metaphorical thinking about states of profound consciousness. The names of these four charts are: "The Land of Mystery," "The River of Consciousness," "The Mountain of Care," and "The Sea of Tranquility." Mathews adapted these four images from ancient Chinese lore, but he expanded on them in his own twentieth-century manner. I have written poems on these four topics, and I share these poems and related commentary in the first four chapters.

The term "Other World" can distort Mathews' meaning if we do not hear the rest of his title: "in the Midst of This World." Indeed, for Mathews there was no "other world" in the sense of the old natural-supernatural dualistic metaphorical system of thinking. Each of these four charts contains clues for describing sixteen states of profound consciousness that may occur in our everyday events of living. The "otherness" of profound consciousness seems "other" to us only because we have become estranged from it. Profound consciousness is our essential humanness.

Contemplative inquiry into profound consciousness is old in the history of humanity. The Upanishads (800 BCE and following) are writings of ancient India that were a turn from a more outward-leaning Vedic thinking toward a more inward, contemplative inquiry. A similar turn toward inwardness can be found in the Prophets of Israel (800 BCE and following).

In both India and the Middle East, reflective civilizations reach back well before 2500 BCE. So we might claim that reflection upon our profound consciousness reaches back before writing—perhaps all the way back to the dawn of the human form of consciousness. We see strong evidence for such awareness in cave paintings 15,000 to 30,000 years old, and in stone art forms older than that. I will be emphasizing much more recent developments in contemplative inquiry into the profound nature of our lives, but I have a longer story in the back of my mind.

I am exploring what it means, has always meant, and will always mean to be profoundly human. I believe that assisting humans in this everlasting quest has been the task of all long-standing religions, at their best. And I am going to define (redefine for many) the word "religion" (that is, "good religion") in terms of our primordial need to access the essence of our humanity and live our lives from that deep place.

# Part One

## Profound Consciousness

In Part One, I begin with the topics of mind, thinking, and consciousness—states of consciousness within the human being, states of consciousness unique to humans, and states of consciousness that humans share with other animals and forms of life. It will be my contention that accessing the most intense layers of human consciousness (our consciousness of being conscious of our profound consciousness) is an experience needed for defining what I mean by "good religion."

This pursuit has to do with ascertaining why we have religion of some sort in virtually every instance of human culture. "Religion" is, of course, being defined in other ways than I will be defining it, and truth of various sorts may be found in many of these other philosophies of religion. I am, however, making a case for my definition.

In addition, we have the problem that religion, being a human creation, has the capacity to be corrupted. In other words, we have the issue of sorting out good from bad religion as well as defining what we ascertain is essential for a definition of "good religion."

I am a practicing Christian and the core aim of this book is to give fresh definition to rediscovering the core revelation of this heritage and thereby updating Christian practice. In Part One, however, I am trying to say something more *universal* about religion, without imposing my Christian experience upon this definition. I can be questioned on this, of course, for I am quite sure that my long study and practice of Christianity is influencing all my thinking. I have, however, studied Hindu heritage and Buddhism to the extent of considering the option of becoming a practicing Buddhist. I have decided that I am a Buddhist-impacted

Christian, rather than a Christian-impacted Buddhist. But I do not wish to impose even that combination on these Part One considerations.

Though my work with religion is surely affected by my various influences, I want to invite the reader to pursue with me in Part One of this book a philosophy of religion that has universal application. I also count this general sense of the social process of religion as an essential prerequisite for defining good theologizing and practice of a Christian sort.

# 1

—

# Out of Your Mind

## *What Is Mind?*

MARK WATTS GATHERED TOGETHER some of his father Alan Watt's best talks, and put them together in a book entitled *Out of Your Mind*.[1] Whether or not you think being "out of your mind" is a good thing or not, my explorations in this chapter are intended to provide some clarity on the concept of "mind" and on being "out of your mind." First of all, being "out of your mind" means a simple recognition that we are living in a *Land of Mystery* that our minds cannot comprehend.

> We live in a Land of Mystery.
> We know nothing about it.
> We don't know where we have come from.
> We don't know where we are going.
> We don't know where we are.
> We are newborn babes.
> We have never been here before.
> We have never seen this before.
> We will never see it again.
> This moment is fresh,
> Unexpected,
> Surprising.
> As this moment moves into the past,
> It cannot be fully remembered.
> All memory is a creation of our minds.
> And our minds cannot fathom the Land of Mystery,

1. Watts, *Out of Your Mind*.

much less remember it.
We experience Mystery Now
And only Now.
Any previous Now is gone forever.
Any yet-to-be Now is not yet born.
We live Now,
only Now,
in a Land of Mystery.

## BEYOND CAUSE-AND-EFFECT THINKING

"Cause and effect" is an interpretation of this Land of Mystery Reality that has always been part of the life of being human. Even in that gut-level form of image-using intelligence that we share with dogs and other animals, we have a pre-intellectual form of cause-and-effect thinking. Trial-and-error thinking assumes the cause-and-effect mode of interpretation. But it has been fairly recent in human history that we have made the cause-and-effect interpretation of Reality the be-all for what Reality with capital "R" essentially is. "Reality," however, in its profound meaning points to a Land of Mystery or Wonder that is beyond our cause-and-effect interpretations.

In other words, realizing that we live in a Land of Mystery includes demoting our cause-and-effects knowledge to what it essentially is—a human form of mental interpretation along with probability interpretations and choice interpretations. Our cause-and-effects interpretation is very useful for understanding much about the past and for making useful predictions for the future. Our lives would be much impoverished without this mode of interpretation of our everyday events. But the Land of Mystery "trumps" cause and effect, so to speak.

Another very popular mode of interpretation of our everyday events is "accident" or "probability." We also call this "chance." "Life," we might say, "is one big gamble." We may ask, "What is the chance of that happening?" When playing a game of dice or cards, we may do some sophisticated thinking about the probability of this or that happening. "Chance" is another mode of interpretation of reality, quite different from cause-and-effect. Chance interpretation is another limited view of this inclusive Land of Mystery.

When Albert Einstein said that he did not believe that "God plays dice with the cosmos," he was stating his preference for the cause-and-effect mode of interpretation. He was even saying that our so-called chance happenings could finally be explained by cause-and-effect thinking. And "God" in his poetry was simply a word for Reality in its always-surprising presence. Physics, however, has proceeded using both *cause* and *chance* modes of interpretation, and physicists have never found a way to unite these two modes into one final theory of physics. In spite of all the effort to find a "theory of everything," our various "string theories" have not yet found grounding in experimental fact.

And on top of that strange awareness, there is yet a third mode of re-alty interpretation that cannot be reduced to either or both of these other two modes of interpretation. In addition to *cause* and *chance, choice* is a mode of interpretation that lies behind our asking questions like, "Why did you do this instead of that?" We assume that even cats can choose whether to jump up on the table or not. We assume that human history can be shifted or promoted by human-made *choices* that are not *caused* and are not simply *probable*, but are freely *chosen*, using a capacity of our existence that we call "freedom." Attempts have been made by some philosophizing minds to reduce the experience of choosing to something that is determined by cause and effect. Such philosophizing does not ac-knowledge that cause-and-effect knowledge is just one of three human modes of thinking about that Land of Mystery we often call "Reality."

A fully comprehensive philosophy of truth can best begin with the axiom that there are at least three modes of human interpretation, no one of which can produce an overall grasp of Reality with a capital "R"—that is, mind cannot grasp that Mysterious Reality that confronts humans in personal and historical events. This Reality both inspires and judges the veracity of each "approximation of reality" that we humans have created with the power of our *freedom*.

Living in the Land of Mystery means seeing each event in our lives as a dialogue of our consciousness with this Reality that is totally mysteri-ous to us—an unknown-ness that never becomes known through our cause-and-effect mode of knowing or through our probability mode of knowing. Our freedom-of-choice mode of thinking is itself an admis-sion that Reality includes this enigma of choosing that is part of being in a Land of Mystery. The *choice* mode of interpretation means noticing that an act of choosing by human consciousness is not caused, and that choosing is not an accident in some probability means of interpretation. "Choice" means an action out of *nothing*—nothing except the enigma or mystery of *freedom* itself given with this Land of Mystery.

## WHAT IS MIND?

The word "mind" is a contemplative reference, not a scientific reference. "Brain" and/or "nervous system" are the scientific terms best suited for indicating our outward study of what we inwardly experience as "mind." We commonly assume that these internal experiences that we call "mind" are related to the external observations of brain cells, nerves, various chemical interactions, electrical signals, and brain waves that we can view externally or scientifically. Great efforts have been made to correlate the truths of our inward contemplations with the truths of our outward observations. We do typically assume one Reality that we attempt to understand from these two quite different angles of human perception.

Some of us have contemplated this matter deeply enough to notice that "inward" and "outward" are simply concepts of our mind used to distinguish between contemplations looking within and observations looking without. We may also have noticed that inward and outward are valid organizations of our thinking about this one overall, ongoing process of happenings. Most of us assume that inward and outward are not two different worlds of Reality, but two ways that our consciousness has for viewing the same ongoing Overall-ness. In other words, outward and inward are two types of rational understanding, rather than two different realities.

Yet this outward and inward organizations of our thinking (scientific research and contemplative inquiry) are essential for understanding the essence of human thinking. Thinking must divide the one realm of Reality into these two realms of thought. This duality in the nature of thinking is another witness that Reality is a Land of Mystery. I will say more on that topic in chapter 3. Just as we are clear that our hearing and our seeing are contacts with One Reality not two, so it is that our scientific research and our contemplative inquiry are two approaches to One Reality.

In our daily living we commonly meld together the truth-content of our outward experiences with the truth-content of our inner experiences into a patchwork of unified stories and predictive patterns that tend to serve our practical needs. Yet if we dare to look closer, we can notice that when we discipline our consciousness to think scientifically, we are focusing only on outward observations—the "objective facts" as we commonly call the "tests" of truth for our scientific thinking. And if we do mediation or listen to music or contemplate, or in other ways, focus on our inward observations of inner phenomena, we test the veracity of this contemplative thinking with what we can notice with our consciousness about our inner life of conscious contents.

## CONTEMPLATIVE INQUIRY

In the following paragraphs, I am asking each of us to look inwardly (i.e., do some contemplative inquiry) and notice that each of us has one consciousness that uses the tools of one mind to create two minds of truth that do not rationally match. My contemplative inquiries lead me to understand that "mind" and "consciousness" can refer to different processes. It is consciousness, not the mind, that is the thinker and the doer. Mind is a tool for consciousness to think with about the inward and outward perspectives on the Reality in which we dwell. Yes, we see Reality through the concepts of our mind, but it is consciousness that has created these concepts and that uses them to organize what is seen by consciousness.

These descriptions of the processes of mind and the processes of consciousness do not imply that we are drops of consciousness trapped in a material body. Consciousness is a temporal dynamic of our living body, but consciousness is a non-mental, enigmatic process that is relating us to a mysterious Overall-ness—a Land of Mystery within which consciousness is one aspect of that larger mysteriousness.

There is no need to imply the presence of a Divine Mind or Absolute Mind to which our finite minds have some sort of access. A human's inner life can be seen as a temporal consciousness using limited mental capacities to develop approximate patterns of truth sufficient for us to survive, thrive, and live our lives. The mind is glorious, but not infinite. It is just flesh-and-blood living cells with lightning-fast interactions being used by an enigmatic consciousness to form environmental and inner awareness that can make plans for future action. These plans are our own temporal creations; they are not to be confused with the Land of Mystery of which mind and consciousness are enigmatic parts.

Our inward awareness is not what we can call "objective facts," but *subjective experiences* of touch, taste, smell, hearing, sight, and other sensory impressions. We also have subjective experiences of what we call body motions, pains, pleasures, emotions, thoughts—inward pictures, strings of words, arrangements of meaning, meaningless gibberish, musical tunes, art memories, passionate beliefs, frames of reference. All these inner elements arise, perhaps grab us, perhaps drift by and pass from awareness. Perhaps we grab onto some of these mental elements and work with them, change them, laugh at them, or whatever.

With an inwardly disciplined consciousness we can "watch" all these inner impressions take place. If we pay very close attention we can notice the noticer—that enigmatic consciousness that does the noticing. This noticer is also the thinker who latches onto the symbol-providing mind and thinks something through to programs of action. This noticer who can notice the noticing defines what I am pointing to with the word "consciousness." This noticer is also the builder of our patterns of "truth." By "truth" I mean the rational order built by consciousness using our mental capacities.

So again, what is mind? A careful focus on our inward experiences can notice that the operations of the mind are not consciousness itself, but a tool of consciousness. It is somewhat like being a person using a computer—although our human mental ability is many times more intricate than a computer. "Mind" is our inner experience of part of our wondrous biological brain. With our inward look we don't see brain cells or energy waves. We see thinking, mathematics, and art-creating capacities being used by our "consciousness."

I will spend the next chapter looking more deeply at what I want to point to with the word "consciousness." And I will look more deeply at "mind" in chapter 3. For now I will simply say that "consciousness" is an enigmatic depth of our being about which we are clearly at a loss for words. "Mind," as we use that term to reference our inward thoughtfulness, is a capacity for words and other symbol-using expressions. We use these mental gifts of our biology to enjoy, play, organize, and conduct our lives. Consciousness uses our mind to build and change our patterns of truth and to carry out our projects of living.

## OUT OF YOUR MIND

So what does it mean to be "out of your mind"? It does not mean being out of your biological body. It does not mean being out of your always-active brain/mind dynamics—our always-busy image-making, symbol-using thinking processes. Being "out of your mind" does not mean being out of the biological truth of having a brain and a nervous system for doing the human form of thinking. Nor does it mean being out of our feelings or out of our sensations. All these forms of activity keep functioning, and they never cease functioning until our death. Nevertheless, being "out of your mind" is a state of awareness that consciousness can notice.

## The Perpetual Infant

In the book *Out of Your Mind*, cited at the beginning of this chapter, Alan Watts suggests the following clue to what it means to be "out of your mind." Watts cites the life of an infant before the learning of words.[2] The infant has all sorts of impressions coming in, and they are fascinating, wondrous, perhaps frightening, but the infant is open to them. She has no screens of rational meaning with which to censor or interpret these impressions. She is "out of her mind" in the sense that she is not yet filled up her memory with mental content—her scientific content, her contemplative content, and whatever other mental content she may someday have.

The infant does not yet realize that her distinguishable experiences have names. Her human society has not yet stimulated that symbol-using potential to begin operation in her already-evolved, well-prepared biology.

For we adult humans, the process of language goes on constantly, along with mathematics, music, dance, story, paintings, and other forms of symbol-using expression. The infant is not yet using symbols to stand for experiences. She is in that sense "out of her mind." There is a wonderful story from the childhood life of Helen Keller (who since infancy was totally blind and deaf). The word "water" was spelled out in one hand while feeling water pouring over the other. Helen later described what dawned on her in that experience was "learning that everything has a name." More words were learned that same day. My point here is that Helen had become six years old without yet activating her naming potential. She was still "out of her mind," somewhat like an infant.

So what does it mean for an adult who has constructed all sorts of mental meaning structures to be "out of your mind"? It does not mean being without structures of thought, meaning, and reason. It does not mean becoming an infant. It can only mean recovering the openness to unformed reality that the infant naturally had. Appropriating this openness in the midst of also being an adult with all those rational patterns in operation means accessing a rare sort of detachment from the presence of these useful mental forms that I am calling "symbols." "Out of your mind" means being unimpeded by mental screens from "seeing" beyond

2. Watts, *Out of Your Mind*, 63.

those screens. Is this possible? Many philosophers and religious innovators in every age on every continent bear witness that this awareness is
possible. I concur.

## OUT OF YOUR SOCIAL ROLES

Being out of our minds includes being out our social roles. This does not
mean that we do not play social roles or that these roles are unimportant.
Nevertheless, all social roles are a sort of game. Playing a social role is like
being in a play or drama for which we have been assigned a role to play.
The role is not *you*. *You* are taking on this role, like playing a game.

For example, I have spent much of my life playing the role of teacher.
It is tempting to say "I am a teacher." But I play many roles. I am not any
of these roles. I simply play them. If I think I am this role of teacher, I may
lack spontaneity in the way I teach.

However, when I am clear that teaching is only a role, only a game,
then I *play* the role. I interact with people. I am spontaneous. I am unpre-
dictable. I am ready to do many different things. It is just a game. Games
are played. Now I may have skills for this game. I may have invented
rules for my game of teaching. Indeed, I have had many different sets of
rules—different whole views of how to play this game. I am still creating
new views, new rules. But all these views and rules are just made up by
me, or copied from others. I am creating this game to play. I play this
part. Teaching is just a game I play. I don't need to be good at it, even
though I am never without what "good at it" means for me. "Good at it" is
just a part of this particular game. "Bad at it," according to my own rules,
is also something I do, but it is just a game, just a role I play in the grand
drama of my life. Also, I don't have to play teacher in every situation. I
am not this role.

All my roles are just a game—husband, father, lover, dishwasher,
floor sweeper, writer, political organizer, or religious practitioner. I had
to give up my role as basketball player when it got too dangerous for
my advanced age. But I still play weight lifter, Tai Chi class member, TV
watcher, and others.

All these games have a degree of seriousness. But none of them have
the seriousness of being who I am. I can *play* these games with a degree
of rest and detachment. I don't have to win. I don't have to lose. I can just

play the games. If I play roles in life as "being me," that means that I am not "out of my mind."

## OUT OF YOUR BELIEFS

Being out of our minds includes being out of our beliefs. Beliefs are not just stray ideas moving through our head. Beliefs are programs of living for which there is an element of commitment. Being out of your mind includes being loose from these commitments to statements of rational content or programs of action. We certainly do commit to statements of truth and to programs of action. But being out of our beliefs means being open to modifications of our beliefs and programs of action. It may mean abandoning specific beliefs and programs of action. In other words, there are no beliefs or programs of action that have dropped into our lives from an Absolute Somewhere. We have chosen these beliefs and programs. They have not chosen us. It can seem that our beliefs and programs have chosen us, when we are attempting to find beliefs and programs of action that give manifestation to our profound humanness. But our created manifestations of our permanent depths are never permanent.

Our so-called religious beliefs may be patterns of symbols that participate in our profound consciousness of that Land of Mystery, but each of these religious symbols are temporal products of a human imagination. In later chapters I will explore more deeply how such symbols can point beyond themselves, indeed beyond rationality as a whole, to Land of Mystery–type experiences.

## OUT OF YOUR SELF

Being out of our minds also includes the most profound detachment of all—detachment from "who we think we are." I am speaking of the very personal realization that our self-image is made of thoughts and words and imagery that we ourselves (with help from our culture) have put together. What a shock this can be to notice that we actually do not know who we are—that no self-image we hold, or will ever hold, will be able to contain the wondrous truth of our actual being. The self-image (or "ego" as we sometimes call it) does not exist as something to be found somewhere in our body or in our psychological dynamics. The ego is only a mind game—a made-up story, a picture, a mental form put together out of a selection of inward and outward noticings plus whatever exaggerations, underestimations, and outright lies we have chosen to include in that picture. The ego is a self-created fiction that may have some uses in navigating our lives, but this self-image needs no defense from us, for it is not who we are. Indeed, it has no substantial verity.

I am always a mystery to be further discovered. I am indeed a mysterious "Atman" embedded entirely in the overall "Brahman" of total Mystery. In other words, both my essential being and the That-ness to which I am inseparably related are entirely beyond my comprehension. These insights are in accord with the ancient contemplative geniuses of Sub-Asia. These insights are also present in Judaism, Christianity, and Islam, when these Middle East–originated religions are deeply understood.

"Out of our mind" also means noticing the limitations in everything we think about the external world of which we are likewise only somewhat conscious. Words never hold Reality as a whole. Our worded or artistically expressed thoughts always exclude more than they include. In every case, our rationally constructed sense of reality is not the Whole Reality that is coming at us, rising in us, surrounding us, sustaining us, affirming us, showing us our ignorance, and blessing us with partial knowledge.

Reality is always immensely more than (and is surprisingly different from) the approximations of reality we have constructed for our practical survival and self-affirmation needs. To be "out of our minds" is to be awakened in a vivid and personal way to this grim, but liberating, truth. "Out of your mind" is a welcome back to the infant you in the midst of your complicated entanglements that you have made of your life so far through your fragmentary efforts to understand the world, who you are, or what you need to do or not do. "Out of your mind" opens you to experiences of your real past, present, and future.

## BEING "OUT OF YOUR MIND" IS NORMAL

Being "out of your mind" makes room for a fuller coming forth of your emotionality, your image-using imagination, your sensory pleasure/pain vividness, and your drive to survive. Also, being "out of your mind" opens the vast space of your consciousness into intensities of awareness that I am calling "profound consciousness." And most surprising of all, being "out of your mind" enriches the accuracy and creativity of your mental consciousness—that capacity that employs symbol-using intelligence to think about everything. Opening to being "out of your mind" is opening to a truth about your existence that *intensifies everything* in your living. In the following chapters, I will explore further all of these enigmas of this Land of Mystery.

## 2

---

# Seven Swirls of Consciousness

## *What Is Consciousness?*

IN OUR TYPICAL CONVERSATIONS we tend to associate consciousness with intellectual intelligence. In addition we have an emotional intelligence, as do all the mammals. We also experience a gut-level intelligence, as do the alligators snakes and frogs. We often use the word "instinct" to point to these more primitive levels of consciousness. We also have an intense awareness that reaches beyond language, mathematic, and the various forms of art. We often use the word "intuition" to point to these deep matters.

So what is consciousness? Consciousness is an enigma—a mystery as huge as the cosmos as a whole. How can a choice of consciousness lift my arm, wiggle my fingers, think my next thought? We simply do not know. But we can look within ourselves and describe what we see there that we can call "consciousness." Here is a set of observations with which to begin: Consciousness can (1) *take in* aspects of Reality, (2) *let be* aspects of Reality, and then (3) *put forth choices* that bend the course of aspects of Reality. Common words for those three processes of consciousness are "knowing," "being," and "doing." I also like these three terms: "attention," "embodiment," and "intention."

Words that refer to consciousness are among the most slippery words of all. This is especially true for words that point to the intense forms of consciousness that are foundational for understanding religion. Following is a poem I have written to awaken awareness of these deeper experiences of being humanly conscious.

Within this Land of Mystery
flows a River of Consciousness—
a flow of attention and freedom.
Consciousness is an enigma in this Land of Mystery.
Consciousness flows through body and mind like a river—
a moisture in the desert of things.
Consciousness is not our pain, pleasure, or rest;
not our desire, emotion, stillness, or passion.
These are like the rocks in the River of Consciousness
Consciousness is a flow through the body and with the body.
Consciousness is an alertness that is also
a freedom to intend and a will to do.
The mind is a tool of consciousness,
providing consciousness with the ability
to reflect upon itself.
But consciousness cannot be contained
within the images and symbols of the mind.
It is an enigma that mind
cannot comprehend—even noticing consciousness
is an act of consciousness using the mind and
flowing like a River in the Land of Mystery.

We can pay attention or not pay attention to selected matters outside or inside our bodies. Paying attention is an aspect of what I am pointing to with the word "consciousness." As I am defining the word "consciousness," it also points to the freedom or capacity for intending that I notice within my power to alter the course of events to a limited degree. Lifting or not lifting my arm is a choice of consciousness. So, for the following study, let us write down in our memory that "consciousness" means at least these two things: (1) *attentionality* or paying attention, and (2) *intentionality* or making choices. A third aspect of consciousness supports these two; let's call it *presence*.

Part of what we know about consciousness derives from watching other living beings act and communicate with one another and with us. Those beings appear to make choices and pay attention. Is my cat conscious, along with all the other mammals I know? I vote yes. Is the turtle crossing my path conscious? I vote yes. What about the grasshopper that moves to the opposite side of a stem to hide from my presence? I vote yes. What about the amoeba that I can view in a microscope? The amoeba seems to make decisions to move from danger and move toward food. A rock does not do this. An amoeba does. Does the amoeba know it does this? Such awareness we need not assume for the amoeba. We say that the amoeba has an "instinct" to survive. Let us view this so-called instinct as an elemental level of consciousness.

Even though we don't have an inside look at the consciousness of another species or even of the consciousness of another human being, we are capable of very powerful inferences from the outward data arriving through our senses. We can guess yes about consciousness being a factor to some degree in all living animals. Consciousness seems more doubtful in a tree or in plants generally. But if we omit bark and wood and consider only leaves and other living parts, we do see tree leaves turning toward the sun. Some plants turn with the sun on a daily basis. Plants appear to "know" how to do this. Unlike a rock, they have some sort of "instinct" to survive and grow. Is this instinct of a tree a form of sentience or consciousness? We humans also have this "instinct" to survive; we share that capacity with a tree. If we say that the instinct to survive is a level of consciousness, then we are saying that we share this level of consciousness with a tree. Such a definition of the word "consciousness" means consciousness is indeed an enigmatic reality in which all living forms participate to some degree.

Let us at least tarry for the moment with the notion that the enigmatic presence we call "consciousness" is present wherever or whenever choices are being made, directions are tried, trial and error takes place. This also means that consciousness is something that evolves—as well as something that is a factor in the process of evolution, along with chance and adaptation to environment. For example, a similar gene pool of mammalian grazers evolved into both bison and horses. Thomas Berry joked that horses became horses through a love of galloping and that the bison became bison through a love of butting. Both choices worked for their survival against the wolves and big cats. Did those pre-horses know what they were choosing? No, and humans also make choices without knowledge of the consequences. The choosing of living beings is a guessing game. As new species become more conscious, those creatures become better at guessing.

Humans have become so conscious that we can even give shape to the frames and quality of our own consciousness. This ability often results in inventing patterns of consciousness about "reality" that are actually believed falsifications leading to consequences detrimental to both survival and happiness. I will say more about this malfunction in later chapters.

## CONSCIOUSNESS AND MIND

"Mind" is closely related to "consciousness" in the following way: the word "mind" is often used, and is best used, to point to the interior experience of consciously viewing from the inside the functioning of what we outwardly view and call our "brain" and "nervous system." "Brain" and "nervous system" are the most appropriate words we use to point to what we can scientifically observe or medically observe as parts of the human body. "Brain" we view as an objective fact. We speak of a "brain surgeon," not a "mind surgeon." Scientifically we observe brain cells, brain waves, nerves, eyes, ears. Inwardly we experience sights, sounds, ideas, logic, theories. And inwardly we experience "mind," as I am going to use that word.

So how is our interiorly experienced "mind" related to our interiorly experienced "consciousness"? However closely related these two aspect of our lives may be, I am going to insist on using the word "conscious-ness" to point to a different set of interior functions than I am pointing to with the word "mind." I am going to reject such language as "con-scious mind" in favor of the phases like "consciousness using the mind" or "mind-enhancing consciousness." Clearly the turtle has a brain, and we can assume a turtle consciousness using an interior mind. The human mind enjoys mental capacities that enhance human consciousness to do greater feats than the turtle. The turtle's life is wondrous compared with anything a human can build. But the human capacities for thought and action are wondrous in areas unimaginable for reptilian life. Some sort of evolutionary leaps have happened in both mammalian and human consciousness.

I am assuming that both the consciousness of the turtle and the consciousness of the human can be distinguished from the brain/mind of the turtle or the brain/mind of the human. Mind is not conscious-ness and consciousness is not mind. This will be a core axiom in this book, and I am intent on spell it out in this second chapter. Of course the biological brain supports consciousness, but when we consciously explore consciousness with our contemplative inquiry, we find it possible to distinguish mind from consciousness.

I am defining "consciousness" as the knower and the doer that uses the "mind" (the mental capacities of the brain and nervous system) to move my arm or think my thoughts. I view consciousness as composed of three dynamics: (1) *taking in* or *attentionality*, (2) *being* or *presence*, and (3) *putting forth* or *intentionality*.

In order to further examine this enigmatic dynamic I am pointing to with the word "consciousness," I am going to reflect upon some poetry from ancient India about seven swirls of consciousness located at seven sites along the spine to the top of the head. These seven "chakras," as they are called, correspond to what I have come to understand scientifically about the evolution of life on planet Earth and what I have come to understand from contemporary philosophy about the image-using and symbol-using mental capacities. In other words, I am using the chakras as a poetic frame for talking about our interior experiences of being conscious. I will also be referencing other life forms in the evolution of life on this planet.

7. Awakenment

6. Third Eye

5. Symbolization

4. Emotion

3. Imagination

2. Sensuality

1. Survival

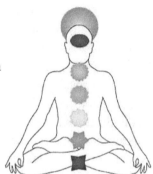

In my description of these seven swirls of consciousness, I am going to use three sources of "wisdom": (1) the ancient poetry of India describing these swirls, (2) evolutionary science, and (3) some contemporary philosophy on the essence of art, language, and mathematics and how these skills, present in humans, are only one of these seven layers of our human consciousness.

With regard to a philosophy of art and language, I am indebted to a groundbreaking book by Susanne K. Langer entitled *Philosophy in a New Key*.[1] She describes how art forms like music, painting, sculpture, and dance are modes of mental expression alongside language and mathematics. Both language and the arts (including the linguistic arts like poetry, story, and drama) are modes of employing a symbol-using mind

---

1. Langer, *Philosophy in a New Key*. See chapters 8 and 9.

that is highly developed in the human species (chakra 5) but barely, if at all, present in a few other now-existing mammals.

Following are my twenty-first-century reflections on this chakra model of consciousness. Many other uses and understands of this ancient poetry exist. This is just my own poetry—my own contemplative inquiry into my own human experiences of consciousness.

## Chakra 1—Survival

The first of these nodes of consciousness is located at the base of the human spine, and deals with a dynamic of aliveness that we share with the earliest forms of life. Aliveness on this planet began with very simple enclosures of life. We humans share this survival impulse of consciousness with these simple cells.

Much later a more complex single-cell life evolved that contained within its enclosure millions of these first simple cells. These complex single cells evolved at least these three ways of energizing their aliveness: sunshine, oxygen, and decaying biological matter. The decay type of single-celled energizers are ancestors to the multicellular forms we recognize as mushrooms and other fungi.

The sunshine-energized single-celled life evolved into multicellular forms of life that we call "plants" and those magnificent "trees." These sunshine forms of aliveness used solar power to break down $CO^2$ and $H^2O$ into carbon, hydrogen, and oxygen—keeping the carbon and hydrogen and releasing the oxygen as a waste product. The wood of trees is mostly carbon taken from the air.

Oxygen was then used by those single cells that are the ancestors of the multicellular forms of life we call "animals." All the cells in our body are descendants of these oxygen-using single-celled beings. Clearly, the amoeba is not a rock or a machine. It is a living and quite mysterious mode of functioning that we may never fully understand. It has a muscle-like skin that can move this tiny being around. It can sense danger and move away, and sense food and move toward it. That skin is its mind as well as its sense organs. These dynamics are elemental characteristics of all animal life. We human animals can identify more easily with the life of an amoeba than we can with a mushroom or a tree. Nevertheless, the mushroom and tree share with us this survival characteristic of consciousness that the chakra model of consciousness is pointing to with the chakra-1 level of consciousness.

It is now being scientifically explored how a forest of trees communicate with one another both through their root contacts and through using chemical means through the air. However that may be, I am defining the word "consciousness" to include this striving to remaining alive that we find in a tree, an amoeba, and a human. In other words, I am willing to view trees as my fellow creatures in this chakra-1 regard.

With this definition of consciousness, aliveness and consciousness become corresponding concepts. Of course, consciousness in a human being includes a level of awareness that has not evolved in an amoeba or tree. I am not projecting the human form of conscious on the amoeba. Rather, I am finding in myself elements of consciousness that I share with the amoeba, and even with a tree.

An amoeba is not conscious of being conscious as we humans clearly are. It is we, not the amoeba, who use the word "consciousness" and take interest in studying this topic. It is we, not the amoeba, who have the facility of words and who consciously know that we were born and that we will die. And it is we who can guess that every cell in our bodies has an amoeba-like level of consciousness. A living cell seeks to survive—to maintain its aliveness. This passion or drive to survive is well developed in the whole human organism and all its parts. We can count on all this rudimentary consciousness to keep us going, with or without our intellectual or intuitive awareness of this elemental chakra 1 level of consciousness.

The chakra-1 level of consciousness can function quickly on our behalf, before we even have time to think about a given danger to our survival. Also, when we are using our more expanded layers of consciousness in choosing to risk our lives for something, we find that we have to strive with our chakra-1 survival instincts as well as with those forces or enemies that may harm us.

## Chakra 2—Sensation

The second of these nodes of consciousness is located in the lower pelvic cage. It is characterized as a drive to avoid pain and find pleasure or to find rest from both pain and pleasure. These sensations come into our consciousness from both our interior environment and our exterior environment. We might speak about this level of consciousness as "sensory awareness," for we humans are aware beings who are capable of using our enlarged consciousness to notice our sensations and how they are different from our thoughts and emotions.

The amoeba does not have our awareness, in thoughts or emotions, but it may have a rudimentary alertness to sensations of pain and pleasure—more than a tree. So, let us guess that chakra 2 consciousness became fully developed in multicellular animal life. It is clear that even the simplest multicellular animal (a worm for instance) has need of chakra 2 awareness. Animal life could not manage its survival without the use of its sensations of the environment and the interior sensations of pain, pleasure, and rest. We humans share in this deep need of our sensations, and for our ever-deepening human awareness of our sensations. Sensations enhance the realism of our overall living.

We humans share with all multicellular animal life a pleasure drive for sex. And this craving for pleasure may sometimes conflict with our drive for individual survival. I watched a documentary movie that included two male bears fighting to mate with a female bear. These two male bears were willing to risk their lives for this opportunity. Chakra 2 is about both some extremely subtle sensations of sight, hearing, and taste and some strong propulsion to live life as fully as possible. This swirl of consciousness can be characterized as a drive for optimal aliveness as seen in the sex lives of insects, alligators, and cats, as well as humans.

## Chakra 3—Imagination

The third of these nodes of consciousness is located about two inches below the rib cage in an area that has come to be called the "solar plexus." All seven chakras can be imaged as located in the spinal column, but each chakra is also characterized as a swirl of consciousness present throughout that vicinity of organs, nerves, and muscles. This third swirl of consciousness might be characterized as an image-driven determination. Its quality is a strength of imagination that has evolved in all animal life.

By "image" I mean a multisensory rerun that has been recorded and stored in the brain's recall system. Each significant moment of an animal's experience of sights, sounds, smells, tastes, touches, and other sensations can be accessible to memory as needed by the temporal choosing animal to interpret current sets of multisensory impacts. This image-using animal memory is composed of stored mental images that can be evoked by the environment. Animals then use signs to communicate with other animals. This complex mode of intelligence enables the animal to know the environment more descriptively and respond more usefully. This chakra 3 gift of consciousness has made complex multicellular animal life possible.

This chakra 3 level of intelligence does not include art or language or mathematics. These symbol-using modes of intelligence do not arise until the evolution of chakra 5 in the human species. No other now living species operates with this human level of consciousness. Nevertheless, it is amazing what animals can do with their pre-symbol-using mode of mental operation. A dog running to join his teeth on a curving frisbee in mid-flight is an example of the power of the image-using form of intelligence.

We can view this imagination-enabled swirl of consciousness in our own bodies. We can notice it doing amazing feats without using our chakra 5 capacities for symbol-using thinking. Here is an example from the wisdom of the baseball player and philosopher Yogi Berra: "When you are batting, don't think, just bat." As I understand this, it means just watch the sensory images coming into your eyes about how fast that ball is coming at you, how it may be curving or not, and let your body begin muscle movements accordingly. You might want to think about this pitcher while you are in the batting circle, but at the plate just be an image-using animal. No symbol-using human thinking is useful.

Here us another example of this fast acting chakra 3 intelligence operating better than our slower moving chakra 5 intelligence. If a stick is perceived by our consciousness to be a snake, our alertness occurs and appropriate action begins before any sort of chakra 5 thought has time enough to become the focus of our consciousness. One day, as I was watering a plant on my porch, a creature leaped out of the pot and raced across the porch. It was only a harmless lizard, but my heart was beating fast and my preparations for flight or fight were in operation before I noticed with my chakra-5 mind what it was.

We humans share this chakra 3–type intelligence with a grasshopper. In my garden I have noticed that a grasshopper can take in my presence and move to the opposite side of the stem that he or she is occupying. A charka 3-type capacity has evolved in insect life, and likewise in primitive worms long before that.

Chakra 3 image-using mental capacity fosters a strong form of determination. We can watch this aggressiveness in an alligator, dog, or cat going for what that animal "figures" will promote its whole organism's welfare, pleasure, or purposes. This gut-level, solar-plexus, imagination-enhanced determination is also a factor that is added to the drives of chakra 1 (survival) and the drives of chakra 2 (pleasure, pain, rest, and the propagation of a species). Humans share with all animal life this chakra 3 quality of consciousness.

## Chakra 4—Emotion

According to the Chakra poetry, the fourth of these nodes of consciousness is located about two inches below where the collar bones join, in the center of the chest in the heart and lungs region. It is referred to as the "heart chakra," but its essence is not about pumping blood, but about the emotional life we refer to with poetry, like heartbreak, heartache, sweetheart, and emotional bonds of all kinds. With such emotional intelligence, mammalian life made a large evolutionary leap beyond the reptiles. Mammals possess a capacity for bonding with their young, with other members of their species, and even with other species—like, for example, humans. Most humans have enjoyed such bonding with dogs, cats, horses, and even porpoises and other water mammals. This emotional force is not strongly developed in reptiles or fish. We do not enjoy emotional responses from our pet snakes or turtles. Primates and humans are strong inheritors of this mammalian emotionality and its interpersonal bonding capacities.

So what are emotions? Emotions are something more than image reruns—though multisensory images are prominently used to express these emotions in both waking and sleeping experiences. Our gifts of emotionality come into play as feeling clues to the living relationships between an animal's consciousness and the environment as understood by the animal that is feeling emotional.

Affection, sadness, peace, longing, and much more characterize this powerful development in animal consciousness. The heart chakra is also famous for its characteristic of bonding and empathy. These bonds of deep attraction when denied are experienced as losses with emotional feelings of sadness. When we encounter rejections, our bonds of deep love can become feelings of deep resentment. All these emotional states can be viewed as operations of a level of consciousness using the feeling capacities of the body to make our way through the complexities and challenges of living. We can trust that our emotions are telling us truths about our living that we need to know. We are gifted with an emotional intelligence that is a strong ally with our other forms of intelligence. We can also trust that our emotions are not permanent states, but passing experiences that come into play, endure a while, and then go away like all temporal things.

## Chakra 5—Symbolization

The fifth of these seven nodes of consciousness is located in the throat area. Speech and art communication characterize this whirl of consciousness. Language using and other symbol using is the key to this dynamic of consciousness. The evolution of the symbol-using mind was a big leap in the intensification of consciousness. The mental *symbols* that comprise language, mathematics, and all the various arts differ greatly from the mental *images* of multisensory reruns described as the essence of chakra 3.

A symbol is a mental entity that gathers together a wide set of multisensory images as well as emotional memories into a new mental entity that most importantly characterizes human intelligence. For example, the symbol "four" can gather together an element of meaning that is in four clouds, four days, or four apples. Symbolization includes not only language but the much more abstract activity called "mathematics" and the more concrete symbolism called "art."

A piece of music is a type of symbolizing that expresses a virtual flow of feelings that can happen in many different concrete situations. A painting or sculpture provides a virtual representation of our experiences of space. Dance is another presentational art that needs no linguistic symbols. Poetry and other linguistic arts combine a use of language with the creation of virtual expressions that are more concrete than prose. In other words, the fifth charka swirl of symbol-using consciousness and communication features not only speech and song, but extends to writing and reading, hearing and composing music, drawing pictures, carving icons, designing rituals, and many other complex performances unique to the human species among other living species.

Symbol-using communication among other symbol-using humans adds a huge amount of strength and power to our living. The great orator, poet, or writer plays a huge role in a human society of consciousness living. Each of us, however limited or renowned, show our strength of consciousness in our powers of communication, including our tone of voice, our pauses, and our choices of words. Symbol using undergirds our ability to build novel cultures, useful economies, and workable political systems.

Clearly, the symbol-using mind and the enhanced consciousness that symbol using enables in our species has been a leap in the evolution of life that distinguishes the human species from the general mammalian family of surviving fellow creatures. Perhaps many of the now extinct, upright-walking primates also shared in this symbol-using gift. Perhaps a few of the smartest living chimpanzees can, with sufficient human help, manifest fragments of this talent. Nevertheless, a three-year-old human child growing up in a human society has a facility with this mode of consciousness that no chimpanzee will ever attain.

That uniqueness being true, it is also true that symbol using has arisen from its earlier antecedents. The healthy human consciousness accesses this symbol-using intelligence in companionship with the earlier chakras of mind-enhanced consciousness. A human would be severely handicapped without his or her emotional intelligence or imaginal intelligence. Symbol using in its most abstract mathematical essence would be helpless and useless without these earlier more concrete means of taking in and putting forth within the real world.

Also, this symbol-using talent has its dangers and drawbacks. Humans can create whole universes of thought, conviction, and action, and can then substitute such overviews for the actual universe that confronts us in our sensations, emotions, and contemplative awareness. When this happens, a state of life is created that goes by names like "estrangement," "inauthenticity," and a long list of religious language like "karma" and "sin." Whatever the name, estrangement or dis-relation with Reality has consequences that we can call "despair." I will say more on the estrangement topic in later chapters.

## Chakra 6—Third-Eye Intuition

The sixth of these nodes of consciousness is located above the physical eyes in the center of the forehead. This swirl of consciousness is poeticized as an invisible third eye that, metaphorically speaking, "sees" beyond images, symbols, talk and writing, music and sculpture, and all other symbol-using expressions of consciousness. Therapists often speak of listening with the "third ear." Both "third eye" and "third ear" are metaphorical speech about the chakra 6 type of consciousness. The word "intuition" can be descriptive of third-eye consciousness, while the word "instinct" is often used to describe chakras 1, 2, 3, and 4. Chakra 5 is the dynamic of consciousness that enables us to use word-type descriptions like instincts and intuitions.

Third-eye awareness is more, not less, conscious than the previous five chakras. In this third-eye "seeing," we are consciously seeing consciousness itself as an independent dynamic of human living—distinguished from thinking or any other image-using or symbol-using mental process. Of course the mind is still operating as reflection upon the environment and on our inward dynamics, including our reflections on mind and consciousness. Yet in chakra 6 consciousness, both the inner and outer realms of experience are being "seen" beyond the limits of our rational screens of language, art, math, and other symbol-using formations.

This gift of awareness may sound completely magical, but this experience is actually quite ordinary. For example, when a scientist moves his whole view of a topic from one overarching paradigm to another overarching paradigm of thought, an irrational gap exists between those two modes of thinking. This gap is a glimpse into the depth of consciousness itself—a depth of awareness that is not the same as the dynamic called "mind" or any content of that mind.

When we intuit some truth that has never yet been experienced or expressed by us, we are experiencing this third-eye swirl of consciousness. When we intuit the consciousness of another person behind or beyond the content of their words and the their behaviors, we may be experiencing this third-eye swirl of consciousness. When we see possibilities in seemingly impossible situations, we may be experiencing this third-eye swirl of consciousness. When we see joy and victory in the midst of grim moments, we may be experiencing this third-eye swirl of consciousness.

In this chakra 6 level of being conscious, we have moved into an arena of consciousness that is the hidden essence of our intelligence—our primal brilliance. This hidden baseline of our *intelligence* is deeper than our scientific research, our contemplative inquiry, or our practical modes of conscious behaviors. We are speaking about an unspeakable *brilliancy* that makes our profound consciousness *profound*. Within this brilliancy we are experiencing the deep spaciousness of our consciousness in which our attentive knowing and our intentional doing are fundamentally located. In chakra 6 awareness, we are shaking hands, so to speak, with the dynamic of consciousness itself.

## Chakra 7—Awakenment

The seventh of these nodes of consciousness is located on the crown of the head just behind the top of the skull. The velocity of this wheel of consciousness has neared the speed of light, metaphorically speaking. Though we might say that we can't speak of it, we do speak of it. We poetize this state of profound consciousness with words like "awakenment" "enlightenment," "nirvana," "rest in Eternity," "the peace that exceeds understanding," "the joy unspeakable," "the enchantment with Being." Only metaphorical thought or poetry will work for speaking about this level of being conscious.

If we must say something more descriptive, we can speak of this stage of consciousness as that "fullness of "wonder" that is beneath the profound knowing and the profound doing that we explored in the third-eye chakra. If we associate the color red with the chakra 1, orange with 2, yellow with 3, green with 4, blue with 5, and blue-black with 6, then chakra 7 is white, containing in itself all the other colors—all the other vibrations or swirls of consciousness. When we experience conscious awareness at this seventh chakra level, we have touched into our raw participation of that field of consciousness that extends beyond our heads and throughout the cosmos. And this same consciousness colors all the other chakras of conscious presence in our human body. I am calling this chakra 7 swirl "profound consciousness" to distinguish it from the other six swirls of consciousness.

Following are some words of description of this awakenment from the clear-headed contemplative inquirer Jon Bernie.

> When we are living in a purely mental world we are not aligned with aliveness. . . . But in these moments when we awaken, when we touch our truth, we fall deeply into alignment, into embodiment. . . . So right now, take a moment to allow yourself to open to this vast space of being. Take this moment to surrender into fullness, into just being aliveness. Letting your body unwind. Letting your heart unwind. Letting your mind unwind. . . . Awakening changes everything. It offers you a new approach to life, a new set of options. That is not to say that your old personality patterns vanish—the personality has a lot of momentum! But even though you may still experience at least some of the same old automatic reactivity, you will find yourself welcoming it rather than pushing it away. You'll see those reactions arising within the space of awareness. You'll see how they work, how they function.

You'll see very, very clearly that your thoughts and reactions are
no longer—and never actually were—who you are.[2]

This passage may make it sound like awakenment is a very ordinary
thing. And it is ordinary in this way: we essentially are this profound
consciousness. But we are only aware of who we are when we are aware
of who we are. This may only be a few moments in our living. So in this
sense, profound consciousness can seem extraordinary. And it is true
that we need to avoid cheapening our understanding of profound consciousness to something less intense—such as other good things that are
better understood as expressions of chakras 1–6.

Finally, I want to underline that all seven chakras are important
parts of our consciousness. While the higher numbered chakras have
a faster spin, a greater intensity of being conscious, the slower spining
chakras are also crucial to the overall health of being conscious. Each
aspect of consciousness enriches all the others. If one of our charkras is
weak or sick, we should consider finding a therapist or a practice that can
assist us to strengthen that part of our being conscious.

## THE DECENT INTO DEPTH AND
## THE RETURN TO THE SURFACE

I want to share another look at defining consciousness with help from
the chakra poetry. Consciousness has already been described as both a
*taking in* of the environment and a *putting forth* into the ever-changeable
environment. The following chart pictures how this taking in and putting
forth takes place at an ever-deeper and more intense way as we move
through the evolution of life and consciousness toward becoming the human version of that life and consciousness.

If consciousness is happening only at the chakra 1 level, then the
taking in of the environment takes place only from the survival level on
this chart, and the putting forth of responses only come from that level as
well. Such is the life of a tree, perhaps. Perhaps an amoeba takes in the
environment at both chakra 1 and chakra 2 levels and makes responses
from that level of consciousness. A multicellular animal takes in the environment at chakra 1, 2, and 3 levels and makes responses from that
level of consciousness. In the case of a cat, the taking in and putting forth
goes still deeper to the chakra 4 level. Yet this intelligent image-using and

2. Bernie, *Unbelievable Happiness of What Is*, 98.

emotion-capable creature has not yet tasted the symbol-using mode of consciousness (chakra 5).

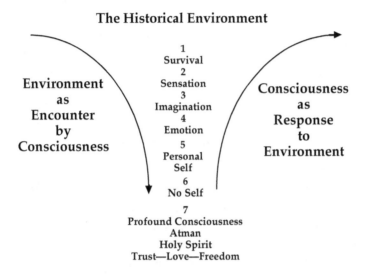

## The Historical Environment

Environment as Encounter by Consciousness

1 Survival
2 Sensation
3 Imagination
4 Emotion
5 Personal Self
6 No Self

Consciousness as Response to Environment

7
Profound Consciousness
Atman
Holy Spirit
Trust—Love—Freedom

For the human, symbol-using consciousness (chakra 5) enables this high-powered creature to create a picture or story of his or her own personal "self." Since self-image is a human creation, it is not a full picture of who we are. We are the enigmatic creator of that self-image. This self-image becomes an operating belief that is assumed, defended, and promoted by "me" as "my" real being.

On this chart I am naming the chakra 6 level of consciousness with the Buddhist term "no-self"—that is, *no personal self*, no actual knowledge of who we are. The third-eye consciousness of chakra 6 can also be described with more content-sounding metaphors, but "no-self" remains a valid description of this state of consciousness. At this level of being conscious, we no longer know who we are, and we never expect to know. We have tapped into the full mystery of consciousness itself, so all our self-images now float helplessly on the jet-black waters of pure mystery.

The chakra 7 metaphors can sound like taking back this sense of sheer mystery, but such is not the case. Chakra 7 is like a firmer embrace of this jet-black mystery that makes the sheer *unknown* feel more lively. "Profound consciousness" is an empty metaphor that says nothing except "none of the above." "Atman," as used in Hindu lore, does explore this level of awareness—emphasizing experiences of an inner spaciousness that unites consciousness with the "that" of Every-thing-ness.

"Holy Spirit," as used in the best of Christian reflections, explores profound consciousness as an active power in our surprisingly able historical responding. "Holy Spirit" can be described with these three profound metaphors that I believe characterize New Testament theologizing: (1) *Ultimate Trust* in the trustworthiness of the Final Mystery; (2) *Universal Love*, a "care" that extends to all beings, both enemies and friends; and (3) *Profound Freedom* from our personality, our self-image, and our fate. I will reflect much more on these Christian terms in later chapters.

## Rewriting the Dictionary

In this and other chapters of this book, I am rewriting the dictionary on certain key words. In the first chapter, I focused on deeper meanings for that key word "mind." In this second chapter I am focusing on deeper meanings for that key word "consciousness." I hope I have underlined a close correspondence between consciousness and aliveness.

Obviously, each of these two words ("mind" and "consciousness") will have multiple meanings for any one person, but I want the reflections of these opening chapters to be part of our swirl of meanings. I want you, the reader, to at least hold on to these definitions for the rest of this book.

In chapter 3 I will be doing similar work with the word "truth." Then in chapter 4 I will be giving fresh meaning to the term "profound consciousness." And in chapter 5 I will be taking on a redefinition of the word "religion."

Some readers may take offense with my using such key words in what may seem to be my own arbitrary way. But such innovations are taking place all the time with every innovative philosopher, scientist, artist, and contemplative inquirer. Also, I am not making my word innovations entirely on my own, but along with many movements in word changes that are already in process all across contemporary culture.

Finally, I am not recommending my changes in word usage only for a few readers. I am attempting to change the use of these key words in every language and culture on Earth. I realize that I am going to need some help with such a big task, and I realize that these hoped-for cultural changes will take some time—long after my death I am sure. Many other innovators have already and will in the future participate in this ongoing innovation of our Reality-accessing linguistic tools.

So, please fasten your seat belts! I am inviting you on a bumpy ride.

# 3

---

# Into Your Four Minds of Truth

## *What Is Truth?*

"TRUTH" IS A SLIPPERY word that requires some definition. My definition may cause more, rather than less, consternation. I am defining "truth" as a formulation of ordered insight—a formulation created by our conscious intentionality, using our symbol-using mind (chakra 5) to provide an expression of order to our experiences of that boundless Mysteriousness we all face. So truth is a finite, temporal, mental formulation initiated by our consciousness through both *taking in* Mysterious Reality and then *putting forth* in the face of Mysterious Reality a bit of approximate representation of Reality in the form of language, mathematics, or art.

This means that there is no Final Truth except our experience of that Mysterious Realty which can never be contained in these human truth approximations created by our finite consciousness using our finite human mind to create approximate "truths" for the somewhat ordered and practical living of our lives. Does this mean that all truth statements are as good as any other truth statements. No, Mysterious Reality judges some truth statements as better than others.

Furthermore, it is important to notice that thoughtfulness about the truth of Realty is required to enact our care—our essential love of self and others. Though care is a gift of our essential nature, care to be caring must be enacted by human consciousness. And enacting care requires thoughtfulness. Here is a poem about care—a care that implies thoughtfulness about the truth of the Mysterious Reality we confront.

Within the Land of Mystery
rises a Mountain of Care –
care for self, care for others,
care for Earth, care for the cosmos,
care that we exist, care that we suffer
care that we may find rest and fulfillment,
care that we may experience our caring
and not grow numb and dead.
It takes no effort to care.
It takes effort not to care.
Care is given with the Land of Mystery.
Care is part of the Mystery of Being.
We care, we just care, we are made of care.
Care is a Mountain because care is so huge,
so challenging to embrace, to climb, to live.
Care is a demand upon us that is more humbling,
more consuming, more humiliating,
than all the authorities, laws, and obligations
of our social existence.
Care is a forced march into the dangers
and the hard work of constructing a life that
is not a passive vegetable growth
nor a wildly aggressive obsession.
Care is an inescapable given, simply there,
yet care is also an assertion of our very being.
It is compassion, devotion, love for all that is given
and for all parts of each given thing, each being.
Like Atlas, we lift the planet day-by-day,
year-by-year, love without end,
in the Land of Mystery.

## ESSENTIAL CARE

This word "care," in the profound consciousness phrase "Mountain of Care," points to the same quality as the word "love," used by the apostle Paul when he claims that love (*agape*) is a greatest of all the gifts of the spirit. "Care," as I am proposing to use that word, points to an outgoing compassion for both self and others that requires extensive thoughtfulness. If we do not care for ourselves, we do not care for others, and if we do not care for others, we do not care for ourselves. Essential care does not have to be divided between self and others. When we access our essential care: we have a boundless amount of care to give to both others and ourselves. Such care is a total attitude of our entire being.

And essential care is not an accomplishment of the caring person, but a gift that is given with our authentic existence. Essentially, we just do care. And we care for the whole mountain range of caring. We do not have to create this care. We only need to surrender to the fact that we do care. Then we will need to decide which particular mountains in the mountain range of our care we choose to prioritize. We have to choose which specific mountains we are going to be guilty of neglecting. We have to choose the roles that we play in caring for our chosen mountains. We will have to choose how to carry out these roles. All this caring requires thoughtfulness—a thoughtfulness that builds guidelines for being our caring being.

## OUT OF YOUR MIND AND INTO
## YOUR FOUR MINDS OF TRUTH

Being "out of your mind" is an adult experience of the openness to Mysterious Reality that we had as an infant. And it means a fresh type of infant-like openness occurring at the same time as participating in adult thoughtfulness about everything that is required of us in the historical caring of our care.

The commission to take on caring action seems initially to contradict the wondrous no-thought-ness of being "out of our minds." Adult life has moved on from being an infant. An infant learns to be thoughtful to live. And as an adult, we move on from one specific thoughtfulness to some more effective specific thoughtfulness in a perpetual revolution of thoughtfulness, thereby manifesting the adult way of remaining "out of your mind." One of the ways we experience this "out of your mind" quality as adults occurs in the gaps between what we have thought and what we are choosing to think next. These gaps are windows into the vast space of being "out of our minds."

The adult life is complex, because we are not limited to one mind of truth at a time. Rather, we have four minds of truth all the time. We have four different ways of being thoughtful that we already have, and will continue to have. We may be unconscious that we have four minds of truth, but they are simply there in our living. Furthermore, each of us can be continually improving each of these four minds of truth in order for each of them to be more supported by our experiences of Reality.

The word "mind" can point to an inner view of our single brain and nervous system. In that sense we have one brain and one mind. Nevertheless, we can also say that we have four "minds of truth." My mind and your mind in approaching the One Reality must construct four different types of truth, resulting in four different systems of thoughtfulness. These four different minds of truth can be joined into one overall project of living, but these four patterns of truth cannot be rationally consistent with one another. I am going to spell this out in detail.

I will demonstrate in this chapter that as long as we live, all four of these minds of truth will exist in our lives. Only within this humbling awareness we can remain "out of our minds" at the same time that we are consciously and intentionally recreating our four minds of truth. So what are these four minds of truth?

The four minds of truth are: (1) the *scientific* or outward-looking fact-based mind, (2) the *contemplative* or inward-looking impression-based mind, (3) the "I-you" or *interpersonal* workability mind, and (4) the social *commonality* or group workability mind.

I will present a partial description of each of these four minds of truth. I will discuss how they are different, how they are each essential, and how no one can live realistically without all four of them. And most important of all, I am also going to demonstrate how each of these four minds of truth are not and can never be rationally consistent with each other.

Taking on these realizations means the end of any hope that we will ever have a consistent and rational universe of lasting meanings. Realism at the outer edges of our current cultural awareness requires us to surrender the notion that "the rational is the real" and replace it with these two far more realistic notions: (1) the rational is never the Real, and (2) the Real exists as a power that affirms some rational designs as more real than other rational designs. I have just outlined a realistic epistemology that I am now going to spell out further.

## Mind 1: The Scientific Approach to Truth

Though there are many pseudo-scientists who use the aura of scientific truth to promote their authoritarian finalities, the true research scientist, of whom there are a vast number, are perpetually open to the unknown.

These honest workers of the scientific approach to truth know that no theory is safe from radical improvements. They know that all scientific knowledge is approximate and that all scientific knowledge remains on the move toward better correspondence with the objective facts of human experience. The best of our recent scientists have come to realize that the more we know about the nature of observable things, the more we don't know. Instead of chipping away at the mystery of nature, scientific progress opens up even more mystery. Science is a journey into an unknown that becomes, thereby, ever more unknown.

This does not mean that one scientific theory is as good as the next one. Rather the sciences are progressive disciplines; the newer accepted theories generally correspond better with the current facts of sensory experience.

And I am not only talking to scientific nerds. All of us participate in scientific knowledge, and in its constantly changing conclusions. And none of us have the privilege of valuing our own opinions over the documented scientific truth. Literary writers and contemplative thinkers can and do validly criticize the limitations of the scientific method; nevertheless, these more contemplative writers all participate in creating their own scientific minds of truth. Anyone who speaks of dinosaurs or black holes or evolution is a scientist of some sort. Indeed, it takes scientific knowledge to make your bed, wash your dishes, water your plants, build your house, etc. There is even a rudimentary, pre-intellectual form of scientific truth used by a cat to find its food bowl. The scientific approach to truth is as unavoidable as breathing. We all have a scientific mind along with three other minds.

## Mind 2: The Contemplative Approach to Truth

Scientific truth is not even half of the human approaches to truth. The contemplative approach to truth is present in all the humanities, in all the arts, and even in the sciences of psychology and biology. For example, psychology is a discipline of learning that straddles the divide between objective science and interior contemplation. Behavioral psychology leans scientific, and depth psychology leans contemplative. Both of these branches of psychology use the scientific and the contemplative approaches to truth. Something similar can be said of the humanities of history and philosophy. We have analytical philosophy and existential philosophy. We have scientific history focused on the exactness of past events, and we have history that has to do future projections in order to make decisions in the present to affect that future.

In the arts, contemplative inquiry dominates the scientific type of truth. Music is an expression of our flow of inner feelings. Painting, sculpture, and architecture provide virtual expressions of our inner experiences of space. Poetry uses outward references as metaphors for inner experiences of living events. Dance gives outward expression to our total experience of space-time bodily movements. Song, novel, and drama combine language with several of the above presentational arts. In other words, a big part of what we know has been derived from the contemplative approach to truth. We cannot even begin to understand religion if we only use the scientific approach to truth to grasp the meaning of our religious rituals, icons, myths, methods, practices, community life, and so on.

Buddhist meditation is perhaps the closest to a pure form of the contemplative approach to truth. In at least one form of this ancient practice, we watch our breath until we create enough stillness and silence to watch our consciousness watching everything that is watchable from this deep interior point of view. Overt Buddhist mediation may not need to be practiced by everyone, but the contemplative approach to truth is not optional. It goes on in every human being all the time, everyday, everywhere. So if we want to intentionally understanding our real lives, contemplative inquiry is an approach to truth we cannot ignore.

The contemplative approach to truth focuses upon looking beyond thinking, yet contemplative inquiry includes thinking about our explorations beyond thought. Expert contemplators quite commonly write whole books on the methods, experiences, and discoveries of their contemplative efforts to see beyond thought. When we contemplators share our contemplations with others, we use language and art forms. We use the imperfections of words and art to share that which is beyond both words and art.

## Contemplation, Inquiry, and Scientific Research

So what are some of the characteristics of the contemplative approach to truth and how does this approach differ from the scientific approach to truth? Measurable time is an essential part of the discipline of physics, and measurable time spills over into all the other sciences. Physics could not exist apart from measured seconds, minutes, years, feet per second, miles per hour, and the speed of light. But in the contemplative approach to truth, our impressions are not measurable, and the time is always and only *now*. In the contemplative approach to truth, the past is but a memory in the *now* of living, and the future is only an anticipation that is happening *now*. Time is a flow of happenings through an enduring *now*. *This now of conscious living is the assumed context for contemplative inquiry.*

Contemplative inquiry is an approach to truth in which consciousness is being aware of the inward impressions of being conscious, and these impressions are always conscious *now*. It is not exactly the case that the conscious watcher is viewing consciousness itself, but consciousness views the flow through the now of experiences of being conscious of whatever consciousness is aware. Time is a flow through this now of awareness. It is upon that flow and its contents that we are contemplating.

In contrast, time in the scientific approach to truth is viewed as an abstract measurable line, and on that line of time is an infinitesimal dot called "the present." This zero-length dot separates past from future. So which view of time is true? Is now a dot of nothing, or is now all there is? This is a primary paradox found in our human thinking about Reality. All those philosophers who have attempted to undo this irrationality in human thinking have failed.

Time can be meaningfully viewed in both of these wildly different ways. This paradox reveals that human thought can never be one consistent system of thoughtfulness that encompasses the whole of Reality. Furthermore, we cannot avoid using both the scientific and the contemplative modes of thinking. Both modes of thinking are built into the reality of being a human thinker and using thought to guide our behavior.

Here is another big difference between these two approaches to truth. The truth of scientific inquiry is tested with public observations of "facts." But in the truth of contemplative inquiry there are no "facts" that a peer group of scientists can together see or hear or smell or taste or feel outwardly. Each contemplative inquirer only sees his or her own solitary awareness. And even the word "sees" is just a metaphor, for no eyes are used, no light rays are involved. This is a mode of truth that reveals the limitations of science and opens up a quest for truth in an entirely different realm of exploration. We can assume that inner phenomena are part of the same overall Realty as the outward facts. But there is no path of reason from one of these two modes of inquiry to the other. They are independent of each other, and they can be said to complete each other as well as compete with other.

Here are some of the unique and surprising discoveries of the contemplative approach to truth: the limitations of the human mind to comprehend Reality; the raw cares of being human and the inevitable frustration of these cares; the omnipresence of the No-thing-ness out of which all things arise and all things return; the omnipresence of the Every-thing-ness within which all things commune; the inseparable essence of living and dying; the futility of fighting with these grim and also wondrous truths of our enigmatic existence.

And here is the most awesome discovery of the contemplative approach to truth: the absence of a reference for all our images of "myself." Whoever I think I am, I am still more and/or quite different than I think.

Also awesome is the omnipresence of raw uncaused freedom in our human makeup. This freedom is foundational in human life in spite of the use of our freedom to refuse to be free. Blaming is most often used method of fleeing our responsibility. Whole books have been written on the flight from freedom. This strange freedom is not all-powerful: we have minimal control over the results of our free choices upon the course of events. Many other powers than my own free decisions impact the future—everyone else's freedom is one of those powers, and the immense powers of the natural world is another.

In the contemplative approach to truth we can also come to see that your or my specific personality pattern is simply habits that our own essential freedom has created from among the cultural options provided to us. Our parent or early caregivers may have provided many poor options for us to choose, but we chose what we chose. We, not our parent, created our personality. Blaming our parents for who we became is simply avoiding responsibility for who we will become as a pattern of personality habits. These patterns are real, and our early childhood formations endure, but they can now be related to differently and compensated for decisively.

Each of the above contemplative awarenesses can result in books of poetry, novels, myths, art forms, personal reports, movements of spirit, religious practices, and much more. My contemplative findings may not resonate with your experience. If so, consider my assertions as places you might go and look for yourself. I have no other authority than my own contemplative inquiry into my own being. And my aim in this chapter is not to sell you on my contemplative findings, but to convince you that contemplative inquiry is a mode of truth finding.

## Mind 3: The Interpersonal Approach to Truth

The entire topic of truth is at least twice as big as the scientific approach and the contemplative approach combined. A third approach to truth that I am now going to describe might be called the "I-Thou" approach to truth, or the "interpersonal intimacy" approach to truth. This interpersonal approach takes at least two persons in order to explore this quest for realism. When one human consciousness looks into the eyes of another human consciousness and sees those eyes looking back, the interpersonal approach to truth is born. This type of truth begins in early childhood, and lives on as a life quality in each and every human being. We are *communal beings* in ways that neither contemplative inquiry nor scientific research can fathom.

Jack Kornfield tells of living the life of being a celibate Buddhist monk for many years, and then leaving that mode of life in order to get married. At the time of leaving his monastery, he was an accomplished teacher of the contemplative approach to truth, but living in this deep and intimate way with another human being proved to be for him an experience that necessitated an additional approach to truth. In a less extreme way, many of us have made this same rather astonishing discovery. It takes a special set of skills to navigate the interpersonal aspects of being human. This type of truth differs widely from our solitary inquires or our scientific excellences.

True intimacy is an awakening that notices that other humans are not simply objects in my universe of scientific knowledge. Nor are others direct participants in my solitary contemplative awareness. Another human is another universe of awareness that is viewing me within their universe of awareness. If a person has little or no sense of intimacy, we call that "narcissism," a state of psychological limitation having to do with being locked into one's own brand of self-imaging. Intimacy is a realm of living that challenges narcissism. Nevertheless, most of the awareness that each human being enjoys has been coaxed or rocked into being by interpersonal meetings with others. In a later chapter, I will dwell further on these meetings as they pertain to our life together in intimate circles, as well as to leadership and followership. I will also explore the meaning of "witnessing love" as a depth care for those with whom we have intimate relations.

Ken Wilber contrasts this third approach to truth with what he calls the "I" approach of contemplative inquiry and the "it" approach of scientific research. He characterizes intimacy as a "we" approach to truth. In addition to the "we" approach of interpersonal living, he also alerted me to a second "we" approach to truth that I will call the "commonality" approach to truth.[1]

## Mind 4: The Commonality Approach to Truth

The English language that I am using to write this essay is an illustration of what I mean by a "commonality" process in our human living. There are many languages, but language of some sort is an essential process in every human society. Art and religious formations, like language, appear in every human society and appear very early in human evolution. These common-life processes come into play in that great leap forward in consciousness that make what we now call human society different from the social relations that characterize the social processes that appear in the other still-living species. Many mammalian species make strong social connections, but these communication processes use the third charka multisensory image-using intelligence rather than the fifth chakra symbol-using intelligence. See chapter 2 for more on that those chakra distinctions.

For a clear discussion of human social processes, we need to distinguish between what we can call "essential social processes" found in every human society and *manifestations* of those essential processes that differ greatly from society to society. For example, the language and art of a Stone Age human society differs greatly form those of medieval Rome or modern New York City. But all these very different societies include the essential processes of language and art.

Here is what I mean by "social processes." A social process is an ongoing activity that human beings do in common or with one another. Religious formation is another essential social process. Religion is a common doing of humans involving rituals, icons, myths, communal life, ethics, and the theoretics that discusses those practices. In chapter 5 I illustrate how religious processes differ from all the other essential

---

1. See Wilber, *Brief History of Everything*, 107. Though Wilber's complex writings have been a source of inspiration to me, I am using my own language, some enrichments from A. H. Almaas on contemplative inquiry, and years of study on the scientific method and the history of religion. So count me, not Wilber, responsible for my language uses.

processes of a human society in their purpose of accessing and expressing profound consciousness living.

Moral fabrics, singular roles, and associative patterns are other social
processes that we might call "essential common-style processes" of a human society. The disciplines of learning, educational structures, and the
methods of nurture are social processes that we might call "the essential
common-sense processes" of a human society. Together with language,
art, and religion, all these essential social processes so far mentioned
might be called "cultural processes." Some sociologists have called these
"social process." I prefer to use the phrase "social processes" to mean the
inclusive set of social processes that includes economic processes, political processes, as well as the cultural processes just mentioned.

*Essential economic processes* can be spelled out to include natural,
human, and technological resources, plus their *production* for human use
and the *distribution* of the resulting products and services to the populations who need or want those benefits.

*Essential political processes* have to do with the processes of group
decision-making. Every organization and every geographical population
make group decisions. They make them in many different ways, but the
need for some sort of operational unity and overall social purpose conducted within some sort of social order is also essential to human social
life. The essential set of political processes includes norms, taboos, laws,
and their means of enforcement. The arguments between the various
types of political manifestation can be severe, but the need for some kind
of commonly designed political processing is an essential aspect of the
common life of every society of human beings.

Defining the essential social processes that appear in every human
society is the *first task* of the commonality approach to truth. Any model
of those essential social processes can be improved, but building such a
model is not optional. We need a model of these essential social processes
that orders or our memory of the past societies, our analysis of the present societies, and our vision for any future society.

The *second task* of the commonality approach to truth is saying what
is true about the current manifestations of the all these essential processes—what is working well; what is oppressive, unjust, out of date, useless, or immoral; and how these manifestations can be improved for the
people living now in this or that particular place. All this is a truth quest
about what would actually work better for advancing the well-being of
people in a specific geographical area or a specific organization of human

life on this planet. Later in this chapter, I am going to say more about the "workability test for truth," but first I want to underline the importance of the commonality approach to truth for all truth seekers.

## THE IMPORTANCE OF COMMONALITY TRUTH

If a society corrupts, twists, or neglects some of the essential processes that comprise a human society, this will lead to a loss of effectiveness or even threaten the survival of that society. All these many essential social processes are an important part of our human social life. Social processes provide an environment for our living along with nature, but social processes are an altogether different sort of environment than the natural facts of physics and biology. Social forms are patterns of living that humans have created, chosen, and enacted. They are constructed with uses of nature and alongside nature, but they are not nature in the scientific sense. So, focusing our minds on the manifest verities of social commonality requires a fourth approach to truth.

I am giving this expanded space to discussing the commonality approach to truth, not because the commonality approach is more important than the other three approaches to truth, but because there is more resistance in our current mindsets and in our current educational institutions to pursuing this commonality quest for truth. In response to our hatred of authoritarian institutions, we have developed a "cult of spontaneity" that neglects thoughtfulness about social affairs. Many of us are rebelling from the challenge to do the needed hard-headed, long-term, big-scope thinking that the commonality approach to truth requires.

It is understandable to find ourselves averse to social structures that are oppressive, corrupt, hopelessly obsolete, and stubborn to change. So, we tend not to trust the truth of even excellent social thought. As a result of such mental neglect, we too often opt for social beliefs that reflect the popular prejudices, our own psychological biases, and plain ignorance of social realities. Though we rightly don't want to be social robots, truth inquiry of the commonality type is required to find our best responses in terms of understanding, preserving, and changing our social structures.

Relevant commonality thinking requires an understanding of the current customs, norms, styles, truths, and sensibilities that we have grown up with in our existing culture. This awareness is the starting place from which we can then choose what to conserve and what to rework.

Our entry into bending the course of social history is not a simple abandonment of inherited thought and practices. It a thought-through replacement of the ongoing mostly unconscious social patterns with better thoughts and practices created by us in opposition to the existing social flow of operations.

Such reality-affirming social truth is seldom welcomed throughout the society. Supporters of the old customs typically resist proposed changes. It is often dangerous to insist upon even obvious progress. Therefore, clear thoughtfulness and good strategy require courage both to conserve the best qualities of a current social order and to meaningfully embody better values in creating better models for a better social order.

## THE MEANING OF "WORKABILITY"

"Better" in the commonality approach to truth means better social workability. "Workability" will be my name for the test for truth in the commonality approach to truth. Like the interpersonal approach to truth, the commonality approach to truth is a "we" approach to truth. Interpersonal workability is about finding interpersonal skills that make personal communication with others workable. Commonality workability has to do with creating workable social forms for the specific cultural, political, and economic processes of a given society at a given time in its history.

In order to be workable, the commonality approach to truth must work in accord with scientific truth, contemplative truth, and interpersonal truth. Having taken in these other three approaches to truth to the best of our abilities, we can then appropriately seek commonality truth for our social conditions, including a realistic range of possibilities for our given society with its historical challenges. Our truth for action includes guesses about future outcomes and the creation of thoughtful paths that may reach the outcomes we can envision and intend.

The amount of stuckness within the inherited ideologies or doctrines of our inherited social commonality is often very strong—so strong that many resist even considering a quest for truth in the commonality mode for truth. Most often we humans simply adopt whatever limited truth or false understandings we find most comforting, and close down any further consideration of commonality truth. Such attitudes, when widespread, will make a society unworkable. So, let us consider further the relationship of the commonality quest for truth with each of the other three quests for truth.

## The Truth of Commonality and the Truth of Science

In order to be workable, the truth of commonality must honor the "facts" as defined in the sciences; nevertheless, commonality truth entails exploring a further realm of content than the facts of science. For example, when we study physics we sometimes talk about the "laws of nature." Such a "law" means a relatively dependable ordering of the experiences of our senses. Such a law tells us what we can expect from future experiences in the outward world of nature. When our senses produce exceptions to this law, then we scientists develop a better law and look for ways to test its truth with the data that is observable by our senses. These dynamics remain true regardless of the complexity of the instruments of observation and the rarified definitions of what we mean by facts. If the new theory is confirmed by these tests of our senses, it becomes the new natural law until our senses, through whatever instruments, observe new facts that counter that new law, thus calling for a still better law.

A social law, however, differs from a natural law in the following way: a social law is created by human beings for the practical purpose of ordering relations among human beings. A human society must make group decisions some way or another in order to be a human society. Such inescapable necessities for social living may be called a "natural law," but the specific social decisions or social laws that order a particular human society are humanly invented social practices that appear to be workable for most, or at least some, members of that society. These social laws are very different from natural laws. We call them both "laws" only because these two types of ordering constitute our overall environment.

In a democratic society the "consent of the governed" is expanded from the type of forced consent that is typical in a top-down, top-serving, authoritarian society. So, what makes a social law valid in the minds of a society's social participants? Validity here is simply what works for ordering that specific society for the time being for that particular assemblage of human beings in that time frame. This test of *workability* is something quite different from a test based on "facts" of nature we find in physics.

Nevertheless, for social workability to be full-blown, we must not deny the natural laws of science. In fact, social ethicists from Thomas

Aquinas to Theodore Roszak claim that society is not working properly if natural law is not being obeyed by its social laws. Roszak's very fine book *Person/Planet* develops an ethics that claims that a workable society must be obedient to the nature of the planet and to the nature of the human beings who compose that society. Otherwise, very bad outcomes for that society occur in the course of time.

A contemporary illustration of what that means is found in the current challenge we call "the climate crisis." The natural scientists have made very clear that burning vast amounts of fossil fuels is having disastrous consequences on our climate and consequently on our weather patterns and other natural features that will lead to upsets in social order, and even threaten humanity's long-term survival. Therefore a politician who denies the climate crisis or does not propose solutions (i.e., social laws) that work to mitigate this emergency are promoting an unworkable society—where "workable" has a wider meaning than what is workable for the wealth of oil investors. Many other scientific facts shape our vision of commonality workability.

The commonality approach to truth also assumes a long-range knowledge of social history—past and future. Historical science helps us build this historical knowledge. Competent historical knowledge has a scientific component. Historical writing is also existential storytelling about past meanings and future possibilities that inform the ongoing decision-making for the practical workability of the society concerned. The historical contributions of science to our projections of future social workability are also important, but science alone does not provide a full test for social workability.

Our tests for a workable commonality include elements of understanding unique to our social commonality decisions. Society is an ongoing group process of decision-making about: (1) the economic processes that distribute produced goods and services that sustain human beings, (2) the political processes that enable ongoing group decisions by people who remember the past and anticipate possible handling of social challenges, and (3) cultural processes that enable humans with the current wisdom from all four approaches to truth. In a democracy these awarenesses need to be widely known if citizens are going to be effective for the enrichment of life, liberty, and the pursuit of informed living within the economic, political, and cultural fabrics of that society. Spending ample resources on education is therefore imperative for a fully workable democracy. Those who starve public education and price university

education out of reach for many citizens are dumbing-down the population, and thereby promoting dictatorship rather than democracy.

We can notice that scientific truth enters into all these decisions, but
the scientific facts are only part of the data that informs good (workable)
decisions for the commonality of that society. There is no such thing as a
scientifically rational society, in spite of what a number of sociologists try
to claim. It takes more than the scientific mode of truth to design a viable
society. It takes what I am calling the "commonality mode of truth."

## The Truth of Commonality
## and the Truth of Contemplation

Contemplative wisdom about our essential humanity also enters into the
discussion about social workability. It is human beings, after all, who are
being ordered into a social order. What we know contemplatively about
being a human being must of necessity enter into our discussion and
decisions about social workability. Nevertheless, the test of workability
that operates within the commonality approach to truth requires more
than our contemplative insights. It requires our scientific consensus, our
contemplative insights, and still more than that. It also requires our understanding of commonality itself and how commonality truth functions
in social history.

## The Truth of Commonality
## and the Truth of Interpersonal Relations

The truth of interpersonal relations and the truth of commonality process have something in common. Both are "we" approaches to truth, as
opposed to the "it" approach of science and the "I" approach of contemplation. Both commonality and interpersonal relations depend on a
workability test for truth. But workability means something different for
each of these two "we" approaches to truth.

The workability of interpersonal relations has to do with successful "I-to-I" or "I-Thou" communications. One personal consciousness is
looking upon and listening to another personal consciousness that is looking and listening back. Workability here means personal sensibilities and
communication skills that work for an authentic "I-Thou" meeting. These
skills depend upon body language, sensory contact, intellectual sharing,

and consciousness resonance. These interpersonal skills are different gifts than the gifts it takes to pursue the commonality approach to truth.

The quest for commonality truth is more scientifically objective, but deals with entities more slippery than scientific facts. Workability for a social order has to do with: (1) the fair distribution of needed and wanted goods and services, (2) an allocation of political power to a range of citizen types and roles of responsibility, and (3) a provision of cultural contents and skills that enable viable participation in that society.

The wisdom for interpersonal workability is important for the commonality struggle, but it is not enough. For us to provide fair, just, and adequate ordering of social care for all persons in our society requires of us some study of our social past and some long-range and large-scope thoughtfulness about the future of our society.

At the same time, our thoughtfulness about interpersonal relations is important input into envisioning the workability of our social vision. For example, when we are working among both men and women in our social change movements, we must deal creatively with the inherited patterns of male entitlement and the oppression of women. Similar interpersonal wisdom also applies to classism, racism, and religious bigotries. All these interpersonal maladies impede the effectiveness of our social commonality reforms and innovations. Human society is created for human beings (along with all the other life forms), and human beings only flourish within societies that allow and foster workable interpersonal relationships.

However critical interpersonal skills are, the commonality quest for truth entails something more. Our thinking, designing, organizing, and block-by-block building of a workable society have an *impersonal* quality as well as the interpersonal one. Commonality truth includes workable laws, customs, and norms that enable a workable society. Commonality truth includes caring for the land, waterways, atmosphere, and other life forms that support human life as well as provide a long-range home for all life. Commonality truth includes a deep sense of history and wisdom about bending history for the betterment of social workability. In the "we" approach of commonality truth, both long-range past and long-range future time considerations make the commonality approach different from the more intimate and immediate person-to-person "we" approach to truth.

Workability can seem to be a flimsy test for the commonality approach to truth, unless we understand that these other three tests of truth are present in defining what true workability means. A well-understood workability test for truth is far more than a mere ego-centered pragmatism. For commonality concerns, workability includes obedience to the other three truth quests. This is true because all four types of truth about our relationship to Reality feed into the commonality approach. The test for commonality workability expands our quest for truth into a consideration of real-time historical results. The call for workability within our commonality vision and action asks us: "Does our action result in realizing our values for a just and feasible social operation?"

## THE RESPONSIBLE THINKER

All four of these minds of truth are present in everyone's life, often unconsciously held, often uncritically adopted. Also, we are seldom aware of all four of these quests for truth, how they differ from one another, or how they relate to one another. Indeed, many of us, much of the time, are not seeking more truth of any sort. We may be passionately stuck or deeply hung up in some segment of approximate wisdom from one or many of these four types of truth.

So what does it mean to be a responsible thinker in this twenty-first-century era in which all truth is understood to be approximate and ever changing? Clearly, being hung up on a set of inherited beliefs is not the answer to the question of responsible thinking. *Dogmatism* is a retreat from giving responsible answers to changing circumstances. Dogmatism is a flight into false securities that will be dismantled over time by the unstoppable forces of Profound Realty. Also, *anti-intellectualism* is not an answer to the question of responsibility. Anti-intellectualism is another form of escape from giving answers and acting out those answers with relative confidence. Anti-intellectualism and dogmatic mindsets are two forms of flight from responsible thinking and action.

The way forward is a deep trust in our ongoing confrontations with Profound Reality and enacting the accompanying realism that honors and celebrates a perpetual insecurity of mental and moral functions. Trusting Reality means a perpetual revolution in thought and action, a thoughtfulness that is never fully confident, an activism that is always partly wrong, and a presence that is still becoming more lucid about being human. Nevertheless, we can proceed with our own degree of "out of our mind" openness and our own partially developed four minds of truth. We can be relatively confident about what we know and what we are called to do to be realistic. And we can be fully confident in our perpetual opportunity for fresh starts—that is, in our forgiveness of self and in our forgiveness of others.

This ongoing trust of Profound Reality can be experienced as an unspeakable joy in the midst of constantly dying to modes of living we may have previously held. Such perpetual insecurity of mind (in all four of our minds of truth) is part of that quality of living I am calling "realistic responsibility" in the care of ourselves, our neighbors, and our living planet of possibilities.

# 4

---

# The Paradoxes of Being Awake

## *What Is Profound Consciousness?*

MARY JANE RUBENSTEIN HAS become my favorite philosopher on what I am calling "profound consciousness" or "being awake." Here is a quote from her book *Strange Wonder* with its wonderful subtitle, *The Closure of Metaphysics and the Opening of Awe.*

> The double movement of wonder takes us out of the world, *only to put us back into the world,* dismantling old possibilities to uncover new ones, exposing as "wind-eggs" all we think we know in order to reveal everything as different—as more itself—than it had been before. Genuine relation and decision, then, do not depend upon closing off wonder into a momentary "spark," but upon keeping it open.[1]

This "momentary spark" view of wonder Rubinstein referred to earlier in her book with this comment about Aristotle:

> It is Aristotle who first proposed a remedy for wonder in the knowledge of cause and effect. He explained that while philosophy begins in thaumaxein [wonder] 'it must in a sense end in something which is the opposite' . . . Aristotle values wonder because it prompts the learner to find the causes of that which confounds him.[2]

---

1. Rubinstein, *Strange Wonder*, 60.
2. Rubinstein, *Strange Wonder*, 32.

This view of the place of wonder persists in the scientific philoso-phizing of 2019. Wonder does inspire thoughtfulness to replace the won-der with rational order—cause and effect, probability patterns, and other means of giving human understanding to what was previously baffling.

But the deeper insight of Rubinstein and, she claims, of Socrates is that wonder can stay open. She further explains that wonder is both what is stunningly attractive and dreadfully repelling. This is why humans are motivated, in the first instance, to replace wonder with order.

Nevertheless, the whole order of any culture of humans might be pictured as a small boat on a vast ocean of wonder. Let us say that when we are born, we are living at the stern of this cultural boat with little sense that there is something more. As we walk toward full adulthood, we come to the prow of this boat moving into the wonder of a mystery that never goes away. We can then retreat into the body of the boat and forget that dreadful sight, or we can work with the possibility of making friends with this permanent wonder—this opening of a wonder or awe before an Awesomeness that is our one and only Reality.

This brings me to my fourth poem—this one about the fourth of Joe Mathews's states-of-being charts: *The Sea of Tranquility*.

In the Land of Mystery
there is a Sea of Tranquility,
a place of Rest amidst the wild waters of life.
The waves may be high, our small boat tossed about,
but there we are with a courageous heart.
It is our heart that is courageous.
We are born with this heart.
We do not achieve it.
We can simply rest within our own living heart,
our own courageous heart that opens vulnerably
to every person and all aspects of that person,
to our own self and every aspect of that self,
to life as a whole with all its terrors and joys.
This is a strange Rest, for no storm can end it,
no challenge of life defeat it,
No loss, no death, no horror of being, no fear
can touch our courageous heart.
We live, if we allow ourselves to truly live
on this wild Sea of Everything in the Tranquility
of our own indestructible courageous heart.
To manifest and fully experience this Tranquility,
we only have to give up the creations of our mind

that we have substituted for this ever-present Peace.
We have only to open to the Land of Mystery
flowing with a River of Consciousness
and containing a Mountain of Care.
Here and here alone do we find the Sea of Tranquility.
Here in the Land of Mystery that our mind
cannot comprehend, create, or control,
here beyond our deepest depth or control
is a Sea of Tranquility
in the Land of Mystery.

The courage to be what we actually are opens to us a deep rest or tranquility, because we have ended striving to be what we are not. This does not mean that we have ended the various ways we work to improve our knowledge, hone our skills, preserve our health, create our places, achieve our goals, and so on. But we have come to realize that none of these temporal achievements handle being our essential humanness. Our true authenticity or *presence* as a human being does not open by simply changing our temporal qualities. This profound *tranquility* comes into play from a deeper level. Tranquility is a gift that comes with our courage to be the exact being we are being gifted to be by Being itself.

Nevertheless, tranquility is not a flight from the putting forth of our own life; rather, it is the strongest putting-forth quality known to human experience. We must embrace tranquility with the full might of our consciousness. Even though tranquility is not an achievement but a surrender to the gift of realism, tranquility is an intentional departure from the strong draw of living within our patterns of estrangement.

*The Sea of Tranquility* poem completes my poetic summaries of Joe Mathews's four profound consciousness states-of-being charts. The experiences described in these four charts compose together a comprehensive portrait of our authenticity. I turn now to the relationships among these four arenas of profound experience. The following diagram pictures these relationships using the wisdom of the Taoist yin-yang complementary dualism to describe their relationships.

|  | yin | yang |  |
|---|---|---|---|
| yin | **The Land of Mystery** | **The River of Consciousness** | yin |
| yang | **The Mountain of Care** | **The Sea of Tranquility** | yang |
|  | yin | yang |  |

The nature of the yin-yang complementary polarity is pictured in the following symbol:

Pictured here is a complementary two-some that completes a whole. For example, white and black are complementary colors on this printed page. With only one or the other there would be no printed page. A more profound example is the polarity of nature and human society. In this case, human society is a "yang" of *putting forth* in union with *taking in* nature's "yin." It is human consciousness that takes in nature and puts forth society. If human society is the dark fish in this circle, we also see a dark dot in the light fish of nature. That dark dot indicates that the nature pole includes a human social component before human consciousness creates overt manifestations of human society. Similarly, the dark fish of society includes a white dot of nature—indicating that creating a human type of society is a natural thing to do. Society and nature are not entirely separate processes. They form a polarity that is fundamentally complementary, rather than conflictual.

Good-bad is a conflictual polarity; such a twosome assumes an either-or choice. "Good," as it appears in the yin-yang vision of Reality,

means accepting the both-and quality of complementary polarities—
such as nature and society. "Bad," in the yin-yang vision, means making
society good and nature bad or making nature good and society bad. In
the yin-yang vision, nature and society form a whole that we might call
"Earth processes." Today, we very much need ways to affirm our various
wholes, rather than insisting on warfare between their complementary
parts. For example, Thomas Berry claimed that humans, in being this
natural planet's self-awareness, can be poeticized as the champagne
whose role is to celebrate the whole life of the planet.

Here is another example: the whole of human consciousness has
within it this complementary polarity: *attentionality* (yin) and *intentionality* (yang). "Attentionality" (or paying attention) means *taking in* reality
to our consciousness. "Intentionality" (or freedom) means *putting forth*
conscious actions that are "reality bending." Both *taking in* and *putting
forth* are acts of consciousness that describe what I mean by the word
"consciousness." Both aspects of consciousness are *real* and also *good* in
the context that consciousness is good.

I turn now to describing the complementary polarities in the above
diagram about Mathews's four arenas of profound consciousness.

## Yin-Yang Polarities within Profound Consciousness

The polarity of the Land of Mystery and the River of Consciousness form
a whole in which the Land of Mystery is the more *taking-in* or yin quality,
while the River of Consciousness is the more *putting-forth* or yang quality of these two aspects of profound consciousness. Poetically speaking,
the River of Consciousness flows in the Land of Mystery.

The Land of Mystery is also yin to the yang of the Mountain of Care.
With the word "care" we are indicating a *putting forth*, even though care
is given with our essential being. Care is manifest by caring our care with
acts of freedom responding to the situations that confront us.

The Sea of Tranquility is the most outright *putting forth* or yang of
all four quadrants of the above chart of profound consciousness. In relation to the Land of Mystery, the Sea of Tranquility is a deep action of
obedience to live in the Land of Mystery. Tranquility comes upon us as
we act to become open to the full mysteriousness of the whole Land of
Mystery. Such surrender to Mystery is *tranquility*.

The Sea of Tranquility is also a *putting forth* or yang in relation to the River of Consciousness—the yin in this relationship pair. The intentional pole of our consciousness is employed in this deepest of all acts of courage to be who we actually are. Applying our intentionality to being our being rather than clinging to our delusions is the deepest of all applications of our intentionality.

And, the Sea of Tranquility is yang in relation to the Mountain of Care. Lifting of the whole Earth of care is already strongly yang, but even more yang is the opting to be open or at ease with the load of such overwhelming care.

Let us turn now to some more complex yin-yang contemplations of this master chart:

The
# Void
of
**No-Thing-Ness**

|  | yin | yang |  |
|---|---|---|---|
| yin | **The Land** <br> **of** <br> **Mystery** | **The River** <br> **of** <br> **Consciousness** | yin |
| yang | **The Mountain** <br> **of** <br> **Care** | **The Sea** <br> **of** <br> **Tranquility** | yang |
|  | yin | yang |  |

The
# Fullness
of
**Every-Thing-Ness**

There is a wider yin-yang polarity between the top two and the bottom two of this chart. The whole of the Land of Mystery and the River of Consciousness I will call "the Void of No-thing-ness." The whole combination of the Mountain of Care and the Sea of Tranquility I will call "the Fullness of Every-thing-ness." In this pair "void" is the yin to the yang of "fullness." The whole of void and fullness is a complementary polarity that I will entitle "Spirit Space."

## THE METAPHOR OF SPIRIT SPACE

The words "void" and "fullness" look like complete opposites, yet void and fullness form another complementary polarity—a yin-yang tension using the metaphor of "inner space" to describe a quality of profound consciousness that I will call "Spirit Space."

We can ground the dynamics of this Spirit Space in our interior experience of having been born and having to die. We live in relationships with the entire cosmos, near and far. From that *fullness* of being alive, we experience the *void* of one day not being here. Each of us was not always here, and each of us will not always be here. A cat does not know this, but we humans do know this, unless we have lost touch with Reality is some extreme way. Perhaps we comfort ourselves by supposing a pre-existence before our birth or expecting a post-existence after our death. But even if we do not treasure such beliefs, we may have sought to forget about this always-present void.

Nevertheless, our impermanence is actually with us always. Realism includes confronting our daily deaths as well as our total extinction. The experience of void travels with us each moment. In subtle ways, the void confronts us in the ongoing character of our relationships with anything or anyone. Dear friends can betray us. Our most treasured ideas about life can be revealed as simply wrong. Each moment contains a death to that moment, and a birth of a next moment that may contain absences to which we cling or challenges we prefer not to face.

As we become aware of our ever-present impermanence, we become aware of the enduring *fullness* within which all things come to be and pass away. It is from this inwardly experienced place of fullness that we experience the presence of void. And our awareness of the void reveals the wonder of fullness. These reflections are not just word games, but descriptions of our profound consciousness as human beings.

In Hindu lore there is a metaphorical story of an accomplished spirit teacher who was walking through the ordinary villages of India when he fell into a hole. This was a very strange hole in that he kept falling and falling until he fell out of the known universe, ending up in a sea of jet-black water with a sky that was moonless and starless, as well as sunless. After a period of being shattered and horrified by this sheer void, he noticed that he was still swimming in some sort of somewhere.

Soon he noticed a huge glowing form swimming near to him. It was a huge human-like being who momentarily reached out a hand, put him in its mouth, and swallowed this still-shocked spirit teacher back into the everyday life from which he had fallen out.

The symbolic meaning of this strange story tells of the human experience of void and fullness. Notice the spatial symbolism used to awaken this experience of Spirit Space.

Perhaps the most gripping vision of the void is the discovery that our image of our own self is a fragmentary construction of our finite minds. Our self-image is a self-created rational construction that serves as a substitute for the real "me." Perhaps our self-image has some usefulness for navigating our culture, but it is at best a fragile approximation of the real me. That approximation is laced with comforting delusions of both weaknesses that do not exist or strengths we only imagine are true.

The Atman of Hindu lore points to the mysterious "Great Me" beyond all the viewpoints of my mind as well as my culture's view of me. Many Buddhists have clarified that this Atman is a "no-self" in terms of anything we know in our experience or can put into words or into forms of art, or into human thoughts of any sort.

Whatever I *think* is "me" is not me. Instead, I am a wondrous Spirit Space of fullness and void to which the human mind can only point with rough metaphors. Such metaphors can point to our experiences of a profound consciousness that neither words nor silence can reach. Yet this profound depth of being profoundly conscious is always present, though often hidden. It can, however, be present to our consciousness. This profound consciousness has a quality of mystery, wonder, or awe that we may want to escape, but this presence of void and fullness is inescapably who I am.

In his book *The Void*, A. H. Almaas speaks of how the clients of his psychological/spiritual counseling tell about what it is like for them when they are loosening from their old self-images. These clients share their experiences of a "pure spaciousness" or an "empty clear space." Almaas gives the following description of this inner space he finds in his clients and in himself:

> The experience is pleasant and freeing, bringing lightheartedness and joy. In the experience of spaciousness and openness, one experiences the absence of emotional heaviness and a release of the sense of burden. There is mental clarity and lucidity of perception. All the senses become sharper, as if cleansed and rejuvenated. The body feels light, relaxed, agile, and buoyant. It is similar to the experience of being in a clear open space with fresh and crisp air—as if on the top of a high mountain on a clear day, or on a broad beach—but it is experienced inside. And ultimately it becomes clear that we are not a subject experiencing this spaciousness—we are the spaciousness.[3]

The above paragraph is Almaas's own poetry about his own experiences, but he is claiming that, as a therapist, he is finding such awareness occurring in his clients. He is telling us something that is not only personal for him, but a widespread experience—indeed, a truth about being authentically human. This spaciousness may be described in many ways, and our experience of it can become more vivid.

Nevertheless, we can take the following as true: beyond the pains of perpetually giving up who we think we are, we can move into a spaciousness that manifests our heart's courage to take in all these humiliations of self and thereby find a powerful type of joy on the back side of these rude discoveries.

## THE METAPHOR OF SPIRIT TIME

It can be said that the religions of Hinduism and Buddhism are especially effective in assisting us to become aware of our Spirit Space. It can also be said that the religions of Judaism, Christianity, and Islam can be especially effective in assisting us to be aware of our "Spirit Time." These three Semitic-originated revelations of authenticity provide metaphors for our profound humanness that are taken from our experiences of time. Many of us may be unwittingly sharing our experiences of Spirit Time through telling our life stories or sharing with others our actual participation in social history.

---

3. Almaas, *Void*, 22.

The following chart is a completion of the previous chart about Spirit Space with metaphors for Spirit Time included. On the left side of this chart, I have added how the combination of the yin of "mystery" and the yang of "care" can be viewed as comprising a whole that I am naming "the Encounter of Connectedness." On the right side of this completed diagram I have added how the combination of the yin of "consciousness" and the yang of "tranquility" can be viewed as comprising a whole I am naming "the Response of Aloneness." Now let us imagine a still larger whole (comprised of "encounter" and "response") using "time" as a metaphor for describing our experience of profound humanness. "Spirit Time" is a name I am using for this whole—a name that contrasts with the whole of "Spirit Space."

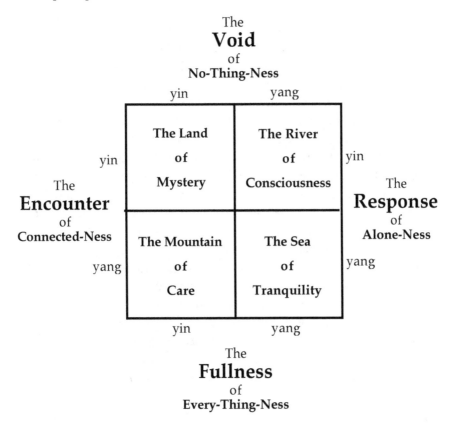

"The Encounter of Connectedness" means something deeper than simply bumping into another temporal being—such as another person, another society, the whole Earth, or even the entire cosmos. This encounter happens in conjunction with some temporal encounter, but only when that temporal encounter is seen in the context of an encounter with the Wholeness of Being. This Wholeness encounter is *taken in* to the profound awareness of a human being (or a community of human beings) and is then *responded to* within the ongoing events of temporal history.

The poems and speeches of Isaiah are an example of this sort of metaphorical thinking about Spirit Time. The scroll of Isaiah was written by at least two different persons. The Isaiah of the early chapters was confronted with the conquest by Assyria of the northern sister kingdom of Israel. These events also posed a threat of conquest to the southern kingdom of Judea. The aristocracy of Judea was in a panic to ally with Egypt as a defense against Assyria. Isaiah advised against that. His speech stated that Assyria was only a rod in the hand of the Wholeness of Being. According to Isaiah this Wholeness defined the actual encounter that Judea was facing. When that Wholeness is finished beating up on these sleepy coastal kingdoms, Assyria too will be handled by that same Wholeness that we people of Judea are now facing.

The king of Judea and his advisors went ahead with a treaty with Egypt; so instead of marching on by the hill of Jerusalem, the Assyrian army stopped by to conquer that tiny kingdom as well. So we find an Assyrian horde of troops surrounding the walls of Jerusalem asking for the king to be thrown over the wall. Isaiah advised simply waiting and doing nothing of the kind. So the Assyrian force waited and waited and waited and suddenly got up and left. Perhaps some other priority called. Perhaps the Assyrian general decided that conquering this city was not worth the cost in soldiers. Whatever their reason, they left. Isaiah's reading of the situation proved accurate. The response of quiet to this dreadful threat was seen by Isaiah as trust in the Wholeness of Being as a power beyond any power possessed by this Assyrian force. Isaiah had been informed in his thinking and action by his memory of how such a trust in the Wholeness of Being had encouraged his slave ancestors to leave Egypt and start a new mode of living. In other words, all humans are always facing possibilities that are not obvious to the customs of thought that most people have absorbed.

The Isaiah story also illustrates the dynamic I have named "the Response of Aloneness." Isaiah was making these decisions of consequence in his own profound aloneness. Isaiah illustrates how our own solitary choices can bend the course of history. This profound aloneness of human freedom is a denial of any sort of fatalism. The power of human freedom is not the only power that is bending history, but we decide things and those decisions matter. We are in dialogue with many other forces that are determining outcomes. But we humans can also access our essential freedom—a freedom that is not an instinct or a personality conditioning. This profound freedom is a gift of our own profound consciousness, a capacity to creation out of no cause but freedom itself. Nor can this free response be explained by some sort of probability calculation. Such freedom is finite in its power to bend history, but it is absolute in its ability to participate in bending history as a deep personal agency or power to change things that is essential to the deep essence of being an alone human.

So through this awakening, we see that human history is not a tale already told—just working its way out. History pays attention to my and your requests. Our choices make a difference. The Wholeness of the Real is granting you and me right now this power of freedom. As you or I operate our solitary freedom, we assist this Wholeness in determining the outcomes that actually take place.

You or I are absolutely alone in this freedom. Even though we are always living among others and have close companions who advise us, each person is also 100 percent alone in making choices in dialogue with the Every-thing-ness that is meeting us and endowing us with this essential freedom. The importance of this freedom for understanding everything about being human must not be underestimated. The Response of Aloneness is built into the essence of our profound consciousness.

The prophet Jeremiah gives us an even clearer illustration of this profound aloneness. I will also tell his story in a fragmentary manner. Following the Assyrian withdrawal from Jerusalem, it became a popular belief that the Wholeness of Being would always protect Jerusalem from conquest. But after the empire of Babylon had conquered the empire of Assyria, a new means of controlling spunky kingdoms was put in place— namely, carrying off the aristocracy and intelligentsia into captivity in Babylon. So when this became likely for Judea, almost no one believed that this would happen to them. "After all," they said, "we are in a covenant with the Wholeness of Being." Jeremiah was an exception to this interpretation of these matters. Therefore, Jeremiah was deeply alone with a very unwelcome message. His painful laments express this aloneness.

Convinced that Jerusalem would indeed be conquered and large numbers of people would be carried off to Babylon, Jeremiah's message of trust in the Wholeness of Being included the announcement that a new covenant with that Wholeness was being offered—a covenant that did not need the existence of a nation for its embodiment. This new covenant would be a covenant written on the heart—that is, on the solitary profoundness of our primal human aloneness—an arrangement written into the inner life of each exiled person heading off to Babylon. Ezekiel and others who went to Babylon carried on this viewpoint. The peoplehood of these exiles was preserved and later some of them returned to rebuild their decimated homeland.

The New Testament writers also used metaphors taken from these "encounter" and "response" metaphors of Spirit Time. The life and death of Jesus was given the Christ title as a statement about these events being a New Exodus from the evil kingdoms of the world into the Kingdom of God. This meant a profound humanness that was detached from the old Adam and Eve and resurrected to a new Adam and Eve—a rebirth that is best understood as the beginning of an ongoing transformation from inauthenticity to authenticity—that is, of being the profound humanness that we humans were constituted to be.

Paul was clear that we who share in this transformation are still "sinners" who are called to press on to the full stature of Christ Jesus. That means to me that this new (or restored) humanity had already come into being, even though it would continue this coming into being over against still more rude awakenings to our hidden layers of estrangement. In a later chapter I will discuss in more detail the deep meanings that are held in these strange symbols of Christianity.

My point in this chapter is that the Spirit Time metaphor (encounter and response) points to a dynamic of profound humanness that is on the same level of profoundness as the Spirit Space metaphor (*void* and *fullness*). The fact that some religious traditions emphasize one of these polarities more than the other need not trouble us. I believe that encounter-and-response thinking about profound humanness is present in the East as well as in the West, even if Eastern luminaries do not emphasize Spirit Time as much as Western luminaries tend to do. Also, we now live in an era in which East and West are learning deeply from each other. For example, Gandhi's Hinduism and Thích Nhất Hạnh's Buddhism clearly use the metaphors of Spirit Time as well as the metaphors of Spirit Space.

However that may be, my vision of a vital and relevant next Christian religious practice will use both the void-and-fullness symbolism of the East along with the encounter-and-response symbolism that is so important to the heritages of Judaism, Christianity, and Islam.

There is still a deep gulf between Eastern and Western religions as they are currently being understood and/or misunderstood. I believe that the fruitfulness of interreligious dialogue between East and West can be further enhanced by exploring further how (1) void and fullness (Spirit Space) and (2) encounter and response (Spirit Time) are related to one another as a complementary duality, rather than as a conflictual either-or.

## THE EAST-WEST DIALOGUE

By "East" and "West" I mean the religious cultures impacted by Taoism, Hinduism, Buddhism, and others of Eastern origin in encounter with the religious cultures impacted by Judaism, Christianity, Islam, and others of Western origins.

In 800–500 BCE there was very little or no dialogue between the prophets of Israel who were making their speeches and recording their scrolls in the geography indicated by Egypt, Israel, Judea, Persia, and Babylon with the teachers and writers of the Upanishads in India or the Taoism of China. When Marco Polo (1254–1324 CE) spent years in China and reported his experiences back in Italy, the cultures of the East were still basically unknown in the West. But in recent centuries masses of spirit-questing Westerners have visited and/or studied in the East to learn from Taoism, Hinduism, Buddhism, etc. In addition, thousands of brilliant Eastern teachers have come to the West to teach Europeans and Americans something Western populations have eagerly sought. Also, this exchange has moved from West to East. Western religions are now well known and often deeply absorbed in the East.

Also, the dialogue between Eastern and Western religions has moved into deeper water—the inner clash of the basic metaphors used in these two very different cultures. We are slowly getting a better understanding of what the basic religious metaphors of each region have accomplished in their home regions, as well as what both sets of metaphors might now accomplish in tandem with each other within every geographical location.

I am convinced that the theologizing and religious practices of a vital and relevant next Christianity will not be adequate for these times without appropriating the Spirit Space emphasis of the East as well as reviving the Spirit Time emphasis of the West. Combining these two depth probes into our humanity has been at least partially pictured in the charts discussed in this chapter. We are, I believe, very close to the beginning of reconciling these two very different religious emphases. The hints outlined in this chapter are far from complete understanding of this complementary polarity.

Nevertheless, I present this chapter as strong clues to a direction for this dialogue to continue. Clearly, there can be found in the depths of our profound consciousness a meaning for both Spirit Space and Spirit Time, provided that we remain clear that both "space" and "time" are images taken from the scientifically explored temporal world and then used *metaphorically* to describe a profound consciousness that we only experience contemplatively.

In the next chapter I will talk about religion more directly and about how religion is related to the states of profound consciousness that I have examined in these first four chapters.

# 5

## The Roots of Religious Practice

### *What Is Religion?*

SO WHERE ARE WE now in Part One of this book? Chapter 1 is about "What Is Mind?" Chapter 2 is about "What is Consciousness?" Chapter 3 is about "What Is Truth?" Chapter 4 is about "What Is Profound Consciousness?" These first four chapters illustrate what I mean by an "awakenment" to profound consciousness. In chapter 5 I explore the topic "What Is Religion?" I will define "religion" in relation to the already explored topic of profound consciousness.

With the word "religion" I am pointing to humanly crafted practices that make awakenment to profound consciousness more likely. Such practices define "good religion," and thereby also define "bad religion." There are many ways for a religion to become corrupt. A relatively innocent way is simply to become out of date—no longer relevant to the contemporary cultural situation. A once-good religion can become meaningless, or at least misleading, simply because it was a useful practice crafted for a different time and place.

A less innocent way for a religion to become corrupt is making claims for a specific religion that ignore the human or temporal quality of every religion. No religion has dropped down from some other realm, risen up from nature, or been put into the mind of a chosen human by some absolute being. Such stories are no more than mythology to express the supposed trustworthiness of some person or text. Religion can be a useful social process, alongside commerce, education, politics, and sewage disposal. Religion is distinguished from these other social processes by its purpose. Following is a story that I have found useful for defining the core purpose of all good religion.

A student of Buddhism asked his teacher if meditation caused enlightenment. "No," said the teacher, "enlightenment is an accident. Meditation only makes you more accident prone."

This insight can be expanded to all religious practices. No religious practice causes the awakenment to profound consciousness. Profound consciousness is who we essentially are, and our awakenment to this profound consciousness is restored to us by the active agency of Profound Reality rescuing us from our estrangements from Profound Reality. This healing event is variously called "illumination," "grace," "salvation," "justification," "sanctification," or something else.

A religious practice can only make us more prone to having such "healing events" happen to us. What we are healed from is our own and our culture's sickness of attempting to rebel or escape from the ever-present Profound Realty from which there can be no escape and with regard to which no rebellion can win. A popular escape today is the assertion that there is no Profound Reality, leaving us to create or cling to whatever view of reality we like better that the Reality that actually confronts us.

This chapter will help illustrate the view that religion arose in human history to meet a real need—namely, overcoming your, my, and our unrealism, illusions, false stories, or some other escape from the truth of our lives—our true depth, our true temporality, our true response-abilities, and many other aspect of our profound consciousness. These assertions amount to an enduring paradox: religion is a temporal social process, and yet religion is a prompt that makes more likely the happening of a profound realism—an "Eternity" in the actual living of an ordinary human life. "Good religion" then means any human practice that meets these requirements of healing our profound lives.

In this chapter, I want to avoid using my own Christian understanding as my criteria for judging all religion. I am seeking a definition of "good religion" that applies to every religion, including Christianity. The explorations outlined in chapters 1–4 were about that, and those awarenesses will now be used as the profound realism in terms of which we can evaluate all religious practices, their moral norms, their theoretics, their communal life, and their mission to our times.

Being a temporal human invention, every religion has both its limitations and its potentials for being twisted into uses that are opposite to the purpose for which good religion comes into being and plays an essential role in human social life. My efforts toward clarifying and illustrating these assertions will be admittedly incomplete, yet my current understanding is the product of a long life of improvements from earlier understandings. My life history suggests to me the possibility of still further improvements during the rest of my life, and in the lives of others for centuries to come. It is a bit puzzling to describe the modest confidence I have on this topic.

## The Religious Math of "2" and the Religious Math of "3"

Before I move to a detailed exploration of the relation between profound consciousness and religious practice, I want to point out that the chart I will use in this chapter will employ a threefold patterning: knowing, being, and doing.

In chapter 4, I used religious symbolism based on a twofold patterning (the Taoist yin-yang complementary dualisms). The fourfold chart of chapter 4 (Land-River-Mountain-Sea) is a double duality.

Christian heritage is famous for using triune modeling. Triune modeling can also be found in Hinduism (e.g., Shiva-Brahma-Vishnu). Triune modeling also shows up in these triplets: attentionality-presence-intentionality as well as trust-love-freedom. The most abstract of these model-organizing triplets is knowing-being-doing. In this modeling, "knowing" means *taking into consciousness*, "being" means *being a state of consciousness*, and "doing" means *consciously putting forth an intended action*. This triplet (knowing, being, doing) names three dynamics of ordinary human consciousness.

Both the dual and the triune modeling of profound consciousness are creations of the human mind. The reality of profound consciousness is an *enigma* beyond any of our human models. We need to keep reminding ourselves that our contemplative thinking about profound consciousness is not the same as our contemplative experience of profound consciousness. Yet such insights into our temporality need not discourage us from thinking about our experiences of profound consciousness. Indeed, the enigma that characterizes this topic can function as a challenge to do more thinking about our experiences of this reality. My modeling in this chapter is simply one attempt at such description.

My thinking in this chapter will focus on nine (3 x 3) states of profound consciousness: (1) three states of *taking in our essential trust* in profound and temporal realism, (2) three states of *our essential presence of care or love* toward profound and temporal realism, and (3) three states of *putting forth our essential freedom* in outgoing actions of historical manifestation of this profound and temporal realism.

In correspondence with each of these nine states of profound consciousness, I will describe a set of religious practices that is most helpful in preparing us to open to and receive that associated state of profound consciousness.

In this chapter I am not yet discussing Christianity as a separate religion. I am describing religion as a human practice that is found in human life. When I refer to Christianity in this chapter, it is in this context of Christianity being one of the many religions that have been created by human beings.

The following chart contains nine states of profound consciousness that are listed inside the large circle. Nine types of religious practices appear outside the large circle, except for the state of profound consciousness that appears in the very center of the chart. The name for that type of religious practices appears at the bottom of the chart. It may help if the reader meditates a bit on this chart—observing its basic relations among all these named elements, and contemplating the poetry used to name these states of profound consciousness and the nine types of religious practices that most closely associate with those nine states of profound consciousness.

Though a specific religious practice may make us accident prone to many of these states of profound consciousness, it remains my intuition that each of these nine types of religious practice is especially useful for accessing one of the nine states of profound consciousness. So on the above chart, I have placed the name for each type of religious practice adjacent to a corresponding aspect of profound consciousness. These associations will help illustrate my main point that religious practices are rightly named "religious" if and only if they are helpful in opening us to one or more of these states of profound consciousness.

I will start my description of these nine states of profound consciousness and their associated sets of religious practices on the left side of the chart. These three states of profound consciousness have to do with the topic of trusting Profound Reality.

# The Practices of Religion

With each of the large bolded words add the modifiers:
## The Practice of_____

Corresponding with the center Circle associate:
## The Practice of Visionary Trance

## I. TRUST

In describing trust as an aspect of profound consciousness, I will discuss knowing trust, being trust, and doing trust. The descriptive name I am giving to knowing trust is "transparent attention." The descriptive name I am giving to being trust is "universal forgiveness." The descriptive name I am giving to doing trust is "effortless letting be."

## 1. Transparent Attention and Profound Dialogue

I am using the word "transparent" to mean looking through our concepts, through our thinking, through our sensing, through our feelings, to the Profound Reality that includes being profoundly conscious. We mostly see Reality through the *screens of our mental concepts*, but consciousness can also see beyond our screens of thought to experiences of consciousness that are not yet conceptualized or given artistic forms. The edge artist or researcher knows this. We get glimpses of this capacity of consciousness when we change our mental screens. Such changes can be like closing down an old universe and entering a new universe. While this is happening, we live in the gap between these two mental universes. This gap is a window into the consciousness that is doing the looking, the thinking, and the doing of our living. This gap is also a window into the Mysterious Over-all-ness of which our consciousness is one part. Once we see these gaps between our changing mental screens, we see that Reality is beyond our screens and that our screens are simply approximations or representations of Reality. With this awareness, the spirit journey called "transparent attention" has begun. Indeed, until transparent attention begins for us, there is no spirit journey.

Transparent attention also involves becoming *aware of our estrangements* from Reality. "Estrangement" here means confusing our ideas about things with the realities that our ideas are attempting to describe. Our ideas can only express a limited realism, and we may prefer a limited realism as part of our attempt or hope to avoid, deny, or escape Profound Reality. Living with the awareness that our ideas are always approximate is part of living in the presence of Profound Reality. Such transparent attention enables us to be a more authentic thinker.

Finally, we are seldom aware of how approximate our ideas about Reality actually are. Reality is so vast compared with what we know that we might view ourselves as 1 percent knowledgeable and more than 99 percent ignorant. This is the nature of Reality and thought. When we view our shelves of read books, we may avoid noticing that. We may have forgotten that at times we have looked into the face of sheer wonders and been content with the dread and fascination of that.

Nevertheless, with our recent technologies and "advanced" thinking, we can easily suppose ourselves to be far more wise than our primitive ancestors, *yet they and we confront the same Mysterious Reality*. We are just viewing from a different place. Sometimes the wildly unusual poetry coming to our view from these primitive humans reflect wisdom about Realty that we have forgotten or never learned.

We sometimes *despair* over the fact that we are *so ignorant*. But such despair is not necessary. We can simply come to terms with the fact that we are *more vulnerable than we thought*. And that is as it should be for a finite creature. We can be *gloriously humble* about our humanity. If we settle into this transparent attention to Absolute Mysteriousness, we will become stronger thinkers and more compassionate actors. Transparent attention is not anti-intellectualism. It is a simple detachment from dogmatic beliefs, reigning theories, unshakable moralities, unalterable plans, etc. Transparent attention means embracing a middle ground of *deep thinking about the finitude of all thinking*.

## The Religious Practice of Profound Dialogue

Ira Progoff wrote extensively about "profound dialogue." He created many workshops and workbooks to aid his workshop members in discovering the deep dialogues that go on in our lives—not only with parents, care takers, siblings, family, and teachers, but with artists, authors, fictitious characters, saints, mentors, anti-heroes, villains, political figures, archetypes, etc.

The Order:Ecumenical of which I was a member provided me with a religious practice we called "seating our meditative council." I was challenged by this exercise to list all the persons in my life history that had deeply affected me in my present living—persons with whom I still consult in my living. For example, here are some of the people who now sit on my meditative council. On the front rows sit prominent Christian theologians like Paul Tillich, Rudolf Bultmann, H. Richard Niebuhr, and Dietrich Bonhoeffer. Close by are philosophers like Susan K. Langer, Søren Kierkegaard, and Jean Paul Sartre; physicists like Richard Feynman; psychologists like Rollo May and A. H. Almaas; equity champions like Martin Luther King Jr. and Malcolm X; feminists like Charlene Spretnak and Mary Daly; ecologists like Thomas Berry, Naomi Klein, Bill McKibben, and David Orr; authors like Herman Hess, J. K. Rollings, Jane Austen, Nikos Kazantzakis, Fyodor Dostoevsky, and Sir Walter Scott; and Buddhists like Jon Bernie, Adyashanti, and Eugene Cash. On some of the back rows of my meditative council sit some anti-heroes like Stalin, Hitler, and Trump.

I do the seating for my meditative council. I can decide who is most important and on what topics. I decide what to take from each counsel member and what to leave. This swarm of voices is my swarm of voices. I seat them as needed, I add new voices, and I constantly change them around to meet changing circumstances. Nevertheless, I am obedient in a freewheeling way to my council. This council often moves me beyond my comfortable constructions and transports me into transparent attention.

Actively referring to my council—rereading, rehearing, re-seeing their art, comparing their advisements and insights—adds up to a religious practice that makes me more accident prone to the accident of profound consciousness—especially the state of profound consciousness I am calling "transparent attention."

## 2. Universal Forgiveness and Boundless Inquiry

*Universal forgiveness* is equally profound as transparent attention. I will not dwell on this state as long as I just did with transparent attention. Here is the essence of this profound inner discovery: there is always a fresh start no matter how much we have messed up. But here is the rub: if I accept the forgiveness and a fresh start from that mysterious Profound Reality for myself, I accept it for everyone—for Donald Trump, for Adolf Hitler, for a shame-filled mother, for a dominating father, for a difficult sibling, for an oppressive companion, for *everyone*. Perhaps the key estrangement for which we each need forgiveness is our own lack of forgiveness for others. Universal forgiveness is not a feeling, nor is it a bare idea, and certainly it is not an excuse. Universal forgiveness is a state of profound consciousness. I am always being offered a fresh start in realism. I am always confronting this question: Do I have the courage to accept my fresh starts? Do I have the courage to accept the possibility of a fresh start for everyone? The experience of a crushing karma is real; I do get stuck in my patterns of unrealism. Nevertheless, this bondage can be broken by the discovery of universal forgiveness. Accepting universal forgiveness includes the awareness that this includes stepping forth into a wider realism. And this includes departing from the unrealism in relation to which universal forgiveness has appeared.

## The Religious Practice of Boundless Inquiry

The practice of journal-keeping is an example of *boundless inquiry.* The journal-keeping I have in mind is a solitary writing practice that is deeper than a mere factual diary. Journal-keeping, as a religious practice, includes reflections on the deep matters of living—including my estrangements from realism, my failures to accept my fresh starts, my discoveries of profoundness, and so on. Looking intently upon our own real experiences reveals the ever-widening truth about the presence of our forgiveness for fresh starts and about the unrealism for which I need forgiveness.

Boundless inquiry can also be a group process. Here is a practice that I have found unusually helpful. In pairs, one person asks the other person a specified question that prompts some depth recall about real living, such as: "When have you not known what to say?" After hearing the answer, the questioner then says "Thank you" and repeats the question, prompting the partner to recall more. This is repeated several more times. Then the roles are exchanged and the questioner becomes the answerer. When this simple practice is honestly done, the participants experience what boundless inquiry means. Such practices can move us into an ever-deeper need for a realization of universal forgiveness, including the fresh starts that this entails. The feelings about such a moment may be quite melting—like being washed in some sort of deep awe. Or not. Perhaps just quiet. Perhaps frightened. Choices are called for to accept the consequences.

## 3. Effortless Letting Be and Holistic Detachment

Being authentic is a *grand surrender.* It takes *no effort* to be authentic. Effort is always needed to stop being authentic. Authenticity is a great relaxation—a rest from the struggle to be something else than who I am in the context of what is actually happening. Letting your actual life be what it is allows you to be your most creative and productive self. Such letting be is not a passive flight from living. Letting be includes letting be our active putting-forth existence as well as our more quiet, patient existence.

The state of *effortless letting be* means viewing our lives as a gift to be *expended* rather than a possession to be defended. Effortless letting be includes accepting that "life and death are two wings on the same bird."[1] You cannot truly fly your life with only one wing. Living without dying is not a real life. Dying without living is not a real life either. Letting be both our drive to live and our necessity to die is a surrender to our profound consciousness.

Effortless letting be means accepting my "righteousness" from Reality as a gift. Authenticity is not an achievement. Authenticity is a gift. We do not invent it or achieve it. We simply accept the gift of authenticity and then live out the consequences of this style of effortless letting be our essential authenticity.

## The Religious Practice of Holistic Detachment

"Holistic detachment" is my name for the religious practice that is most helpful for accessing effortless letting be. Giving up any absolute need for status, for wealth, for acceptance among our peers is the core of holistic detachment. Detachment is the opposite of clinging. Holistic detachment means being open to life and to the joy of living, as well as to the seriousness of expending our life through dying our life for the causes that truly matter to us.

As a religious practice, holistic detachment is often a group practice. It can be a vow of poverty as part of living in a monastic order. It can be some other pattern of living simply—perhaps just a good economic model for your whole life expenditure, perhaps just keeping good records of your expenditures and your income. Such simple details about our economic living can be a religious practice. This may surprise many people. It is evident, however, that thoughtlessness and indulgence is quite the opposite of the religious practice I am calling "holistic detachment."

## II. FREEDOM

Freedom as a quality of profound consciousness is described on the right side of the above chart. I will discuss knowing freedom, being freedom, and doing freedom. The descriptive name I am giving to knowing freedom is "primal merging." The descriptive name I am giving to being freedom is "inherent purity." The descriptive name I am giving to doing freedom is "attuned working."

---

1. Rumi.

## 4. Primal Merging and Persistent Intentions

*Primal merging* has to with allowing your essential freedom to flower. Freedom is not an achievement, but a surrender. We can even consider freedom as an obedience—putting into action our capacity to make choices based on free responsibility alone. The truth is that we are all fleeing freedom into fatalism or sloth. The truth also is that our essential lives are response-able. Because we are able to respond, we are responsible for everything. Our freedom is always there to do something about whatever we are facing. As the baseball player Yogi Berra once philosophized, "When you come to a fork in the road, take it."

Many people do not want such response-ability to be true. We often prefer to be a safe robot of our culture or peer group. Or we opt to be a victim of our druthers or addictions—anything except taking on our essential, free response-ability. Primal merging means surrendering to the gift of freedom as an essential quality of our being. One of the inconvenient truths is that freedom has to be enacted, done, intended, put to work. This truth gets buried and forgotten in our unconscious flight from freedom. Freedom has to be enacted or it becomes bondage to this or that flight from freedom.

We flee from our essential freedom because enacting our freedom undermines who we think we are. Who we think we are is always an approximation at best, and a hoax at worst. *We do not know who we are.* We are beyond our comprehension. We are basically ignorant about what we can know or what we can be or what we can do. We can surprise ourselves. *Surprise* is who we are. *Freedom* is a surprise with which we can continually surprise ourselves. Primal merging is a surrender to this permanent state of a *surprising freedom.*

### The Religious Practice of Persistent Intentions

All the long-established world religions do the religious practice of *persistent intentions* in some manner. Jews, Christians, and Muslims call it "prayer." Christian prayer can be well understood as ritual acts of freedom that tend to open our ordinary living to our essential freedom. For example, in the story of Jesus in the Garden of Gethsemane, we see him preparing to face his impending trial, crucifixion, and death. That is what prayer is—choosing how to handle the next thing. Christian heritage has

broken down the types of prayer into these four types: petition, intercession, confession, and gratitude.

Petitionary prayer is about making persistent intentions for our
own authentic living and general well being. Intercessory prayer is about
making persistent intentions for other people and for the various social
topics and causes that grasp us. Confessionary prayer is about making
persistent intentions that open myself to my estrangements, despairs,
and other failings and flights from responsibility. Gratitudinal prayer is
about making persistent intentions that open myself to my thankfulness
for all the sustaining gifts for my living, including my forgiveness and my
fresh starts in realism. Such gratitude is the willingness to live victori-
ously, whatever life we are being given. The opposite of being grateful is
despairing over our lives. In each moment of our lives, our deep freedom
is challenged to be grateful or not. Freedom's deepest challenge is to be
grateful for freedom itself and for the life issues within which this freedom is constrained to operate.

Whole books are needed to clarify the depth and wonder of these
practices of persistent intention. These simple religious practices make
more likely an accessing of our ongoing *primal merging* with our essential freedom.


## 5. Inherent Purity and Full-Body Ex-formation

*Inherent purity* means actions that originate from the clear space of
*freedom*. Inherent purity means living *beyond good and evil*—beyond
the stories of the superego that holds our oughts, duties, customs, and
morals; beyond the approval of our parents, offspring, friends and other
social peers; beyond all the libraries of ethical thought; beyond all the
preferences of our own bodies, minds, and habits. Inherent purity means
finding our native wildness, outside of our current society, and outside
our imagined alternative societies. This aspect of freedom turns up in
many religions. Buddhism, Judaism, and Islam are all strong on this deep
freedom, as is Christianity. The second and third chapters of the Bible tell
a story about Adam and Eve. This story can be viewed as a myth about
our fall into impurity from the inherent purity of our freedom.

Adam and Eve ate from the tree of the knowledge of good and evil.
That is not the tree of knowledge, but the tree of illusion—the illusion
that we know good and evil. Even though our parents taught us good and

evil, our culture taught us good and evil, and our own internalized superego screams good and evil at us as a constant instruction, we humans are still ignorant of good and evil. We are not "like God" (like Eternity), knowing good and evil.

We may not want to accept that there is a Profound Reality that does, metaphorically speaking, know good and evil. But the accurate implication of this ancient myth is that Ultimate Reality is the true "Judge" about good and evil, and that we humans do not possess and will never possess such eternal wisdom. So eating from that tree means a fall into illusion, believing our socially conditioned superego over the Profound Reality we actually confront and might be consciously experiencing in every event of our lives. This commonly committed crime against realism sends us out of the garden of inherent purity into the wilderness of unrighteousness, wreckage, hypocrisy, arrogance, ruthlessness, and eventually to some very dry desert of despair.

So that does it mean to live in the Inherent purity of value ignorance? It means noticing that all our specific, real-world decisions are ambiguous—choices between "right" and "right" and between "wrong" and "wrong" in terms of the many principles, laws, values, goals, and ends with which we are familiar. We are always being called to leap into the dark in terms of having a fully true justification for our actions. To say that differently, our essential freedom is our only justification. Full ethical risk is our inherent purity. We can act in freedom without regret because we live in the presence of a Reality that forgives us before, during, and after each deed we make.

This does not mean, however, a license to follow our own druthers, desires, or arrogance, for that would not be the realism within which freedom lives. This inherent purity of freedom does not mean an end to our thoughtfulness about what we do. Indeed, we think more carefully when living in this deep freedom, because we know that we will never know a fully justified decision. As Dietrich Bonhoseffer put it, we "observe, judge, weigh up, decide, and act"[2] without a justification of our choices. Freedom is exposed when we realize that all our choices are ambiguous—that after all our careful thinking, each decision is a leap beyond the justifications of that thinking. This freedom is our inherent purity.

2. Bonhoeffer, *Ethics*, 248.

## The Religious Practice of Full-Body Ex-formation

Freedom is a type of dance of our whole being—a full body putting forth of our lives. The following workshop leaders have given me a deeper sense of what a religious practice looks like that emphasizes accessing inherent purity. I have done several workshops with the Sufi dance teacher Dunya. She teaches her classes to move from our body center to the rhythm and emotion of some highly expressive music. Such movements access and express some freedom—freedom from our mind's control and the habits of our body. She taught us to make creative movements that are very small to some full-body Sufi twirling.

My second example is learning to do "ex-formation" from Cynthia Winton-Henry and Phil Porter, the founders of a movement called "Interplay." "Ex-formation" is the opposite of "information." Instead of taking in information, these two innovators playfully trick their classes to risk creative ex-formation—putting forth our lives before others. For example, they might ask each member of a group do a few minutes of fake opera. Or we might be asked to tell a story about something in a loud voice or high voice or low voice. One of my favorite "rituals" that they invented is entitled "Dance, Talk, Three." Each member of a small group does this ex-formation three times: a brief whole-body dance followed by a brief talk about whatever comes to mind. These simple exercises assist us to exit our slaveries to mindsets and body habits and allow space for our creative freedom to be further uncovered. I am suggesting that such practices open us to accessing our inherent purity aspect of profound freedom.

## 6. Attuned Working and Historical Engagement

We only exercise our freedom in the time-bound situations of our actual lives. Profound Reality is working, and I am working in the midst of the flow of temporal events provided to me by Profound Reality. I am compelled to respond in some way or another, free or enslaved by my personal patterns. Freedom is an *attuned working* to my real confrontations. Freedom is given along with the situations in which we are being given that freedom. This profound freedom is an *obedience* to making free choices in our given situations. The exercise of our freedom can alter those situations, but what those alternations turn out to be is almost always a surprise to us. I am constantly being given new and strange situations to which I must attune and respond. Freedom is an attuned obedience to being who I am in the situations that are being given to me. Attuned working is an obedient freedom I employ in my "I-Thou" dialogue with Profound Reality.

## *The Religious Practice of Historical Engagement*

We do not often think of *historical engagement* as a religious practice; nevertheless, simply being part of something real and needed is enriching at the profound consciousness level. For example, in the 1960s I chose to go to Jackson, Mississippi and march in that troubled place with Martin Luther King Jr. As I walked down that street, I saw people of all colors on their porches—some curious, some angry, and some bored. There were also stern-looking police officers on all the corners, and there was a remarkable collection of people marching along beside me. Reflecting on this later, I became clear that this was a religious practice that may have had spirit impacts for all of us involved. I am willing to propose that engagement in history-bending of any clearly relevant sort is a religious practice that accesses our essential freedom, especially the attuned working aspect of our essential freedom.

# III. CARE

I am going to describe care or love as a third major aspect of our profound consciousness. In this section I will discuss knowing care, being care, and doing care. The descriptive name I am giving to knowing care is "autonomous strength." The descriptive name I am giving to being care is "enchantment with being." The descriptive name I am giving to doing care is "outgoing compassion."

## 7. Autonomous Strength and Foundational Meditation

*Autonomous strength* is a state of profound consciousness that has to do with discovery of my true self—discovery of the love of my true self as part of my love of overall realism. A true love of self is more complicated and profound than simply indulging in my druthers, fears, lies, and other means of flight from my real life. Autonomous strength includes an affirmation of my weaknesses, rather than my fabricated strengths.

Autonomous strength is an affirmation of my strengths, rather than my fabricated weaknesses.

In Hindu lore there is a goddess named Kali who holds a sword and wears human skulls on her belt. She is represented as a goddess of destruction, but a deeper understanding of her significance is the "destroyer of falsehood"—false self, false world—all our illusions about life in general. This understanding makes her a goddess of love for our essential self. We are invited by her symbolism to be Kali—to take out our own sword of truth and chop off the head of any falseness that comes our way. We are invited to be a warrior for truth—tough on lies, delusions, escapes, excuses, blaming, and anything else that diminishes the honesty of our living. In that sense, Kali is a symbol of our autonomous strength—loving being our true selves.

Being Kali can be frightening, for we do fear parting with our delusions and excuses as well as our habits of blaming others for our own failures, mistakes, and weaknesses. We can also be frightened to discover the greatness of our existence, the autonomous strength that is our true profoundness. However frightening autonomous strength may be, it is also liberating and empowering. Autonomous strength means a full flowering and strengthening of our authentic humanity.

## The Religious Practice of Foundational Meditation

*Foundational meditation* is a religious practice that most especially associates with the autonomous strength aspect of profound humanness. Mediation practice can be awakening to many aspects of our profound consciousness, but autonomous strength is certainly one. The awakened Buddhists are the experts on this religious practice. Foundational meditation appears in other religious practices, often called by other names: yoga, contemplation, spirit dance, Tai Chi.

In Buddhist practice, meditation has to do with being silent enough and still enough to allow our consciousness to sit by and watch our breathing breathe. In doing so we also watch our feelings feel, our thinking think, and our being be. Foundational meditation is a discipline or practice that can assist us to make convincing discoveries about the nature of consciousness. By simply sitting in this super-aware way and not engaging in our thoughts or believing our thoughts, but simply watching our thinking think, we may awaken to being our being.

If our consciousness wanders off into mental spins, as it usually does, the discipline of Buddhist meditation challenges us to simply *choose* to return to watching our breath. Watching the breath is not the most important feature of this practice. The breath is used as a tool of discovery. As we watch our consciousness watching our breath, we are becoming aware of consciousness itself. And we may be led to discovering the strength of our profound consciousness. As we become aware of this mysterious *whoever* that is doing this watching, we are becoming aware of *who we really are*, rather than who we think we are. Who we really are shows up as a *vast awareness* and a *great activist* potentiality, a being who is mysterious beyond our understanding. This autonomous strength is who we are.

## 8. Outgoing Compassion and Devotional Singularity

I am skipping from the bottom of the chart on "autonomous strength" to the top of the chart on "outgoing compassion," leaving the center circle, "enchantment with being," to discuss last. If autonomous strength is about deep care for ourselves, outgoing compassion is about that same deep care for others.

*Outgoing compassion* is not indulging others in their lies, addictions, and other escapes from their Autonomous strength. In outgoing compassion, we are caring for others in ways that promote their finding the profound consciousness that they are suppressing with their estrangements. Our care includes assisting others to be aware of their estrangements, and their doorways back to realism—the life of true aliveness, joy, peace, autonomous strength, and yes, outgoing compassion for others. This is very different from being a support for other people's falseness. Outgoing compassion means being a slayer of falseness in others, as well as in ourselves.

At the same time, outgoing compassion is a state of outgoing care for every neighbor with whom we are neighbored, whatever their state of estrangement and however horrifically that estrangement is manifesting. Real persons can show up both caring in some areas and hate-filled in others. Outgoing compassion walks a strange path of loving each and every person for their potential for profound humanness in spite of their tragic estrangements from that profoundness. Outgoing compassion also manifests as care for the structures of society that support and care for everyone—fostering justice in the social structures of human life.

## The Religious Practice of Devotional Singularity

*Devotional singularity* is a religious practice that helps us access our out-going compassion. This is a hard practice to clearly understand. It has to do with regularity in the practice of a specific set of religious symbols. Those symbols might be Buddhist or Hindu, Jewish, Christian, Islamic, or something else. But whatever our choice of a religious practice, de-votional singularity means practicing that religion every day, every week, every year, for the rest of our life or until we change our religious practice. A complete religious practice is a group experience as well as a solitary experience. Good religion is communal as well as solitary. Strange as it may seem at first, a devoted religious practice enables us to access our outgoing compassion for other human beings as well as for other animals, plants, and this planet as a whole. Good religion regularly and intently practiced makes us more prone to the accident of accessing our compassion for others. This is one of the ways that good religion is extraordinarily practical, rather than an escape from the issues of our personal and social lives.

## 9. Enchantment with Being and Visionary Trance

*Enchantment with being* is a state of profound consciousness that might be said to be central to the other eight aspects of profound consciousness. Profound consciousness is actually one reality. The nine aspects described in this chapter are parts of a rational topology of this one overall chakra of humanness that I am calling "profound consciousness" or "awaken-ment to Profound Reality."

This ninth aspect of profound consciousness can be described as the intensification of the other eight aspects of profound consciousness. Enchantment with being is a love of the overall Land of Mystery that includes everything else. Indeed, the symbol "Land of Mystery" points to the Every-thing-ness that is also the No-thing-ness out of which all mere things come and to which all mere things return.

So what does it mean to be enchanted with this Land of Mystery? Enchantment with a lover or with a job or with a place to live are all fa-miliar to us, but enchantment with being expands infinitely the meaning of "enchantment." This ninth state of profound consciousness is a love for that Absolute Mysteriousness that engulfs everything. Such love means a love of realism—a love for complete realism, however challenging or horrifying the particulars of that confronting realism may be. When we access our enchantment with being, we are accessing a deep passion for being truthful, realistic, and honest about everything, and courageously so. This ninth state of profound consciousness is a kind of *glow* that enriches the other eight states of profound consciousness.

## The Religious Practice of Visionary Trance

*Visionary trance* is the religious practice that is most effective in opening us to the conscious state of enchantment with being. We often associate trance with the practice of primitive shaman, Holy Rollers, the early Quakers, and other sorts of trance-evoking religious communities. Most of us have been suspicious of such practices. We may, however, have participated in visionary trance processes that seemed less weird to us. Perhaps we have participated in a drumming circle in which we were "carried away," as we sometimes call it. Or perhaps we have experienced a dance-a-thon or songfest that created a trance-like state.

Coming away from a lengthy religious retreat, we might have found ourselves in a trance-like distance from our ordinary lives. For example, at the end of a several-day Almaas-inspired workshop that I attended, the workshop planners had anticipated that we would be in a trance-like state. So they had planned a last session that was focused on preparing us for reentry into our ordinary lives. Perhaps these frequently experienced trance-like experiences will help us see the ordinariness of visionary trance practices.

I also hope these examples will assist us to appreciate those ancient shaman who promoted flights of trance out of their ordinary world in order to conduct rights of passage for their youth or healing events for the troubled in spirit. Perhaps we can identify somewhat with leaving the reality of the ordinary world altogether in order to reenter that same ordinary world with a new perspective on practically living our actual lives. Though such appreciation can be meaningful to us, trance practices still present us with a need to sort out the genuine from the superstitious.

Nevertheless, I still view the religious practice of trance inducement to be a religious practice that is most closely associated with preparing the trance participant for the accident of accessing his or her enchantment with being.

## CONCLUDING COMMENTS

This concludes my descriptions of these nine aspects of profound consciousness and the related nine types of religious practice. Each of these pairs can prepare us for an awakening to these nine aspects of our profound consciousness. If you do not identify with all of these examples, any one of them can illustrate the main point of this chapter—a human practice can be defined as "religion" (that is, "good religion") if and only if it functions to assist humans to become more open to their profound consciousness of Profound Reality.

Using our own experiences of profound consciousness, we can critique our dealings with religious practices. A religious practice is good or bad religion—strong or weak, relevant or out of date, priceless or demonic—in relation to its usefulness in opening us to our deepest lives.

Finally, I want to underline that a religious practice is something that we do—something that we *practice* doing on a regular basis. Religious practice also includes our thinking or theoretics about our practices, but religion is not simply ideas or doctrines or beliefs of any sort. Rather, our religious thinking is part of our practice of doing our religion. Also, part of our practice is the communal life within which our practices and our thinking about those practices take place.

Part Two of this book is about the Christian religious practice of theologizing. The above general definition of "religious practice" will help us gain a fresh grasp of the meaning of doing Christian theologizing.

# Part Two

## Christian Theologizing

IN PART ONE, I focused on topics that are relevant for the renewal of any religion, if "good religion" means practices that make more likely the accessing of our essential humanity. Here is a one-sentence summary of Part One: *If your religious practice does not assist you to transcend your culture, then your practice is not religion at all; it is just some sort of support group for living in the status quo of your culture.*

True religion assists you to leave your cultural and thereby enter into the essential truth of human existence. True religion also enables you to return to your culture as a transformer of that culture. The resulting cultural transformations of that return are all temporal changes, for culture is temporal. Authentic religion is a temporal process very similar to language and art, but distinguishing itself by being geared toward opening us to the Eternal.

I turn now to the Christian religion—a "next" practice of this religion that opens us to the Eternal. In Part Two of this book, I will be examining the more theoretical topics of a renewed form of Christianity, and then in Part Three I will be examining the more communal and ethical aspects of a renewed form of this practice.

I do not deny that many of the current forms of Christianity have become destructive, or at least irrelevant to the twenty-first century. And Christianity is only one religion among many other religions. Not only must a next Christian religion not claim to be the best religion, but also a next Christian religion is called to be open to being enriched by other-than-Christian practices. I do claim, however, that Christianity is a heritage that is worth recovering for this era. I intend to show that the original breakthrough that spawned Christianity makes a valuable contribution to interreligious dialogue and cooperation.

My critical approach to Christian heritage includes far more than another theology to place alongside current theologies. Rather, I will demonstrate a method of "theologizing." I will maintain that there is no such thing as an altogether right or unchanging Christian theology. By "theologizing" I mean an ongoing action by a community of people, rather than any sort of fixed position or dogma.

I am inviting the reader to join me in a type of theologizing that is intended to be consensus-building for a viable and vital future for Christian practice. One criterion for my critique of current Christian practice was laid out in Part One—being a viable and vital religion for this cultural era. A second criterion of my critique is faithfulness to the Jesus Christ revelatory event. I will be elaborating how the Jesus Christ event was a unique disclosure of the friendliness of Profound Reality and how this revelation is a blessing toward being restored to the realistic living of our lives.

# 6

---

# The Death of Heavenly God-Talk

My mentor for twenty years, Joe Mathews, was a graduate student and long-term friend of H. Richard Niebuhr. "Perpetual revolution" is a phrase and an emphasis that Mathews took from Niebuhr and passed on to me. This phrase was applied to all social structures, but especially to the perpetual revolution in religious forms. The word "God" and words like it have been in perpetual revolution all the way back to Moses and all the way forward to any radical new edition of Christianity.

One of Mathews's favorite spins was about how Spirit cries out, "Give me form," and how the form that we give to Spirit can never contain the Spirit that cried out for form. For example, the first sermon I ever gave was on the topic of Christian love. I chose as my text, "Let love be genuine." That talk held some spirit truth, but I have come to see that Christian love is far more wondrous than that small insight. In a recent talk I emphasized love as "care" and how such love is like Atlas holding up the planet, a very heavy "mountain of care."

The word "God" indicates another topic that is still in process of clarifying for me. During the last two decades I have done a great deal of thinking and living in relation to this topic. Here is a list of questions that are still open questions that I and many others continue asking and answering again and again.

## Four Sets of "God" Questions

Set 1: "God" as a concept within two-realm God-talk (i.e., traditional theism):

How is two-realm God-talk dead?

When was two-realm God-talk alive?

How and why did two-realm God-talk die?

Why is this "death" crucial for future realism?

Set 2: "God" as a discussion about Reality:

What is Profound Reality?

How do we know Profound Reality?

How does Profound Reality differ from our rational pictures of reality?

How is Profound Reality true for every human?

How is Profound Reality related to religious practice?

Set 3: "God" as a devotional word that adds no content to Profound Reality:

What does devotional language add to our experience of Profound Reality?

What use of the word "God" is needed in a revitalized practice of Judaism, Christianity, or Islam?

In this devotional sense, is there a post-two-realm theologizing?

Is such theologizing restricted to devotional communities?

How does Christian theologizing relate to the disciplines of learning?

Set 4: God" as a discussion of all devotional words for Profound Reality:

Is the Great Goddess of deep antiquity a devotional word for Profound Reality?

Are "Yahweh," "Our Father Almighty," and "Allah" devotional words?

What words for a "God-devotion to Profound Reality" do we find in: Hinduism? Buddhism? Taoism? Native American lore? African lore? And more?

In this chapter I am going to deal with the first two sets of questions—that is, questions on "God" as two-realm God-talk and questions on "God" as Reality. In chapter 7, I will deal with the third set of questions—that is, questions on "God" as a devotional word that adds no content to Profound Reality. Then in chapter 8 I will deal with the fourth set of questions—that is, questions on "God" as the Great Goddess and other poetry.

## "GOD" AS A CONCEPT WITHIN TWO-REALM GOD-TALK (I.E., TRADITIONAL THEISM)

How is two-realm God-talk dead?

When was two-realm God-talk alive?

How and why did two-realm God-talk die?

Why is this "death" crucial for future realism?

### How Is Two-Realm God-Talk Dead?

Some members of the Christian community speak of "the death of God" or even "the end of theology." I take the view that "the death of God" does not refer to an end of all use of the word "God." I, along with others, understand "the death-of-God" discussion as pointing to the end of something temporal—namely, the obsolescence of an ancient metaphor of religious thinking held in the word "transcendence." For over two thousand years Christian theologizing has used this familiar metaphorical narrative—a "story-time" imagination about a transcendent realm in which God, angels, devils, gods, goddesses, and other story-time characters are living in an other-than-ordinary "realm" and "coming" from that "realm" to "act" within our ordinary human space and time. This not-of-this-world "heavenly" realm is metaphorical talk, not scientific truth.

Being metaphorical, however, is not the problem. Metaphor is a common form of expression for the contemplative approach to truth. Every religion uses metaphors, cryptic parables, koans, icons, and the like. The problem for us today is not the use of metaphors, but the continued use of a now-obsolete metaphor—the double-deck metaphor of heaven and earth, spirit and matter, supernatural and natural, etc. This use is further complicated by taking that metaphor literally (that is, scientifically).

Is there an alternative to the transcendent metaphorical system of religious reflection that allows us to interpret the word "God" for our time? Yes, and this includes rescuing for contemporary discussion words like Yahweh, Allah, divine, Thou, and others that we find in biblical texts and in the other writings of Judaism, Christianity and Islam. I will illustrate how we can translate all of this heritage from the double-deck metaphorical expressions to single-realm metaphors that speak meaningfully to our times.

I will focus on Christian texts, but these issues appear for Jews and Muslims as well. Many Jewish, Christian, and Muslim interpreters are now many decades into this basic issue. We can see this shift very strongly in the writings of Rudolf Bultmann, who insists that we point with the word "God" to something we actually experience in our everyday lives. Paul Tillich added to this discussion the very important insight that good Christian theology cannot mean by the word "God" a being alongside other beings—"God" must point to the "Ground of Being." As Tillich seeks to describe our experience or our "Ground of Being," he points with poetry to the mystery, depth, and greatness of our existence.

My long-term teacher and mentor Joseph Mathews used the following metaphorical picture to illumine the Eternal depth of our temporal existence. Imagine living within temporality symbolized by a sheet of paper. A spot on this paper begins to turn brown and then bursts into flame. Living in this paper, we don't actually experience the match that is held under the paper, but we certainly do experience the browning and burning of our temporal world. So this match would be something that is only available to our metaphorical imagination. We have no actual experience of the match; we only experienced the browning and burning.

I am going to use the term "Profound Reality" (or "Reality" with a capital "R") to refer to the "Source" of this "browning" and "burning" of temporal stuff. By this I do not mean visiting another realm. I mean a profound happening within temporal stuff that is the essence of temporal stuff being temporal. This happening is not a change in the temporal stuff, but a change in our conscious attitude toward all temporal stuff. This happening cannot be described using the scientific approach to truth, but we can describe this experience using the inner truth of our experiences of dread and fascination, plus the courage to stand within what we might call an "awe experience"—that is, an experience of profound consciousness of a wonder-filled Wholeness or Awesomeness.

Dread, fascination, and courage are categories for our contemplative description of our experiences of "awe" or "wonder." In other words, an "awe experience" includes a dread of the unfamiliar Land of Mystery, a fascination drawing us into that Land of Mystery, and the courage to live such intensity. And this "awe" is both an inward experience of being awed and an outward experience of encountering the Awesome. So an experience of awe can fill all outward space as well as all inward space. A whole group of people can manifest together a whole roomful of awe, but only the awed ones notice that this room is full of awe. In that secret sense, the awed ones see a wonder-filled Awesomeness that sources the awe. This Awesomeness may also be called "the Eternal." This new concept of the Eternal is not a picture of some divine space other than temporal space/time; it is a profoundness of actual subjective experience that is inaccessible to scientific objectivity without in any way contradicting the validity of scientific knowledge.

Our awe experiences do not necessitate the assumption of a Divine Being in some parallel universe, but we can intuit why early generations talked that way. We can see now how all our awe/wonder goes on in this one universe of our everyday experience. This train of observation and thoughtfulness implies a distinction between the Awesome and the awe/wonder that is described in terms of dread, fascination, and courage.

This new metaphorical system helps us in our twenty-first-century culture to interpret stories like Moses and the burning bush. Here we have a temporal bush and we have a temporal Moses and we have a temporal state of consciousness within Moses. What then is on fire? This strange fire is burning up Moses' understanding of who Moses is, of what bushes are, of how Reality works, and of what Moses might do with the remainder of his life. Moses found all of this to be in flames that did not consume Moses or the bush. So interpreted, this is a vivid story about a breakthrough of the Awesome in a temporal moment of a temporal human life. It is a subjective experience of Profound Reality or the Eternal that manifests in this temporal sheet of paper.

The Moses stories associate Moses' bush experience with memories of these people's stories about the "God" of Abraham, Isaac, and Jacob. The people that Moses led out of Egypt may indeed have had a religious tradition in common that the burning bush moment brought back to life. Whatever was historically happening in this dim antiquity, the Moses story has lived on and it can be rescued for our time if we associate the "God" of Moses with the term "Profound Reality."

When we associate the word "God" with the words "Profound Reality," we are interpreting both of these symbols in a fresh way. The term "Profound Reality" roots "God" in the personal experiences in our everyday lives. And the word "God" renders "Profound Reality" a trustworthy experience that we can deem friendly (or we can view it as *love* for humans like you and me.) Trusting the friendliness of Profound Reality renders realism the best-case scenario for living our temporal lives.

It is important for us to remain clear that Profound Reality is a Land of Mystery that the human mind cannot fathom. This profound depth of Reality can be said to be invisible even though Profound Reality shines through the passing temporal events that are visible to eye and mind. An ordinary bush can burn with the extraordinary. A temporal event can burn with Eternity. A finite human being can glow with the presence of Eternity.

This Eternity need not be imaged as another space that is separate from the ordinary space/time of our living. Our human experience of the Eternal is met in the temporal flow and only in the temporal flow. There is no Eternal place to which we are going some day. The Eternal is an interiorly perceived event happening now, and only now.

Furthermore, this fresh view of Eternity does not imply contempt for the temporal. Rather, this understanding of "Eternal" implies a fulfillment for each and every ordinary temporal event of our lives. Each temporal event has an Eternal depth or glow or burn. Eyes and ears cannot see or hear the Eternal, and mind cannot grasp in mental symbols this Eternal connection. Only our enigmatic consciousness can "see" the Eternal, and in this context of thought "see," "seeing," and "seen" are metaphorical uses of these temporal words to point to a *That* which is not temporal.

In this fresh context, words like "ordinary" and "extraordinary," "temporal" and "Eternal" are viewed as categories of human perception. We live in one, and only one, realm of Reality, with many temporally viewed aspects of that Eternal Reality.

## The Enigma of Oneness

The Oneness of Profound Reality is not seen by eye or mind. We do not "see" Oneness directly. Oneness is in part a devotional category. Oneness means that we are devoted to serve all aspects of our Real experience, rather than viewing the Real as part friendly and part enemy. In this One-ness point of view, the only enemy is our estrangement from the One Profound Reality within which our own person and all other persons actually do dwell.

The Oneness-of-Reality point of view within Christian faith is not a denial of the diversity of our experiences of the Eternal or the diversity of our experiences of the temporal. Differentiation and multiplicity characterize our temporal lives. Multiplicity can even characterizes our God-talk. In the God-talk of the Bible, there are many angels or servants of the One that express and carry out the actions of the One. But this Oneness is maintained in spite of this manyness in our ways of experiencing the Eternal. In the opening verses of the Bible, the One God says to some angels, "Let there be light!" and this is done by the One's many servant forces. Such poetry was intended to preserve the Oneness of Reality, not to fragment the Oneness of Reality that is being obeyed in a true grasp of Christian faith.

In the current philosophical world, we find the frequently held view that no experience of Oneness exists—that we only experience multiplicity. Multiplicity does indeed define the temporal aspect of this temporal/Eternal polarity. Every temporal thing comes into being, has its time, and then passes out of being alongside things that do not pass out of being yet. So, every temporal thing is a thing among the many things. "Temporality" and "multiplicity" are words that define the same set of experiences.

"Eternal" and "Oneness" are also words that define the same experience. And when we experience temporality as indeed temporal and fully impermanent, that means that we are standing in the presence of the Eternal—the Oneness of Awesome Mystery. Paradoxical as this may sound, if there is a "place" in our consciousness from which we can see temporality, that is also the "place" in our consciousness where we are experiencing the Eternal. In the human sense, a cat does not "see" temporality: she does not know that she was born or that she is doomed to die. But you and I do, or at least can. And that awareness of our temporality is an experience of the Eternal. If this sounds irrational, it is because it is. The Land of Mystery in which we dwell is indeed irrational in the sense that it is beyond the powers of the human mind to encompass.

Let us also notice that the scientific approach to truth deals only with the temporal—that is, only with facts formulated from the experiences of our senses. We have to use the contemplative approach to truth to "see" the Eternal. The Eternal is an experience of our enigmatic consciousness, not of our eyes, ears, nose, tongue, or skin. Consciousness can see the temporal and the Eternal, the impermanent and the permanent, the passing and the lasting, the multiple and the Oneness. Science as science has no way to talk about subjectivity, or about the enigma of consciousness, or about our profound consciousness of this One Profound Reality.

Without this elemental experience of Eternal Oneness in the midst of the temporal manyness, we have no way to understand Western religions anew. This Oneness quality pervades all three of those religions. From "Hear Oh Israel, our God is One" to Islam's "There are no gods but the One," we find a firm dedication to Oneness. And this same Oneness is included in the witness of Christianity, even though this heritage has explored Oneness as *an experience with three faces*. But those three faces, which I will discuss fully in a later chapter, are faces of our one experience of the Oneness that is the boundary of our experiencing.

Here is a first clue toward understanding this threefold aspect of our experience of the One. God, the Almighty, can point to our experience of an awesome Otherness. Holy Spirit can point to our experience of Awe within our own consciousness. The third aspect of that one experience is that community of the temporal human awed ones who embody the awe and live in obedience to the Awesome. So, the Awesome, the awe, and the awed ones give us a hint of how one experience of One Profound Reality has three "faces." Such a view of this Oneness and its three faces does not necessitate a second story to the universe where we can imagine three "persons" sitting beside each other. Christian theologizing can proceed with triune thinking without returning to "heavenly God-talk."

Finally, here is how we remain clear about what this death of heavenly God-talk means: (1) we remain clear that two-realm God-talk was always metaphorical talk when such God-talk was still alive and (2) we remain clear that a new metaphorical talk can express the same human experiences that Christians pointed to when they were using the now-obsolete story of a heavenly King with his angels in a universe next door.

## When Was Two-Realm God-Talk Alive?

How far back do we find humans using the two-story mythology? The Australian Aborigines have preserved a very old human culture. I am guessing that their use of the term "dream time" as distinguished from "ordinary time" reflects a two-story mythology that may be twenty-five thousand years old. The Great Goddess devotion of human antiquity is at least that old. Even though her story is very earthy, her personification makes her a character in a story time that is being used as a symbol for a devotion to the Profound Reality of our Land of Mystery experiences. Though the religious poetry of these ancients may not have had the intellectual sophistication we can muster today, it remains plausible that the experiences to which these ancients were witnessing were deeply human and were being articulated using a two-realm quality of metaphorical speech and art.

Since pre-civilization antiquity provides no written records, we have to consult archeological evidence and writings written much later. So, we don't know with certainty how early the aliveness of two-realm God-talk began. But we do know that it is older than any verse of the Bible.

Also, we may need to explore how the Axial Period (approximately 800–322 BCE) of deepening consciousness made this separation between nature and super-nature more vivid. We can grasp how, for that time, this increased vividness was a progressive step in human lucidity about the mysterious truth of human existence.

As Christians we certainly have to come to terms with how the aliveness of second-story God-talk remained firmly in play through the lifetimes of Luther and Wesley and other such luminaries until the nineteenth century of the Common Era. Nietzsche, Kierkegaard, and Dostoevsky did not kill the two-realm God-talk; they simply noticed that the old metaphor was dead. They articulated their sophisticated awareness of this consequential historic happening as the cultural death of the two-realm God-talk.

## How and Why Did Two-Realm God-Talk Die?

Quite likely, there are many good answers to this question of which I am not aware, but here are three answers that seem probable to me:

(1) The advent of modern science brought with it a skepticism about all metaphorical thinking. Since the contemplative approach to truth is almost entirely metaphorical in its expressions, it was easy for objective-thinking scientists to reject metaphorical expressions altogether as superstitions arising from our subjectivity. Superstition is often present in human subjectivity, but it is not truthful to give all artistic and religious expressions a back seat to scientific discovery, thought, and technological

usefulness. The contempt for two-story God-talk became especially strong when these metaphors were taken literally (that is, made to compete with scientific literalism). Heaven, angel visitations, devils crawling around in our psyches, virgin birth stories, indeed the whole two-realm mode of thought, when taken literally, is simply not true in the sensibilities of our scientific culture.

(2) Even when those old metaphors are understood to be metaphors that were meaningful at one time to human contemplative quests, the two-realm metaphorical picture still has drawbacks to the lucid-minded, democracy-affirming, freedom-loving individual citizen in the modern world. For example, the "Kingdom of God" is a primary metaphor in the teachings of Jesus, yet "kingdom" clashes with our democracy-loving sensibilities and with our emphasis on human freedom. Many if not most modern people cannot support the myth of a Divine King for symbolizing Profound Reality. We tend to oppose authoritarian rulers here on Earth, and so we tend to lack the old longings for a good earthly king that might be used to symbolize a friendly Profound Reality that calls us to our essential freedom and demand freedom of us.

(3) Our modern uncovering of the vast possibilities of human agency to bend history has exposed modern minds to the depths of our essential freedom. This tends to make any sort of determinism an enemy of our common sense. So, if "God" is to mean an Almighty Someone in a parallel universe telling us what to think or making our decisions for us, we are thereby robbed of truth we know about our own freedom that we can choose this or that destiny for ourselves and for our planet.

We know that there are no inevitable outcomes to human history. Both optimism and pessimism are left in the dust by the discovery that we humans can bend history both constructively and destructively. As we face our challenging choices, we cannot wait for some outside force to take care of us or make our choices for us. If we are to have a relationship with an all-powerful Reality, it will have to be a Power that provides us this profound freedom and allows us choices that have consequences.

These factors are among the factors that have killed the usefulness of that old metaphor of a Supernatural King acting upon us from a parallel space.

## Why Is This Death of the Old Metaphor
## Crucial for Future Realism?

First of all, any plausible theologizing will need to be clear that the old metaphor was a metaphor, not a set of literally true statements dropped down from a heavenly space. Such superstition is being meaningfully rejected by thoughtful members of our culture. Scientifically aware persons will tend to reject literalistic fantasies. Even those who are not scientifically literate will tend to reject any statements that do not accord with their daily experiences. We next theologians will have to walk the razor's edge of honoring science fully while also exposing the limitations of the scientific approach to truth, as well as the validity and importance of the contemplative approach to truth.

We will also need to train ourselves and others with facility to use one-realm metaphors, rather than two-realm metaphors. Once learned, these new tools allow a deeper listening to the Christian Bible's older metaphorical expressions and that can show us how we can reword those texts for our era. We can, with surprising ease, translate those two-realm metaphorical expressions into our one-realm metaphorical expressions that speak to thinking and freedom-loving people today. The single-realm interpretation of biblical texts can call forth in ordinary people a vast ocean of truth that is currently being lost in the panic to interpret those scriptures in a literalistic manner.

Further, we will be required to explore with people the truth of the "determined yet free" paradox in an accurate way. Here is a way of understanding and sharing that paradox: *Profound Reality, our God-devotion, determines humans to be free and thereby to share in determining the future along with all the other determining forces.*

Human freedom does indeed bend history. Metaphorically speaking, Reality "calls upon" humans to do this history-bending in ways that are realistic and just. We can say that Profound Reality determines everything only if we include in this vision the insight that Profound Reality is determining humans to be a finite freedom that is also a determining force in the course of things. This does not mean we humans can determine the exact consequences of our choices, but we can choose courses of action that we then surrender to Profound Reality—the determiner of all consequences. Such thinking is needed for making plausible both (1) the presence of human responsibility and (2) the presence of an all-powerful Profound Reality in dialogue with which our free obedience and obedient freedom is engaged. This includes an attitude toward the future that is neither pessimistic nor optimistic, but simply aware that the present contains real alternatives that are yet to be determined.

"God" can then be a word that shapes our view of Profound Reality into a Demanding Friendliness. The word "God," as I will explore fully in later chapters, includes an acceptance of the possibility for humans to trust Profound Reality and thereby to view realistic living as the best-case scenario for our lives.

Also, in a later chapter, I will explore how the Exodus revelatory event, and the Jesus Christ revelatory event, and the event of Moham-med's dawnings, each in their own way witness to the "friendliness" of Profound Reality toward human beings.

I turn now to my second set of questions:

## "GOD" AS A DISCUSSION ABOUT REALITY:

What is Profound Reality?

How do we know Profound Reality?

How does Profound Reality differ from our rational pictures of reality?

How is Profound Reality true for every human?

How is Profound Reality related to religious practice?

### What Is Profound Reality?

I began this book with five chapters, each of which contributed to a de-scription of profound consciousness. To understand the concept of "Pro-found Reality" we need to be clear that profound consciousness is part of Profound Reality. Profound Reality is also that about which profound consciousness is conscious. Our consciousness, both ordinary and pro-found, is still a temporal process. Profound Reality encompasses all tem-poral processes, including consciousness, and this includes our profound consciousness of Profound Reality. Profound consciousness, though temporal, is profound in the sense that it is an awareness of Profound Reality that is not temporal. Profound Reality is eternal, inaccessible to finite human minds, yet accessible to our temporal human consciousness when this temporal consciousness is in a profound consciousness state of awareness.

## How Do We Know Profound Reality?

Whenever we are experiencing profound consciousness, we are being touched by Profound Reality. As we respond in profound consciousness to Profound Reality, we create metaphorical expressions about being touched by Profound Reality. In so responding, we are touching Profound Reality back. This experience of being touched by Profound Reality and touching Profound Reality back is what "profound" means. This being touched by Profound Reality and touching back is the profound aspect of the contemplative approach to truth. I will illustrate this being touched and touching back with a slight rewording of Psalm 90:

> Profound Reality has been our place of safety
>    from generation to generation.
> Before there were mountains
>    or the earth or humankind,
> Profound Reality was Reality from eon to eon.
>
> Profound Reality turns humankind to dust.
>    "Turn back to dust" says Reality to all
>    offspring of the human species.
>
> But for Profound Reality, a thousand years is like a day.
>
> We, however, pass by like a short watch in the night.
> We fade to nothing like a dream at daybreak,
> like grass which springs up in the morning
>    and is withered away by nightfall.
>
> It is as if Profound Reality were angry with us.
>    We are brought to an end.
>    We are silenced in mid-speech.
>
> Profound Reality lays bare our unrealistic living.
> Our desires to be immortal are unmasked as illusions.
>
> As all our days pass by, each one is marked
>    by this dark shadow of sternness.
> Our years expire, each with a deep sigh.
>
> Seventy years is the span of our life,
>    eighty if our strength holds.

Yet the hurrying years are labor and sorrow.
So quickly they pass and are forgotten.

We who know Profound Reality are those who also feel
   Reality's stern unrelenting power.

So let us allow Profound Reality to teach us,
   to count and value each of our days.
Only then, will we be truly wise.

Let us notice both the gifts to us and the limitations of us are aspects of our touch with Profound Reality. Touching Profound Reality back is most clear in the prayer for wisdom in the closing verses of this psalm.

There is a bit of objective science in this psalm, but mostly it is a contemplative report. Our stern limitations and our wisdom about them are contemplative reports, not simply scientific knowledge. To humans who use only the scientific approach to truth, the meaning of the words "consciousness," "profound consciousness," and "Profound Reality" are inaccessible. A scientist can also be a contemplative being. In the midst of scientific work, a scientist can have experiences of wonder or awe that mean being touched by Profound Reality and touching back. Yet we do not touch Profound Reality through the scientific approach to truth. We touch only temporal processes when we focus on objective observations. To touch the Eternal we must do contemplative inquiry.

The truth of science is very important, but it only touches the temporal, never the Eternal. As a figure within mathematics, "infinity" is not a human touch with Profound Reality. Mathematical infinity is only a piece of rational order created by the human mind. Mathematics is not about Profound Reality at all; mathematics is only an outgrowth of the remarkable capacity for order created by the human mind. That some of our mathematical creations correspond to temporal process may help explain why we evolved this capacity for mathematics.

*All human creations are temporal. In order to touch Profound Reality, we have to contemplate how our direct inner conscious experience of temporality is also a direct inner conscious experience of the Eternal—of the untemporal, unchanging, overall Oneness of Profound Reality.*

## How Does Profound Reality Differ
## from Our Rational Pictures of Reality?

All of our rational pictures of Reality are temporal creations by temporal human beings. This temporality applies to all our rational reports about (descriptions of) our profound consciousness of Profound Reality. Profound Reality is not temporal. Our theologies, myths, symbols, rituals, and icons never encompass Profound Reality. These human-invented symbols may participate in our experiences of Profound Reality, but Profound Reality is forever mysterious—beyond human thinking. Our languages and art forms can approximate reality well enough for us to escape dangers, get fed, sleep, rise, work, play, etc., but these rational forms cannot contain Reality with a capital "R."

There are rational approximations of Reality that are *better* than other rational approximations of Reality. For example, Einsteinian physics is a better approximation of Reality than Newtonian physics because "Reality says so." When the planet Mercury does not follow a Newtonian predicted obit around the sun, that is Reality speaking. When light rays bend around a galaxy of stars, that is Reality speaking. When an atomic bomb blows a small island to pieces, that is Reality telling us that mass times the speed of light squared is a better understanding of mass and energy than Newtonian physics could account for. Newtonian approximations have proven inferior to Einsteinian approximations by a wide margin to a wide audience of thinking observers.

"If all we have are approximations of Reality," we might ask, "does this Profound Reality even exist?" And if it does "exist," are we supposing a next-door universe of Spirit? "No" is my answer to this last question. "Yes" is my answer to the first question—we do have the possibility of a real experience of Profound Reality. We can consciously experience Profound Reality in the midst of our everyday ordinary temporal lives.

Here is how a teacher of mine, Joseph W. Mathews, dealt with this question of experiencing Profound Reality. The following story happened in 1954 at the Perkins School of Theology in Dallas, Texas. Some miles south of Dallas is a city called Waxahachie. Joe spoke about visiting this unusual city of Waxahachie, and then he said, "If you haven't been to Waxahachie, you haven't been to Waxahachie." He applied this parable to experiencing Profound Reality.

With regard to having an experience of this Eternal Profound Reality, you may have been to Waxahachie but did not know it was Waxahachie.

For example, if you have ever experienced the total temporality of your existence—body, emotions, thoughts, consciousness, everything—then you have been to Waxahachie—that is, you have experienced the *Void* the Absolute Oblivion—that is, the total impermanence of all temporal aspects. This Void is an aspect of Eternity—of Profound Reality. *Fullness* is another aspect of Eternity. The remarkable interconnectedness of a whole cosmos of amazing processes, including our tiny unlikely existence, is an experience of the Every-thing-ness of Profound Reality.

Perhaps an updated statement of Jesus' eight beatitudes or *blessings* may help us remember if we have ever been to Waxahachie. Here is my bit of thoughtfulness about the essential paradox in each of these renowned sayings.

B1. Those who are humiliated by the loss of all things are visiting the Eternal.

B2. Those who mourn the loss of all things are tasting Eternal comfort.

B3. Those who own nothing, own the entire Earth as a gift from Eternity.

B4. Those who hunger and thirst for rightness are being fully fed by Eternity.

B5. Those who forgive everyone are forgiven of everything by Eternity.

B6. Those who are pristinely honest of heart can view the Eternity.

B7. Those who reconcile others with realistic living walk with Eternity.

B8. Those who suffer opposition for living the full truth of realism are walking and talking exemplars of Eternity.

## How Is Profound Reality True for Every Human?

It is only our temporal qualities that make each of us unique. Profound Reality is the very same for every human being because it is Eternal. Our bodies are unique. Our cultures differ greatly throughout the planet. Our religious practices differ. Our insights and models about Profound Reality are temporal and they can differ. The very words "Profound Reality" are temporal words. My definitions of these words are temporal. But what I am pointing to with these two words is not temporal. Profound Reality is none of these temporal things. Profound Reality is eternal.

Because Profound Reality is eternal, every conscious being can confront the same Profound Reality. We can have our own words for Profound Reality. We can have our own paragraphs seeking to point to Profound Reality. But with all our many temporal ways of pointing, we humans can be pointing to the same Profound Reality—or it is not Profound Reality to which we are pointing. This is not a word game. This is a clarification about what the words "Profound Reality" mean in this context.

For example, I was teaching an eight-week course in Australia in which eight Australian Aborigine adults from an Outback Presbyterian mission were in attendance. They had learned English and how to function in twentieth-century Australia, but they still breathed a culture that was more alien to me than I had ever encountered. I was not always sure that I was making contact with these eight people, though I was amazed at the insights that some of the women expressed.

One morning after I had given a talk on the Land of Mystery, a jet-black slim Aborigine man came forward and said to me, "When you give a talk like that, I can hear you in my own stories." I had no idea what stories he was referencing, but I did get it as I looked into his eyes and saw him looking back at me, that we were of the same humanity, capable of the same profound consciousness of the same Profound Reality.

## How Is Profound Reality Related to Religious Practice?

In chapter 5, I gave many specific illustrations of religious practices that can assist or provoke the likelihood of experiencing a profound consciousness of Profound Reality. I was thereby defining religion. Religion is not a set ideas or a set of moral maxims. Religion is a practice—an ongoing action of a group of human beings. So defined, religion is a temporal set of humanly invented practices. Those practices are supported by temporal religious theoretics that give understanding and support to these practices. This makes Christian theologizing a part of Christian practice. Christian ethics is also part of Christian practice. These temporal theoretics and ethics are supported by temporal communities of human beings who do these practices in the context of that community's theoretics. Therefore, religion—like education, agriculture, or politics—is one among the many temporal social processes.

What distinguishes religion from these other social processes is the purpose of doing a religious practice. That purpose is assisting humans to become more likely to experience Profound Reality in their own subjectivity—that is, being aware of that same Eternal Profound Reality that confronts us all

This enigmatic Profound Reality is not a passive something that needs to be looked for somewhere. Profound Reality is, metaphorically speaking, like a huge, fast-moving truck loaded with iron bars that is running into us in each and every moment of our lives. This encounter is not always violent, but it includes our injuries and our death. It is true that the ending of our lives is not the only experience we have of Profound Reality. A simple rainbow, a falling meteor, a blooming flower can also be an occasion for having our entire sensitive being run over by Profound Reality.

## A Concluding Question

What does the word "God" or "Yahweh" or "Allah" add to the word "Profound Reality"? That question is the topic of the next chapter.

# 7

---

# A Contentless Monotheism of Devotion

In this chapter I am continuing my exploration of the list of questions begun in chapter 6. The set of questions for this chapter focuses on our twenty-first-century use of the word "God" as a word of devotion to Profound Reality.

## "GOD" AS A DEVOTIONAL WORD THAT ADDS NO CONTENT TO PROFOUND REALITY

What does devotional language add to our experience of Profound Reality?

What use of the word "God" is needed in a revitalized practice of Judaism, Christianity, or Islam?

In this devotional sense, is there a post-two-realm theologizing?

Is such theologizing restricted to devotional communities?

How does Christian theologizing relate to the disciplines of learning?

### What Does Devotional Language Add to Our Experience of Profound Reality?

Devotional language like "God," "Christ," "Holy Spirit," "grace," and even "sin" adds nothing to our understanding of Profound Reality. These words only add devotion to that Mysterious Profoundness that we never fully understand. Devotion is *contentless*, rationally speaking. This contentless devotion is about a *relationship* with whatever content real life is offering us.

Both "sin" and "God" can be viewed as words of devotion concerning the same Profound Reality. "Sin" is the devotion "No" to Profound Reality, and "God" is the devotion "Yes" to Profound Reality. We are all involved in both "Yes" and "No." We all quite often reject, fight, and attempt to flee Profound Reality, from which no escape is possible. Sin is a paradoxical escape from the inescapable, a fight with the undefeatable, and a denial of the undeniable. Sin, therefore, results in despair, because it is a hopeless project of living. Yet consciousness of our despair can be viewed as a good outcome from the perspective of Christian "faith in God," for consciousness of our despair is a doorway to "faith in God." When we so understand this core Christian vocabulary as devotional words, we can see that these words add no sensory, mental, or emotional content to the Profound Reality we face. They only add some words for our expression of commitment within our deepest consciousness to take in and live every bit of content that Reality brings us.

The challenge or offense in this basic message comes up around the fact that both life and death are part of the Reality we finite creatures face. This challenge also means affirming both possibility and limitation, both ease and suffering, both despair and our liberation from despair.

## What Use of the Word "God" Is Needed in a Revitalized Practice of Judaism, Christianity, or Islam?

I view these three long-practiced religions as three viewpoints on the mysterious Abyss of Profound Reality. Each of these three religious heritages is rooted in an event that reveals the trustworthiness or friendliness of Profound Reality. In each of these three sets of religions, the word "God" (and words like it) holds the meaning of *trust in* or devotion to Profound Reality. "God" is a devotional word that adds nothing to Profound Reality except devotion. So we can say that the word "God" is *contentless*. To call Profound Reality "God" is a transformation in human consciousness, not a transformation in Profound Reality. Of course, for the person involved in such a transformation, everything is transformed in its meaning for that person.

What does it mean to add *devotion* to this Absolute Abyss of Profound Mystery that I am holding with the term "Profound Reality"? "Sweetheart" is also a devotional word, but unlike the devotional word "God," "Sweetheart" does not usually carry the meaning of "ultimate concern." Paul Tillich points out that "God" is a devotional word that means an *ultimate concern* for *Ultimate Reality*.

When we are oriented in our ultimate concern toward a temporal reality or a set of temporal realities, that devotional attitude is understood as "idolatry" in Jewish and Christian theologizing. In Islamic theologizing, "infidelity to Allah" is used as much or more than "idolatry," but the meaning is the same.

Here is an example of idolatry that we easily recognize. If nationalism is functioning as our God-devotion, that means practicing an ultimate concern for a temporal power. That devotion is idolatry in Christianity, Judaism, and Islam. The same can be said for choosing money or status for our ultimate concern—that is, for our God-devotion. When we have chosen these idols, we are stuck with our choice in a bondage that is now choosing us. We have opted for a life of slavery to a limited scope of Reality from which only the Full Reality can rescue us.

Here is a second type of violation of being ultimately devoted to Ultimate Reality—having a limited concern for that ultimate Mysterious Reality that requires an ultimate concern. That would mean attempting to make our devotion to Profound Reality merely one devotion among many, rather than the devotional context for all our other devotions. A singularity of devotion to Profound Reality means making this inclusive realism prior to our temporal devotions to family, work, pleasure, pain avoidance, ego enhancement, nation, race, gender, sex, and so on. Herein is the meaning of the first of the Ten Commandments: realism requires an ultimate concern for the truly Ultimate.

## In This Devotional Sense, Is There a Post-Two-Realm Theologizing?

"Yes" is my short answer. Such theologizing becomes a study of Reality in the context of a devoted-to-Reality mode of living. Such theologizing describes what it means to live in a permanent openness to changing our mind about what is real. Such openness is a positive quality for any true research scientist or any true prophet or poet who is addressing a culture's ethical delusions. Radical Christian theologizing is similar: a permanent affirmation of openness to the Absolute Mysteriousness pointed to by the capitalized word "Reality" or "Profound Reality." I am using this two-word symbol to distinguish the "reality" created by humans from the "Reality" that creates humans and their creativity.

Not all poetry is Christian theologizing, but all true Christian theologizing is a type of poetry. Here is a poem I will use to illustrate the poetic nature of Christian theologizing:

### God?

God is the Stillness in which all motions move.
God is the Silence in which all sounds resound.
God is the Peace in which all conflicts transpire.
God is the Nonbeing in which all beings be.
God is the Emptiness in which all filling fills.
God is the Mystery in which all knowing knows.
God is the Un-manifest in which all manifestations manifest.

God is the Immensity in which all parts partake.
God is the Solidity through which all thereness is there.
God is the Fullness with which all fulfillment is filled.
God is the Intimate Presence in which all secrets are exposed.
God is the Inescapable from which all fleeing flees.
God is the Home to which all returning returns.
God is the Welcome into which all estrangement is received.

God is not a being,
and God has no form,
neither personal nor impersonal.
There can be no model of God
in which God is contained,
for God contains all
and is the Source of all.

God is the Isness
within which all that is Is.

## Is Such Theologizing Restricted
## to Devotional Communities?

"Yes again" is my short answer. "God," "Allah," "Yahweh," "Lord" and even "Thou" (as an address to Eternity) are words that only have meaning to a religious group of practitioners—a subculture that uses these words for devotional purposes. Only within such a community of devotion can theologizing or God-talk have a serious meaning and impact. Without such a subculture of people who are open to being a community of trust in Profound Reality, the word "God" can have no meaningful power for our actual living. As a word in a rational worldview, "God" is what has died—and died forever. This death of heavenly God-talk means that all those old God-centered worldviews must now be reunderstood as devotional expressions of trust communities, rather than rational creations like science, philosophy, or art.

## How Does Christian Theologizing Relate to the Disciplines of Learning?

The form of Christian theologizing being described in this chapter has no need of conflict with any of the disciplines of learning, but theologizing does need to be distinguished from the other disciplines of learning. The reason for this lack of conflict is that the disciplines of learning create *content* statements about aspects of Reality, while theologizing is *contentless*. Theologizing adds no rational content to any discipline; it only adds the relationship of devotion to the content each discipline of learning explores.

### Physics

This contentless nature of theology is most clear in its relationship with physics. Physics is a study of the temporal aspects of the natural cosmos. Interior feelings or other experiences of consciousness have no part in the study of physics. Physics is about outwardly observable facts, created and ordered by the human mind to make the phenomena of nature more predictable. The physicist, of course, has an interior world. The physicist spends time in this inner world of mathematics and other thoughtfulness and reflects on the relationship of such thinking to the process of scientific testing for further objective truth. The physicist can be filled with wonder or awe before the expanding mysterious awesomeness of the natural world—as well as before humanity's ever-changing knowledge of that world of wonder. But the specific study of the physicist is not about awe or wonder. Theologizing, on the other hand, is very much about awe and wonder.

Contentless Christian theologizing can accept as reality the content that physics discovers. The focus of Christian theologizing is about the relationship of our God-devotion to the implications of whatever content the physicist discovers—a Big Bang beginning, black holes, space/time oddities, nuclear explosions, whatever. The first chapter of the Christian Bible is not about natural origins or evolution or any other scientific topic. Those writers were simply using the science of that day to write some poetry. Genesis 1 is poetry about the goodness of our natural existence, however that existence is best conceived. The seeming conflict of contemporary physics with biblical poetry can be resolved by simply understanding the truth of biblical poetry as a different quest for truth than the scientific quest for truth.

## Psychology

Psychology has more overlap with Christian theologizing than physics. Psychology, as a science, observes human behavior and human reports on their experiences, but those reports are themselves contemplative observations rather than facts in the physics sense. Those reports are about a contemplative approach to truth that psychology shares with religion. Even the behavioral psychologists reflect upon the dynamics of the inner life of humans. The inner life is the specialty of the existential forms of psychology, pioneered by people like Viktor Frankl and Rollo May, as well as gestalt therapists like Fritz Perls, Laura Perls, and Paul Goodman. This focus on our inward life is also pursued by therapists like A. H. Almaas who relate psychology with spirit practices. A theologian like Paul Tillich can also qualify as a depth psychologist. His book *The Courage to Be* is an example of a psychological work that probes profound consciousness levels of this topic. Søren Kierkegaard can be included in this group of psychology-emphasizing theologians. His *The Sickness unto Death* and *The Concept of Dread* are good examples of psychological/spirit combinations.

Someone can be a good existential therapist without also being a spirit leader, though many therapists do combine their practice as psychologists with lessons learned from Eastern and Western religions. A. H. Almaas explicitly combines his carefully crafted psychology with his unique spirit practice built from many religious sources, such as Buddhist and Sufi. I know Buddhist teachers who use Almaas practices as part of their Buddhism. I have come to use Almaas practices as part of my Christian practice. In my definition of religion, a religious practice and a so-called "spirit practice" are one and the same thing. Also, we need to be aware that all religions have borrowed practices from other religions and spirit movements, and will continue to do so.

Nevertheless, in spite of this close relation between some psychologies and some spirit practices, I want to maintain that Christian theologizing is a discipline that is significantly different from a discipline of psychology. Psychology deals with specific contents of our cultures, our personalities, and our human biologies, while a Christian form of theologizing, of the type I am conceiving here, adds nothing in the way of psychological content. Such theologizing is about what it means to be devoted to a "Yes" relation as opposed to a "No" relation to whatever realism a psychology brings into human consciousness. The "Yes" of trust in Reality and the "No" of despair over Reality are either-or options for relating to whatever content a discipline of learning brings to light. All psychologies are in an ever-changing (perhaps wisdom-growing) state, while the core topic of theologizing is about this enduring "Yes" or "No" *contentless* relatedness to our current rational content veracities.

## History

Like psychology, the discipline of history entails another straddling of the scientific and the contemplative approaches to truth. We can speak of two quite different branches or aspects of the modern discipline of history: *scientific* history (What are the historical facts?) and *existential* history (What can be learned from the past in order to project possibilities for the future that illuminate decisions to be made in the present?). A third branch or aspect of modern history has been called "rational history"—having to do with meaning overviews—such as the Middle Ages, the Protestant Era, the Industrial Age, the Atomic Age, the Axial Period of religious deepening, etc.

Christian theologizing is very much about interpreting the meaning of historical events. Much of the Bible is a type of historical fiction that dwells upon much interpreted happenings that affect choices rather than seeking what modern historians would call "historical facts." The history emphasis of the Bible is a form of existential history—that is, it is about myths, legends, and other narratives that interpret the meaning of events rather than being a disciplined science of factual happenings. The biblical writers remember the past for the sake of anticipating the future as guidance for decision-making in the present. For example, the faith of Israel is rooted in the trust that Profound Reality is always acting Exodus-wise, bringing forth possibilities for liberation that are genuinely new and unprecedented.

Contemporary Christian theologizing is tasked with honoring both scientific factual history and the historical nature of the biblical writings. While the Bible can be a source for scientific history, the lessons of the Bible on the topic of history are more about that type of contemporary historical study we call "existential." For example, an Old Testament writer may speak of hearing God speaking messages like "I set before you life and death, choose life and live."

Like the Old Testament, the New Testament is also about historical interpretations and choices that bend history. "The Kingdom of God" is a communal *arriving* in history as well as a future communal *coming* in history—this "Reign of Reality" is breaking into the existing norms of our historical living with alternative possibilities for being human. The crucifixion and resurrection symbols, as presented in the New Testament texts, reflects a historical turning point that sheds light on what is happening in every event that happens today, tomorrow, and forever.

In this vein of historical thoughtfulness, contemporary Christian theologizing has an overlap with contemporary existential history. Christian theologizing, in order to make responsible decisions in the now of living, adds no content in facts or rational overviews. Rather, contemporary theologizing can provide contentless affirmation of the meaning of history as the meeting of a friendly Mystery that is providing possibilities for more realistic living. Whatever is happening, we are always facing choices between unrealisms that lead to the hell of despair and realisms that lead to favorable outcomes for ourselves and our descendants. Again, the discipline of Christian theology adds only this contentless devotion to realism—that is, responses toward the factual contents of ongoing history, explored and codified by the modern discipline of history.

## Philosophy

Contemporary philosophy has another important overlap with Christian theologizing. Here we must be very precise in defining philosophy as a temporal discipline of learning, rather than a quasi-religion—a philosophy of life that serves as a metaphysics of all truth. The discipline of philosophy need never claim to be an overview of thought having some sort of absoluteness or permanence. Philosophy, like physics, psychology, or history, creates ever-changing perspectives, even about religion.

All the human disciplines of learning, including philosophy, can create useful overviews that benefit our human cultures with our human need for meaning, order, and practicality, but these overviews can no longer be associated with a term like "metaphysics" or any other claim to absoluteness. Some new word like "meta-view" will have to do. All the disciplines of leaning are building a cultural consensus with regard to how to think and act as a given society in a given moment of history. Philosophy is a temporal process. Religious developments are also temporal processes. Christian theology is a temporal process interacting with all the other disciplines of learning, but in these interactions, Christian theologizing adds no content to the discussion except the unqualified "Yes" to realism.

Christian theologizing has had and will continue to have an especially close tie with philosophy, because philosophy can best be understood as the ongoing process of creating an overview or meta-view of all the other disciplines of learning. So how do we even distinguish philosophizing from theologizing?

Theologizing presuppose a devotion to Profound Reality. A philosopher may have such a devotion to Profound Reality, but his or her job as a philosophizer is different from his or her job as a Christian theologizer. The same person may do both jobs. Søren Kierkegaard clearly did both. His philosophizing served his theologizing, and his theologizing undergirded his philosophizing, but which was which?

Here is my approach to that tricky question. Philosophy builds rational overviews for a culture of human thought. For this type of philosophy I sometimes use the German-derived term "meta-bilt philosophy," rather than "metaphysics," because I see modern philosophy retiring the word "metaphysics." I also want to retire "metaphysics" from my Christian theologizing perspective, because that word contains an overtone of two-story thinking. I am insisting that there is no "meta-" (no meaning world that is *before*) to physics, or biology, or psychology, or anthropology, or history, or the arts. Philosophical overviews are cultural creations of usefulness for now. All the disciplines of learning, including philosophy, are finite, approximate, temporary, impermanent, progressive, changing overviews of human meaning. We have no permanent meaning of life that the rational minds of humanity can encompass.

Christian theologizing differs in its overview thinking form philosophy in the sense that theologizing is creating an overview of symbols of devotion relating us to the Profound Reality we meet in each and every event of human experience. Christian theologizing discusses our devotion to that Profound Reality. If a theologian adds something to our rational knowledge about Reality, he or she is doing philosophy or some other discipline of learning.

Also, theologizing needs to be defined as the thoughtfulness of a community of religious practice. For example Jewish theologizing works out the implications of the Exodus revelation. Christian theologizing works out the implications of the Jesus-viewed-as-Messiah revelation. And Islamic theologizing works out the implications of the Qur'an visions. Each of these theologizing enterprises is done by a community of trust in that revelation concerning how humanity is related to Profound Reality. I am going to spell out the meaning of "revelation" in a later chapter. For now, I simply want to help us notice that theologizing is not just another philosophy, but a servant of a devotional community. Theologizing must learn from philosophy whatever philosophy has to teach about Reality because theologizing is serving a community of people committed to Profound Reality and all the attending realisms implied by that devotion.

Philosophy as philosophy need not imply a Christian devotion or any other sort of religious or secular devotion. Philosophy can be done in a strictly secular manner—devoid of any dealing with personal devotion other than a general devotion to truthfulness. Indeed, I have attempted to do a philosophy of profound consciousness and religion in Part One of this book with as much objectivity as I can muster. Only in Part Two have I shifted to exploring the meaning of a Christian devotion to Profound Reality as appropriate for this century of Christian history. Obviously, every philosopher will have a devotion of some sort, at least a devotion to wisdom. But the devotion hidden in the meaning of that philosopher's devotion of "wisdom" may be very different from the devotion implied in an informed and relevant Christian theologizing.

Christian theologizing can seem like just another philosophizing. Yet because Christian theologizing adds no rational content about Reality to the discussion with philosophy, we can assert a huge difference for theologizing. As already explored with the word "God," Christian theologizing adds only a Christian devotion to the philosophical discussion. If a Christian theologian adds some fresh insight in the philosophical over-view of Reality, that theologian is being a philosopher, not a theologian.

As competent philosophers, we never arrive at a metaphysics that takes the place of a Christian theologizing, because in a good contempo-rary philosophy, there is no longer any such thing as a metaphysics. There are only relative meta-views useful for a specific culture at a specific time in history. Plato's so-called metaphysics is actually only a meta-view for his Greek culture in his time in history. The now-visible "cultural relativity" is a philosophical discovery in today's culture. There are no final views. Paul Tillich, acting as a philosopher, characterized the core anxiety of our era as "the anxiety of meaninglessness." I believe that this statement is consistent with the cultural occurrence of the awareness of cultural relativity. We, at least many of us, are now seeing that no culture has ever or will ever provide humans with the metaphysical "meaning of it all."

Christianly speaking, meaninglessness is our Profound Reality–given wholesome situation—that is, never to have the final answers to anything is our one and only good life. Even our questions are finite and passing. And this need not mean contempt for our curiosity or for our mental work to push the edges of our understanding. We do not have to meet the limitations of the human mind with pique.

The Christian theologizing that I am articulating affirms fully this discovery in contemporary philosophy of an unlimited Mysteriousness and its accompanying Wonder. I view Wonder as an aspect of any meet-ing with the Profound Reality of Christianity's God-devotion. This sort of theologizing views the finitude of the human mind as good, and sees in this finitude no cause for discouragement about our mental life. The widespread *anti-intellectualism* of our times is promoted by a *rigidity of mind* that *supposes final answers*. Openly living in the ever-expanding Land of Mystery is not only the intellectually honest thing to do, it is also a true affirmation of our intellectual life—our perpetual journey into the depths of mystery.

In order to have in the midst of our life's mental absurdities a last-ing meaning for our lives, we will have to renounce having some sort of contact with a thought world of rational finality and open our lives to a perpetual sequence of events of awakening that provide our con-sciousness with ever-new opportunities to trust a profoundly Mysterious Reality. Such trust is an ever-renewed leap into the dark night of total Mysteriousness. We have no proof of reason for this trust. Such trust pre-cedes even our thinking about the meaning of the word "trust." It is our thinking about "trust" that distinguishes Christian theologizing from our philosophizing or from any other discipline of human learning.

Such a demotion of the human disciplines of learning is best understood as *flexibility* or as a *healing* of our dogmatic, arrogant, rationalistic, authoritarian bigotries. When God-talk is about a "Yes" to Profound Reality, we enter into a life-long journey of being curious about that Boundless Mystery that is now our only dependable companion. Even the word "dependable" now has a mysterious meaning. We live "by faith alone" as dear Luther put it.

## So Where Are We with All These God-Questions?

A devotion to Profound Reality includes a devotion to profound consciousness, but a devotion to profound consciousness does not necessarily include a devotion to Profound Reality. I can imagine someone opting for a last gasp of a devotion to temporality by being devoted to profound consciousness. Profound conscious is no less temporal than frog consciousness or cat consciousness or human consciousness in its more pedestrian forms. Profound consciousness is an aspect of the Eternal only in the sense that profound consciousness is consciousness of the Eternal.

A devotion to Profound Reality includes a devotion to profound consciousness as well as a devotion to the frogs and frog consciousness, to the oceans, the soils, the elephants, the polar bears, the sky, the climate, and to the course of history. And a devotion to Profound Reality includes the sacrifice of the whole of human consciousness to that much larger devotion to Profound Reality. Luke pictures Jesus saying these last words just before dying, "Father, I commend my spirit into your hands" (Luke 23:46, J.B. Phillips). This verse means to me, "Profound Reality, My God, to you I deliver up my profound consciousness." Such devotion of profound consciousness to Profound Reality is the Holy Spirit—a third component of the experience of the standing before Profound Reality as our God-devotion, in all the harsh and ecstatic Wonder of that devotion.

The bottom line of the Christian God-devotion is sacrificing our temporality to the Eternal—sometimes called "living both our living and our dying as gifts from the Eternal." We might also say, "Christian sainthood means giving back our given lives to the Giver of our lives." This is the *contentless* devotion that I am writing this chapter to clarify, or at least to partly clarify. This devotion characterizes the whole Christian life, not just the last moment of it.

This God-devotion I am describing is not limited to Christianity. Certainly, Judaism and Islam have borne witness to the same God-devotion. The devotional forms or religious symbols are different, but the object of devotion is the same. Indeed, the health of these three religious heritages, and the peace among them, is dependent upon a vast majority of these billions of religious practitioners rediscovering their own form of God-devotion to the same Profound Reality. Such rediscovery includes rediscovering their religious uniqueness as Jews, Christians, and Muslims. Religious uniqueness is a temporal quality like hair color or foot length. Rediscovering the Eternal and devotion to the Eternal is a deeper matter than finding our religious uniqueness. Making a religion our God-devotion has been a favorite idolatry of all times. Indeed, "my religion" is the idolatrous devotion that has been the most hell-raising of all estrangements from our essential devotion to Profound Reality.

If we do not seek this eternal level of mutual discovery in our interreligious dialogue among these three Abrahamic religions, our dialogue will be superficial. We cannot talk about better relations among Jews and Muslims, Muslims and Christians, or Christians and Jews without manifesting a deeper awareness of our God-devotion to Profound Reality. Obviously, what we are touching upon is an issue that has to do with "peace on Earth" as well as with the spirit healing of many individual lives.

This truly massive vision of "peace on Earth" includes our Christian relations with Hindus, Buddhists, Taoists, Confucianists, and many others, as well as with the many religious combinations of all the above religions. In chapter 4, I touched upon the depth of the dialogue between Eastern and Western religions. There is no truly vital next Christian practice that does not include concern for this dialogue with and this mutual renewal of both Eastern and Western religions on planet Earth.

This does not mean asking all persons on Earth to practice some form of Christianity. It means asking all persons on Earth to be devoted to trusting in the friendliness of Profound Reality and thereby living realistic lives. Since any temporal religion can be both effective and demonic, each religion will always be a temporal battlefield between authentic and inauthentic living. A true "peace on Earth" has to do with calling forth the happening of human authenticity in millions of human lives, rather than continuing with our various delusions.

In the next chapter, I am going to probe further the many languages of devotion that may be used to serve this deep unity I am pointing to with a God-devotion to Profound Reality.

# 8

---

# The Great Goddess and Other Poetry

THIS IS THE THIRD chapter on the use of the word "God" in the Arabic-originated religions of Judaism, Christianity, and Islam. Chapter 6 examined the death of heavenly God-talk. Chapter 6 also explored further the concept of Profound Reality that we meet only in the flow of time. In chapter 7 we explored the word "God" as a devotional word for Profound Reality, a word that adds no content to Profound Reality. God is still dead as a philosophical concept or metaphysical idea. In that sense God is *contentless*, adding nothing to the discussion except devotion to what can already be discussed.

Devotional words are a crucial aspect of any and all religious practices, but devotional words are not descriptions of our experiences of the Profound Reality to which these symbols express devotion. They are expressions of our attitudes, passions, or loyalty toward Profound Reality. Emotions are involved in all our devotions, but many sorts of emotion can attend a living commitment to realism. Almost any emotion may be involved in our Profound Reality devotion. For example, anger toward those who have contempt for one's God-devotion is expressed in Psalm 139. The fear of Profound Reality is a very prominent emotion noted in the Bible—this sort of fear is also called "dread" or "anxiety" or "horror" or "awe" or "wonder." The "wonderful" need not always be beautiful. "The fear of God" is often used in biblical writings as a universal term for the God-devotion.

So, emotional feelings cannot be the core meaning of our devotional words. The devotion meant is a deep choice of commitment or loyalty toward living realistically in the presence of Profound Reality.

This commitment can express itself through the whole range of emotional qualities.

Also, in the Bible we find many devotional words that work along with the word "God." Some devotional words are variations on the word "God"—such as "Lord" "Yahweh," "Elohim," or simply "Thou." Other devotional words are used in the Bible to enrich this relatedness to Profound Reality: "Foundation," "Rock," "Shepherd," "Father," "Mother." It is said that Yahweh cares for her "chicks" like a "Mother Hen." The word "Father" may be seen to simply mean a *friendliness* of *parental care* from Profound Reality. "Mother" would certainly do as well for that—perhaps better. In the patriarchal age, maleness meant power, and Profound Reality is the final power.

But in the Great Goddess antiquity, She was the final power. And this insight raises the question of this chapter, about non-biblical devotional words for Profound Reality. Here is the fourth and last set of God-questions listed in chapter 6.

## "GOD" AS A DISCUSSION OF ALL DEVOTIONAL WORDS FOR PROFOUND REALITY

Is the Great Goddess of deep antiquity a devotional word for Reality?

Are "Yahweh," "Our Father Almighty," and "Allah" devotional words?

What words for a "God-devotion to Profound Reality" do we find in: Hinduism? Buddhism? Taoism? Native American lore? African lore? And more?

### Is the Great Goddess of Deep Antiquity a Devotional Word for Reality?

"Yes" is my simple answer to this question. Charlene Spretnak, in her well-researched book *The Goddesses of Ancient Greece*, documents the important point that the goddesses we find in the classical period of Greece are patriarchal goddesses within the Zeus pantheon. These goddesses, Spretnak claims, have a quite different character than the Great Goddess of deep antiquity, along with all her many mythical daughters who expand upon the human imagination of the Great Goddess.

Though the Great Goddess had a down-to-Earth quality, this does not mean that She was merely a symbol for the temporal processes of nature. The Great Goddess was seen as a "Great Womb" from which all things had come, the "Breasts" at which we are being fed, and the "Tomb" into which we return. The Great Goddess is echoed somewhat in our image of Mother Nature, but her role in the most ancient religious symbolism called for a positive relationship with the Every-thing-ness. I will contend that she is a symbol of loyalty to the same Profound Reality I have been exploring in previous chapters. Here is a quotation from Charlene Spretnak on this topic:

> Perhaps the earliest Paleolithic statues, dating from 25,000 B.C.E., are expressions of the female body as a living microcosm of the larger experiences of cyclic change, birth, renewal, and nurture. In time these energies became embodied in the sacred presence of the Great Goddess, the encompassing matrix of female power. On her surface she produced food, into her womb she received the dead. Rituals in her honor took place in womb-like caves, often with vulva-like entrances and long, slippery corridors; both the cave entrances and grave sites were often painted with blood-like red ochre, a clay used as pigment. As society evolved, so did the powers of the Goddess. She was revered as the source of life, death, and rebirth; as the giver of the arts, divine wisdom, and just law, and as the protector of peace and the nurturer of growth. She was *all forces, active and passive, creative and destructive, fierce and gentle.*[1]

Notice that the biblical Yahweh is also characterized as "*all forces, active and passive, creative and destructive, fierce and gentle.*" With the phrase "the Great Goddess of deep antiquity" we are referring to a mode of religious devotion that was specifically feminine, a symbolism of devotion that preceded the patriarchal takeover of human society in which "he" symbolism replaced "she" symbolism for our devotion to Profound Reality. This feminine style of religious symbolism may reach back more than twenty-five thousand years, and has never died out entirely.

So let us imagine ourselves shortly after 4500 BCE in the city-state of Uruk, located in the upper region of the Tigress and Euphrates River basin in what is now Iraq. Uruk and surroundings may be considered the first full-blown "civilization" with a centralized state structure in contrast with pre-civilization societies of both hunter-gatherer and settled-village

---

1. Spretnak, *Lost Goddesses of Early Greece*, 19–20 (italics added).

types. In the city of Uruk, the Great Goddess was the core religious practice, according to our best archeological guesses. This means that the
application of hierarchy to male-female relations had not yet occurred.
Likely, men were not the head of everything, and women were not second class. This society was content with picturing the Final Reality as a
Great Mother. In fact, it is likely that the Great Goddess intelligentsia or
priesthood was the top layer of that social structure. The pre-royal king/
queen-type elites were still a lower layer along with warriors, merchants,
and peasants on down the social pyramid of the civilizational hierarchy.

Great Goddess priesthoods gave leadership to this form of civilization for another two thousand years in out-of-the-way places like Crete.
Women in Crete were not only respected but were given roles of authority not typical in patriarchal societies. This is more than guesses, for we
have frescos in Crete that show these roles for women.

By 3500 BCE, we find in southern Mesopotamia a city named Ur
that was thoroughly patriarchal; the kings were on top of the hierarchy
and male Gods dominated the mythology. By 1800 BCE we have written
mythology in that area, then called "Babylon." We find a myth about the
male God Marduk cutting the Earth Mother in two and making half of
her the sky and the other half the land. Also, we can guess that by this
time the myth-makers and intelligentsia were no longer the top layer of
society; they were reduced to a lower-layer status serving the kings and
their patriarchal style of civilization.

Over a thousand years later, Plato still dreamed of making the intelligentsia this top layer of civilization. Throughout the Western Middle
Ages, male Christian popes and bishops fought with the male kings and
emperors for top-layer status in the civilizational hierarchies. The kingly
rule prevailed, however, even when significantly limited by the religious
hierarchy. Meanwhile, any leftovers of Great Goddess priesthoods were
pushed to the extreme peripheries of the planet. Like a secret, forgotten
by all but a few, these Great Goddess devotees lived in the gaps of a thoroughgoing patriarchal culture.

During the patriarchal era, most men and women understood little
of the power of the woman's body and her child-bearing capacities as
symbolic material for our relations with Profound Reality. This oppression within the social mythology had its parallels in oppressive social
consequences for women and nature. India left larger spaces than Europe
for the Great Goddess leftovers, but India also became a thoroughgoing
patriarchal society, as well as a rigidly hierarchical class operation.

The above paragraphs are storytelling, based on facts I find credible, but the actual feel of pre-civilization history is an ongoing project of ever-better guesses. Even if some of these historical details are incorrect, this clear overview will stand: *patriarchy was not always here and patriarchy need not always be here.* Patriarchy is not nature, but is entirely optional for our future. This understanding is absolutely crucial as an ethical guideline for the life and practice of a viable next Christianity.

A post-patriarchal transition within Christianity will not be easy, for until very recently Judaism, Christianity, and Islam have been fully adapted to intensely patriarchal cultures with patriarchal roots that go back to at least 3500 BCE. So when, in about 1800 BCE, the tribes of people symbolized by Abraham and Sarah left the city of Ur and journeyed to that promised land, patriarchy in that part of the world was already at least 1,700 years old. When Moses left Egypt (about 1300 BCE), patriarchy was at least 2,200 years old. In the entire period from 1000 BCE to 120 CE, when both Old and New Testaments were written, no person in that part of the world ever hear of a pre-patriarchal society. Though some of Israel's surrounding societies—Egyptian, Canaanite, Babylonian, and others—had goddesses that were enthusiastically revered, these Goddess practices were part of patriarchal societies. These Goddess-revering societies that surrounded Israel were no less patriarchal than Israel. The religious conflict between Israel and the Canaanites was not about patriarchy, it was about monotheism versus polytheism—that is, it was a conflict between devotion to the One Profound Reality and a manyness of devotions to a pantheon of temporal powers.

Overcoming patriarchy is a very recent challenge, and it still remains to be shown that monotheism can or cannot survive the end of patriarchy. A continuation of oneness in ultimate devotion to the One Profound Reality requires that Christianity, as well as Judaism and Islam, repent of thousands of years of adaptations to patriarchy—including all-too-frequent intensifications of the violence of patriarchy. We post-patriarchal Christians need to repent of even our heritage's minimalist moderations of patriarchy. I am visualizing a new form of monotheistic devotion to Profound Reality that can move forward without any sort of commitment to patriarchal cultural patterns.

Such a Christian repentance of patriarchy is very radical. It includes repenting of Jesus' behavior in calling Profound Reality "Abba" or "Papa" and choosing twelve men for his movement leaders. Jesus clearly respected women, spoke with women, and brought healing to the lives of many women; nevertheless, even Jesus adapted his practices to patriarchy. Paul too adapted to patriarchy, even though he also respected women beyond the norm; he even defended Christian women from their Christian husbands.

The basic norms and customs of patriarchy, however, were not removed by Jesus or Paul or any other New Testament saint. Patriarchal cultural habits were not removable in that era of history. It is we who are now challenged with the possibility of a post-patriarchal society— a type of possibility that H. Richard Niebuhr might have called "a new aspect of God's will." In his work on the responsibility of the church for society, Niebuhr spoke of being pioneers in our ethics, rather than the last and safest holdouts for the older moral conclusions. By "God's will" he spoke not of determinism, but of the expansion of our freedom within the events of history. He applied the phrase "new aspect of God's will" to the abolition of slavery and its racism aftershocks.[2] Had Niebuhr lived to experience what we now know, he would surely have included the abolition of patriarchy as another "new aspect of God's will." Certainly, a vital next form of Christianity will experience the call to be "pioneers" in the abolition of patriarchy.

If Christians are going to move beyond patriarchy, we can no longer chant "Our Father who art in heaven" in our Christian liturgy. And it is not a sufficient solution to chant "Our Mother who are in heaven" instead. Profound Reality, to which these devotional symbols "Father" or "Mother" might express devotion, is not in any sense male or female. Even when we use a gender-neutral term like "Thou," we are not saying that Profound Reality is a person. Nor does this mean that Profound Reality is an "it" or non-person. Profound Reality is not a temporal thing about which the human mind can have a picture. Profound Realty is Absolute Mystery. We can only picture our devotion to Profound Reality, not Profound Reality. "I-Thou" or "I-It" are both devotional poetry created by human beings. Neither poem is saying anything descriptive about Profound Reality. All devotional words are temporal options for expressing devotion, never descriptions of Profound Reality. Such words are never capable of characterizing the uncharacterizable Profound Reality. Only within this devotional view of God-talk can we see that it is true

---

2. See the last section of H. Richard Niebuhr's essay "The Responsibility of the Church for Society," recently published in *The Responsibility of the Church for Society and Other Essays*.

that the "Great Goddess," as a devotional word for Profound Reality, can add richness to our religious rituals, icons, myths, and discursive speech.

## Are "Yahweh," "The Father Almighty," and "Allah" Devotional Words?

Yes, each of these words are symbols within a set of symbols that indicate devotion to Profound Reality. "Yahweh" is a Hebrew word that when orally pronounced has a sound that symbolizes an Awe experience. To get a sense of this, say out loud the syllable "yah" on an in-breath and say the syllable "weh" on the out-breath. Or say "yah" on the out-breath and "weh" on the in-breath. The same trick can be done with the word "Allah." Both of these words of address to Profound Reality describe, not Profound Reality, but our encounter with the awesome quality of Profound Reality. The Hebrew word "Elohim" has a more general meaning. All the Canaanite gods and goddesses are "Elohim." "Elohim" has the generic meaning of God-devotion. The Canaanite gods and goddesses are expressions of devotion to some aspect of human life. The phrase "Yahweh is my Elohim" means "Profound Reality is my God-devotion" (my ultimate concern).

"The Father Almighty," like "Yahweh" and "Allah," has a devotion meaning. All three of these symbols are part of a male-emphasis culture's symbol system of devotion in relation to Profound Reality. None of these words are descriptions of Profound Reality. There can be no description of Profound Reality, no image of Profound Reality, no model of Profound Reality. Profound Reality is a Land of Mystery, a Black Abyss from which no light comes. "Land" and "abyss" are also human poetic symbols. "The finger that points to the moon is not the moon." And the finger of devotional words that point to Profound Reality is not Profound Reality.

The Great Goddess rediscovery is deeply important, but only if we remain clear that this symbolism is not a description of Profound Reality. The Great Goddess is a female-emphasis culture's symbol of devotion to Profound Reality. The Great Goddess has other similarities with Yahweh. The angels of Yahweh and the daughters of the Goddess are all aspects of a oneness of devotion to a Oneness of Reality. These daughters are aspects of the One, just as Yahweh's angels are aspects of the One.

These similarities are so important that we can, poetically speaking, say that Yahweh was the Great Goddess dressed in male attire.

Many women living in patriarchal culture, such as Joan of Ark, dressed as males to avoid rape or accomplish something that only males were permitted to do. So let us, for a moment, imagine a rather weird myth for our times in which the Great Goddess dresses as a male, Yahweh, in order to get by under patriarchal circumstances and to accomplish something not permitted to a Goddess. In the Middle Ages, the rise of devotional attention to Mary was quite likely a quest for a feminine picture of a Jesus exemplar. Some contemporary Christian feminists are also willing to explore a feminine savior as well as a feminine mode of devotion to the Final Mystery.

Such mythical talk, however, must not minimize the great difference in human consequences of having a devotional symbol system for Profound Reality that was woman-oriented, rather than man-oriented. The eclipse of the Great Goddess was a huge cultural shift with dire consequences for baseline attitudes toward women and nature, as well as warping the lives of men as well. We must also clarify that this was not a shift from matriarchy to patriarchy. There never was a matriarchy in the sense of a suppression of the male body and its unique gifts. The Great Goddess presided over a mode of gender equity that we might thankfully reinstate. Patriarchy, however, was an oppression, an illusory entitlement for males that has been destructive and now needs to be fully corrected.

Finally, we must not confuse two-story symbolism with patriarchal symbolism. Both need to be abandoned. Let us be careful to notice that the Great Goddess symbolism and the Yahweh symbolism were both two-story. Both were stories about fictional "characters" in a fictional other realm. Our widespread contempt of nature is not due to the male symbology itself, but to the literalization of a good spirit realm over against a less-good material or temporal realm. When the Old Testament Yahweh is understood in the actual Old Testament context, we find that the Yahweh devotion is also nature affirming. Many psalms and genesis myths express this love of nature clearly. So while it is good to recover our love of nature with help from the Great Goddess mythology, we could also recover our love of nature with a proper understanding of Yahweh.

## What Words for a "God-Devotion to Profound Reality" Do We Find in: Hinduism? Buddhism? Taoism? Native American Lore? African Lore? And More?

Hinduism is such a vast array of poetic pointers to real experiences that almost any contemplative insight can be found somewhere in that religious heritage. I think, however, that the richness of the Hindu tradition is hidden to us unless we notice that many of these devotional words express devotion to Profound Reality. "Brahman" and "Atman" are two such words. The fact that there are two such words is saying something about both words. "Brahman" is about our devotion to every experience we can call a "that" in our outward view of human consciousness. "Atman" is about our devotion to every experience we can call an "I" in our inner consciousness. So when the Upanishad philosopher says "That I Am," he or she is saying that every inner and every outer experience of consciousness is an experience of One Reality and of devotion to that One Reality. The overlap of this "That I Am" devotion with a well-understood Western monotheistic devotion is extensive.

Original Buddhism was like a protestant movement within Hinduism. Original Buddhism included a critique of the term "Atman"—seeing this Great Self concept as a temptation to believe that the human self was something substantial. Early Buddhism claimed that the "true self" is not something that can be found somewhere in our inner space. That is, a truth we can discover in a serious contemplative practice is that we do not know and will never know *who I am*. This "not knowing" my own self is part of the experience of enlightenment. In other words, I am and you are an absolute mysteriousness of self that is equal to absolute mysteriousness of the inclusive Brahman. In other words: profound consciousness is as mysterious as Profound Reality.

We may find it both a horror and a glory that our own human consciousness is a complete enigma, a black abyss as boundless as the black abyss of the Brahman Profound Reality. I now find it freeing that both you and I are "no self" with respect to anything we have ever thought or will ever think about *who we are*. Furthermore, it is useless to speculate about the final essence of the overarching cosmos, Profound Reality, or Brahman.

The above-described Buddhist quest for enlightenment amounts to a great devotion to truth. Such a quest is a positive devotion to truth that is expressed by the very word "enlightenment." Such truth is not called "endarkenment." Buddhist practice, at its best, is a devotion to Profound Reality.

In the ancient religious ferment of China, we also find devotional words directed toward Profound Reality. The tradition we call "Taoism" spawned many poets besides Lao Tzu. Here is part of a poem by Chaung Tzu as translated by Thomas Merton. These verses end for me any argument as to whether the depths of Taoism point to what I am calling "Profound Reality."

> Tao is beyond words
> And beyond things.
> It is not expressed
> Either in word or in silence.
> Where there is no longer word or silence
> Tao is apprehended.[3]

Implied in this and other such poems, the "Eternal Tao" is a mode of devotion to Profound Reality. Though Taoist thinking is a type of dualism in which a yin-yang pair of factors implies a *whole* of which this particular yin and yang are two complementary parts, such a quest for truth is actually an emphasis upon wholes not parts. The Eternal Tao is what we have when the most inclusive dual parts reveal one Whole. I am using here the capitalized word "Whole" to indicate the Oneness of Profound Reality being indicated in the above poetic verses. A devotion to Profound Realty is implied in this poetry, for Taoist practice assumes a love of realism that extends to a love or devotion to that Eternal Way of Profound Reality.

Finally, what words for a God-devotion to Profound Reality do we find in Native American and African-originated religious lore? I have done enough reading of Native American and African religious writings to believe that devotional words for Profound Reality did definitely evolve in these two regions of the planet. I do not find myself competent to write a brief generalization about those heritages as I have risked doing above for Hinduism, Buddhism, and Taoism. Nevertheless, I am convinced that such discoveries can be found.

Indeed, our exploration of religious heritages in every scope of geography can reach back so far in time that I can ask this question: *Have human beings always had devotional words for Profound Reality?* If that is

---

3. Merton, *Way of Chaung Tzu*, 152.

true, it may be because not having devotional words for Profound Reality is a survival risk for an entire human culture.

## How Far Back, How Far Forward?

Certainly, devotional words for Profound Reality are not limited to Jewish, Christian, and Islamic cultures. If it is indeed true that an ultimate devotion to Profound Reality is a universal experience, possible for all humans, then it should not be surprising if we learn that the human form of consciousness came into being along with an alertness to the presence of Profound Reality. If that is so, it may also prove plausible for us to speculate that a devotion to Profound Reality was required to move on from those initial experiences of baffling Awe into the very first inventions of human culture. And such a speculation also implies that a devotion to Profound Reality is required to move on from the human culture we have to a next more realistic culture of human living.

# 9

## The Meaning of Revelation

WHAT DO WE MEAN by the word "revelation"? What does "revelation" reveal about what? How does revelation reveal? What happens to those persons who *take in* the revelation? From H. Richard Niebuhr I have learned to speak of three faces of the event of revelation.[1] The following spins are my words, not his.

### The First Face of Revelation—The About What?

Let us imagine ourselves looking into that absolutely black hole of Mystery, so black that no sight into it is possible, and so silent that no sound is coming from it. This sightless, soundless, stillness, blackness of totally Mysterious No-thing-ness is the *first face* of any sound grasp of the Jewish, Christian, or Muslim revelation. I am using the symbol "blackness" as having nothing to do with face color. To the extent that "blackness" has become a cultural coding, I am intending to say that "black is beautiful." That is, I am affirming that the absence of the "light" of consciousness is a positive aspect of our lives, a description of the Finally Real. We can even suggest that estrangement from the darkness of Mystery is one of the roots of White-culture racism. The *first face* is also the Fullness or Every-thing-ness in which all things exist and the Total Demand upon our limited consciousness.

---

1. Niebuhr, *Meaning of Revelation.*

## The Second Face of Revelation—The Viewpoint

The *second face* of revelation in the above three religions of Arabic origin is a human viewpoint on the human encounter with this Absolute Mysteriousness that we meet in the everywhere and every-moment course of human living. Most of us are somewhat familiar with these viewpoints on the Abyss of Mystery: the exodus story, the cross-resurrection story, and the Mohammedan or Qur'an story. Each of these stories witness to a revelatory event—a historical event that reveals a faith *viewpoint* about that Absolute Mystery we encounter in every event. Such a viewpoint when taken on as a lived faith becomes a historically revolutionary movement of people who respond to living in the light of their revelation.

Each of these three monotheistic viewpoints puts a human-created face on the Abyss of Mystery—a face that is *for us*—a viewpoint that reveals a trustworthiness of this Abyss of Mystery. The words "God," "Allah," "Yahweh," "Father," "Mother," "Friend," "Shepherd," "Foundation," "Rock," and other such devotional words are ways of symbolizing a friendly face on this enduring Abyss. Such faces communicate to us: "The Abyss of Mystery is trustworthy. The Abyss loves us. The Abyss is the only encounter worthy of our total obedience."

In different ways each of these three sets of monotheistic world religions speak of the trustworthiness of the Mysterious Abyss. Each of these primal revelatory events is a "showing" to its faithful adherents of a truth about what is being experienced by humans in every event that is happening to them. The exodus from slavery in Egypt reveals a *friendly face* on the Abyss of Mystery out of which all happenings are arising. I will explore the exodus revelation shortly, but before I do I want to mention the *third face* of every revelation.

## The Third Face of Revelation—The Authenticity

The *third face* of revelation is the quality of consciousness that bubbles up in those human beings who trust their respective revelation of Abyss trustworthiness. This quality is called by many names, including: "authenticity," "profound humanness," "Spirit," "Holy Spirit," "Freedom," "love," "tranquility," "rest," "peace," "joy," and more. These deep interior states are variously described, but the underlying truth being expressed has to do with a bond with the Abyss and with Abyss-experiencing humanity. That bond includes a social ethics that promotes justice for all humankind—as well as for other species of life and for the whole Earth.

With this three-faced definition of revelation in mind, I will explore further the exodus viewpoint, the cross and resurrection viewpoint, and the Qur'an viewpoint. Obviously, these insights are my own takes on these three revelations, which remain ongoing quests for living implications for me and for everyone involved in any one of these basic viewpoints.

## The Exodus Viewpoint on the Abyss

So what happened to those slaves that Moses led out of Egypt? This more-than-three-thousand-year-old event is now covered with centuries of story, myth, and interpretations to the extent that any scientifically historical accuracy about what actually happened is obscured. Let us assume the following bare-bones approximation of the outward historical facts:

An unusually aware, sensitive, and perhaps educated member of the Hebraic slave community was moved to lead a significant number of his Hebraic companions out of a severely hierarchical Egyptian society. They fled into the wilderness, where a new vision of law-writing was established, based on the vision that Mysterious Reality allowed such free action to change the course of history. Though based on some cultural memory, this was a shift in life interpretation for these Egyptian enculturated slaves. So huge was this shift that it took Moses and others forty years, so the story goes, to wash Egypt out of this people and prepare them to fight for a more promising place on Earth for their revelation and their emerging peoplehood.

A more existentially rooted story-time rendering of this transformative event begins with how a man named Moses got so angry over a member of his people being mistreated by an Egyptian soldier that he killed that soldier and had to flee to the outback to hide from the authorities. Then one day, so the story goes, Moses came upon a bush that was blazing with a strange type of fire. Temporal bushes burn up, but this bush was not being consumed. It remained the same bush in spite of this strange conflagration. This was surely Moses' poetry for a very real inner happening to Moses himself. His own "who he thought he was" was being burned up, yet he was not consumed. The poetry continued: he said that the whole scene became holy and that the bush spoke to him about rescuing his people from their slavery. This was the last thing in the world he wanted to do. He raised the fact that his speech-making talent was far inferior to his brother's. "Take him then," said the bush, "but be clear that I am speaking to you, not him. You will have to do the speaking to your brother. You are the one I am calling to this task. Your brother is not here for this awakening in your being." After a bit more excuse-making, Moses set forth to carry out this challenging calling.

So when a series of cracks in the seams of Egyptian society offered an opportunity to slip out, Moses had already prepared the people to do so. We do not have to believe the exaggerated storytelling that elaborated these events. I don't believe that Moses ever had an audience with the Pharaoh. I don't doubt that in his dream life Moses may have said to Pharaoh, "Let my people go." Also, I don't doubt that plagues happened in Egypt. Such things happen to many societies. The extent of this plagued society and the relation of that to this slave escape was surely exaggerated as the exodus storytelling developed.

Anyhow, on one highly opportune day, a fairly large group of slaves got underway before the Egyptian CIA noticed them, alerted the authorities, and got a detachment of fast-moving military chariots in pursuit. I believe that the real historical miracle was something like the chariots getting bogged down in the mud of the Reed Sea rather than walls of water as pictured in an exodus movie or in a biblical story. But however that was, the big happening was that this group, like many others, actually escaped. It is likely that most of those other escaping groups did not find a way to survive in the challenging wilderness. They did not have a Moses who could explain to them how Reality was *for them*. Moses told them to remember the exodus and how to remember it. I can imagine Moses saying, "Let us view our freedom from slavery as an ongoing realism that applies to the situation at hand. Here are five ways to not forget the Exodus and five more ways on how we need to treat one another if we are to be true to what we have learned about being freedom-loving people who can dare the impossible and win."

Herein was a revelation about how Mysterious Reality *is* and how humans who *are true to this truth* will find their "higher angels" in their own inner depths and then from those profound states find ways to "bend" history. Elijah, Elisha, Amos, Hosea, Isaiah, Jeremiah, and others accessed for themselves the Moses-initiated vision about the friendliness of the Abyss of Mystery and applied that viewpoint to their contemporary situations. This expanded the relevance of the exodus experience for all humankind.

## The Cross and Resurrection Viewpoint on the Abyss

John the Baptist and Jesus also applied the exodus experience to their situation. Jesus carried out his loyalty to the Mosaic revelation to such an extent that his followers called the result the "new exodus." John the Baptist washed people of their era of estrangement in the Jordan River. I believe he picked that place for his washings from the Joshua stories of old. Jesus emphasized an "exodus" from the entire kingdom of Satan toward the Kingdom of God on Earth. This new exodus for humanity was described in the first century using the symbols of cross and resurrection. The cross was a new washing from the world of estrangement, and the resurrection was a happening in the lives of the disciples—a promised land of new humanity. In truth, cross and resurrection are two aspects of the same happening.

This new exodus viewpoint was not entirely inconsistent with the old exodus viewpoint. Both were viewpoints on the same Abyss of Mystery. Furthermore, the prophets of old, the person of Moses, and his mode of law-writing were all revered as valid insofar as these revelations were viewed through this fresh cross/resurrection viewpoint. The Jewish-born and Greek-educated preacher named Paul viewed the faith of Abraham as Christian faith, a faith that preceded law-writing, a faith that Paul saw as support for his vision that our core trust in the ever-present Abyss of Mystery precedes our law-writing.

The cross/resurrection viewpoint on the Abyss of Mystery has been buried in many layers of literalization, superstition, and downright foolishness. Digging these symbols out of the muck for our time requires some intense thought. How can we understand why these symbols have had such a profound hold on so many people? In order to approach the deep power of this revelation, we need to tell the story of Jesus and his followers in an inward, existentially profound way. And we need to tell the story from the perspective of the disciples. We don't actually have the perspective of Jesus, except what we can glean from his teachings remembered and interpreted by these disciples.

First of all, what we know scientifically about Jesus is minimal. We only know what Jesus said and did through those who tell us about what he said and did. And that first layer of telling is way down beneath several other layers of telling. Mark's gospel is the earliest New Testament book we have about the life of Jesus, and Mark has cross and resurrection in mind from his opening verses. Mark is focused on opening up a revelatory witness that includes resurrection. The earliest Christians, then Paul, and then Mark spell out this revelation seen through the cross-and-resurrection mode of visioning. Mark was not crafting a biography of Jesus. A biography of Jesus we do not have, will never have, and do not need to have to understand the cross/resurrection revelation.

Again, we need to see the cross/resurrection revelation from the perspective of the disciples, rather than from the perspective of Jesus—whose perspective we do not have. These disciples, according to these stories, left everything to follow this remarkable truth-telling man who was exciting the masses and offending the religious authorities. They slowly learned a great deal about truth-telling, and had some experiences with truth-telling themselves. Their expectations for this leader grew to cosmic proportions. But then something very surprising happened—the grim torture to death of their mentor. Their expectations about what following Jesus meant and would mean for them were dashed in this untimely and downright demeaning death of this good man. At first they could not see how this could possibly be a positive experience of revelation of anything more illuminating than how cruel human beings can be. The cross was a death experience for the disciples, a deep-river crossing.

The resurrection was also an experience of the disciples, not an experience of Jesus. We actually have no words of Jesus about what it was like to come back from the dead. It was the disciples who came back from the dead—from the death experience of having lost all hope for authentic living. Resurrection for the disciples was an experience that turned the cross into a deliverance from estrangement. The resurrection happening turned the cross into a "Jordan River crossing"—into a "promised land." The resurrection realization turned despair into a "doorway" through which one might walk to an experience of true authenticity.

If we see the resurrection as an objective corpse walking about, eating fish, disappearing and other weird things, we are missing the whole point of what was happening to these living humans—these living women and men who were experiencing this resurrection—who were becoming in themselves the resurrection of Jesus. This was not a happening to the corpse of Jesus. The corpse-of-Jesus stories are poetry about what was happening to these still-living disciples.

The disciples saw the Life of Jesus in one another—in the living, walking, eating, talking, humans who were now carrying on the Life of Jesus in the acts of the apostles and their followers and in all their walking, talking, eating, bonding, child-raising, preaching, organizing, and other actions.

What had died in the cross/resurrection revelatory happening was what these followers of Jesus thought they were following. They died to who they thought they were, what they thought Reality was, as well as what they thought was going on or could go on. In other words, they died to their illusions—their estrangements from the Abyss of Reality.

Is this really true to the New Testament witness? "Yes" is my answer. The way the gospel of Mark ends and the way Luke put together the twenty-fourth chapter of his narrative make clear to me that the resurrection was being viewed as a happening to the followers of Jesus. Here is a bit of my poetry on this point:

> Resurrection is about me!
> I always sort of knew that.
> Why else would I care about it?
>
> And resurrection is not about life after my death.
> Resurrection happens now.
> Was that not so for Mary, Peter, and Paul?
>
> So what was it that had died in them or me—
> that made a resurrection possible?
> What died was who I thought I was,
> what I thought reality was,
> what I thought thought was,
> what I thought WAS was and IS is.
>
> This grand GIFT
> is given at the tomb.
> No wonder those women in Mark's narrative
> fled from the tomb in terror
> saying nothing to anyone.

The resurrection was the dawning that the death experience of the cross was a doorway—that the loss of everything they thought and expected for Jesus and themselves was an illusion. This oblivion experience had paradoxically led them into the very Life of Jesus—that is, a resurgence into authentic life, the life for which we are all made, and the life from which all of us are well skilled in fleeing. This is also the life that these disciples had been fascinated with in the figure of Jesus. They were now themselves the Life that they had left everything to follow.

What had happened in the cross/resurrection revelation was that ordinary weak and estranged women and men became the "Life of Jesus." Did not Paul and others talk of being "in Christ," of being "the Body of Christ"? As the wildly creative gospel writer John had Jesus say to his disciples before leaving them: "*You will do greater things than I*." When John wrote this gospel these disciples had already done great things— transformed the lives of tens of thousands of people, broken out of the Palestinian container, and written books that are still read today.

The probability is strong that Jesus was an actual historical person whose characteristics are reflected in the New Testament stories. But it is also true that in all four gospels Jesus is a fictitious character in a master narrative about cross and resurrection. Mark, Matthew, and Luke keep a bit of historical realism in their storytelling, but John is writing a whole-scale fictionalized piece of radical-edge theologizing. It is important to realize that all four of these storytellers were cross/resurrection visionaries witnessing through their stories to a revelatory viewpoint on the Final Abyss of Mystery that all of us meet every day of our lives. Their Jesus characterizations were attempts to exemplify in a rather outlandish form of fiction what a profoundly authentic human looks like when walking, talking, and impacting other human beings. The disciples in these stories are also fictional characters who exemplify the journey toward the cross/resurrection revelation.

In Mark's story the cross/resurrection happening clearly occurred in the life of Jesus when John the Baptizer dunked Jesus in the River Jordan. This ritual meant being washed from attachment to that era of oppressions and hypocrisy—then being lifted up from this sea of death into a new mission of life that was going to be as costly for Jesus as it was for John. Following Jesus means taking up our own unique cross experiences that we will live when experiencing our resurrection in this still estranged world of humans among whom we will have to live and to whom we will be called to love with the expenditure of our lives. Living the resurrection is living the cross, and living the cross is living the resurrection. These are core elements is this revelation of the friendliness of the Abyss of Profound Reality.

So now, when we read the New Testament stories about Jesus, we are reading about a resurrected type of human-leading dumbbell disciples like you and me through the deep-river crossing of the cross to the life of resurrection. This is the good news. This is the gospel feast. This is the revelation of the New Testament about the Abyss of Mystery and how that Mystery loves us—loves us by leading us through the deep river of dying to a campground of Life on the other side of this death.

Christians are called not only to take in this revelation for their own lives, but to witness to this revelation—to preach it, to proclaim it to the last person on Earth. What do they proclaim? They call it "the Word of God"—a communication from the Abyss of Mystery.

## The Qur'an Viewpoint on the Abyss

Six centuries after the crucifixion of Jesus, Mohammed communicated a fresh viewpoint on this same Abyss of Mysterious Reality. The Islamic viewpoint into this Abyss of Reality is a revelation that is less well understood than the other two, at least in the United States. Mohammed, however, saw both Judaism and Christianity as allies in his primary fight with polytheistic forms of religion. He had less trouble allying with Jews than with Christians. Mohammed could not see how the Constantinian Christianity he encountered was genuine monotheism, rather than a worship of three gods. Mohammed was clear that neither he, nor Jesus, nor Moses were in any sense God.

I doubt that Mohammed was ever exposed to anyone who suggested to him anything close to what I am developing in this essay—namely, that each of these monotheistic religions have three faces to their revelation. Here is how even Islam is triune—(1) the Abyss face, (2) the Qur'an face, and (3) the profound humanness face that flows from that viewpoint into the Abyss of Mysterious Reality.

I will not develop this thesis further; I only want to indicate something crucial for Christians—namely, that Islam, deeply perceived, is an ally, rather than an enemy, to Christian monotheism. Jews, Christians, and Muslims can work together against humanity's true enemies—the shallowness, oppression, and hatred that is present in this estranged world that we all face.

Estrangements among these three religious heritages can be healed if we go deep enough into how all of us can be friends of the same Abyss of Mystery as that Mystery is encountering all of us in the historical events of the twenty-first century.

# 10

Rereading the Old Testament

IF TWENTY-FIRST-CENTURY CHRISTIANS ARE going to use the term "Old Testament," we must be clear that "Old" here does not mean "obsolete," or "transcended" or "less than," or "replaced by the New Testament." "Old" simply means "former." And "Testament" does not mean a set of texts: it means a "devotional covenant with Profound Reality."

What we are calling the "Old Testament" (plus perhaps a few later writings) was the only scripture that Jesus had. It was the only scripture that Paul had. Both Jesus and Paul were loyal Jews who only knew of one covenant, the exodus covenant with Yahweh—a covenant that had been renewed many times in many previous situations (the work of Jeremiah being the most celebrated occasion). Jesus and Paul may have known they were doing some fresh interpreting of the exodus covenant, but they did not view what they were doing as a new covenanting. And they certainly did not see what they were doing as creating a new religion. All that came later.

At some point in the first century, these Christ-Way communities began to speak of themselves as a "new exodus." This, however, did not mean doing away with the exodus covenant or with the ancient scriptures. It is very important to notice that the main body of the Christian movement in the second century insisted on keeping the Old Testament as their scripture and considered a man named Marcion as out of Christian bounds for suggesting that the Old Testament and its God were obsolete religion. Marcion viewed his form of Christianity as more "spiritual" than the Old Testament and as a full replacement for those older texts. Marcion's position was relegated to the sidelines by the ongoing core of the Christian development. Yet, many people today still take a view very similar to Marcion's view.

It is true that Christianity did become a new covenanting with Profound Reality. The cross/resurrection covenanting was viewed as a fresh viewpoint on the friendliness or trustworthiness of Profound Reality. This amounted to a shift in the style of their God-devotion, but not a shift in the Profound Reality to which their devotion was directed. Looking through this new viewpoint, the older exodus viewpoint was reinterpreted, but still included. New symbols and rituals were made central—the bread-wine feeding and baptismal water washing celebrated this new covenanting. *What we Christians today need to understand most about this new covenant was that it was a covenant with the same God—that is, with the same Profound Reality.*

Christians tend to see the exodus through cross-resurrection eyes, and Jews tend to see cross-resurrection through exodus eyes. Who knows which eyes are best? And both sets of eyes see a wide-range scope of the same things. Christianity and Judaism are sister religions in a very deep way. Our sibling fights are mostly the result of corrupt religion on one or both sides of this sisterhood. Some of those fights were and are simply serious misunderstandings of one another.

## THE EXODUS TURNING POINT

The exodus event is central to understanding the whole Old Testament story. The myths, stories, and legends we find in the book of Genesis were written after the exodus event, and reflect the exodus revelation in the way these stories were told. The date of the exodus has been hotly debated, but for the sake of my narrative of the Old Testament story, I am going go with the most recent of the proposed dates (1290 BCE). The most ancient writings now contained in both Genesis and Exodus were likely written sometime between 1000 and 962 BCE. There are scraps of poetry and story that may date earlier, but those bits and pieces have been fully integrated into later writings.

This means that the exodus event probably happened about three hundred years before the story of the exodus took on the written form recorded in our Bibles. Like Genesis, the book of Exodus has been expanded, revised, and combined many times over five or six centuries. Nevertheless, as a re-membered and re-membered and re-membered event, the exodus remains the turning point in basic revelation that characterizes the whole Old Testament collection of memories. So I will begin with the exodus vision that I have already described in chapter 9, and then move forward in time with a retelling of the revelatory story of exodus-wise living.

After telling the post-exodus story and its contemporary meaning, I will turn to an overview of the book of Genesis (the beginnings). These myths and narratives are about events that are supposed to have happened before the exodus, but Genesis is actually a book of post-exodus memories.

Though Genesis is mostly a book of cryptic myths and outlandish legends, this book is about the most profound matters of the whole Bible. Though Genesis is placed at the beginning of the Bible, this placement does not mean that the insights are the oldest or least evolved. Some of its written materials may be as early as 1000 BCE, but even the antiquity of these oldest stories does not mean that they are less profound than the later writings. The book of Genesis probes three major topics: (1) the goodness of nature and human nature, (2) the estrangement from our good humanity, and (3) the dynamics of becoming our human goodness once again. These three topics are very old and forever relevant.

## THE EXODUS AND FOLLOWING

I will be telling the post-exodus story in a fashion that focuses on the concept of covenant with Profound Reality—a covenant that is spelled out in patterns of social order for the covenanting group. In the biblical sense, "covenant" is a tough-minded agreement made among a group of people living and thinking together in a specific, historical situation. Such a covenant is a temporal construction, but the covenant is being made with Profound Reality by a particular temporal group of humans. Such a view of "covenant" is both a religious practice and an evolving "constitution" for ongoing sociological construction. A biblical covenant is a group action that is both a "testament" of their faith and a social formation for living together in a trusting relationship with Profound Reality. Since this Profound Reality is being met in history, this covenant also has to do with living a life of realism within existing historical situations.

## The Sinai Story

The exodus covenant with Profound Reality began taking historical shape when Moses organized Hebrew slaves for an escape from Egypt. We don't actually know anything about how this was done, but Moses somehow accomplished this very tough challenge. I imagine that he was persuasive in telling his story about being called to conduct this escape at the burning bush by the God of their ancestors.

This covenanting took on a more specific form on the other side of the successful escape. At Sinai, so the story goes, Moses laid out the covenant that made the exodus the beginning of a whole new style of life. We don't know, historically speaking, the exact form of that original covenant. What we have in Exodus 20 in those now-famous Ten Commandments is a story told about this covenanting several hundred years later. The whole book of Exodus is a type of historical fiction, somewhat like that of Sir Walter Scott, only without Scott's interest in being plausible. Such biblical writing is hard for modern people to grasp correctly, because it is not accurate scientific history, and yet it is based on events in history that actually happened. These stories were told and retold in dramatic ways that spoke to the current historical life of those listening to the stories. Such writings give permission to continue telling these stories in our own imaginative ways, while still being true to the core truth of their original tellings.

For example, imagine Moses at Sinai with two handfuls of very simple statements that Moses held up to the assembled people. The first handful of five sayings had to do with remembering and maintaining the purity of the post-Egyptian revelation of Profound Reality's friendliness. The second handful had to do with how such a Profound Realty–loyal community could survive and not fly apart in living their social lives in these trying wilderness conditions. This wilderness was not a forest, but a desert with no lakes, no rivers, and skimpy vegetation, much of it good only for goats. And according to our story, they survived as a continuous community under these conditions for the next forty years.

If there is any doubt that this Sinai event was a profound consciousness experience, listen carefully to this poetry from Exodus 20:18–21. My rewordings of the New English Bible are in brackets.

> When the people saw how it thundered and the lightning flashed, when they heard the trumpet sounding and the mountain smoking, they trembled and stood at a distance. "Speak

to us yourself," they said to Moses, "but if [Profound Reality] speaks to us, we shall die." Moses answered, "Do not be afraid, [Profound Reality is present] only to test you, so that [the dread of Profound Reality] may remain with you and keep you from [un-realism]. [Nevertheless], the people stood at a distance while [only] Moses approached the dark cloud where [Profound Reality was manifesting].

As well as being an awe-filling presence, Moses must have been a tough-minded sociologist and politician. Let us imagine him as a cross between Franklin D. Roosevelt and Che Guevara. He endured as the glue for this people for forty years, living under trying conditions with a bunch of rough-minded ex-slaves who were victims of extensive Egyptian social conditioning—a conditioning that had to be replaced with something better. Apparently, Moses was flinty, fair, and persistent to a fault. Likely, he was also something of a military leader who inspired the necessary courage for hand-to-hand sword work in defense from the other marauding and desperate tribes of humans roaming this desert. Perhaps we can plausibly guess such characteristics for this obviously talented and dedicated leader.

## The Deep River Crossing

After Moses' death the leadership of this now large band of men, women, and children passed on to another flinty, optimistic, charismatically speaking character, named Joshua. Joshua challenged these desert people to cross the River Jordan and capture a lasting place for themselves and their culture in a "Promised Land" where there are lakes and rivers and sea shores, fish, fertile soil, agriculture, and the like. This was a big challenge because this land of promise was already occupied with many tribes of people who were already warring with each other for a piece of this pie. So Joshua and his community are assuming that they are now strong enough, many enough, tough enough, and courageous enough to kill, conquer, and incite fear enough among those already settled folk to establish a space for these newcomers.

Joshua's violent tactics for securing and culturally purifying a place for this Mosaic people to prosper may be a difficult offense to our modern morality. But this very offense can point out to us that these biblical stories are not about specific beliefs we have to hold, or a final morality for all times, but about something far deeper—including the truth that these stern conquests were how we ever came to hear about the Mosaic break-through. These conquests also had to do with what the Mosaic break-through was all about—a courageous life in service of Profound Reality.

The Jordan River crossing was a challenge requiring a recovenant-ing at the river's edge for a new sort of life. Crossing the River Jordan be-came a symbol for a deep inner transformation—crossing a deep river of change and risking our lives—leaving an old style of living, and washing our spirits for a brand new chapter in our living. Spiritual songs written by the slave churches of the U.S. South still reflect this symbolism. In the song "Swing Low, Sweet Chariot" we hear these words: "I looked over Jordan and what did I see, a band of angels coming after me." Here are words from the song "Deep River":

> Deep river
> My home is over Jordan
> Deep river, Lord,
> I want to cross over into campground
>
> Oh don't you want to go
> to that gospel feast
> that promised land
> where all is peace.[1]

## The Network of Judges

It is not fair for us to characterize these early Israelites as war-like mon-sters compared with we moderns. Machine-gun slaughter, explosive devices, and nuclear bombs had not yet been invented. In that early post–Jordan River–crossing period, the type of ongoing warfare was a way of life for all occupants of this space of geography at that time in history. The tough fights of these Mosaic-enriched people maintained the social transmission of the exodus wisdom for the storytellers, poetry writers, and prophets who came later.

Once established in this land, a further covenanting of these people was created—a network of trusted "judges" whose role was to resolve tribal differences, maintain the Mosaic traditions, and inspire alliances to fight the many battles for their ongoing survival. A woman, Deborah,

---

1. This song was first mentioned in print in 1876, when it was published in the first edition of *The Story of the Jubilee Singers: With Their Songs*, by J. B. T. Marsh, page 230.

was one of these judges—this included her being a military leader. These judges and their military exploits fought and won a role in history for the Mosaic heritage.

This tribal alliance pattern existed for many years before a next convenanting of their lives proved advisable to most of the people—namely, having a king and a more powerful military like the other social powers within that increasingly internationalized crossroads. Many thoughtful members opposed this shift, but again, the survival of the Mosaic heritage may have depended upon it.

## Having a King

Their first king, Saul, was an experienced warrior, but not a man with the personal qualities that were needed to do well with this new job of being a king. David, who according to our stories was an unusually resourceful person, began his public story as a charismatic guerilla leader who conquered Saul's kingdom from within, and created a stronger and more Mosaic type of rulership that replaced the ineffective kingship of Saul. David, so the historical fiction goes, was not only a military strategist and an inspiring leader, but a musician, a poet, a songwriter, a student of historical tradition, and even a liturgical reformer.

Like many monarchs with unchecked power, David's kingly status allowed him to steal a beautiful married woman and place her husband on the front lines, where he was killed. When the prophet Nathan tricked him into experiencing his guilt over this deed, instead of doubling down and having Nathan exiled or killed, David became actually grieved over what he had done, repented, and made changes in his ongoing behavior.

The Davidic kingdom became a strong symbol of historical success for the Mosaic peoplehood. Though our archeological efforts can find no proof that such a kingdom ever existed, the historical fiction about this Davidic kingdom and its humanly flawed king was told with such empathy and plausibility that it is hard for me to believe that a real person with some of these rare qualities did not exist shortly after 1000 BCE. The historical David certainly did not write all the psalms as later traditions have held, but such a religious and art-loving king may indeed have published the first official songbook, to which so many beautiful poems were added in the following centuries.

David's son Solomon, so the story goes, was an unusually bright politician, a homespun philosopher, and a competent wealth manager. He did not write the whole book of Proverbs, but it is plausible that such a leader did bring this new kingdom to its high point in social wealth and stability. When Solomon died, the kingdom split into the southern kingdom of Judea and the northern kingdom of Israel. In this new situation, there emerged a few reasonably good kings and some very bad kings. In this period a new type of religious leader arose—the prophet.

## The Major Prophets

The Major Prophet was not a magical predictor of future events, but a reader of history through the eyes of the Mosaic revelation—a spokesperson and writer who was capable of being a severe and accurate social critic, poetic verbalizer, popular educator, and frequent limiter of kings. It was these prophets dealing with real-world issues who brought the Mosaic revelation into its international standing. To this day the stories, writings, and wisdom of these "Major Prophets" (Amos, Hosea, Isaiah, Micah, Jeremiah, Ezekiel, and Second Isaiah) compare with the authors of the Upanishads, the Buddha, Lao Tzu, Confucius, Zoroaster, and other luminaries living in this same basic time period—a period named by Karl Jaspers the Axial Period (roughly 800–322 BCE if we include Socrates, Plato, and Aristotle). These centuries are a time of spirit deepening—a revolution in inwardness that transformed the quality of the civilizations those awarenesses affected.

Across a large portion of the planet, earlier civilizations underwent a deep critique from this fresh perspective. We can generalize the essence of this social shift as a deeper consciousness about profound solitude and Profound Reality that stretched the limits of the pre-Axial style of civilization, which were uniform, closed systems of narrowly permitted thought and action. The Major Prophets of the Old Testament accomplished for the people of Moses the kind of deepening that Lao Tzu did for China and the Buddha did for India. Such deepening had historical ramifications in many directions and for hundreds of years following. To these spirited explorers, we owe a debt of gratitude for our understanding of the autonomous power of the individual person and for our capacities for ongoing critique of our cultural configurations based on our experience of a Profound Reality that is more than the contents of our human-made cultural canopy.

Jeremiah is a vivid example. He is living at the time of the conquest of Judea by the Babylonian Empire and the complete destruction of Jeremiah's home nation. The entire elite population was carried off into exile in Babylon. Jeremiah, facing these grim events, spoke of a new covenant with Profound Reality—one "written on our hearts." That message included the deep awareness that losing the nation as the historical manifestation of Mosaic peoplehood was not the end of being "the People of God"—the ones devoted to the One Profound Reality. The role of this people in history could be carried on as exiles in Babylon. Jeremiah, in spite of being an interpreter of an extremely grim social situation, was an incredibly optimistic voice—in addition to facing up to the obvious grimness that few wanted to take in, Jeremiah proclaimed a deep quality of hope. This hope had an Axial Period quality that was lived on in Babylon captivity with help from Ezekiel and others. When the Persian conquests allowed exiles to return to their homelands, these exodus people in exile were inspired by Second Isaiah to return to Palestine as rebuilders of a fresh Israeli nationhood and its ancient mission to the world.

The Babylonian exile was not a period of religious vacuum for these exiles. Perhaps the first chapter of the Bible was written there. Certainly many of the psalms express that "covenant of the heart"—the personally deep impulse given by Jeremiah and others. Following is some of that new-covenant-style Old-Testament poetry from Psalm 139:13–18, from the New English Bible, reworded a bit by me. This psalm is also an exploration of how to use the symbol "Thou" or "You" as a devotional word for our relationship with Profound Reality.

> Where can I escape from *Your* Awe?
>   Where can I go to flee from *Your* Awesomeness?
> If I climb to the Moon or journey to Mars, *You* are there.
>   If I lower my body into my Earthy grave.
>   *You* are there as well.
> If I take flight to the edge of the morning,
>   or make my home at the far edge of the western ocean,
>   even there *Your* handwork grabs me.
> If I say, "Certainly darkness will cover me up,
>   night will conceal me,"
>   yet darkness is not dark to *You*.
>   Night is as luminous as day
>   dark and light are the same for *You*.

It was *You* who fashioned my inward parts;
  *You* knitted me together in my mother's womb.
I praise *You*, because *You* fill me with Awe.
  *You* are wonder-full, and so are *Your* works.
*You* know me, through and through;
  my body is no mystery to *You*,
  or how I was secretly kneaded into shape
  and patterned in the depths of the Earth.
*You* saw my limbs yet unformed in the womb
  and in *Your* records they were all recorded,
  day-by-day they were fashioned,
  not one limb was late in growing.
How deep I find *Your* thoughtfulness, O my God!
  How inexhaustible are *Your* topics!
  Can I count them? They outnumber the grains of sand!
  To finish the count my years would have to equal *Yours*!

Clearly, this psalmist is expressing an emotionally intense, personal relationship with the Eternal Source of every detail of our temporality. Not only our infanthood, childhood, and adulthood, but also our life in the womb has been lived within the loving care for us by this Profound "Thou" of our personal God-devotion. Such personal intimacy with Yahweh reflects what Jeremiah was pointing to with a "new covenant written upon our hearts."

## The Christ-Way Covenant

Early Christianity picked up on Jeremiah's "new covenant" symbolism and applied it to the death/resurrection revelation that the early followers of Jesus saw in the life and death of Jesus. The "New Testament" (i.e., new covenant) writings spell out a new covenant with Yahweh, the God of Moses, Amos, Jeremiah, etc. This recovenanting was a fresh mode of responding to the same Yahweh by those Christ-Way Jews. This new covenant was built upon Jeremiah's covenant of the heart; perhaps the New Testament covenant was an even more personal—an intimate "I-Papa" symbolized relationship with that same invisible, inescapable Profound Reality presence.

A large amount of recent Christian theologizing has claimed that the Old Testament was about a different God than the New Testament. This is not so! The new covenant of Christianity was no more and no less than another new covenant with the very same Profound Reality. This new covenant was not about a new God, but about a new relationship of devotion with the same Profound Reality. Only in the sense of a new patterning of the God-devotion was this covenant new.

The Old Testament remains Christian scripture—every word of it. All the verses that trouble us so much are troubling to us because they are written by temporal human beings living in another time in human history. We contemporary interpreters of those ancient scriptures are not required to hold the same moral judgments as those writers or to believe the same beliefs of those writers or to enact the same deeds that they did. To be the people of this God, we are only required to hear the Word of Eternity in those temporal writings. Every sentence of that absolutely human text is Christian scripture. Even the textual corruptions are corruptions of a Christian text. All texts—including Christian texts, including this text that I am writing—are finite texts, corruptible texts, texts that can be misunderstood, texts that can be wrong about this or that. All texts are finite texts. No text has dropped down from the Eternal. No text has been dictated by some absolutely dependable Source. All our alienations from the scriptural status of the Old Testament texts are rooted in our own flawed means of interpreting these texts.

Of crucial importance is the now-frequent complaint that the Old Testament texts are patriarchal—that is, that they assume the rule of men over women, of male story over female story, of second-class status and opportunity for women. These observations are simply true. Every word of the Old Testament texts, as well as the New Testament texts, is saturated in patriarchal social forms and beliefs. How could this have been otherwise? Every text written in that block of time within that region of civilization was patriarchal. Only hints of viewpoints different from those norms leaked into these texts here and there.

We are looking into the face of another paradox that good Christian theologizing must learn to embrace. Even a patriarchal text can carry the Word of God. But that Word, interpreted for our time, will have to be stripped of patriarchal customs, names, attire, and ongoing oppressions found in these biblical texts. Any viable future for Christianity will have a patriarchal Bible that we interpret in a post-patriarchal fashion. This way of interpretation is only a problem if we persist in understanding these texts in a literalistic rule-making means of interpretation.

The new covenant of these Christ-Way Jews was very new in this way: it shifted the central symbols from the exodus event to the event of cross/resurrection. Though this was called a "new exodus," it established a different core liturgy—the feasting on bread and wine as symbolic of taking in the holy life laid down as our primal healing. It also promoted the ritual of being washed from the eon of estrangement, a ritual adopted from the still-revered John the Baptist. I will write more on these topics in later chapters, but for now let us finish our look at these older Christian scriptures with a look at the book of Genesis.

## BEFORE THE EXODUS

In a story sense, the book of Genesis is a long look backward from life lived after the exodus into the long past that leads up to the exodus. While the book of Genesis is mostly origin myths and legends, it is about three of the most profound topics in the entire Old Testament: (1) the goodness of nature and human nature, (2) the estrangement of humans from that good nature, and (3) the antiquity of exodus-wise sainthood—in which these old rough saints are portrayed as breakthroughs of trust in Profound Reality living among a human species that is deeply estranged from Profound Reality.

### The Genesis of Nature

#### *Genesis 1:1—2:4*

*In the beginning Profound Reality, our devotion, created both beyond the sky and down to the ground—i.e. everything.*

(A SLIGHT REWORDING OF GENESIS 1:1)

The word "beginning" assumes time and the beginning of time. Assumed here is a "time" when there was no time—that is, the beginning of time, the beginning of the temporal—of temporal things that have a beginning and an end. Clearly, we are in a form of talk called "myth." The Creator of the creation is a mythic story with an upper and a lower stage of events: the eternal stage where the Creator and angels dwell, and the temporal stage where things begin and things end. "Things," in this general sense, include humans, human society, animals, plants, soils, rocks, Earth, air, water, stars—all impermanent things changing through what we call "time." According to the biblical myth, anything that is changing is a creature of this Eternal Creator that/who/it/she/he never changes, never begins, never ends.

So this Creator is not a thing among other things. This Creator is not just one more temporal actor among other temporal actors, for that would make the Creator a thing among other things. In this biblical myth the Creator is only a fictitious character in a human made-up story—one character among many characters. To take this story literally would make the Creator a thing among other things, but that is not the meaning of this myth for the living of our real lives.

In our contemporary biblical interpretation, we begin with the plain fact that a literal interpretation of this Eternal realm where this Creator character lives is not plausible for thinking Christians, Jews, Muslims, or anyone else who chooses to live realistically in the twenty-first century. Indeed, the Eternal realm is now and always was just a piece of poetry, just story-time talk. The Eternal Creator is a story-time metaphor for that human experience of Profound Reality encountered in the midst of our temporal personal historical events. We meet the actual Eternal Creator nowhere else than in the temporal events of passing things.

The manyness of things, according to the story of Genesis 1:1, has been *sourced* by an Eternal Creator, and these ever-changing things will continue to be sourced by this ongoing Eternal Creator. In other words, every experience of our lives is an encounter with this Creator—whether that event is a sunrise or a mosquito bite, that event is sourced by this Profound Reality, here told about in some story-time talk about an Eternal Creator.

Our consciousness may not be engaged in noticing this profound depth within each temporal event. We can speak of some events as special in the sense that our consciousness is awakened in these special events to this Eternal Depth that is eternally there in all events. The whole Old Testament grounds our experience of this Eternal Creator in history, in the ongoing temporal story of we humans moving through time. Some events are more revelatory to humans than other events, but all events are the preoccupation of the book of Genesis.

After introducing us to this Creator/creation metaphor, the book of Genesis gives us a seven-day mythic creation story using 500 BCE science to tell us one central lesson: that everything the Creator is creating is good for human beings—for all of us and for all our human living for all time. In other words, your and my whole life and all that it has contained, does contain, or will ever contain is good for you and for me. That means that our human druthers are not what makes any event good in this final sense. Gentle breezes are good for us, but so are tornadoes and hurricanes. Kittens are good for us, but so are mosquitoes and snakes. With respect of our druthers, this is not so. But in Bible-talk, we are talking about good with respect to our authenticity, our realism, our human essence, our best-case scenario for living our one temporal life.

Also implied here is this: our flight from Profound Reality is bad for us. Our fight with Profound Reality is bad for us. Our defiant resignation to Profound Reality is also bad for us. Basically, it is bad for us to reject Reality and create a reality we like better, and then pretend that this self-created delusion is real. These considerations move us to chapters 2 and 3 of our Christian Bible.

## The Genesis of Sin

### Genesis 2:5—11:9

In Genesis 2 and 3 we have a much older creation story than Genesis 1. In this second creation story, the Creator reaches into the dirt to create the human, and then the Creator walks in the garden in the cool of the day to talk to this first couple. This rather humorously told story moves quickly into a strange story about the first two human beings eating from the tree of the knowledge of good and evil. They were not eating from the tree of knowledge. This was not a step up in consciousness or aliveness. This was a step into the death of their authenticity.

Adam and Eve ate illusion, something no cat can do. With our wondrous symbol-using intelligence, we humans can create a delusory worldview in which we believe we know good and evil. The Genesis myth implies that only Profound Reality (the Absolute Mystery) knows good and evil. However wondrous we humans are, we are "not God" in the sense of knowing good and evil with absoluteness. We are ignorant of good and evil in the absolute sense.

We do know good and evil in relation to this or that temporal value, but we do not know good and evil in relation to Profound Reality. Rather, humans commonly insist on living their lives on the basis of some humanly created set of values with which we judge the events of our lives. This Genesis story assumes the reverse—that Profound Reality judges our values for their realism. Taking in the meaning of this myth means being open to greater realism, rather than being stuck in the ruts of our values with which we close off reality.

Nevertheless, it can seem strange to see ourselves as essentially ignorant of good and evil. Our parents taught us good and evil. Our church, synagogue, or mosque taught us good and evil. Our police department taught us good and evil. Our schools taught us good and evil. Our whole human culture continues to teach us good and evil.

So why is this knowing good and evil a delusion that leads us to the death of our authenticity? I will begin with what we might call an extreme example. Adolf Hitler fashioned a view of good and evil that envisioned good as being a member of the Aryan race with all its many excellences, and envisioned bad as being polluted by the Jewish people and their damnable God. Hitler's crude but charismatic certainty about good and evil was already latent among a wider population, enabling this proclaimed delusion of good and evil to become a social power that gave permission for the horrific holocaust.

The Nuremberg war trials forged an interpretation of these events that contributed to making the very word "holocaust" a symbol for the most extreme violation of our human authenticity. Some have argued that the Jewish holocaust was such a horrific revelation of our human potential for depravity that nothing like this had ever happened to humanity before. But is that true? Adolf Hitler himself claimed that one of the places that taught him the most about how to conduct the holocaust was the manner in which the European settlers in North America handled their Native American population. And let us also mention the appalling slave trade and slave use by Europeans of the African population. Also we must not overlook the twelfth-to-mid-fifteenth-century Christian church Inquisition waged against the supposed threat of pagan-leaning women and other so-called heretics. The Inquisition horror continued into the Late Middle Ages and early Renaissance. The scope of the Inquisition mode of evil expanded in the early life of Protestant Reformation and the Catholic Counter-Reformation. Because of its publicly open and severe cruelty as well as the length of time that this horror endured, one might conclude that it was an even worse assault on human authenticity than the Jewish holocaust.

These are only a few of the examples of how our symbol-using human capacities can be used to create universes of good and evil knowledge that are damaging to ourselves, our authenticity, and all that we touch. So understood, the Adam-and-Eve forbidden tree is about a very dangerous type of eating—*taking in* to our lives delusions about good and evil.

In recalling Hitler and others, we must not let our own selves off the hook. In our personal lives, each of us has our own quite private and well-excused fabrications of good and evil knowledge. We can all discover life-long patterns of our own good and evil convictions, and perhaps we have lived long enough to see the damaging consequences of some of our own foolhardy convictions about good and evil.

Devotion to Profound Reality is a strong affirmation of the human, but devotion to Profound Reality is not humanism. All forms of rationalism are forms of humanism, for rationalism means an idolatry of human reason. All forms of anthropocentrism that make humans the center of value with respect to the planet are forms of humanism, and thus are violations of devotion to Profound Reality. On the other hand, any contempt for humanity is also a violation of our devotion to Profound Reality. We need not violate humans in the name of some sort of love for the planet. Humans are the super-aware part of the planet. Human are assigned by Profound Reality to celebrate the entire planet, including its humans.

Living beyond good and evil is not a negation of the human need for moral order, laws, and lawfulness in human society. This human capacity for evil is one key reason we need law and order. Every society must construct and enforce appropriate norms and just laws, and thereby name some of those evils that must be restrained for society to function.

While we find these social restraints on the corruptions of human living important, it remains true that our essential human authenticity is free from the tyranny of any law or any moral order or any custom, or any patterns of good and evil that the human being might create. This freedom from all norms, combined with a trust of Profound Reality and the resulting care or love for all things, is our human essence. Our human corruption of that essence, however horrific and dangerous, does not entirely bury our human essence. Though we find ourselves estranged from our affirmation of Profound Reality by some idolatry to our own creations of good and evil, we can also find ourselves perpetually restored to our ignorance of good and evil by that invincible Profound Reality and by once again opting for devotion to that realism.

Is all this depth of realization actually contained in these second and third chapters of this ancient book of Genesis? I am convinced that this is so. And there is more. Our ignorance of good and evil can also be called "freedom." Our choices are all risks of creation out of nothing dependable. All choices are ambiguous. There is no sure morality, no sure belief system, no sure conception of justice, no sure doctrine of religion. We really do live in a Land of Mystery. Living in that openness to Mystery is our only authentic righteousness.

We humans, with our essential freedom, construct temporal patterns for our societies that are never a final good and evil, but these social patterns can be part of our practical fight for authentic living. Some of our social patterns express our deep authenticity better than other social patterns. And many of our social patterns are rooted in a view of good and evil that contradicts our authenticity. And even with our best sense of justice, we are not "like God." Our certainties are not certain. Any knowledge of good and evil that we claim to be ultimate is a delusional feasting on the deadly fruits from the forbidden-to-humanity tree of the knowledge of good and evil.

So where are we as a human species in terms of living realistically before Profound Reality? Many of the psalms are poetic expressions about this deep topic of human estrangement from Profound Reality. Psalm 53 is an example of a poem on estrangement. The poetry of the psalms was written using that now-obsolete double-deck metaphorical language and other language that is strange to our modern minds. Following is Psalm 53, to which I have done a small amount of contemporary rewording—adaptations that I believe do not change its ancient meaning about our human existence that is present in this psalm:

> The un-contemplative ignoramus says in his or her heart,
> "There is no Profound Reality."
> How corrupt humans are—how depraved and loathsome;
> not one does anything good!
>
> From the Profound Reality perspective,
> none acts wisely, none seeks Profound Reality.
> All are estranged; all are rotten to the core.
> Not one does anything good, not even one.
>
> So shall these fools not rue their course,
> these evildoers who devour the People of God,
> as humans devour their bread?
> Shall they never call upon Profound Reality, our God?
>
> The People of God can visualize these rebels experiencing dire alarm,
> when Profound Reality scatters them,
> when the crimes of the estranged are frustrated,

when Profound Reality rejects them.

If only Israel's own faithfulness might arise in this place!
Let Profound Reality restore the People of God!
Let the people of Jacob rejoice!
Let the people of Israel be glad!

Not all the psalms are about this widespread estrangement from Profound Reality, but none deny it. Nor is the whole book of Genesis only about the presence of rebellion from Profound Realty. Only in chapters 2–11 of Genesis is estrangement the basic topic. After eating from the forbidden tree, humanity, personified as Cain, slays his brother Abel—acting upon an anger that is "crouching at his door"—an angry envy over Abel's more effective religious practices.

Next, we are shown how the masses of humanity become so corrupt that God is said to be sorry about creating them—only one boatload of humans and other animals is saved to start over after this huge flood of chaotic waters washes over the surface of the Earth.

Then in chapter 11 we find the story of humanity building a tower as high as heaven itself. This is not pleasing to Reality. So, this one-language communication system breaks down. This quest to eliminate diversity runs into a wall. Humans were split into many language groups—each "speaking their own truth" in many different ways and places.

Finally, in chapter 12 we begin to read stories about Abraham and Sarah, who exemplify an initial Genesis picture of biblical sainthood. This sainthood does not have to do with beliefs or morals or twenty-first-century relevance. Genesis sainthood has to do with trust in Profound Reality. These two people are not self-made heroes. They are just ordinary humans—estranged humans called to realism. They left the city of Ur, not knowing where they were going or what they would find, trusting in the promise of trusting Reality. However wild and strange these stories can seem, they are about the restoration of our humanity from our estrangement from Profound Reality—a Reality that never goes away, but confronts the lives of everyone all the time.

Before I move to these stories about this strange hope for a restored realism among humans, I need to say more about estrangement from Profound Reality. If Profound Reality is Absolute Mystery and truth is always temporal, impermanent, changing, and never certain, how can we find for our lives a confident truth over against untruth? How do we get beyond the "he said"/"she said" tangle of disagreements? Here is the biblical answer to the kind of truth that accounts for our having timely convictions and solid calls for historical action: *Profound Reality is also "speaking" to both parties in any disagreement.* Profound Reality can speak through the scientific approach to truth. Profound Reality can also speak through the contemplative approach to truth. And Profound Reality can speak through the intimacy and commonality approaches as well. (See chapter 3 for more on this topic.)

Here is an example from the scientific approach to truth. When our consciousness stands in that gap of understanding between the Newtonian universe and the Einsteinian universe, Reality speaks in favor of Einstein. Why? Because the facts support this newer way of understanding nature. We can have a similar experience with our various conceptualizations of truth when using the other three approaches to truth. Profound Reality is speaking to us in every event. We can disagree about what Reality is saying or about how best to say what we are hearing from Reality, but Reality is always speaking. It only takes finding our profound-consciousness "ears" to notice that Profound Reality is speaking and to have some intuitions about what Profound Reality is saying. Each event is an event that is truly happening, and every event includes Profound Reality as its backlight or background speaking to us. The finite nature of our reasoning does not prevent this experience of Profound Reality from being possible. The rational is never the real in any full sense, but Realty is always judging some of our thoughtfulness as more real than other efforts of our thoughtfulness. Every truth is an old cultural custom or a new cultural custom, yet no truth is merely cultural. How do we know when "Reality says so"? We can never understand the Bible (Old or New Covenant), unless we understand in our own experience what it means to say, "Profound Reality says so!"

## The Genesis of Sainthood

### *Genesis 12:1—50:26*

Both Jews and Christians claim Abraham and Sarah as their spirit grandparents. Muslims distinguish themselves slightly by claiming Abraham and Hagar as their spirit grandparents. The Abraham-and-Sarah stories are about the mythic beginning of the recovery of human authenticity in the midst of this ongoing world of estranged humans—a deep sickness and profound woe that includes Abraham and Sarah themselves.

Nevertheless, this flawed couple, according to our biblical story, left the hierarchal and oppressive city of Ur in southern Mesopotamia, going they knew not where—simply trusting in an inwardly sensed promise that they "heard" from the Mystery of It All that they would be the parents of a people more numerous than the sand grains on the seashore. This is just a story, remember, but this is how that story goes.

Maintaining faith in this promise has been hard for them both. Sarah is now past the age of childbearing, and Abraham is also an old man. So when those mysterious messengers brought the news that a child was on the way, Sarah laughed in their faces, and Abraham, apparently, just stared dumbfounded. A child did come—a miracle gift as all children actually are. They named him Isaac.

Then this story goes off the rails when Abraham gets the message that all gifts have to be given back to the Giver, including Isaac. Anyone who has lost a child knows the grief of such news, but Abraham maintained his trust in the promise even after he grasped that the gift of Isaac (upon whom his life promise was hanging) had to be given back to the Giver. Indeed, Abraham was called to be the knife that returned even this gift, his only son, to the Giver. Without daring to tell Sarah or Isaac, he set out to obey Profound Reality—still trusting in the promise from Profound Reality of his preposterous hope.

As the story works out, another alternative to actually killing Isaac came into view, but Abraham had already given back the gift of Isaac to the Giver of Isaac. Abraham's obedience was complete. His faith in God's promise to make his seed as many as the sand grains was still intact. Indeed, Abraham's detachment from all the temporal evidence that questioned his preposterous trust in the Eternal was the seed that Abraham passed on to be multiplied like seaside sand.

So here is our initial definition of biblical sainthood: give all your gifts back to the Giver. Whoever finds his or her capacity to do this giving back is a spirit descendent of Abraham and Sarah. Sarah's part in this story was not told very well in the storytelling done by the last three thousand years of patriarchal storytellers; nevertheless, she is part of this story as women always are, even when they are neglected in the storytelling.

The Abraham-and-Sarah stories are, after all, just stories—stories that have been told and retold and changed over hundreds of years. But these stories have carried on the seed of giving our gifts back to the Giver. This is the primal Jewish and Christian picture of sainthood. We sometimes call this giving back "love" or "compassion" or "lovingkindness."

Paul claims that this love of expending your whole life for the cause of realism is the greatest gift of the spirit. Mohammed, I believe, understood this radical love in a similar way.

In the following Genesis stories, this seed of giving back one's gifts to the Giver is itself the gift that is passed along. Isaac grew up, married Rebecca, and she bore twin sons. Esau was born first and then Jacob. Isaac's giving back does not seem too impressive. He dug some wells and settled in, but he passes along the seed of giving our gifts back to the Giver. Isaac was not a very good father. He favored one son over the other. Perhaps he thought Esau would be a better carrier of the Abrahamic faith. The storytellers also suggest that Isaac identified more with Esau's hairy outdoor ruggedness than with Jacob's more smooth-skinned body and scheming thoughtfulness. Rebecca (and Reality too, apparently) disagreed with Isaac. As this unusual biblical story goes, the woman character had a better grasp on Reality than the man character. With help from Rebecca, Jacob tricked Isaac out of a blessing intended for Esau, and the story proceeds with Jacob carrying on the Abrahamic legacy. Herein is a lesson for us: *We never know what Profound Reality will do, or who Profound Reality will choose to do what.*

Anyhow, while still a teenager, Jacob, with help from Rebecca, was forced to flee his brother's anger and leave home at, let's say, about sixteen. So he is walking across the country alone with only a staff and some sandwiches to live with his uncle Laban. While sleeping that first night all alone with a rock for a pillow, Jacob had a gripping dream about Profound Reality and the promise made to Abraham. The next morning he made a pact with "the God of his fathers" to devote himself and his gifts back to the Giver, if he could just be kept safe until he got to Laban's house. So in this personally intense way, Jacob became the custodian of the Abrahamic legacy.

Laban had two daughters: Rachel, whom Jacob dearly loved, and Leah, whom Laban tricked Jacob into marrying first, and then working another seven years for Rachel. Years later, Jacob left Laban, taking his two wives, a flock of children, and many sheep he had "fleeced" out of Laban. On his way, he learns that he was going to intersect with his estranged brother coming his way with three hundred men. So this was the night for his all-night wrestling match with an angel of Profound Reality. The next morning Jacob, having changed his name to Israel ("God-struggler"), met Esau. With Jacob's diplomatic realism in full operation, he made friends with Esau, and then got on his way before Esau changed his mind. This is a story worthy of many sermons that I will not include. Anyhow, the main point of this story is that Jacob found his essential freedom, operated carefully with his brother, giving up his old trickster lifestyle, and took on that new name Israel—one who strives with Profound Reality and thereby wins his life.

So what does biblical sainthood look like? It means seeing yourself out of control by a Mystery you don't understand, and yet seeing yourself responsible for everything that happens to you. This Genesis sainthood means seeing yourself as a dialogue with a Power infinitely greater than you, and yet seeing it as a friendly Power that is giving you the freedom you use to choose your still unknown destiny.

I won't tell the rest of the Genesis story, except to say that the Abrahamic style was passed on again, mainly through Joseph. After the Hebrew people had become slaves in Egypt, some of them were open to be aroused to their Abrahamic origins by Moses, whose story is in the second book of the Bible, entitled Exodus.

All these Genesis tales of sainthood are just stories made up after the exodus, but these stories still witness to a fascination with history, and with trusting the God we meet in history. These stories are witnesses to the notion that this exodus faithfulness has a deep past and an open future. These stories also tell us that our estrangements from Reality are deep and deadly, but not our absolute fate. Opportunities for fresh starts in realism do occur, and we can choose to take these paths and bend the future toward realism for ourselves, our species, and Earth.

As Christian theologians thousands of years later have put it: *We Christian saints are sinners saved by grace.* In spite of horrific bad turns, we can reverse course toward finding bits and pieces of our authenticity, which include finding our appropriate humility and our compassion for other humans. Today, this compassion has extended to this fragile planet. Our freedom will contribute to the destiny of the life on this planet, for better or for worse, and we will need to decide what "better or worse" means.

## THE CONTEMPORARY ADDRESS
## OF THE OLD TESTAMENT

One key address of the Old Testament to contemporary churchgoers and skeptics alike has to do with what it means to have "faith in God."

## Faith in God

Most contemporary practitioners of a Christian religion understand "faith in God" to mean having beliefs of some sort—perhaps a set of doctrines, or having a theological position, or at least knowing a true morality that clarifies right and wrong. We even use "having a faith" to mean having a religious practice.

In the core message of the Old Testament, however, having faith in God means *action*—a response of the whole person in the flow of time. Faith in God means packing up a bag of possessions and your children and following Moses out of Egyptian slavery into a desert and living there for forty years—working Egyptian culture out of your bones and replacing that mode of life with a singular obedience to Profound Reality. Faith in God means gathering with thousands at the edge of the River Jordan for a recovenanting for a new life—crossing this river holding up babies and swords out the water, and camping on the other side, making final preparations for conquering a place for yourselves among already warring factions. Faith in God means hearing prophet after prophet challenge you to give up some familiar way of life and attempt something better. Faith in God means persistence in preserving the lessons of the past and building new lessons never recorded before. *Faith in God means action—action of the whole person in the flow of time.*

## The Temporality of Morality

It is not true that the Old Testament is basically a law book, a rule book, a guide book for our moral lives. It is true that four out of the first five books of the Bible are almost nothing but laws. The book of Exodus is at least half about Moses as law-giver. Leviticus, Numbers, and Deuteronomy are almost entirely laws, rules, norms, customs, and morality. We are right to be bored and often critical of what we find there. These books are not guidelines for our moral and ethical lives today. They are a record of the ever-changing moral implications of living one's faith in Profound Reality in real situations. These Old Testament situations no longer exist.

What we might learn from this vast sea of teachings is how to create laws, morality, and norms for our own social situations today. We find nothing in these books about the use of nuclear energy or the avoidance of nuclear war. We find nothing about handling a climate crisis that could end life as we know it. And Moses did not write all five of these books as some traditions imply. If they can be called "books of Moses," it is only in the sense that the inspiration of Moses about law-writing was reasserted over the period of about eight hundred years that it took to write these five books.

All this was law-writing for different historical situations. Every new situation requires a new set of laws, norms, moralities, customs, or advisements. No law or morality drops down from heaven, or grows up from nature, or is a set of justice statements found is some idea world. Moses did not impose absolute laws on his community. He invented new laws and customs within the context of being loyal to an Eternal Mystery that continued to judge and inspire his understandings and efforts toward best-case behaviors. *Until we see the human nature of all morality, we have no hope of understanding or respecting these primal books of the Old Testament or making use of them for our own moral efforts.*

## The End of Patriarchy

In spite of the fact that all the Old Testament lessons about faith in God are embedded in patriarchal and hierarchal social forms, living exodus-wise today includes an exodus from the patriarchal social forms that we have inherited. Enacting the exodus faith today also includes forging post-patriarchal modes of sociality in both our secular patterns and our religious fabrics.

Let us not overlook the fact that many of our prominent feminists are also some manner of Christian or Jew. (Increasing number of Muslims, Hindus, Buddhists and others are also catching the flame of the feminist opposition to the patriarchal pasts of all our longstanding religions.) The post-patriarchal turn in time is a fresh prophetic call from that Profound Reality that we meet in the flow of history. *Today, faith in God includes being a feminist,* whatever our own personal gender may be. Feminism is a new prophetic edge of the commands of Profound Reality. How do we know that? Our God-devotion to Profound Reality says so through the events of our lives.

## Ecology

The Old Testament texts are also a call for love of the human body and the natural world. The first chapter of Genesis and many of the psalms are especially clear about loving this Earth. No support is given in these texts for our longing for escape from material existence, or to justify our technological overpowering and/or polluting of our natural places and resources. Religious philosophers have been right when they have said that Judaism and Christianity are among the most "materialistic" of all religions. This is only true, however, if "materialistic" means "down to Earth," rather than simply having more money and more things. A love of the natural Earth is totally consistent with a love of Profound Reality. *Ecological commitment is supported, not opposed, by a clear grasp of the Old Testament view of faithfulness to Profound Realty.* It is also true that a literalization of the supernatural poetry of the Old Testament tempts us to an anti-ecological attitude that demeans our temporal life and excuses our responsibility for temporal life here and now on planet Earth.

## Clear Communication

The Old Testament also tells us something about the use of words as healing agents. The psalm writers and prophets have composed poetry that, when reworded only slightly for our time, is as good as any wordsmithing in the history of language. We can learn how to best proclaim the deep truths of which language is capable by reading these very old texts.

In conclusion, here is the understanding that I propose thinking Christians take from this chapter: *The Old Testament texts are Christian scripture, and there can be no future of a vital and viable Christian practice without these texts.*

# 11

## The Doorway of Despair

Thus the state of our whole life is estrangement from others and ourselves, because we are estranged from the Ground of our being . . . We are separated from the mystery, the depth, and the greatness of our existence. We hear the voice of that depth; but our ears are closed. We feel that something radical, total, and unconditioned is demanded of us; but we rebel against it, try to escape its urgency, and will not accept its promise.

We cannot escape, however. If that something is the Ground of our being, we are bound to it for all eternity, just as we are bound to ourselves and to all other life. We always remain in the power of that from which we are estranged. That fact brings us to the ultimate depth of sin: separated and yet bound, estranged and yet belonging, destroyed and yet preserved, the state which is called despair. Despair means that there is no escape. Despair is "the sickness unto death." But the terrible thing about the sickness of despair is that we cannot be released, not even through open or hidden suicide. For we all know that we are bound eternally and inescapably to the Ground of our being. The abyss of separation is not always visible. But it has become more visible to our generation than to the preceding generations, because of our feeling of meaninglessness, emptiness, doubt, and cynicism—all expressions of despair, of our separation from the roots and the meaning of our life. Sin in its most profound sense, sin, as despair, abounds amongst us.[1]

IN THIS EXCERPT FROM Paul Tillich's classic sermon on sin and grace, "You Are Accepted," Tillich rescues the word "sin" from its false meanings of immorality and disbelief. Tillich gives us a fresh way to understand sin as

1. Tillich, *Shaking of the Foundations*, 159–60.

estrangement from the Ground of our being. This mysterious Ground I am calling "Profound Reality." Tillich claims that this estrangement from the Ground of our Being is the primal estrangement that leads to our estrangement from others, and our estrangement from our own selves. And Tillich claims that such estrangement leads to despair, because this Ground that we attempt we flee is inescapable.

Tillich's use of the word "despair" alludes to a book written a century earlier by Søren Kierkegaard—*The Sickness unto Death*. Kierkegaard's book on despair is perhaps the most profound volume ever written on that topic. Tillich and Kierkegaard agree that the manifestations of sin are best described as a state of human consciousness called "despair." They also agree, I believe, that this despair is a result of our hopeless attempts to flee Profound Reality, or to win a fight with Profound Reality, or at least to justify ourselves with an active or passive sort of resignation that protests that Profound Reality is "no damned good."

Kierkegaard's perspective on sin also clarifies the word "faith." Sin is the opposite of faith, where "faith" is understood to mean trust in that inescapable Profound Reality in relation to which sin is an estrangement. Faith, so understood, is not a belief of the mind, but an action of the entire person. Faith is a "true deed" that alters our whole life, says Rudolf Bultmann. Faith is the deed of leaping into a radical realism in response to Profound Reality. Tillich also clarifies that faith begins as the deed of "accepting our acceptance" (our forgiveness) from the Ground of Being from which we are estranged and in relation to which we are in despair. Such faith is a choice to pass through the doorway of despair into our authentic life.

The state of despair is deeper than feeling grumpy, sad, or panicky. Despair is not a feeling, but a state of consciousness. Despair is the most horrific state of hopelessness that we can imagine—often less to be desired than death. So all sorts of grim feelings may accompany being in despair. Indeed, human beings quite often commit suicide rather than endure a life of despair. Kierkegaard, a resident of Denmark, has been viewed as the "dismal Dane" for even discussing this topic of despair. Actually, however, Kierkegaard is one of humanity's greatest optimists. He reveals our despair to be a doorway to our authenticity. He sees despair as a fragile sickness of spirit that shows us the way to health—to the fullness of our essential possibilities of being human.

Trust in Profound Reality is our spirit health. We must not cheapen this understanding of faith. Trusting Profound Reality is the last resort for most human beings. We often try everything else first. Faith is the health we strongly seek only when we discover that every other trust is a path toward despair—a path that arrives sooner or later to an open hopelessness, complete with suicidal implications.

## KIERKEGAARDIAN DESPAIR
## AND BUDDHIST DUKKHA

The universality of Kierkegaard's insights on despair can be illustrated by a comparison with what I consider to be the best understanding of the Buddhist term "dukkha" (often translated "suffering"). Following are the Four Noble Truths (the truths of the Noble Ones) stated in accord with what I take to be an accurate contemporary recovery of these classical truths of Buddhism:

1. *Dukkha* is a profound unsatisfactoriness that is more than the plain fact of suffering the impermanence of all things. Dukkha is a "second arrow" of our suffering that results from our craving and clinging to things that are impermanent.

2. *Samudaya* is the origin of dukkha. Dukkha arises from a craving for or clinging to these impermanent or temporal things and the states of consciousness that result. This clinging produces a "karma" or "fate" that keeps us trapped in an ever-renewed "destiny" of dissatisfaction.

3. *Niroda* is the cessation of dukkha. By stopping our craving/clinging, nirvana is attained, no more karma is produced, and this dukkha dissatisfaction no longer arises.

4. *Magga* is the path to the cessation of, or liberation from, dukkha. By following the Buddha's Eightfold Path of restraining oneself, cultivating discipline, and practicing mindfulness and meditation, our craving and clinging will sometimes stop, enabling this dukkha/ dissatisfaction to no longer dominate our lives.

These Four Noble Truths provide a conceptual framework for introducing and explaining much Buddhist thought, and its lasting power in the history of religion.

Søren Kierkegaard defines despair as our dis-relation with Reality— our unwillingness to live the perpetually changing realities of our lives. Kierkegaard is using a different framework of thought than the Buddha, but his "Christian" insights into our human existence are much closer to the above expressions of Buddhism than is often noticed. Here is my Kierkegaardian rewording of the Four Noble Truths:

1. Despair is the core malfunction of human existence.

2. The origin or source of despair is our unwillingness to open to our real lives, however pleasant or unpleasant, safe or challenging, our real lives may be.

3. Despair can be healed by noticing that despair provides a doorway back to satisfactory realism by enabling us to notice precisely how this current despair is caused by our specific cravings and clingings to images of life and programs of living that we are substituting for our real lives.

4. The cessation of despair may cease through religious practices that prepare our consciousness for the possibility of trusting our real life as our best-case scenario—that means abandoning ourselves into being perpetually awakened by Profound Reality to our unrealism and to being accepted home to our wholesome realism, in spite of all our departures from such noble and satisfactory living.

In the first three of these four truths, the Kierkegaardian descriptions of these experiences are very similar to the Buddhist ones. "Dukkha" and "despair" are close in meaning—perhaps different terms for an identical reference.

The Fourth Noble Truth in both my Buddhist and my Kierkegaardian summaries is about religious practices. Buddhist and Christian religious practices differ. Buddhist practices tend to emphasize the meditative practices of silence and stillness, while Christian practices tend to be more verbal—more structured in sermons, discussions, rituals, and social responses.

Both Buddhist and Christian practices, however, have a similar purpose—making spirit realization more likely. As the Buddhists sometimes say, "Mediation does not cause enlightenment; it only makes the accident of enlightenment more likely." Lutheran and post-Kierkegaardian theologizing often note that salvation is a gift of grace from Profound Reality—certainly not an achievement of our religious practices. Both "gift" and "accident" can point to the same basic awareness of the relation between religious practices and spirit realization. Our essential goodness comes into manifestation by the power of Reality, rather than by human achievement. We humans have only to accept this blessing and live out its possibilities.

Christian faith or trust is about the action of accepting these blessings of possibility for a radical realism given to us from the depths of Profound Reality. The possibility of faith is not created by human actions. Faith is given, and then faith is enacted as an active life of faith constructed by the person of faith. An action of faith is a surrender to the possibility of being our essential trust in realism that is being given to us by the Ground of our Being.

Furthermore, faith comes as an actual possibility to one of us only when our despair of our ongoing life appears to us as a doorway through which we can walk back to a more realistic mode of living. As persons of faith, each of us, all by ourselves, must choose to walk through that doorway of despair to a new life of greater realism. This is the Kierkegaardian optimism: our spirit sickness (despair) shows us the doorway to our spirit health. When we see how we are creating our own despair, we can also see the possibility of faith—that trust in Profound Reality that heals our despair over the Profound Reality that we are confronting.

## MORE ON THE DOORWAY OF DESPAIR

Let's start with a deeper examination of Buddhist meditation. Buddhist meditation can be defined as a concentration of consciousness upon the breath, upon the current ongoing flow of living in the enduring *now* of being aware. In the midst of such mediation, we notice thinking, emotional feelings, and sensations from our body and its environment happening to our consciousness. The discipline of meditation amounts to maintaining our attention to these ongoing processes without being distracted by our thoughts about these processes or any other factor of our imagination. We simply sit (or walk) in this persistent concentration of consciousness upon being conscious of the impermanent factors flowing through our lives. This amounts to a discipline of intense realism, in which we keep coming back and back and back to our now-existing reality from our inevitable departures into our "imagination."

I want to claim that doing this discipline of meditation includes the ongoing choice to trust in the prime value of realism and to mistrust the substitutes for realism that our minds keep churning up. Buddhists call this "mindfulness," but such "mindfulness" does not mean what Western philosophy calls "thoughtfulness." Buddhist mindfulness is actually a discipline of the consciousness using the mind to notice our conscious awareness of what is real—including our passions, which are using our mind to construct substitutes for our awareness of what is real.

So understood, the discipline of meditation can be viewed as an exercise in trusting Profound Reality—the flow of events that are happening to our consciousness. The act of doing the discipline of meditation is an act of trusting that this practice may lead us to overcoming our despair or dukkha. Connection with the really Real heals despair, for despair is the result of losing touch with Reality. It is this tension between Reality and illusion that results in the tragedy of despair.

## STUCK IN THE DITCH OF DESPAIR

Driving home from a track meet with three companions, I hit a low spot with water all across the road, and the car spun around and backed into a drainage ditch on the right side of the road. We were all safe, but there was no way out of that ditch until a truck came by whose driver was willing to connect a chain and pull us out.

If we use the analogy of the roadway of realism with deep ditches of illusion on both sides of the road, then despair is one of those ditches into which we have driven our lives and get stuck there, needing help from Reality to return to the roadway of Reality. If the truck of Reality does not come along and pull us out of our ditch, we will have to stay there, because this ditch is precisely a loss of our essential freedom that we have negated by driving into the ditch.

This ditch of estrangement is not a "natural" state, for we can be restored to our essential nature, and thereby become even more clear about our nature, having lost it for a time and having gotten it back. But when we are in this ditch of despair it seems eternal, because in using our freedom to create this ditch of unreality, we have lost the freedom that comes with being in tune with Reality. It is precisely a restoration of this lost freedom that is needed to get out of our ditch of despair. So despair has the quality of a fate or karma or bondage to living in the delusion that we have created and thereby become. Even in our ditch we experience some freedom to do this or that, but we do not have the freedom to get out of this ditch of unreality that has become our operating selfhood. Despair is a state of being helplessly stuck in being who we are not. For delivery from being stuck in our mistaken selves, we need help. We are helplessly sick—sick in despair—and we need a doctor.

Kierkegaard uses "sickness" as his analogy for discussing despair. The opposite of this sickness is the health of faith or trust in the roadway of realism as the best-case scenario for our lives. Our driving off the highway into the ditches of despair sickness came about by poor driving, not by cosmic cause and effect. We are responsible for our mistrust of Profound Reality; nevertheless, now that we have mistrusted Profound Reality, we live in a ditch of mistrust within which we are stuck. Mistrust has become our whole life; we have become blind, or almost blind, to any possibility other than the unreality in which we are stuck. In this mistrusting state we have lost our power to choose trust. Mistrust is a ditch out of which we must be helped by Reality to return to the roadway of realism.

Fortunately for us, the possibility of help is always present, because Reality is always present. But Reality is not present to the ditch dweller until Reality comes into our particular ditch and shows us the *ditchness* of our lives, and then leads us out of our particular ditch; that is, out of who we think we are into who we essentially are, which includes our freedom to stay on the highway of realism. When we look closely to such an experience, we can see that we are led through the doorway of despair over our false life into our true, or somewhat truer, life.

We can resist this leading into health, for we have to be willing to be led out of our ditch. This healing may seem humiliating to our self-made deluded falseness. We may greave over loosing this old false self. Nevertheless, this humbling path is the only way out of our despair-laced ditches of unreality.

On the other side of accepting this humiliating path of healing, we can have the happy realization of our Reality dependence for our own realism—a deep gratitude for this gift of realism from beloved Reality—a gift we dearly need to live a despair-free life. The word "God" and the prayer-useful word "Thou" can now attach itself to this beloved Profound Reality that we have mostly fled or even hated.

## ILLUSTRATING THESE DYNAMICS
## WITH LIFE STORIES

Life-story illustrations may help clarify the dynamics just discussed. Telling a personal story is a complicated and stange effort, for we never remember anything that has happened to us completely. So telling a life story is always somewhat fictional; nevertheless, we can be true to the dynamics of what happened without being exact. Here is one of my events of healing that happened many years ago.

I was devoted to a mentor who had greatly helped me. I was, I might say, stuck in my need for his approval. For a summer program that we were conducting together, I was assigned to give a lecture on a topic that I had never talked about before. I kept going to talk with this mentor about this talk that I was preparing. About the third time I went to ask him something, he said, "Do you want me to give this talk to someone else?" "No," I said, and left without another word or another visit for help. This simple rebuke cast me into the awareness of my unrealism about not trusting in my own experience concerning what needed to be said in this talk. I walked through the doorway of this humiliation, and gave this talk with little sense of need for anyone's approval for it. The talk went fine—not perfect, but good enough. This had a long-range effect on my relationshop with my own confidence, as well as my relationship with this mentor. I could now better take from him what was good for me and not take from him what was not good for me. This may seem like a small change, but it was actually rather big for me personally.

Stories that we find in novels and plays, though fictional, can be true to life experiences of healing that illustrate these spirit-healing dynamics. Here is an example from a New Testament story about Zacchaeus (Luke 19:1–10). This story was a sort of fiction—whatever happened in real time, it was told and retold for several decades. So I feel free to tell it in my own way.

A Jewish man named Zacchaeus has been working as a Roman tax collector, and he had taken enough off the top to become rich. Being a tax collector in that system meant taking from the taxed what the Roman govenor required, plus more for the collector's own upkeep. This was a style of operation that tempted abuse. This man was clearly guilty of abuses, and let's guess that he felt a bit uncomfortable about that. He was also upopular among his fellow Jews.

Nevertheless, he was Jew enough that he was interested in a revered Jewish teacher who was coming down the road. Being too short to see over people, he ran down the road and climbed a sycamore tree to see Jesus. When Jesus came close enough to see him up there, he called out, "Zacchaeus, hurry up and come down, I must be your guest for lunch today." Zacchaeus was so impressed with the implied forgiveness in this request, that he came right down. Before hurrying off to fix lunch, he said to Jesus, "Look sir, I will give half of my property to the poor. And if I have swindled anybody, I will pay him back four times as much." Jesus says to him and to the shocked crowd, "Healing has come to this household today."

So what happened in this man's life? The drama of acceptance communicated by this revered teacher brought to his consciousness the grim despair of his own life, and he walked through that doorway into a fresh start for a new style of living. Members of the crowd also had their own lives examined. Their view that "big sinners" like this man were hopeless took a beating. This beating revealed some of that crowd's own despair about this strange truth of ever-present possiblities for deep personal change. Perhaps this revelation became a doorway for some of them for their own way forward.

## DESCRIBING THE DITCHES OF SPIRIT SICKNESS

The topic of despair and its healing is a far deeper topic than a couple of illustrations can explore. In his classic book *The Sickness unto Death*, Søren Kierkegaard illuminated many of the various qualites of despair sickness. In using the word "despair" to identify the root nature of spirit pathology, Kierkegaard shows us that our primary "evil" or "sin" is a fragile reality. In his exploration of despair, he shows us hope under any and all circumstances—making clear to us that however deep our despair, it is a castle of cards that can come tumbling down in the twinkling of an eye. While despair is, indeed, a deep ditch from which we cannot extricate ourselves, the Ground of our Being stands ready to deliver us. Our deliverance is always possible, because Profound Reality is always more powerful than the unreality that is the cause of our despair.

In the opening pages of *The Sickness unto Death*, Søren Kierkegaard gives an abstract, almost comically worded definition of our true self or spirit. But this definition is no joke: Kierkegaard is describing in this comedy of images a profound view of the essential human.[2]

Kierkegaard defines "self" or "spirit" not as a substance, but as relation between two paradoxical factors: the temporal and the Eternal. If we picture a line of relationship drawn from our everyday temporal specifics all the way to our encounter with the Mysterious Eternity we encounter in the flow of time, we have the first aspect of Kierkegaard's picture of the true self. Secondly, we hear him say that this relatedness is not the temporal or the Eternal, but a third term that has a self-aware capacity to relate to itself. Here is my diagram of Kierkegaard's definition of true self or spirit:

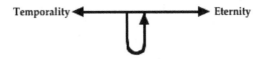

This means that the true self is not a supernatural ghost substance living inside my finite body or psyche. Spirit is a set of relationships (symbolized by the lines in the above diagram). Kierkegaard goes on to say that this temporal-to-Eternal relatedness has two ways of relating to itself: (1) willingly to be itself or (2) unwilling to be itself. Kierkegaard then insists that the self has not constituted itself, but has been constituted by "another." By "another" he means the Eternal Source of all temporal process. This Wholly Other has constituted the human to be this strange complex relatedness that has the capacity and the necessity to relate to its own self.

For Kierkegaard this model defines health and sickness for the human spirit: (1) health means willingly being ourselves as constituted and (2) sickness means what results from refusing to be ourself as constituted. There are many forms of spirit pathology, but all of them, according to Kierkegaard, are forms of despair. Despair is a state of sickness that results because our refusing to be ourself takes place in a cosmos within which there is no escape from being this temporal-to-Eternal relationship that each human being is constituted to be. So here is his abstract definition of despair: attempting to be what one is not, while the self that one truly is persists in opposing this falseness. The persisting reality of the true self stands in opposition to our every attempt to flee or fight being what we

---

2. Kierkegaard, *Fear and Trembling and The Sickness unto Death*, 146 and 147.

truly are. When this opposition is consciously experienced, it is experienced as fleeing the inescapable or fighting the undefeatable—hense, it is a complete hopelessness. It is a state of conscious despair.

## No Duality, Just an Either-Or Choice

Kierkegaard's model of the authentic self does not imply a duality in Reality. It only implies a polarity in the human experience of Reality. The polarity of temporal and Eternal is part of our human experience; nevertheless, it is a human experience of One Reality, not two realities. The temporal does not battle the Eternal: it is the Eternal that makes all temporal factors impermanent. And it is our being conscious of our temporality that enables us to experience the Eternal.

A popular view is that the Eternal is a pleasant thing that replaces the bad thing of being temporal. This is not the view of Kierkegaard, or of Amos, Isaiah, Jeremiah, Jesus, Paul, John, Augustine, Hildegard of Bingen, Thomas Aquinas, Julian of Norwich, Teresa of Avila, St. John of the Cross, Martin Luther, John Wesley, Johnathan Edwards, and ever so many other witnesses in the radical monotheism stream, including Mohammad. Fully understood, the radical monotheism heritage affirms all of Profound Reality—all of the Eternal and all of temporality's ups and downs, successes and failures, births and deaths. Each temporal item is a part of the overall flow of time in which we are embedded. This means that each event in time is an encounter with the overall Oneness of Eternity. We might say that "Eternity" means whatever is turning the wheel of time. So profound are these core awareness that I want to share the following poem to further say these unsayable sayings.

A Non-Dual Contemplation
The temporal and the Eternal
are aspects of the same
human experience!

If you speak of the Eternal
as separate from the temporal
you have reduced the Eternal
to another temporal realm.

If you speak of the temporal
as missing the Eternal
you have not yet experienced

the temporal.

The impermanent and the Permanent
are aspects of the same
human experience.

If you speak of the Permanent
as separate from the impermanence
you have reduced the Permanent
to another realm of impermanence.

If you speak of the impermanent
as missing the Permanent
you have not yet experienced
the impermanent.

The manyness and the Oneness
are aspects of the same
human experience.

If you speak of the Oneness
as separate from the manyness
you have reduced the Oneness
to a another part of the realm of manyness.

If you speak of the manyness
as missing the Oneness
you have not yet experienced
the manyness.

Who you are and who I am
is this relation between
the temporal and the Eternal—
a relation that is consciously
relating Yes or No to
the temporal/Eternal relation!

Herein is our non-dual
Kierkegaardianism!

## THE SPIRIT THERAPIST'S MANUAL ON DESPAIR

Kierkegaard examines despair in relation to our consciousness of despair and our consciousness of what despair is. Following is a brief description of Kierkegaard's typology of six types of despair. These types are examinined in relation to our consciousness of our despair and of our conscious relationships with our despair.

## 1. Unconscious of Despair

First of all, Kierkegaard describes how a human being can be unconscious of the despair that he or she is stuck in. When there is no awareness of profound consciousness (spirit), there is no awareness of despair. Nevertheless, for a human, this very unawareness of spirit is also a form of despair. Kierkegaard calls this state of despair "pure immediacy," for such a person is totally outward in their consciousness, with no inward refectiveness. Such a person only rarely exists. Also, this state of despair is the most tragic of all states of despair, for such a person does not even know that he or she is sick of a deadly sickness—the "sickness unto death."

## 2. Immediacy Plus Some Consciousness of Despair

Kierkegaard's second category of despair is still "immediacy" in the sense of being outwardly oriented and basically unaware of spirit or despair. Unlike the first category of despair, some awareness of spirit and despair is being experienced. But this despairer thinks that his or her despair is a minor flaw that will go away if some outward condition is changed. Many literary characters depict this state. Perhaps Willie Loman in *Death of a Salesman* would be a good example. The butler in the movie *The Remains of the Day* would be another. Kierkegaard satirizes this pattern of living—portraying it as like unto a person who has a smoking fireplace in his living room. He opens windows, walks around the block, comes back to his easy chair, sits down again, and proceeds with living as if no smoke of despair ever occured. Kierkegaard thought that most people in his century had this relation to their despair.

## 3. Despair as a Painful Introverted Secret

In this third type of despair, there is a keen awareness of being an inward self and a self who is in despair. This person is in despair over the self, a self conceived to be weak because of its painful despair. This person is in despair over being a weak person who can and does despair. But because this despairer is proud or wants to be proud, this weak self wishes not to

expose the weak despairing self to others. This keenly aware and consciously despairing self has become a secret, which the estranged person
tries to keep hidden from everyone by living in an outward cocoon of
respectability. This lie of unexposure creates an even deeper despair that
can issue one day in suicide. If you have ever been surprised at the suicide
of some seemingly well-adjusted and successful person, you may have
met one of these skillfully secretive despairers.

You might have noticed this person being quite circumspect, sharing very little or doing so with extreme care. He or she may be a very
agreeable person, never conflictual or argumentative, never rocking any
boat that might lead to his or her exposure of that weak-feeling and pain-
fully despairing self.

The capacity of this rather rare person to handle the extreme pains
of despair would suprise many people. That this pain could be so strong
that this seeming capable person would take his or her own life seems
unthinkable to many of us. In fact, from the outside the issues that this
person is in despair over can seem trivial, but to this person these seemingly trival flaws are experienced as a challenge to whatever it is that currently makes life worth living for this person.

## 4. The Despairing Plunge into Outward Living

The conscious and despairing person just described may resolve the
choice to continue living by making a *plunge* into outward living—a
plunge in which the estranged self seeks to forget itself and its despair in
noble work or in sensual excesses. This way of being an outward person is
different from the outwardness of immediacy. Here outwardness is a desperate compulsion, an attempt to bury from consciousness both spirit and
despair, yet leaving an all too clear trace of itself as a despairing presence.

Literature is full of portrayals of this type of despairer. The 1996
Academy Award for best actor was presented to Nicolas Cage for portraying a man so intent on drinking himself to death even though he
had forgotten why he started drinking. The compulsively driven younger
sister in the movie *Georgia* is another example of a plunging despairer. A
plunger can use sex, love, food, distractions of many sorts, as well as the
now-widespread use of drugs.

Sensual distraction is only one of the patterns taken by this form of
despairer. Kierkegaard says that the despairing plunger can also attempt

to lose his or her painful spirit consciousness by plunging into noble work. Movies sometimes touch on the compulsive noble work of some workaholic lawyer, doctor, or public figure, but these movies seldom portray fully the inwardly despairing nature of this sort of plunging. There is nothing wrong with hard work or noble work; the unfortunate direction involved here is the compulsive nature of this work—a compulsion that leaves a telling trace of desperation. Suppressing a despairing self is more valued than the work that is being achieved. This noble plunger is seeking to escape from being the despair-sick being that he or she actually is.

## 5. The Despair of Active Defiance

Both secretiveness and plunging become obviously futile as one becomes more conscious. As consciousness inceases, a more highly conscious form of despair may be formed by the despairing human. This despairing person can form a stronger and more conscious manifestation of despair rather than turn to a faith willingness to be in accord with Reality. He or she, in this *active-defiant* despair, has renounced the weakness of shame over the despairing self or the plunge into forgetfulness, and become instead an openly defiant protest against the way human life actually is. This is viewed by this despairing person as becoming strong—a "strong self" who chooses the self that he or she shall be.

Kierkegaard explains why this strong state is still a fragile state. The active-defiant person attempts to be a king who has invented his or her own kingdom of reality and selfhood. This passionate, energetic, powerful spirit lives a deeply ironical existence, for his or her whole mode of being is sustained by a defiant self who could, with a single choice, turn this whole kingdom of living into no-thing-ness. The defiant person's own selfhood, since it is constituted and sustained by the defiant person's own energy, is a pseudo-self, living in a pseudo-reality created by this continuing act of defiance. Yet, real Reality and the real self of this defiant person remain present as a threat of immediate extinction to the pseudo-self and its pseudo-reality. Hence, the state of active defiance is a state of despair in spite of (indeed because of) the despairing energy of its own defiance.

Herman Melville in his novel *Moby Dick* paints an unforgettable picture of the eerie false strength of an actively defiant despairing person. Captain Ahab, who lost a leg earlier in an encounter with a huge white whale called Moby Dick, is consumed with the compulsion to defeat this creature of the deeps who has "made him half a man." It is hard to miss the symbolism here. The whale is a mediator of the undefeatable majesty of Profound Reality. Ahab, rather than accept his one-leggedness as his real and only destiny, rebels against his finitude and aims to defeat the Eternal symbolized by this huge white whale. In death itself, he fights on in this defiant style, waving to those who remain to follow him in still further defiance. Which they do. The first mate gives defiance a slightly new style of crass instrumentalism, and continues the quest to defeat the undefeatable. Perhaps Herman Melville was aware that industrial civilization was playing out this story—destroying an entire planetary biosphere rather than surrendering to being our human limitations. And when the whaling vessel of industrial civilization sinks into the deeps, will there then be any aware being who lives to tell the tale?

Defiant forms of despair appear in our real-world history as well as in our fiction. Most of our strongman antiheros are candidates for this type of despair. Hitler and Stalin certainly lead the list. But such hightly visible figures are not the only examples of men or women who make up their own protest against Reality and attempt to be that protest in a shameless, self-absorbed manner of this futile ridiculous quest to create a substitute self with its substitute reality. I myself am capable of creating a brand-name that I confuse with the mystery of "me."

## 6. The Despair of Passive Defiance

Finally, Kierkegaard describes a state of being in despair that is even more conscious and intentional than active defiance. He calls it "*passive defiance*." The passively defiant person knows that he or she is a spirit being constituted by the Wholeness of Being, but uses his or her own despair as an excuse for remaining in despair. The passively defiant person wills to be a mistake made by the Wholeness of Being—a mistake that proves that the Wholeness of Being is a very poor Maker. This may look like being super humble, but it is actually a style of immense pride. This despairer is so insistant on being something other than he or she is that this very pride becomes a jammed lock of defiance toward the entire setup of the cosmos of Reality. This sort of rage is seldom met with, even in literature, but we can intuit its possible presence in some of those deeply estranged characters depicted in the novels of Charles Dickens. Kierkegaard satirizes this person as similar to a bit of written text that has become consciousness and believes itself to be a mistake (even if within the larger composition it is not a mistake at all). Then this "mistake" insists on being this mistake as proof that the writer of the whole text is a very poor writer.

## FINAL OBSERVATIONS

All six of these types of despair are fragile states. Whatever be the stage of our consciousness, whatever be the specific form of our despairing estrangement, our estrangement is fragile, for all estrangement is a pseudo-reality, a pretense reality fighting against the fullness of Profound Reality and of our own authentic spirit existence—our own profound consciousness. Reality always wins this fight in the end, so estrangement is fragile. The more we become aware of our states of estrangement, the more we become aware of our despair. Awareness of our estrangement means entering into a self-conscious state of despair. Such awareness of estrangement and its despairing hopelessness is the threshold or the doorway to health. We can pass through this door into the health of willing to be the life we actually are. And we are accepted—that is, we are indeed forgiven of all our foolish estrangements and thereby face a fresh start in realism. We can surrender to this fresh start in realistic living even if this realism is something quite different from the opinioins of our peer group or the present norms of our society. We can accept our acceptance. Such willingness to be real Kierkegaard calls "faith" or "trust."

Let us notice that Kierkegaard's spirit health is something different than a mere increase in consciousness. The immediate person, though slight in consciousness, can become a person of faith by becoming open to be more conscious and more willing to be a self, a self that despairs, and a self that can be healed of despair. At the other exteme, the defiant despairer is very conscious, but still in despair, using this greater consciousness to be even more despairing—an open commitment to the dark side of despair, and often a leader of others along this deadly path. He or she can end this spirit suicide with a simple surrender to realism. The only cost in parting with a false self and its false reality is living with this newfound health in a world of estranged humans who may ignore, reject, or seek to harm such authenticity.

*Spirit health is a different dynamic than simply becoming more conscious. Spirit health is a willingness, with whatever degree of consciousness we have, to be who we really are within the cosmos of historicity that we actually experience with the powers of consciousness that we possess at this time in our lives.*

With his description of despair, Søren Kierkegaard has not only clarified for us what despair is, he has also given the therapist in us all a spirit doctor's manual on spirit sicknesses. He has given us a fresh way of theologizing—a mode of thinking and living that has been expanded upon by Paul Tillich, Dietrich Bonhoeffer, H. Richard Niebuhr, Rudolf Bultmann, and many others. Perhaps it is true that we "thinking Christians" are not fully entitled to call ourselves "thinking Christians" until we have at least taken in the basic insights of Søren Kierkegaard's *The Sickness unto Death.*

In the next chapter, I turn to an examination of another set of crucial New Testament symbols—cross and resurrection. I will seek to clarify how our clarity about despair and its healing helps us clarify these often-misunderstood symbols.

# 12

## Who Created Christianity?

THE HISTORICAL FIGURE JESUS of Nazareth is believed to have lived in the vicinity of 3 BCE to 30 CE. Such a person is an important figure in the founding of Christianity, but Jesus did not found a religion. He was born, lived, and died a Jew. The founding of Christianity is more complex than the founding of Islam or Buddhism.

Mohammad can be called the original founder of Islam—referred to as such by the many other founding figures of the set of religions we call "Islam." He was born in 570 CE and died June 8, 632 at the age of sixtyt-two.

Gautama Buddha is believed to have lived and taught mostly in the northeastern part of ancient India sometime between the sixth and fourth centuries BCE. He is also known as "Siddhārtha Gautama" or simply "the Buddha," a title that meant "the Awake One." He was a monk, mendicant, sage, and teacher on whose teachings Buddhism was founded. All of this can be said with relative historical certainty.

But such historical certainty we do not have about Jesus of Nazareth. And our most accurate historical science does not find him to be a religious founder. He was born, lived, and died a Jew. We might credit Simon Peter, several men named James, several women named Mary, and others as the Christian founders, but they were also Jews and remained so. Perhaps we could call them "Christ-Way Jews," for they did revere Jesus as the Messiah.

Paul was also a Christ-Way Jew, and his Mediterranean communities were likewise Christ-Way Jews. Paul worked in relation to the Jewish synagogues as well as with Gentile persons attracted to Judaism. Paul conducted a controversial innovation among these Christ-Way

Jews—namely, allowing Gentile men of obvious Christ-Way spirit to be full members of Paul's baptized circles without being circumcised. Was this the founding of Christianity? Looking backward, Paul's work was seen as a step toward founding a new religion. His letters became part of the founding documents of that new religion. Nevertheless, during Paul's lifetime, no new religion was created.

The founding writings that set the direction for a new practice of religion that branched into various sets of religions (Eastern Orthodox, Roman Catholic, Protestant, and others) were four unique pieces of literature called "gospels." These books head the collection we call the "New Testament." The supposed authors of these books are referred to as Matthew, Mark, Luke, and John.

Mark is the earliest text of the four. Few New Testament scholars dispute that. So Mark can be said to have invented this unique type of literature called a "gospel" (a "good news" proclamation about a hero figure named Jesus). While Mark created a lasting comprehensive story about Jesus, this was not a biography about the historical Jesus, but a fictional hero narrative about the meaning of Jesus as the crucified and resurrected Messiah, and also viewed as "the Son of God."

Mark's narrative was so innovative and powerful that two more versions of this narrative, Matthew and Luke-Acts, were soon put to paper. They used Mark as a model and copied much of his wording. Their additions amounted to additional theological discussion on topics dear to these two theologians. Matthew leaned toward traditional Judaism—Jesus as rabbi, a teacher of new teachings. Luke leaned toward the Gentile wing of this emerging religion—the innovator of big changes for humanity at large.

If we want to appoint one person as the founder of Christianity, I believe it would have to be the writer of the gospel of Mark. It is his remarkable piece of writing that set the direction for what came to be called the "Christian religion."

Mark was a follower of Paul, and his theology reflects strongly Paul's influence. Mark was deeply embedded in Hellenistic Judaism: the Old Testament was the only scripture Mark had. The letters of Paul and other writings were not yet "scripture." Mark was pulling together a deep synthesis of insights from three decades of Christ-Way living. Mark's language and allusions are strongly rooted in a Greek translation of the older Hebrew scriptures.

## THAT STILL-WILDER FOURTH GOSPEL

The last of the four gospels was written toward the end of the first century. Its author, whom we call "John," broke the norms for gospel creation. He created a new form of theological fiction adapted to the core questions of the Greek-speaking east end of the Roman Empire. All four of these gospels were theological fiction created from four significantly different theological perspectives. The first three were somewhat close to being a form of historical fiction. The gospel of John broke those bounds. John's gospel is almost pure fiction, theological drama writing—a grand stage play with characters made up by the author. John is still telling a Jesus hero narrative, and this writer is still grounded in the basic Hebraic point of view. John, however, is writing for people who know almost nothing about the Old Testament or Jewish pageants. Following is my interpretive rewording of the first fourteen verses of John's gospel. I have put my rewording in brackets.

> When all things began, the Word already was. (John 1:1, New English Bible)

"Word" is a translation of the Greek word "*logos*," which can also be roughly translated as "the meaning of it all." Assuming that understanding, here is how we might read the opening fourteen verses of this remarkable theological work:

> When all things began, [the Meaning of It All] already was. [The Meaning of It All] dwelt with [the Power of It All], and what [the Power of It All] was, [the Meaning of It All] also was. [The Meaning of It All] then, was with [the Power of It All] at the beginning, and through [the Meaning of It All], all things came to be. No single thing was created without [the Meaning of It All]. All that came to be was alive with the life of [the Meaning of It All]. And that life was the light of being human. This light shines on in the dark, and the darkness has never mastered it.
>
> There appeared a man named John, sent by [the Power of It All]. He came as a witness to testify to [the Meaning of It All], that all humans might become [trusting humans] through [the Meaning of It All]. John was not himself [the Meaning of It All]; he came to bear witness to [the Meaning of It All]. [The Meaning of It All], which enlightens every human, was even then coming into the world.
>
> [The Meaning of It All] was already in the world; but the world, though it owed its being to [the Meaning of It All], did

not recognize [the Meaning of It All]. He [speaking of the Meaning of It All] entered his own realm, and his own realm would not receive him. But to all who did receive [the Meaning of It All], to all who have yielded him their allegiance, he gave the right to become offspring of [the Power of It All], not born of any human stock, or by the fleshly desire of a human father, but the offspring of [the Power of It All (i.e., virgin born)].

So, [the Meaning of It All] became [human, earthling]; [the Meaning of It All] came to dwell among us, and we saw his glory, such glory [awe] that befits the only offspring of the [awesome Power of It All]—full of grace and truth. (New English Bible, with interpretations)

In the context of John's gospel, "grace" means healing power, and "truth" means an awareness within our deep or profound human consciousness that is incapable of formation in our rational minds—namely, that the Power-of-it-all can meet us in a mere human being. Surely such a statement as statement is absurd. In chapter 3 I explored how Truth with a capital "T" is an absolute Mystery. This awareness is present in John's gospel. In the above passage, we are hearing that this Absolute Mystery of this capital-"T" sort of Truth is being made known to human consciousness. That is John is speaking of a profound revelation of what is capital-"T" True for all humans, in all times, in all cultures, and in all places.

Yet this revelation does not empty the Mystery of its mysteriousness to the human mind. The revelation reveals to us that the Mystery's relation to us humans is friendliness, or "love" as John is constantly saying. In those humans who receive the revelation that this Absolute Mysteriousness loves us, those humans find that their own state of profound consciousness becomes love for everybody. Both the essence of the Mystery and the essence of our humanity is revealed by this revelation. We can experience in our own profound consciousness this relation of profound trust in this Profound Mystery viewed by us as a love for us. And as John claims, this dynamic was already in operation at the beginning of the cosmos.

## MARK'S ALSO-STRANGE WRITING

Keeping in mind this fourfold history of gospel-writing, let us return our attention to the gospel of Mark. We see in this first gospel a very different style of theologizing than we find in John. For Mark, the Messiah nature of Jesus is presented as a deep secret. The meaning of "resurrection" is also a secret whose meaning is only hinted at the very end of the gospel. This hint implies that resurrection must become a human experience for you or me before we can understand what Mark means by the word "resurrection." Similarly, "the Son of God" symbolism is also treated as a deep secret known only to the demons who are in dread of their extinction before the human presence of the Jesus exemplar.

Throughout Mark's narrative, the masses of people and even the disciples of Jesus remain "dumb" about "resurrection," as well as about the meaning of this ordinary-extraordinary peasant, Jesus, being "the Christ" or "Son of God." This secretiveness also applies to these followers being "a new covenant with God"—a people who require a whole new sort of religious practice. One of Mark's parables claims that this *new wine* of cross-resurrection spirit requires new religious *wineskins* of symbolism that can hold that spirit. These deep secrets only begin to become entirely plain to other-than-Jesus characters in the closing verses of Mark's narrative, when three women disciples flee from the empty tomb of Jesus in terror.

This truly strange story about these three shocked women ends the original gospel. For we readers experiencing Mark's abrupt ending, the secret of resurrection remains something to be discovered in our own inner depths. We are challenged by Mark to look at his strange storytelling more closely to discover within our own inner authority the meaning of resurrection. Mark has dumped on his readers this secret of why the tomb of Jesus is empty. It is empty because these women are now "the Body of Jesus"—a body that will soon include some men as well.

These women are now asked by the angel to head for Galilee, where Mark's story has begin and where the men have already fled. Galilee is "the place of healing," the place where demons have been cast out, blindness cured, and more. Mark is asking us to read this whole narrative again, asking ourselves this question: "What does it look like for me to be resurrected?" Mark's entire text is one long parable, seeing the meaning of which requires us to undergo deep change in our own person. Herein is the meaning of the Markan secret. Herein is the meaning of the Christian revelation. Herein is the meaning of the symbols of cross and resurrection.

All four gospels have something in common that distinguishes these four writings from most other first-century narratives about Jesus—namely, a focus on these two symbols: cross and resurrection. Not only is crucifixion and resurrection an explicit content in these gospels, but also these two symbols are alluded to in many hidden ways—such as taking in bread and wine, eating magical loaves, and being washed in the River Jordan and raised up from this water a reborn being. We also see resurrection in the story of a twelve-year-old girl, presumed dead, being raised up and given something to eat. We even see death and resurrection in the story about a man being lowered down through a hole made in the roof of a house into a room with Jesus, who forgives this man's sin and causes an argument with the old heads of that religion. In the first three gospels such allusions go on all the way through these narratives. In the gospel of John, written by a different sort of theologian for a different audience, the author is more direct. He has Jesus say brash things like, "I am the resurrection and the life"; "I am the bread of life that has come down from heaven"; "I am the way, the truth, and the life."

## CROSS AND RESURRECTION

It is fair to say that the symbols of *cross* and *resurrection* are as central to an understanding of the Christian revelation as *meditation* and *enlightenment* are to an understanding of Buddhism. Yet both cross and resurrection seem cryptic, even weird, to many people today.

Members of our current scientific culture may be excused for having no grasp at all of the resurrection symbol. We have to move beyond our scientific minds and be contemplative inquirers in order to experience and thereby see the meaning of "resurrection." When we are honest, most of us view the literal return to life of a three-day-old corpse to be superstition. Yet that meaning of resurrection has been told as the meaning of the resurrection symbol by many interpreters. Mark did not see resurrection in this literal way. A literal return from the dead means nothing deeply religious to Mark or to you or to me. If such an event were to happen today, it would be open to hundreds of speculative explanations, none of which would be profoundly or convincingly religious.

Mark's understanding of the cross is equally opaque in our culture. Some modern authors even accuse Christianity of promoting a morbid preoccupation with death, suffering, and tragedy. The crucifix, or even a bare cross, is viewed as meaningless as a hangman's noose or a guillotine. But for Mark the horror of the cross is seen as priceless food for the soul. How can that be? Surely, we have need of some thoughtful exploration if we are to grasp the meaning of this "good news"—this gospel of Mark.

The good news that Mark is announcing needs a deep dive of contemplative inquiry into our own inner existence.

In the first thirteen verses of Mark's narrative, an experience of resurrection happens to an ordinary man named Jesus (from Nazareth—not Bethlehem, the city of David, or Jerusalem, the cultural center). For the rest of Mark's narrative, Jesus is what a resurrected human looks like—walking, talking, eating, sleeping, praying, healing others, challenging the status quo, and facing the consequences of rejection by an estranged humanity. The literary character of Jesus in Mark's gospel is an exemplar of living the resurrected life, and of doing so unto death.

Meanwhile, the disciples in Mark's narrative are what it looks like to be on a journey toward resurrection. They are dramatized as ignorant about the meaning of both cross and resurrection. They are on a journey toward those revelations. We can view Mark's narrative as about two journeys—both of which can take place in our own life journey: (1) the journey of spirit awakening that is taking place in the lives of the disciples, and (2) the journey of the spirit-awake human, which Jesus represents. This is what resurrection looks like in action. Jesus' presence, words, and actions are dramatizing the qualities of the resurrected human—how such a presence among others is healing to what most ails us all. The full meaning of the resurrection will remain Mark's secret until chapter 16, but cross and resurrection are primary symbols in Mark's narrative from beginning to end.

Again, both of these journeys can go on in the lives of all of us: (1) we, like the disciples, can journey toward full enlightenment (cross-and-resurrection living); and (2) we, like Jesus, can resolve to live our cross-and-resurrection life (our enlightenment, our profound humanness) in the real world, in the historical challenges of our time and place.

In other words, we are invited to identify with both Jesus and the disciples in Mark's narrative. As resurrected women and men, we, like Jesus, can expend our new life of profound humanness for the healing and well-being of others. This expending is not a religious duty; it is a surrender to being our profound care for others, as well as for ourselves.

In Luke's second book, the Acts of the Apostles, we see more about the journey of living the life of resurrected humans in stories of persons other than Jesus. Peter, Paul, and other men and women are presented by Luke as further resurrection exemplars. Luke wants us to get the message that we who live "in Christ" are living the resurrection life as well as Jesus. Indeed, we are to *be the resurrection of Jesus*. We are called to be the body that rose on Easter morning. And that is what Mark is asking us to understand when he ends his narrative with three women fleeing the tomb in dread. If we do not associate both dread and fascination with the experience of resurrection, we do not yet understand what resurrection means. It is indeed dreadful to be Jesus—to be the ongoing Body of Christ that is called to the task of healing humanity and leading humanity in the journey from estrangement to authenticity.

It is easier for most of us to identify with the disciples who are moving toward resurrection step by step through the course of Mark's story. We can also easily identify with the crowds who are intrigued, but puzzled, by Jesus' parables. We can even identify with those persons who reject Jesus outright and consider this whole calling to be outrageous, silly, or plain wrong.

Mark's Jesus uses parables to provoke the sleeping into noticing their sleepiness and into seeking more truth. Then, to his more committed disciples, Mark's Jesus explains his parables further, expecting them to catch on to their own profound humanness sooner than the crowds.

Mark is assuming that the readers of his gospel will be carried along, like the disciples, toward the total unraveling of their egoism to an embodiment of the resurrected life that was walking and talking among them in the body of Jesus, and later in the body of the church, which came to be referred to as the "Body of Christ"—that is, the body of the resurrected one. So in Mark's narrative, we are entitled to identify with Jesus ministering to his blind followers, as well as identifying with the blind followers to whom Jesus is ministering.

So, as we read Mark's gospel, we need to keep in mind the originality and imagination of this remarkable person we are calling "Mark." We are dialoguing with Mark, not with Jesus. Jesus is a character in Mark's story. We are in a conversation with Mark in the same way that we are in conversation with J. K. Rowling, rather than Harry Potter, when we are reading a Harry Potter novel. Of course, we can have a conversation with Harry Potter as one of Rowling's characters. Similarly, we can have a conversation with Jesus as one of Mark's characters.

So, in our contemporary Christian theologizing about cross and resurrection, we need to keep in mind this spirit or profound-consciousness meaning of these ancient symbols. Clearly the original inventors and proclaimers of these symbols were not operating like scientific-minded literalists. They were storytellers assisting us to get a deep inner truth.

Identifying with Jesus in his crucifixion is a prominent theme in Paul's letters. He states in various ways that we, who are members of the Body of Christ, were crucified with Christ that we may also be raised with him to newness of life. Paul seems very clear that this strange cross-resurrection experience can happen to you or me—can happen now, not merely someday. Resurrection is the other side of the cross, or the cross is the front side of the resurrection. This dual "secret" is discoverable by you or me or anyone else.

## LUKE 24 ON THE MEANING OF RESURRECTION

But does the New Testament really support the view that resurrection is a possibility for everyone, and that resurrection is something far more than a literal coming back to life of the corpse of Jesus? Many New Testament stories seem to insist on a real, earthly, physical presence of the resurrected body of Jesus. Nevertheless, it is quite plausible to assume that the physical body of Christ that was raised in the physical bodies of the disciples breathing the Jesus quality of living. Luke 24 is a clear example of this disciple's-body understanding the New Testament storytelling on resurrection. I am going to comment on the following verses of Luke 24, which make clear that the resurrection of Jesus is a happening to the disciples, not to the corpse of the historical Jesus of Nazareth.

In the twenty-fourth chapter of the gospel of Luke, we see two of Jesus' followers walking away from Jerusalem. All their hopes have been totally disappointed. What they expected of Jesus had not been realized, because of his untimely and cruel death. It was Sunday morning and some women had reported a vision of angels who had said Jesus was alive, but this report had not impressed these two despairing travelers. Here they are on a seven-mile walk away from Jerusalem toward a village called Emmaus:

> As they went, they were deep in conversation about everything that had happened. While they were absorbed in their serious talk and discussion, Jesus himself approached and walked along with them, but something prevented them from recognizing him. Then he spoke to them, "What is all this discussion that you are having on your walk?"
>
> They stopped, their faces drawn with misery, and the one called Cleopas replied, "You must be the only stranger in

Jerusalem who hasn't heard all the things that have happened there recently!"

"What things?" asked Jesus.

"Oh, all about Jesus, from Nazareth. There was a man—a prophet strong in what he did and what he said—in God's eyes as well as the people's. Haven't you heard how our chief priests and rulers handed him over for execution and had him crucified? But we were hoping he was the one who was to come and set Israel free." (Luke 24:13–35, J. B. Phillips)

This last sentence is surely one of the most despairing sentences in the Bible. These two people had hoped that Jesus was the Messiah, the Christ, but they could not see how anything that had happened had any such significance. They were leaving the scene of this horror of human cruelty. They were having a deep oblivion experience. A very great hope was being frustrated. They were in despair over this negation. Nevertheless, they kept talking to this unknown person who appeared beside them.

> "Yes, and as if that were not enough, it's getting on for three days since all this happened; and some of our womenfolk have disturbed us profoundly. For they went to the tomb at dawn and then, when they couldn't find his body, they said that they had had a vision of angels who said that he was alive. Some of our people went straight off to the tomb and found things just as the women had described them—but they didn't see *him!*"

I find it very interesting that these two disciples found this report about the resurrection of Jesus totally meaningless. The resurrection of Jesus does not become meaningful to these two disciples until it happens to them as a transforming event in their lives. This story continues with this unrecognized Jesus giving these two totally distraught persons a lesson on their religious tradition.

> Then he himself spoke to them, "Aren't you failing to understand, and slow to believe in all that the prophets have said? Was it not inevitable that Christ should suffer like that and so find his glory?" Then beginning with Moses and all the prophets, he explained to them everything in the scriptures that referred to himself.

According to Luke's resurrected Jesus, here was the crux of the matter: the meaning of "the Christ" was being totally transformed. A Christ who was going to stay out of trouble and get us out of trouble had not come. Why should we expect such a thing? Did all the "saints" of the past stay out of trouble? Did we not have the stories of how they all passed through oblivion experiences? Does the tradition really support the idea that we are going to be rescued by some Messiah from having to live our real lives in the Now of living? Is Reality so hard for us that we have to walk away from it? What has the life and death of Jesus really showed us about living our lives? The next line in this passage has both metaphorical and factual meaning.

> They were by now approaching the village to which they were going. He gave the impression that he meant to go on further, but they stopped him with the words, "Do stay with us. It is nearly evening and soon the day will be over." So he went indoors to stay with them. Then it happened!

"Then it happened!" Happened to whom? Happened to these two disciples. What happened? They saw!

> While he was sitting at table with them, he took the loaf, gave thanks, broke it and passed it to them. Their eyes opened wide and they knew him! But he vanished from their sight. Then they said to each other, "Weren't our hearts glowing [on fire] while he was with us on the road, and when he made the scriptures so plain to us?" And they got to their feet without delay and turned back to Jerusalem.

What did they see? They saw Jesus in a whole new light. They saw that Jesus was the Christ with a whole new understanding of what "Christ" meant. They saw their heritage in a new light. They saw their future in a new light. They saw their whole lives in a new light. They had obviously overcome their despair, for they were motivated to live their actual lives. That same night, they walked seven miles back to Jerusalem! Such an experience of seeing all things and doing all things anew was the experience that Luke was identifying as "the resurrection of Jesus, the Christ."

This story makes it very clear that Luke understood that the resurrection was an event that happened to the disciples. It was not an event that happened to Jesus, except to the "Jesus" in the memory of the disciples. Or we might say that the resurrection had happened to the "Jesus" that the disciples had become and were still becoming. There is no focus in this story on what happened to Jesus of Nazareth. These disciples don't quiz Jesus about his unusual postmortem adventures. Nor does Jesus volunteer to hold such a discussion. He simply disappears, as he at the same time appears in the living of these disciples.

## THE NO-MESSIAH MESSIAH

The meaning of the resurrection of Jesus in the lives of these first Christians included seeing that this no good, dead Messiah was the Messiah after all. Jesus was certainly not a Messiah who got humans out of having to live their real lives. At first sight, Jesus did not change anything! Rome still ruled the Jews. Everybody still died. Wicked people still occupied high places. Good people still got crucified. In terms of what everyone expected (and in terms of what we may still expect), Jesus was no Messiah at all.

But then comes this incredible inversion of the messianic image: the Messiah is the very one who makes it clear to us that there is no Messiah of the expected type, and that there never will be such a Messiah. This news is somewhat like the story of some people who had been waiting for hours at a particular street corner for a bus. Then, a man comes along and tells them, "There is no bus that stops at this corner." This was unsettling news, but it was also good news: these people could now stop wasting their lives waiting for what would never come. We do not need to wait for someone to improve the basic conditions of human life before we can live and live abundantly, including taking on changing the conditions of social life that need changing, as well as working with the readiness of ourselves and others to be able to make the big changes that our social conditions are calling for. We can live now with whatever our abilities are in whatever times of challenge we are facing.

## THE QUEST FOR THE HISTORICAL JESUS

It remains difficult for both conservative and liberal Christians to accept the truth that the Jesus that Mark is asking us to follow is a fictitious character in Mark's story—a humanly constructed hero figure in a made-up narrative. The historical Jesus of Nazareth is an important scientific quest—indeed, it has been a quite successful quest. This careful historical work has mined a number of the earliest sentences spoken by Jesus or about the historical Jesus from these first three gospels. These oldest sentences are well short of a biography of Jesus, for they are all memories of post-resurrection men and women who count themselves as the resurrected body of Jesus and who phrase their memory of Jesus in that light.

Not all, but many of the Christian theologians who have been passionate about the quest for the historical Jesus were interested in finding

grist for a religion that is pure and simple and devoid of the cryptic symbols that are so prevalent in the four gospels that head the New Testament
canon. This scholarship has revealed a plausible approximation of what
we can historically know about the historical Jesus, and many have found
these findings disturbing.

Our best scientific historical scholars have revealed a Jesus who
trusted as his God-devotion the same Yahweh that was trusted by the
authors of the ancient Hebrew scriptures and the people who first lived
those messages. Jesus understood himself to be meeting this all-powerful
Reality in every event of his life—a meal with his friends or his torture
to death on the next morning. Furthermore, like those who called themselves "Pharisees," Jesus believed in a final judgment at the end of time,
when those who are right in their God-trusting relationship will be resurrected to everlasting honor and those who are not right in this God-
trusting relationship will be raised to everlasting despair. In other words,
in the end no one gets away with anything. Reality is always coming, and
Reality always wins in the end.

In addition, when Jesus proclaimed that "the Kingdom of God was
at hand," he meant that the expected end-of-time judgment was already
under way, breaking forth in the unraveling and the healing of the lives of
those who were hearing his proclamation of forgiveness and a fresh start
for their specific lives.

In his book *Jesus and the Word*, Rudolf Bultmann takes on that earliest layer of New Testament formation, and gives each sentence of it a lasting existential interpretation for our lives today. For example, Bultmann
sees in Jesus' sayings a crisis of decision—a call to choose for or against
living our authentic life.

Even the end-of-the-world-coming of the Kingdom of God is
shown by Bultmann to be something that each of us can experience in
moments of our real lives. Bultmann has broken the code for translating
this ancient mythic talk of New Testament theologizing into contemporary talk that speaks to the depth of our human living within this time
and this place.


## A Sociological Gospel

It is also important for us to notice that New Testament talk about "the
end of the world" and "the Kingdom of God" uses sociological metaphors.

Most people today are more accustomed to using psychological meta-phors in their religious thinking. The New Testament talk about "the end of the world" is in part an allusion to the impermanent nature of the Roman Empire and its tyrannical "Roman peace" (Perhaps many of us had or still have a similar gratitude for the impermanence of the era of Nazi Germany). Or as ecologists we may be hopeful or thankful for the impermanence of our current world program that is thoughtlessly alter-ing a once-gorgeous Earth into an ecological ruin.

The vision of stars falling from sky in the last days speak of the im-permanence of nature as a whole. Jesus' talk about the Kingdom of God happening now is talk about the advent of a sociological transformation beginning at once in the hearts and minds of living persons. Jesus goes on to say that this Kingdom is like tiny seeds that are capable of becoming huge trees of living justice, love for each other, creative solutions of moral honesty, and good practices all around. All this talk is using sociological metaphors that have deep spirit meaning for our whole lives.

These sociological metaphors can seem to contradict the fact that Jesus was also a person of solitary prayer—spending long hours alone away form the masses and the disciples. How are we to understand this? In the Hebraic heritage, prayer is not a withdrawal from the world, but a practice aimed toward better living in the world. This carries over into Christian heritage, where prayer is not only confession and gratitude, but also petitions for our own strength of living and specific intercessions for the well-being of others. In other words, solitary prayer can have a sociological meaning.

So we can guess that the alone time of Jesus was not an abandon-ment or a minimization of the sociological aspects of human living. It was a preparation for that social living. The Garden of Gethsemane story is certainly about preparation for living the coming trial and execution with the courageous and tactical excellence depicted in the passion nar-ratives. This emphasis on both solitude and sociological ministry need not be seen as contradictory. Our solitude can be sociological and our sociological living can include solitude.

## THE END-OF-TIME HERO STORY

In these first three gospels, the meanings of both "resurrection" and the "Christ" designation have an end-of-time overtone. In Mark's hero story, resurrection and the Christ designation are one and the same secret. We miss the whole point of Mark's narrative if we do not see that both resurrection and membership in the body of Christ are states of being that are offered to each and every human being as the core purpose of the narrative. End-of-time symbols are meaningless unless we see what they are pointing to in our own profound consciousness that can be accessed by us now.

These seemingly strange symbols are not rational dogmas that we Christian believe and other people don't. These symbols are expressions of, or descriptions of, states of being that every human being can experience. In many other-than-Christian religious heritages, we can find overlapping meaning with these end-of-time symbols of the Bible. For example, the "end of time" is a symbol that resonates with what Buddhist devotees symbolize with the term "impermanence." Time itself has impermanence build into it.

## Son of Man, Son of God

The New Testament is full of paradoxes. One of the most important paradoxes is that Jesus is both a "Son of God" (Offspring of Eternity) and an ordinary temporal human, facing every temptation and every limitation that any of us confront. Also, "Son of God" is a description of the essential life that is the birthright of all of us. Though we real-world humans have lost our Offspring-of-Eternity essence and need to be restored, our essence is, nevertheless, Jesus-like—that is, both human and divine. It is only our self-inflicted estrangements from that essence that makes us different from Mark's Jesus hero figure, who always keeps in touch with his divinity.

Whatever our face color, our gender, our education, or our successes, it is easy to conclude that you and I are nothing special. Each of us is just one more dying animal. This is absolutely true of each of us, and it was true of Jesus. He was a human being alongside you and me. To say that you or me or Jesus is "the Son of God" is to say that each of us is something special, but what is that specialness?

The historical Jesus did not refer to himself as "the Son of God," or even "the Christ." He preferred the term "the son of Adam," also stated "the son of man." The meaning of this symbol is not changed if we update it to "the offspring of Adam and Eve." But this "son of man" symbol, as used in the context of Jesus' first-century Jewish culture, is not so easy to understand. In that cultural context, "the son of man" was a figure who was coming at the wind-up of time. We can take this to mean that "the son of man" means "the true human"—a humanity that differs from the fallen Adam and Eve.

Also, we need to be clear that "son of man" implies that our true humanity has been lost through our twisted perspectives, our delusions, our corruptions—all of which result in a loss of our humanity. "The son of man" is something special indeed, if it refers to our profound consciousness of being fully human. It makes sense that Jesus was remembered as someone who identified with that coming fulfillment, that return to our authenticity, that replacement of our fallenness with our essential humanness.

Such an understanding, however, does not mean "humanism"—the worship of humanity as our God. Nor does it mean the evolution of a new species of Homo sapiens. "The son of man" symbol is not about a time-bound change in our nature. "The son of man" symbol is about a restoration of a profound humanness that has always been, is now, and will ever be our true nature. But this nature has been lost. Without that understanding, our theologizing means nothing more than a worship of the human species, which may be judged as better than a worship of the White race or the U.S. nation, but it is still the worship of a temporal animal that is nothing special.

In the origins of Christian theologizing, these four symbols merged: *son of man, resurrection, Christ,* and *Son of God.* The resurrection was about the arrival now of the son of man; not only was Jesus himself the son of man arriving, but this arrival was also in all those who were healed by his words, presence, and deeds. To be *resurrected* from the death of our despair is the same thing as *the son of man* arriving. This event is also the arrival of the *Messiah* or *Christ.*

"Son of God" is the most difficult symbol of the four, for we are troubled to an extreme degree about the symbol "God." But if "God" means devotion to Profound Realty as spelled out in so many previous chapters of this book, then we can intuit a correspondence between devotion to Profound Reality and participation in profound consciousness. If "Son of God" means devotion to Profound Reality and "son of man" means participation in profound consciousness, then these two symbols are pointing to aspects of the same thing.

*The paradox of the divine and human "natures" of Jesus, or of you or of me, means that facing a human who is devoted to Profound Reality is also an experience of the presence of Profound Reality in this profoundly consciousness human.*

In the next chapter, I will explore how the entire Christian Trinity can be stated in a universal, every-person manner.

# 13

## An Interreligious Trinity

QUITE EARLY CHRISTIAN THEOLOGIZING became triune in the systematic layout of its thoughtfulness. Twenty-first-century Christian theologizing has moved beyond the heavenly-realm storytelling that has dominated the last three thousand years of Jewish and Christian thinking. This contemporary shift in theologizing includes viewing the Trinity as three aspects of one experience that happens in our everyday lives.

Rather than thinking of three *persons* sitting close to each other in heaven, Christian thought is now exploring three *faces* of one revelatory event. Moving into this new style of theologizing, we can discover that this experiential view of the Trinity is also present in religions other than Christianity.

This vision of a triune mode of thinking that is independent of any religion and that can be stated in language that is not Christian helps us in our interreligious dialogue. It also helps us with our Christian witnessing to aware persons in our twenty-first-century culture. Here is a chart using non-Christian language that reflects this experiential view of triune dynamics that also show up in Christian theologizing.

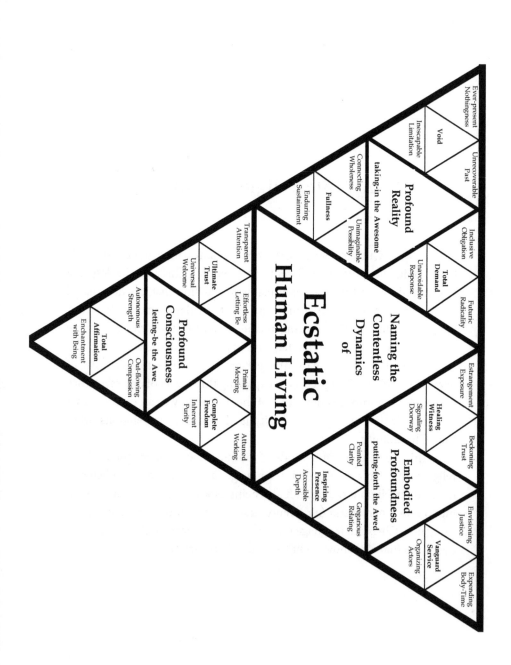

# TAKING IN THE AWESOME
# LETTING BE THE AWE
# PUTTING FORTH THE AWED ONES

These three phrases provide a sense of how one experience can have three aspects: (1) *taking in* the awesome *Profound Realty*, which (2) opens us to *letting be* the awe of *profound consciousness* and (3) allows us to enact *putting forth* the life of the awed ones in an *embodied profoundness*.

Toward the end of this chapter, I will explore how Christian language and thoughtfulness are related to this secularly named triangular array of experiences. First, I will describe the meaning of the poetry I have used on this secularly worded triangular chart.

Please meditate a bit on the above chart, its poetry, and its mathematical construction. The name in the middle of each triangle is a name for a whole that is comprised of three inclusive subparts that are cited in the names of the breakout aspects of that triangle. The three subparts are ordered in this way: the upper left subpart of each triangle is about *taking in*, the lower center subpart is about *letting be*, and the upper right subpart is about *putting forth*. This mathematical arrangement is congruent with (1) *knowing* aspects of that whole, (2) *being* a manifestation of that whole, and (3) *doing* the living out of that whole.

Also, I want to underline that this triangle is a human-created model that can therefore be improved, as is true of all rational models. Over a period of decades, I have improved this triangular model, and I may continue doing so. Much reading and much personal experience have gone into this model of experiences I have had and that you may also have had.

Paradoxically, this is a rational model for human experiences that are rationally nameless. These are twenty-seven profound dynamics of *ecstatic human living*. In other words, each of these names is poetry for human experiences that transcend that poetry. I am working with metaphors that can perhaps awaken experiences of our essential human consciousness. I will begin with the lower third of the above triangular model.

## WHO AM I ESSENTIALLY?

### Letting Be the Awe of Profound Consciousness

The nine subcategories of profound consciousness named on the lower third the above triangular model are answers to the question, "Who am I essentially?" "Profound consciousness" means the depth of being human, for which we have typically substituted our own personality construction and our own self-created brand or self-image that we tell ourselves that we are.

The "profound consciousness" third of the above triangle of experiences was illustrated in the first five chapters of this book. Chapter 5 contains a paragraph or two on each of the nine third-level titles that appear as the breakout topics of the "profound consciousness" third of the above master triangle. I will not spell out the meaning of those categories in this chapter. The reader can explore that part of the above master triangle by rereading chapter 5.

I will, however, spell out the breakout categories of the other two first-level triangles of the above master triangle: "Profound Reality" and "embodied profoundness."

## NINE BLIND MEN DESCRIBE
## THE ETERNAL ELEPHANT

### Taking in the Awesomeness of Profound Reality

You may recall the story of a group of blind men touching an elephant and coming away with very different impressions of the elephant. That is the idea behind the following list of nine different impressions of the same Overall Eternity or Profound Reality. Each of these human experiences of the One Eternal Elephant do not exhaust the mystery of the Elephant. In spite of all our experiences of this Elephant, we remain basically blind. So let us suppose that we are all nine of these blind humans who are touching each of these nine distinguishable body parts on the Eternal Elephant of Profound Reality. Here are my names for these nine aspects of our experience of Profound Reality.

#### Experiences of the Void

1. Ever-Present No-thing-ness
2. Inescapable Limitation
3. Unrecoverable Past

#### Experiences of the Fullness

4. Connecting Wholeness
5. Enduring Sustainment

6. Unimaginable Possibility

**Experiences of the Total Demand**

7. Inclusive Obligation
8. Unavoidable Response
9. Futuric Radicality

# The Void

When human consciousness runs into the impenetrable Mystery, we are experiencing the Void—the No-thing-ness out of which all things emerge and into which all things return.

## 1. The Experience of the Void as Ever-Present No-thing-ness

The experience of dying, or simply knowing that we will, reveals an important truth about our whole lives and the whole of Reality—the truth about our finitude. We feel this experience as a terrific emptiness. Our consciousness is confronting the Void into which our consciousness cannot enter. We often crawl into our personality "box" and thereby close off our consciousness of dying. An awareness of dying is not given space in our box of self-created personality limitations. In our own half-conscious way, we tend to assume that we are the exception to the rule that all things die. Nevertheless, we are born out of the Void, out of a black hole of No-thing-ness, and we return to that Void. As Nikos Kazantzakis put it, "We come from a dark abyss, we end in a dark abyss, and we call the luminous interval life."[1] And as we walk from birth to death, the Infinite Void walks with us. Carlos Castaneda once suggested that death is a constant companion walking just behind our left shoulder. If we turn our head quickly, perhaps we can catch a glimpse of this constant companion.

## 2. The Experience of the Void as Inescapable Limitation

*Inescapable limitation* means that we are never secure, no matter how much money we have, how smart we are, how much we have accomplished, how many people love us, or how much effort we have expended

1. Kazantzakis, *Saviors of God*, 43.

toward being good. All our pleasant moments do not last. Every item in our lives that we might consider necessary for our happiness is vulnerable to loss. In our tightest relationships, we can be cast into utter aloneness. Our knowledge is constantly shown to be far less than complete. Our accomplishments fail to last. Even our own good opinion of ourselves can be upended by our own behavior.

### 3. The Experience of the Void as Unrecoverable Past

The past is gone, unrecoverable. We often say, "What is past is past," but we do not always believe it. We try to hang on to the *gone*, rather than allow ourselves to mourn such inevitable losses and face the future, however unfamiliar or unwelcome that future may be. Whatever we had yesterday, we no longer have today, at least not in the same way. Whoever we were yesterday, we no longer are today. Even though there are continuities, there are also big differences. Think back ten or twenty years. Who were we then? Life in the now of living is a continual departure from earlier moments of now that never return. Perhaps we are a person who used to play basketball every week as our fun exercise program. Now that is gone. Perhaps we are a couple who used to care for four children. Now they are grown. Perhaps we know of politicians and citizens who want to "make America great again"—but who are in truth refusing to be aware that a White, racist, sexist America is not recoverable. The past, whatever it was, is always gone.

## The Fullness

In addition to experiences of the Void, the Profound Elephant also offers experiences of *Fullness*. We encounter an Every-thing-ness in which all things coexist, including we ourselves and all the things we like and don't like. We are sustained by this overarching Fullness. And this Fullness impacts us as a future of possibilities that challenge our best expectations and visions of the possible. What is truly possible can be shocking to our narrow vision, our lazy living, and our clinging to worn-out patterns.

## 4. The Experience of the Fullness of Connecting Wholeness

The unfathomable Profound Reality comes toward us as the *connectedness* of all things. The gravity of the sun, moon, and Earth shapes the space-time in which we live. The light of distant galaxies reaches our telescopes. In the more intimate aspects of our lives, all the people we know are residents in our own heads, haunting us, instructing us, demanding responses from us. Even our freedom is given to us as a part of that Wholeness within which we play out our limited roles. If we use our freedom to separate ourselves from this community with all things, we create an unreality. Connecting wholeness is both a glorious gift and an inescapable demand upon our lives. We are indeed only a singular *part* of the whole, but that means being a part of the *whole* is also our reality. Our partness in this larger whole is inescapable.

## 5. The Experience of the Fullness of Enduring Sustainment

We are also blessed by an *enduring sustainment* that is just as crucial as all the other impressions of Eternity. Whatever is sustaining the sun, moon, and stars is also sustaining you and me. We began our lives through no effort of our own. A woman gave us birth. A cosmos gave us this woman, and the man who sired us. We have a cosmos to live in through no effort of our own. Our very desires, longings, and drives are gifts from this enduring sustainment. When we insist on being a separate person isolated in our own little box of self-constructed personality, we take for granted the enduring sustainment upon which we entirely depend. When we are open to being our true being, enduring sustainment welcomes us home to our true lives, our true nature, our actual spirit journey. Notice the birds; they are fed. Observe the field flowers; they are clothed. So are we, until we are not. And the extent to which we are not sustained as we would like to be sustained does not change the simple truth that *we are sustained*. But we are not always grateful for having a life at all. We often ignore this simply truth of our actuality—*we are sustained*.

## 6. The Experience of the Fullness of Unimaginable Possibility

We also face this overwhelming Fullness as the gift of *unimaginable possibility*. When we insist on living in our self-constructed "box," we eventually run out of possibilities. Hopelessness ensues. Despair yells out loud or hides in our unconsciousness. The boxed person cannot see most of his or her actual possibilities—cannot even imagine them. Imagination is restrained by the box. The appearance of unimaginable possibility brings us this truth: *There is always another way to look at every matter.* Reality is always more than we thought. Consider a professional athlete who sustains a career-ending injury. As long as being a professional athlete is seen as the whole game, only despair is possible. But Reality is always there with other possibilities for living a realistic life. Consider a military power that is unable to win its wars without destroying itself. There are other possibilities for that nation—practicing cooperative participation and meaningful negotiations. Possibilities, previously unimagined, can appear for each of us in all aspects of our personal and social lives.

## The Total Demand

In addition to experiences of the Void and the Fullness, the Eternal Elephant also offers experiences of the *Total Demand* upon our free responsibility. Being a part of the whole includes an inclusive obligation to and for that whole. Responding to my challenges is not an option. I have to respond. Refusing to respond is a response. And the future is never a rigid fate. The future contains radical options to any status quo.

### 7. *The Experience of the Total Demand of Inclusive Obligation*

The future that is coming at us is not simply my or your individual future; it is the *inclusive* future that contains everybody and everything. We face together everything that humanity faces—Muslim fundamentalists and Muslim moderates, Israeli fundamentalists and Israeli moderates, an earthquake in Pakistan, a tsunami in Asia, an AIDS pandemic in Africa, the growth of oil usage, the needs of women all over the world to find a greater place of dignity and participation, the needs of the poor all over the world to have even the simplest form of life, liberty, and the pursuit of happiness. Because we *can* respond to all these things, we are *response-able.* We are responsible for our responses, thereby we are responsible for everything. Nikos Kazantzakis pointed to this experience with this bit of poetry: "Learn to obey. Only he who obeys a rhythm superior to his own is free. Learn to command. Only he who can give commands may represent me here on earth. Love responsibility. Say: 'It is my duty, and mine alone, to save the earth. If it is not saved, then I alone am to blame.'"[2] Surely, this is *inclusive obligation* speaking.

## 8. The Experience of the Total Demand of Unavoidable Response

The future is moving towards us as an uncompromising demand for response. The actual content of that response has options, but response is necessary. We don't have the option of standing on the sidelines of history. We are in history. We respond to the encounters that time brings, and these responses have historical consequences. We can attempt to back away from a responsible role in life, but that response is our response to history, and it has its historical consequences. The dawning of *unavoidable response* reveals to us that embracing responsibility is what realistic living includes. Realism includes the ongoing primal choice between: (1) intentionally responding or (2) backing away into forgetfulness, perhaps even trying to be unconscious. The experience of responding intentionally is more like a *surrender* than a heroic *effort*. We are often *struggling* to be unintentional—to deny our freedom. Intentionality requires no struggle. Intentionality is a *liberation*—an unmerited gift of our true being. This gift can be enacted or fought. Enacting real life is enacting our freedom, our intentionality, our choice-making from the depth of mystery. Fighting real life is a struggle to not be free—to not be response-able.

## 9. The Experience of the Total Demand of Futuric Radicality

We do not control the Reality to which we must respond. Our response is made within the limits and possibilities of an impending and irresistible future. We live in an enduring enigmatic *now*, but this now is embedded in the flow of time. The specific qualities of our own experiences include the flow of time moving toward our living now with or without our consent. We cannot stop time. We cannot avoid new challenges. We can, however, act; we can move forward into the real options of our impending future. *Futuric radicality* is an unavoidable truth about our real lives. The word "radicality" points to the fact that none of us can be fully

2. Kazantzakis, *Saviors of God*, 68.

conservative. If we opt to live realistically, we are thrust into continual change. There are different qualities of change—huge and small, tough and not so tough—but our familiar habits are being undermined by the challenging future that relentlessly approaches us with new options. Let the climate crisis be our example: moderating that crisis will entail changing almost everything. Being realistic about this impending future will mean being an outsider who breaks the norms of fossil fuel living and seeks ways to move that assign oil, gas, and coal to the sidelines of social use. This includes avoiding propaganda that is seeking to capture us with the illusion that we can be stable and safe in some currently existing status quo.

This completes my rough description of our experience of Profound Reality as an unavoidable and mysterious Powerfulness encountering us in the temporal flow of our lives. Notice that I have not described Profound Reality itself, but only nine modes of experiencing Profound Reality. Profound Reality is unknown and remains unknown after our conscious experiences of Profound Reality. Each of us are all nine of these blind men who touch and are touched by this inescapable Eternal Elephant. Though we may be specializing in two or three of these blind-men experiences, all nine of these aspects of the Eternal Elephant are real-life encounters that are happening to us in the flow of temporal events—that is, in the every-moment happenings of our actual lives. Our actual lives are being touched by this mysterious Eternal Elephant, and we do or can touch back. There is no escape from these touches; there is only our denial to being open to being touched. Now for the upper-right third of the overall triangle.

## NINE MODES OF SPIRIT ACTION

### Putting Forth the Awed Ones of Embodied Profoundness

The subcategories of the upper-right third of the triangular model are:

Taking in the Healing Witness

Being the Inspiring Presence

Putting Forth the Vanguard Service

I am going to describe these three topics in a general way that shows how they apply to all people, whatever their religious practice or their lack of a religious practice may be. There are many means of manifesting these dynamics, giving them names, and thinking about them. In this chapter, I will be giving only a sketch of these dynamics.

In Part Three of this book, I will say more about these topics as they are manifested or can be manifested in a fresh style of Christian practice. Such specific illustrations and recommendations will not be included in this chapter. Instead, I will briefly define each of these second-level and third-level categories of the Embodied Profoundness triangle.

*Taking in the healing witness* has to do with: (1) taking in the exposure of our *estrangement* from Profound Reality; (2) hearing the good news about the *doorway* of despair, about our forgiveness, about our welcome home to our authentic life; and (3) obeying the call that *beckons* us to trust in the Profound Reality that opens our living to our caring and to our essential freedom to historically care our care.

Some exposition on these three dynamics was spelled out in chapter 11, "A Doorway Called Despair." These cosmic dynamics are not only true for Christians, these are universal dynamics that are present for all humans—whatever religion they do or do not practice. I am seeking to understand these dynamics in a way that reaches beyond the cocoon of Christian language and practices. I am insisting that such an understanding is necessary in order to both renew Christian practice and make our interreligious dialogue a conversation worth pursuing.

*Being the inspiring presence* has to do with (1) the *pointed clarity* of saying what we mean and meaning what we say, plus (2) being a listener who has the *accessible depth* to hear each human (however glorious, tragic, or horrific their life may be), and (3) being the *gregarious relating* that courageously engages others without being intimidated by our fear of the consequences of our action or by our habitual preference for safe withdrawal.

"Presence" is not an excuse for not being active, it is a quality within all of our actions as well as within all of our inactions. In fact, the presence I mean is itself an action—an intention to be our being to the fullest extent we can and doing so with and among others. The power of presence, so enacted, must not be underestimated. All of our historically significant religious "saints" manifest the presence I am talking about. Many of our political leaders, renowned teachers, news anchors, as well as our store clerks, nurses, construction workers, farmers, cab divers, and more may manifest this presence.

*Putting forth the vanguard service* has to do with (1) *envisioning both witness and justice* from the point of view of our radical realism, plus (2) *organizing the actors* for social movements that put both truth and justice in place, and (3) *expending body-time* in the knowledge that all we have is time and a living body that is going to be expended for something and that might as well be expended for causes that count for something more than our own survival and pampering.

I well spell out some of the details of doing vanguard service in Part Three of this book. What I am emphasizing now is that vanguard service is also a dynamic for all human beings, not just Christians. Furthermore, the Christian concern for truth and justice is enacted alongside and with other persons of good will who are also called to pursue truth and justice. There is no such thing as a Christian justice. There is just justice worked out by awake people living in a time and place. We help create and support the cultural norms of morality, the enforceable laws, and the overall administration of justice for that time and place.

The idea that there is something called "justice" hanging around in a heavenly realm or in a metaphysical mind-space is a delusion that is most often being used to justify some obsolete status quo, or some reactionary return to an even-less-realistic pattern of some falsely remembered past.

Realistic justice is invented by humans seeking a doable realism for their current society in the midst of a specific set of historical and environmental challenges. I will be saying more about this topic in Part Three of this book, but I want to underline now the meaning of the word "justice" as used in this entire book. *Justice is an ongoing innovation by radical human freedom operating in a historical situation. Anyone coming to the question of justice from a fixed notion of Buddhist justice or Christian justice or Jewish justice or Muslim justice, etc., must be seriously challenged to consider the pursuit of a realistic justice for our actual societies in this interreligious, complicated, and unprecedented era.*

This completes, for now, my elaborations on these twenty-seven inseparable dynamics pointed to in the above triangular model. The poetry on this temporal model is my own, but the experiences that are being pointed to with these carefully chosen words are basic humanity for everyone. I must insist that this universality is true, even though it is also true that better descriptions of these experiences are possible.

You may or may not take delight in this "triangular mathematics" uncovered in our classical Christian thoughtfulness. So, it might be helpful to say that this triune mathematics is only a table of contents for the whole book of Christian thinking and living. As any physicist might say, "Mathematics is not the juice of physics. The juice of physics is in our experiences of the physical world." Something similar is true of the above discussion. The juice is not in the triune mathematics. The juice is in the vast human experience that *grounds* these abstract bits of poetry in the real world of human living.

The above descriptive paragraphs are like koans or parables. The readers have to see for themselves in their own lives the meanings that are meant. Furthermore, these experiences happen to humans using other language than the poetry that I have used in this book. The philosophy of religion is an ongoing pursuit of truth—always open to still more insight.

I turn now to a discussion of the difference between a description of these twenty-seven states of experience, and the role of Christian symbols to express a devotion to the human living of these states of realism in an affirmative and creative fashion.

## DESCRIPTIVE AND DEVOTIONAL SYMBOLS

Profound Reality—Profound Consciousness—Embodied Profoundness
Awesome—Awe—Awed Ones

*The above are descriptive symbols; the following are devotional symbols:*

Yahweh, the Creator—Spirit of Yahweh—People of Yahweh
Almighty God—Holy Spirit—Body of Christ
Father/Mother—New Birth—Son/Daughter

What do these devotional Jewish and Christian symbols add to the topics of *Profound Reality, profound consciousness*, and *embodied profoundness*? The biblical symbols do not add further description of our experiences of these dynamics; the biblical symbols only add *devotion* to these described experiences. Christian theologians and writers sometimes add further description to Profound Reality, but if they do so, they do so as philosophers of religion. As devoted presenters of the Christian revelation,

Christian theologians only add Christian-language-worded devotion to the living of these experiences that everyone may experience.

My claim that the above triangular model is a quest for universality on the topic of religion does not deny that all of my descriptions are partial. Indeed, each of these twenty-seven topics can become an ever-expanding library of description. In spite of the fact that my descriptions are limited, they are limited descriptions of what is profoundly unlimited—that is, about what is essential to being human. These twenty-seven descriptions illuminate the possibility of a triune modeling of any religious heritage. This does not, however, mean that a triune modeling is the only good mode of modeling (for example, see my use of the yin-yang dualistic mode of modeling used in chapter 4).

Every long-standing religion has succeeded in being long-standing by its usefulness in assisting humans to access some or all of these twenty-seven experiences and also call for living the described verities in actual historical human lives. So let us ask again, what does classical Christian language add to these twenty-seven dynamics of description? Christian theologizing of the type I am promoting adds only devotion—a devotion that is personal and has often used personal symbols to express that devotion. This does not mean that Profound Reality is a Big Person, male or female, animal or human. Such literalism is the ruin of any valid religion. Devotional language does not describe the Real; it only expresses devotion to the Real. With all this in mind, I will describe in more detail the role of Christian language.

In the heritage of Christian devotion to Profound Reality, Christian theologizing has gathered this sort of devotional language: "*God, the Father Almighty—the all-powerful Creator of nature and history.*" These symbols do not describe Profound Reality; they only express devotion to Profound Reality. We can express the same devotion if we say: "*Great Goddess, the Mother Almighty—the all-powerful Birther of nature and history.*" And many other devotional metaphors will do.

The metaphor of "power," however, is descriptive of Profound Reality. "Time marches on" is another expression of power. We cannot stop time. "Gravity keeps on" is an another expressions of power. It is important that we not view an oppression of humanity in our understanding of the power of God. The "power of God" simply means our human limitations and possibilities. The first face of the Christian devotion is devotion to *God, the Unlimitedly Strong.* The second face of the Christian devotion is devotion to *God, the Humanly Weak*—a humanly *embodied profoundness* complete with a crucified Messiah.

In the heritage of Christian devotion to embodied profoundness, Christian theologizing tells and interprets *the story of a specific finite human being, Jesus, who is born of a woman, who is limited, who is tempted as all human beings are tempted; a human who eats-eliminates, talks, walk, prays, sleeps, and who is crucified by his historical enemies.* This is not *God, the all-powerful.* This is *God, the weak.* Our human participation in the resurrected Body of Christ is a participation in God, the weak. We who are called to becoming members of the Body of Christ will likewise be expended on behalf of all humans and on behalf of all the aliveness of the entire planet Earth. Our body and blood will be mixed with the body and blood of Jesus. This giving back of our own body and blood (our own life) to the Giver of our life is perhaps the core *offense* of the Christian call to devotion. But then again, it is also the core *glory* and *blessing* of this devotion. The blessing is stated in the Eighth Beatitude: "*How blest are those who have suffered persecution for the cause of right, for the Kingdom of God is theirs.* [That is, the Reign of Reality has come on Earth to you.] . . . *Accept it with gladness and exultation . . . in the same way they persecuted the prophets before you*" (Matthew 5:10–12, NEB).

In the heritage of Christian devotion to Profound Consciousness, Christian theologizing has gathered the language of "Holy Spirit." These two familiar words add no content to profound consciousness, except to say that profound consciousness is "holy." "Holy Spirit" is devotional language used to express devotion to profound consciousness being our active consciousness. Such devotional symbolizing means that whatever state of awe we experience is good for us, including the dread as well as the fascination and the courage to live these intensities of ultimate trust, love of everyone, and total freedom. This journey into Christ will mean a continual ripping apart who we thought we were and letting who we really are be exposed and lived.

In the lower third of the mastery triangle, the subparts of profound consciousness are "ultimate trust," "total affirmation," and "complete freedom." The explicitly Christian terms for asserting the *holiness* of these experiences are: "faith," "love," and "freedom" (in which "freedom" includes "hope"). "Faith" is a *knowing,* a *taking in,* a *trusting* of Profound Reality. "Love" is an active *letting be,* a *presence,* an *affirming* of every neighboring being in the context of affirming the neighboring action of the Infinite.

"Freedom" is a *doing*, a *putting forth*, an *anticipation* or hope for bending the course of history and occasioning the healing of human lives.

This Holy Spirit devotion to profound consciousness is also the *Spirit of Jesus, the Christ* as well as the *Spirit of the Almighty*. Profound consciousness is a given by Profound Reality. *Yahweh pours out his Spirit.* Profound consciousness is also specifically presented to us in the embodied profoundness of a human presence filled with the Holy Spirit of profound consciousness. In medieval theologizing, it was said by some that "the Holy Spirit flows from both the Father and the Son." I have just suggested a clue as to what that old bit of theologizing could mean.

## Theologizing—a Group Task

The devotional theologizing just outlined is a group task of thoughtfulness that goes on in a Christian community of devotion. The Christian religion is an action or practice of a human religious community that seeks the gift or grace that enables humans to enjoy the saintliness indicated by that devotional language. Christian theologizing is shared with the world as part of the Christian community's witness to the world, but it adds nothing of rational content to the ongoing work of philosophical insight that will also be used in the ongoing general discussion by humans who do or do not practice a Christian religion. The only addition made by specifically Christian thoughtfulness is our description of what devotion to realism looks like in actual living of real life. A good philosopher can describe realism; a good theologian is focused on assisting humans toward a surrender to the affirmation of realism, rather then fleeing from realism into some sort of fight with realism.

Being Christianly religious might, however, make one a philosopher who can recognize realistic philosophy and perhaps add realism to the philosophical discussion. But in doing so, a Christian is simply one more philosopher. Such an addition is not Christian theologizing as such, but simply being a better secular philosopher because of a Christian commitment to realism. Also, such a person who is both philosopher and Christian theologian will tend to use his or her philosophizing to do better theologizing, as well as use his or her theologizing to do better philosophizing.

Also, Christian theologizing is a communal thoughtfulness about nothing else than devotion to radical realism, and this is done in a community of language and heritage rooted in the event going by names like "Jesus Christ" and "cross/resurrection." It is this devotional communal language that distinguishes theologizing from philosophizing. This distinction is important in order to avoiding a reduction of Christian theologizing to some current philosophy of life.

This distinction is also important for helping contemporary Christians respect Christian theologians living in the past who used a different (and now out of date) philosophy. For example, it is not appropriate for us to base our critique of Thomas Aquinas' theology only on his use of the philosophy of Aristotle. Nor is it appropriate to critique Augustine's theology only because he used the philosophy of Plotinus. Our contemporary theologizing must learn to dialogue with the theology of these earlier "saints" in the history of Christian theologizing, in spite of the fact that we must be critical of their philosophizing in order to even hear well their contributions to our twenty-first-century theologizing.

I want to underline that Christian theologizing is a group process conducted by bands of devoted Christians. Christian theology is not a discipline of learning that goes on in the general community. Of course everyone can read and discuss Christian theology. But no one gets to call themselves a "Christian theologian" unless they share in the devotion that is the one and only topic of Christian theologizing.

## A CHRISTIAN TRINITY SUMMATION

*God, the Almighty* = Profound Realty, the Power of It All—an ever-present Presence to our profound consciousness.

- Profound Reality is the *Timelessness* met in the flow of time.

- Profound Reality is the *Permanent* within the impermanence of all temporal things.

- Profound Reality is the *Every-thing-ness* within the manyness of things.

- Profound Reality is the *No-thing-ness* from which all things come and all things return.

The word "God" adds no content to Profound Reality except a devotion to this Profound Reality.

*God, the Holy Spirit* = the profound consciousness that is conscious of Profound Reality.

- We never see Profound Reality with our senses.

- We never see Profound Reality with our emotional intelligence.

- We never see Profound Reality with our mental intelligence.

- We only see Profound Reality with our profound consciousness.

And the word "God" adds only devotion to our experience of the enigma of profound consciousness.

*God, the Body of Christ* = that part of the human species that affirms and lives from the experience of Profound Reality in the state of profound consciousness. Again, the word "God" adds only devotion to being this "called" body of people.

The Christian revelation is now and has always been a call to perpetual revolution in thought, presence, and action. So, there are still further bumps on this bumpy ride toward a next Christianity. Part Three of this book is about the communal life, nurture, and mission of a viable and vital next Christian practice. These sociological aspects of being Christian today will be reflected upon through the mode of theologizing presented in Part Two.

# Part Three

## Christian Practices

IN PART THREE OF this book I deal with the more ethical and communal aspects of initiating the designing and building of a viable and vital next Christian Practice. The philosophy of religion of Part One and the theologizing of Part Two are key contexts for the more ethical and communal reflections of Part Three.

In Part One, "good religion" was defined as *practices* that make more likely the accessing of our essential humanity—our enlightenment, our profound consciousness of Profound Realty. This means that religion is a human action—a practical and continuous action, not simply a set of ideas. Our religious theoretics is part of our religious practice.

In Part Two, I have explored key theoretical edges for reshaping Christianity theologizing for a world that is in deep rejection of the old metaphors that have defined the Christian religion. This theologizing has also been concerned with recovering a meaningful relationship with the core symbols and history of Christian heritage. Our fresh theologizing also assists us with reshaping a next expression of Christian practice for our contemporary times.

Now in Part Three, I will explore some of the key topics for actualizing down-to-Earth, twenty-first-century possibilities for a relevant and inspiring version of a next Christian religious practice. The next six chapters are mostly about Christian ethics. The last four chapters are mostly about a viable form for a vital next Christian communal life.

# Part Three

## Christian Practice

# 14

## The Friendliness of Trees

"Carbon capture" is a discussion that has come into play as a means of moderating the burning of fossil fuels. Mostly this idea has been used as an excuse for expanding our burning of fossil fuels. Furthermore, the human-made technologies so far suggested for carbons capture are as nothing compared with the natural engines we already have. An old-growth forest does more carbon capture, does it more quickly, and stores it more permanently than any human invention we can imagine.

Every tree trunk is mostly carbon taken from the atmosphere. And these trees and other plants are solar powered. When single-celled life first became solar powered, the atmosphere of this planet was in excess of 70 percent carbon dioxide. How did $CO_2$ get to be that friendly 300 parts per million or so—which is less than about 0.041 percent by volume of the atmosphere? The trees and other plants did this. They turned $CO_2$ into tree trunks, stems, and leaves, and other carbon sinks. Immense amounts of this biomass turned into coal, petroleum, and natural gas, safely hidden away in the bowels of the Earth. This is what carbon capture looks like. The whole industrial world was built on reversing this process, putting carbon back into the atmosphere. We have pushed the limits of what can be safely done with this rearrangement of Earth realities. So, instead of promoting a technological fix called "carbon capture" to justify burning more carbon, we can reverse the damage we have done by rapidly curtailing the burning of carbon, stopping the decimation of forests, and planting more trees that are not to be harvested.

Indeed, let us go outdoors and hug a tree. Let this be one of our new Christian rituals. Let us become tree-huggers in one way or another, and welcome the contempt of those uninformed citizens who have made "tree-hugging" a term for silliness.

Of course, ritualizing our friendship with trees is only the beginning. The realistic response of Christian practice will be to preserve old-growth forests from the lumber companies and make clear-cutting tree treasures a serious crime. Most of all, "love shall find a way" to energize our society with sunshine capture and wind turbine winding, rather than any further reversing of those millions of years of effective carbon capture. Culturally, we must learn to see our trees as family members of life on Earth. Without them there would be no life as we know it.

It may seem strange for me to begin Part Three on a next sociological form for Christianity talking about trees. Here is the reason: The most primary ethical consideration in a twenty-first-century Christian ethics is the climate crisis and the hundred or so other ecological emergencies that attend that most urgent and radical calling to change our entire energy system. Christian ethics shapes our mission of loving the planet and every person, creature, and thing upon it. The mission of love shapes the internal life of Christian religious practice. So the new sociological form of a next Christianity begins with a new attitude toward trees.

## EARTH HISTORY

The Earth's rocky physicality plus its liquids and atmospheric aspects are all made of stardust from a long emergence of about 13.8 billion years. Life on this planet began about 3.5 billion years ago. Science cannot tell us how or why that happened. Maybe the possibility of life is somehow built into the rocks, the atoms, and the force fields of our so-called physical world. This cosmos may not be as "rocky" as our limited imagination tends to hold. I am guessing that life and consciousness are a form of physicality that does not fit neatly into our current physics.

We can, however, tell the story of life on Earth with facts from our scientific study of Earth history. Life began with simple cells of life that were no more than enclosures of mineral-rich fluid swimming with big molecules. These tiny cells had a capacity and drive for survival and for expanded aliveness. The success of these simple cells improved and diversified for about 1.5 billion years before the aliveness drive was expanded into the more complex cells (eukaryotes). These cells contained millions of simpler cells enclosed in a more evolved skin. These larger and more complex single-celled life forms still exist today (amoebas, for example).

About a half billion years later (we are now up to about 1.5 billion years ago), some of these complex cells morphed into multicellular organisms of at least three types based on mutations long ago devised by those complex single-celled beings.

Some of these complex single-celled forms powered themselves entirely on the energy of decaying biological matter. Fungi and mushrooms are multicellular life forms that carry on this means of energizing

A second of these three energizing options evolved chlorophyll and other photosynthetic agents that powered these cells with sunshine. These sun-powered cells evolved into multicellular sea weeds, bushes, grasses, and trees. These sunshine life forms not only turned $CO_2$ into carbon carcasses, heavy stems, wood, coal, petroleum, and natural gas, but also in the process released oxygen as a waste product. Oxygen is now up to about 20 percent of the atmosphere.

This abundance of oxygen enabled the flourishing of life forms that burned oxygen instead of using sunshine. We call the multicellular forms of this third energizing option "animals." These oxygen-powered species have the advantage of moving around within whatever environments can provide that precious oxygen. Many of the oxygen-powered cells don't have to be stuck in wet minerals or stand in the sun. Animal life forms can depend upon the solar-powered, carbon-capturing life forms to supply their needed oxygen, as well as cool the planet and moderate the weather.

Therefore, if we humans want to support life on this planet, one of the ways to do that is to plant more trees and be sure that every tree we chop down goes for a use that is more important than that living tree is already performing for the whole planet. Human life is fully entwined within all the rest of the living forms on this planet. These life forms are not here for our use only, but are here for our use in the context that we work for their care and protection from ourselves and other factors. Here is a wonderful bit of poetic prose on this overall topic:

> You and the tree in your back yard come from a common ances-
> tor. A billion and a half years ago, the two of you parted ways.
> But even now, after an immense journey in separate directions,
> that tree and you still share a quarter of your genes . . . [1]

---

1. Powers, *Overstory*, 445. This quotation comes from a novel, but the science behind these poetic words is correct.

Life on this planet is one huge piece of wonder. Trees have produced and preserve the entire experiment of aliveness on this planet. We even share with these plentiful life forms that first chakra of consciousness (see chapter 2). The *sentience* of trees seems extremely alien to us. Trees perform their wonders without our animal types of consciousness that we call "sensory awareness"—enjoying felt contacts, pleasures, and pains, as well as sight, hearing, smelling, and tasting. Animal life forms have also evolved image-using intelligence, emotional intelligence, and then in humans that symbol-using intelligence like math, language, and art as well as the consciousness of being conscious of our consciousness.

Humans are now in charge of life on Earth in ways that humans never experienced before. The Bible was correct in noticing that humans were given power over the other life forms. Recently, we have badly misunderstood that simple truism to mean permission to overuse and misuse this abundance. We are now becoming aware that this immense power to shape planetary life means responsibility for this entire planet and its life.

Industrial civilization has brought us many benefits, but it has also brought us, and is still bringing us, ecological horror of unimaginable proportions. Our rulership of this planet has entered a new era. We have a name for this era: the Anthropocene—the era in which the *anthropos* species is a major force in Earth history.

## THE PURPOSE OF TREES

Using narrow, human-centered value systems, we might assume that the purpose of trees is to shade our houses, increase the value of our property, provide our lumber, kindling, and perhaps money for our checkbooks. So it is a big shift in understanding to see that the purpose of trees is to make life possible for all forms of life, including our own. So if we were to have in our property a two-thousand-year-old, seven-story-high tree, we need to ask this question: "Is there any other use for that tree that is better than what it is already doing?"

Other such questions abound: "Is clear cutting a whole hillside of trees a crime against life on Earth, including your life and mine?" "Should we favor laws against doing such things, laws that are actually enforced against tree owners and lumber companies?" Way too slowly, we humans are becoming aware of our connectedness with the friendliness of trees, and our responsibilities for these fellow creatures.

Furthermore, it not only in our economic and political arenas that we need to take better care of trees. The cultural arena is also crucial. We need to get much better acquainted with our tree companions, our plant companions, our fungal companions, our animal companions, as well as the many hundreds of thousands of human cultures on this highly diverse planet. We must learn to love the diversity of life with a passion similar to our love for sex, food, and family. We must count White nationalism or any other so-called nationalism as criminal and downright silly. All nations are now called to care for the whole planet of living beings and human types. All nations are called to reign in their profiteers to a level of sanity beyond classism, racism, sexism, humanism, and any other self-exaltation that leaves behind the whole-Earth reality through which and only through which we are meeting that Profound Reality, our God-devotion.

Together, we humans need to know about all these living companions in order to play our proper role in this now existing Anthropocene Era. We can learn things from the long past of living forms on this Earth, and we are called now to grapple with the well-being of all life on Earth for the next thousand years. Even though this next millennium is only one scene in a 3,500,000-millenia scene-story of life on Earth, the quality of future Earth has already been delivered into human hands. How are we doing? We are not doing very well as yet.

How did our responsibilities expand so much? We humans caused this by becoming the most powerful for good and powerfully destructive species on the planet. We moved from being a few million upright-walking, extra-smart primates roaming the heart of Africa to being 7.7 billion and still increasing humans, each with huge capacities for planetary results—helpful or hindering. This self-chosen status is now a calling for responses that were unthinkable two centuries ago. This is what we mean by the Anthropocene Era. We humans have become the most consequential species determining the history of life on this fragile sphere.

We are just barely catching on that we humans are really in charge here, and that our old roles are now obsolete. The Earth is no longer a boundless ball of resources for us to use for our narrow ends. This planet is now our responsibility. Who treats their home like a dump site for trash? Do we even know about those whole islands of plastic bottles swimming in our oceans? Considering our popular ideas about economic growth—do we know that such thinking has become preposterous? The idea of unending, unmanaged growth is now nothing but an excuse for not doing what we need to do. How can a finite planet support unlimited growth in service of a fast-growing species, each member of which is programmed to want to be a millionaire?

We are way too slowly catching on to the fact that big tax cuts for the millionaires and billionaires means way more of us will be living paycheck to paycheck and a still larger number of us having no paycheck at all. Safety from gun violence, healthcare for everyone, and college education for our children—these simple baselines are impossible as long as our economic thinking remains a huge monopoly game where the "winners take all" and the rest go broke.

Our current economics fosters an ever-more authoritarian government that is financed by and protects the ever-increasing power of the wealthy. This encourages corruption and allows the planet to become too downgraded to support this ethically wretched form of injustice. Such a destiny is not inevitable; it is simply being chosen. And those choices are being excused by unrealistic thinking.

Let the recent story of old-growth forests be our sign of how already grim the results of our unchanged plans are becoming. If we had a time-lapse movie from outer space of the planet over the last couple of centuries, we would see a shocking amount of forest shrinkage. These old-growth forests that have been giving us our oxygen and being our carbon sink are passing away. In addition we are burning our ancient carbon storage of biomass in the form of coal, petroleum, and natural gas at an ever-increasing rate that has already altered the climate and is producing horrific and very costly results in floods, droughts, mud slides, and more—consequences that our wealthy citizens and corporations are refusing to pay for. Instead, the costs of the climate crisis are being dumped on the poor and the middle classes. This will result in forms of social chaos that will simply be untenable for rich and poor alike.

One prominent traditional delusion is that there are big, friendly capital owners who are generously providing us with good jobs and supporting solutions to our real problems. But the jobs being provided by the current big institutions are whatever jobs are needed to secure the lives of our current millionaires, not what jobs actually need to be done— such as the good jobs that would shift our energy system from fossil fuels to sunshine, end the need for coal mining, oil exploration, and nuclear power plants, plus protect our old-growth forests from ruin with good tree management. Is this impossible? Not really, the future is open.

## THE CORE OF OUR CRISES

Here is the core of our crises: we need new rules for our economic game. Basic rules for a human economy are always provided by governments, and are best provided by democratic governments that serve the interests of everyone. We need fully democratic governments that are responsive to all the people—governments that make our laws and enforce those laws with competent democratic power, free from any form of economic corruption. Basically, what we have now are ecologically blind rich people who have no other purpose than becoming richer, together with billions of somewhat less blind poor people who are doing ecologically destructive things just to survive another day.

Current economic systems are playing a winner-take-all, monopoly-game economics—a game in which the biggest winners drive all the other players out of the game. Playing monopoly on a game board may be fun for some, but in a real-life world such a game will destroy itself, poor and rich alike, as well as a planet fit for human habitation. *We need new rules* for our economic game; we need them now.

Anyone who insists that letting everyone do whatever advantages them while pretending that everything will work out best for everybody needs to be sent back to school—a school worth attending. The claim that wealth going to the top will then trickle down for everyone is simply not true: centuries of historical facts prove otherwise. Nevertheless, this is one of the persistent lie-infested mindsets that is marching us toward the cliffs of doom.

A fully democratic government that is enforcing workable overall rules does not need to micromanage the entire economy. Some of what we have learned in the Industrial Era can be retained. Innovations made at local and regional areas can still transpire if the overall rules of this now-planetary economic game are the overall rules that benefit every human with a chance for life, as well as benefit the trees, the frogs, and the bees. We don't need to call this new economy "communism," or "democratic socialism," or "capitalism." We can learn from all these experiments in economic order, but let's just call this new economy "an economy as if Earth matters" or "an economy that works for everyone." Waking up to these real factors and new visions of social operation is already decades tardy.

Here is the place to start: phasing out fossil-fuel burning in a manner that does not lay the cost for this on working people. As long as we have big money ruling the world, nothing adequate will be done on the climate crisis. A vision has already been presented in the U.S. Congress that is strongly supported by presidential candidates and a large number of congressional representatives. This vision is wonderfully named the "Green New Deal." Here is the gist of it: Like the Franklin D. Roosevelt New Deal, it is a massive trillion-dollar jobs program, but not for jobs that preserve the old economy, rather for new and better jobs that build a solar and wind economy. It is an update on what FDR successfully did almost a century ago. A new economy has to be built. We cannot depend upon the current fossil fuel corporations to do this in the right way. This is a role for a democratic government that puts public interests and Earth interests before any sort of foolishness or tempting corruption. Our best minds—and a lot of them—have to lead this social shift, and do so persistently over a long expanse of time.

Of course the fossil fuel industries are going to protest such a plan. We will have to neutralize their enormous power. We can greatly expand the disinvestment movement, deny them government perks and subsidies. We could even demand from the leadership of every fossil fuel company that they present to the government their plan for phasing out their product. In other words, we can rationally insist on there being responsible transition-fuel companies, rather than being reactionary ideologues who think they are entitled to expand the sort of business they currently do, no matter what the consequences. Also, the false perspectives with which our culture has been saturated will need to be satirized by every sane comedian. We will have to use whatever popular power we can muster to force cooperation with this necessary direction of march.

## BUT HOW?

When conservatives and cautious liberals ask, "But how can this be done?," they mean this question as doubt that this can be done, or they mean these words as an excuse for not doing it. When progressives ask, "How can this be done?," they are asking for information and inspiration on getting this done. I am speaking to all these various perspectives with the following insights.

Phasing out fossil fuels and phasing in a solar-and-wind energy base is already underway. Solar energy is already cheaper than coal and nuclear and will soon be cheaper than petroleum and natural gas. The sun is a boundless energy source. More sunshine hits this planet every day than humans will ever need. Our means of turning this enormous sun energy source into electricity and hydrogen tanks is improving every year. These are the solutions for storing vast amount of energy in order to power our needs when the sun does not shine or the wind does not blow. Batteries are becoming better and cheaper, and several million vehicles with big batteries can store a lot of energy. Batteries are too heavy for some purposes; but liquefied hydrogen tanks can fuel airplanes, so experts say, more cheaply and safely than jet fuel.[2] Indeed, hydrogen and electricity can transfer sun and wind power to every possible need that humans can devise. The only thing missing is the infrastructure to support this new economy, and even that is well underway and technologically possible to do in a decade under full-speed conditions.

Conservation of energy is a big part of the energy transition period, but our long-range prospects do not have to be viewed as hardships of any sort. The amount of sunshine is virtually boundless. Trees and other plants are already efficient in using sunshine to capture carbon and release oxygen. We can use, rather than fight with, the natural world. This principle has implications for agriculture—using more perennial plants rather than plants we have to plant every year and fertilize with petroleum products. Our future is mostly limited by a failure of imagination. The ethics of a next Christianity will seek to be years ahead of current political possibilities.

We expect there to be a transition period between gasoline stations and power plugs for our car and truck batteries, plus exchange stores for our hydrogen tanks. The core issue is fostering pubic enthusiasm and our political will to get rapid motion going for this huge change. We need to do that now before the old system shuts everything down, including itself. Fossil fuel companies possess enormous wealth with which to oppose this shift: they are already using their available wealth to stop progress in every way they can. Democratic governments will need to use law enforcement to restrain these companies.

Already well underway is a disinvestment movement in the fossil fuel industries. This movement is already having a significant effect, and there is no limit to the effect it could have. Political empowerment in national and state governments is also underway. The Green New Deal is a set of doable programs that can build momentum for this shift and create jobs, as well as put in place the fabric of economic structures that will be needed.

2. See Scott, *Smelling Land*.

## TOO HARD?

Conservative forces are already speaking their panic that this shift is too hard to do. "How are we going to pay for it?" is their most prominent rant. We are going to pay for it the same way we paid for World War II, the Civil War, the Vietnam War, etc. We just gave a trillion dollars or so in tax cuts to people who did not need them. Conservative forces complain about big government and big deficits, but they have no qualms about making their own profit sources bigger by reducing Social Security, Medicare, Medicaid, public parks, education funding, governing effectiveness, and even the Post Office. The core issue is what public money goes for. The climate crisis is so clearly the top priority. And a massive jobs program like the Green New Deal actually grows the part of the economy that needs to be grown.

## MONEY MAKES THE WORLD GO ROUND, THE WORLD GO ROUND, THE WORLD GO ROUND

The Earth, of course, goes around fine without any influence from our minute human exchange systems. But inside the ever-present exchange system of our current economic processes, we may feel like "money does make the world go round." Everyone is competing with everyone else to see how much of our human labor and our planet's goods can be turned into money. Actually, most of us receive a very small part of the money that our labor creates, and we do not have sufficient democratic power to participate adequately in the decisions that figure out how to distribute the money our labor creates.

Those billionaires who claim to have earned their billions often overlook the fact that thousands of people have directly labored to earn the money that these billionaires have taken "off the top." If we count all the labor it takes to build the infrastructures, then hundreds of millions of people have earned most of the money that a billionaire owns and controls. The highways, bridges, railroads, internet, electric systems, police departments, fire departments, post offices, and much more have helped each rich person acquire his or her riches. Such reflections reveal the truth that most of a billionaire's money is actually *public-earned money.* Why should he or she control all that wealth? Are billionaires really the wisest and most just citizens?

A good economy is not a monopoly game in which "winners take all." The good economy is a service organization that all of us would be trying to make work for everyone. This is not a radical idea; it is the commonsense view—providing opportunity for every person, and careful care for the planet. This is not strange. It is our failure to do this that is truly strange.

All of us are turning Earth resources into money, and giving too little back to the Earth. A fully democratic government could be giving back to the Earth important parts of our taxed funds to keep Earth functioning well for all of us. Keeping our oxygen producers and carbon sinks working well would be a top priority. Keeping the overall temperature down to safe levels would be another huge priority. Keeping the diversity of species in good shape would be another. All of us should be glad to give generously to the cause of having a planet and an economy that works for everyone.

The good economy, roughly outlined above, is consistent with loving Profound Reality with all our heart, strength, mind, and consciousness—as well as our neighbors as ourselves. Loving God and neighbor includes providing for and taking joy in paying fair and appropriate taxes, as well as spending those taxes carefully for human well-being and ecological richness. The slightest corruption in the use of those precious funds should be as taboo as genocide.

In conclusion, I underline once more: trees are huge associates in the cause of Earth aliveness. So, let us go into our back yard, or our neighbor's yard, or down the street, and give one of those trees a big hug. If anyone asks us why we are doing this, we can tell them about *the friendliness of trees*, a critical part of our Earth family.

# 15

## His-Story, Her-Story and a New Story

ANOTHER REASON WE CHRISTIANS have not yet completed our full revolution in Christian practice for this era of human life is that we have not yet handled the full extent to which Christians still cling to patriarchal patterns for women and men—thereby warping all our interpersonal relations. This clinging to our deeply patriarchal Christian past is so pronounced among most Christians that many people, especially women, doubt the possibility of a post-patriarchal future for this religion.

Can there be a viable, vital post-patriarchal next Christianity? Can our religious practices overcome patriarchy in attitude, theology, liturgy, and life together, as well as in our internal politics and outgoing mission? This will not be a minor change, for it affects everything sociological and communal in a next Christian life together as well as within that body's mission to all those still patriarchal cultures on this troubled planet.

My title for this chapter may be a bit cryptic. Here is my meaning: history is very important in the theology and practice of Christianity, as well as in Judaism and Islam. All three of these religions are rooted in meeting Profound Reality, their God-devotion in the events of history. Patriarchal dismantlement has become a crucial topic for these religions, because they have spent their whole histories in a type of storytelling we can call "*his-story.*" During this long period of patriarchy—history-telling has been mostly about kings and a few patriarchy-style queens. Literature has been mostly written by men. Some unusually talented women have risen to the top of the cultural discussion, but often with styles that have trimmed off much of the deep gifts of women—the interpersonal intensities, the deep symbolism of the birthing of human life, and a raw grasp of natural embodiment that characterized the woman imagery we find in pre-patriarchal cultures.

In other words, *"her-story"* has been inadequately told. We need to hear with power her-story in all three of its basic eras: (1) what it was like for women in pre-patriarchal societies, (2) what it was like for women during patriarchy, and (3) what it is becoming like and can be like for women in post-patriarchal societies. This whole story cannot be told in this one chapter of this book, even if I were able to do so, which I am not.

The pre-patriarchy part of her-story is difficult to tell accurately, or even to know what accurate means. When patriarchy began sometime before 3500 BCE, we were still in the pre-writing period. So we are deriving the early part of *her-story* from archeological sites and from the echoes of that early period that are present in the written works of later periods. In chapter 8, I summarized aspects of this pre-patriarchy her-story as part of my discussion of the Great Goddess devotion that impacted cultures during that antiquity.

In this chapter, I focus on a few examples of her-story in medieval European history, as those stories pertain to Christian leadership women. And then I am going to provide some thoughts on the future of *her-story* for Christianity-practicing women and men going forward in Christian life together and in the Christian mission toward the dismantlement of patriarchy.

By "his-story" I mean the story of man, where consciously or unconsciously the word "man" is used to include woman as an adjunct to man. His-story includes male commoners and heads of households, as well as male leaders and rulers—kings, presidents, religious innovators, intellectuals, inventors, writers, artists, architects, engineers, generals, and every other role of leadership that patriarchal civilization has had to offer men.

During the era of patriarchy, only a few gifted women played top roles of leadership within the typical his-story mode of history-telling and history-making. Here are a three examples of such Christian leadership women during the Middle Ages:

Hildegard of Bingen (1098–1179) was a German Benedictine abbess, theologian, and writer, who was perhaps the closest we have had to a women pope. She was the teacher of popes, and one of the most influential persons of her era. She was a lover of nature to the point of impressing contemporary ecologists. To establish her place in society, she was constrained to give up marriage and children in order to secure her depth of education and her strong role in that society.

Julian of Norwich (1342–1416) was an English anchoress and an influential Christian mystic and theologian, still widely read today. She lived her life in a solitary cell in order to make a place for herself in that patriarchal world.

Teresa of Avila (1515–1582) was a strict Spanish Carmelite nun, an author and theologian of the contemplative life. She organized a Carmelite religious order reform. She was a primary teacher of John of the Cross. Both she and John were important for the whole Reformation era. They are both still influential today among both Catholics and Protestants.

The lives of these three remarkable women illustrate how difficult it was for a woman to be a big player in medieval history. Women have made progress during the modern era, but they must still fight with patriarchal residues that remain strong in our twenty-first-century cultures.

We have only recently begun to tell her-story, to hear her perspective on the patriarchal era as well as *"her"* vision for a post-patriarchy future. Her-story of the near past of the feminine recovery is still being told, and we have barely begun shaping the future for women and men on planet Earth.

## WOMEN AND MEN IN
## FUTURE CHRISTIAN PRACTICE

Millions of women are now climbing out of that deep pit of neglect and oppression, and they are pulling the men and the tone of human culture along with them. So, what do we do now within our next viable and vital practices of Christianity? At their best Christians have been, and they still are called to be, "first-comers" in history on behalf of all, rather than the last people on the new beaches of history. So to fulfill this promise, Christians are called to be feminists of the most advanced sort.

The theology developed in Part Two of this book can be a breath of fresh air for women. Here is why: to surrender our lives to Profound Reality means not to surrender our lives to a man or to a patriarchal culture. It means *not* surrendering our lives to any temporal reality. Our temporal loyalties are all temporary and open to only penultimate surrenders of loyalty. The moral certainties of the past are now barely interesting in the light of this awareness that there are no laws or moralities or norms that are not rules created by humans. We can, therefore, be open to a wide range of rules for ourselves as women or as men. We can be open to creating new norms for our whole societies that include this openness for fundamental changes in human customs with regard to the roles played by individual women and men.

Surely, Christian reformers must hope for and help build those gender-equity human cultures that will no longer simply tell *his-story,* but will tell a *new story* through and through—a story in which both women and men contribute their differences, but live and contribute within a thoroughgoing commitment to new attitudes and social fabrics that affirm full gender equity. We are facing in the passing of patriarchy a big change—huge like the abolition of slavery. This new story for women and men has economic and political aspects, but unlike other big changes, this change is essentially a cultural empowerment, a psychological healing, an intimacy revolution, and yes, a religious transformation that changes our religious theoretics, our religious practices, every liturgy, and all the devotional words used in our relations with Profound Reality. These changes will be more, not less, than we expect.

Most of the prominent Christian male theologians of the twentieth century were males who were still using the word "man" to mean both men and women. These same men were significantly affected by the rise of women's issues, but their journey into her-story was incomplete. A revolutionary form of her-story began to surface in the 1970s with *Ms.* magazine and other culture-wide events, yet in 2020 we still have billions of humans who have not even begun their journey from his-story to her-story, or to any sort of adequate new story on this topic.

Large numbers of men and women are in open rebellion against making this huge change. There are still U.S. women, now working outside the home in previously male-occupied jobs, who nevertheless view the prospect of a women president unthinkable. The "king" or "male president" symbolism still has a strong hold on many psyches. Indeed, all of us are still in the process of completing this journey from patriarchal hangovers to full equity, and this will likely be a prominent issue for another century.

Like racism, sexism is a cultural disease spread far and deep through every culture in ways that are only recently becoming conscious. Healing for this malady is something more than individuals alone can do. We are all racists and sexists until this is corrected in the institutions and cultural patterns of our societies. This may take another hundred years.

Nevertheless, this deep gender-equity shift will take a prominent place in Christian ethics for any fully elaborated next Christian practice.

The social mission of a viable and vital next Christian practice will feature overcoming patriarchy, sexism, and women's oppression as no less critical than overcoming racism, classism, or handling our ecology crises. A full manifestation of her-story in the lives of all persons and in all the institutions of every society is one among the many key social transformations. Indeed, the above-named social transformations can only be brought to completion together, not separately in any sort of exclusion from one another.

## SO WHAT DOES HER-STORY MEAN FOR THE NURTURE LIFE OF A NEXT CHRISTIANITY?

Christianity has been so immersed in patriarchy for its entire history that many women and men have been doubtful about a cure for this religion. Every sentence of Scripture has to be reinterpreted and often cleaned up for oral reading. Here is an example. In Genesis 2:21–24 we have a patriarchy-influenced myth in which the Profound Reality (God) is taking a rib from Adam and making Eve out of it. This story follows after the same God had scooped up "some dust from the ground" and created man. No self-respecting women today can think of herself as a rib of man. After all, it is the plain truth that all men and women are born from the womb-human. So we are quite within our rights to correct this old myth in our liturgical practices, or at least see this story for what it is—poetry with a patriarchal hangover.

The only thing we might keep from this Genesis myth is its concluding emphasis that men and women are of one flesh (that is, not an alien species, or imports from different planets). If we want to play with a new origin myth for these two genders, we might picture our fictitious Adam and Eve emerging together from the womb of a very ancient species of upright-walking chimpanzee. While we are at it, we will need to envision the skin color of this original pair as jet-black with African-like features. This is more than a guess; our DNA science has concluded that all of our races of humans have a common ancestor in an African Eve.

Almost all of our Christian liturgy has to be rewritten. "Our Father" just won't do for our devotional relation with Profound Reality. And the word "man" can no longer mean "human." Much of the best classical liturgy can be updated into powerful contemporary poetry. But for starters at least, we need to be simple and relevant to our times. We need to be straightforward with the words we use in any ritual we want to be nurturing for twenty-first-century humans.

Every aspect of communal life has to be overhauled. Profound intimacy between men and women, women and women, men and men, gay and straight, and any other gender relations have to be worked through for every circle of Christian practice. The depth of intimacy in these future circles need to be profoundly honest in order to do the quality of spirit nurture we will need for our life together and our mission to planet Earth.

As we come to see the profound common nature that resides beneath all our estrangements, we can also see the possibilities of healing these gender estrangements. Such small-group interpersonal experiences may feel threatening to our stuck egos, but that is what our Christian nurture is for—to rescue us from our ego traps and reveal to one another how authentic humanness in every person breathes the same Holy Spirit of *trust*, *care*, and *freedom*.

## SO WHAT DOES HER-STORY MEAN FOR THE OUTWARD MISSION OF A NEXT CHRISTIANITY?

Movements like ecofeminism point to this unified approach to both loving the Earth and loving its women. Ecofeminism understands that the forces that oppress women and the forces that oppress the Earth are the same forces. Racism, classism, poverty, religious bigotry, and other corruptions are mixed into this same stew of essential changes. These prime maladies of our social life reinforce each other, and their healing heals each other.

Many people still resist women's leadership, support sexist politicians, and even protect sex abusers. Too few Christian communities do an adequate study of ecofeminism and ecological solutions, or conduct a lifestyle of responsible living in a geographical place of action. In general, Christian practitioners are not yet fully alert to the deep connections of our oppression of women and our oppression of nature. So in addition to telling her-story and grounding that story ecologically, we will need to engage in understanding the intricacies of intimate relations, mutual respect, and the empathy required not only for organizing a new circle of Christian life together but also for the Christian mission to society as a whole.

We are called to explore topics like romantic love, sex, marriage, and child-raising. We are in for a long journey of healing within Christian group life and its ongoing mission to the planet at large. Indeed, this reshaping of our group life together informs the qualities of our outward mission.

Her-story is a topic that is especially relevant for religions like Judaism, Christianity, and Islam that are, at their best, rooted in a love of history. Today, Christians need to pay special attention to *her-story within our encounters with Profound Reality—that is, with our God.* A shift away from the patriarchy of our Christian past is a transformation that Christians cannot avoid, if they are to be true to our own heritage, as well as sharing the radical gifts of Christianity for building a viable and vital future for humanity.

In the world at large, there can no such thing as a full democracy without the full participation of women. And there can be no such thing as an equitable economy without equal pay for equal work for women. Indeed, there is no possibility of resolving the climate crisis and other ecological emergencies without women and men who together understand that *her-story* and the *planet's story* are entangled stories.

Before I examine further the importance of her-story for our practice of Christian love for all humanity and the planet, I will examine in chapter 16 "Post-Civilization Christianity," and in chapter 17 "The Dead End of Christendom."

# 16

---

# Post-Civilization Christianity

FOR SOME READERS THIS may be the most controversial chapter of this book. The notion of replacing civilization with an alternative mode of social organization is still a radical proposal, even though Kenneth Boulding suggested it as early as 1965 in his book *The Meaning of the 20th Century: The Great Transition*.[1] Nevertheless, most social ethics writers call for a better civilization, rather than for the replacement of civilization with a whole new mode of social organization.

Indeed, the whole idea of modes of social organization may sound strange to many people. The common mind often assumes that "civilized society" and "acceptable society" mean the same thing. In Boulding's typology of social modes, there are three major modes of human social organization: pre-civilization, civilization, and post-civilization. (There are many subtypes within each of these three types.)

All three of these modes of society exist today and may always exist, so I will be using the suffixes pre- and post- to distinguish these three types in terms of their time of origin. What I am calling "civilization" began about 4500 BCE and became a majority mode of social organization much later. Civilization now dominates the planet, and the beginnings of a replacement for civilization began, let us say, with the democratic revolutions of the eigtheenth century.

However strange this perspective may seem, I will be insisting in this chapter that the social mission of a viable and vital next Christianity

---

1. *The Meaning of the 20th Century* is a prophetic book that has stood up well for six decades.

is *dismantling civilization* and assisting in the design and building of a mode of society that replaces civilization as the majority social habitation for humanity. Here is a list of the questions that I am going to explore in this chapter:

What is civilization?

What are the gifts of civilization?

What have been the downsides of civilization?

Why must civilization be phased out and replaced with something better?

How can this vast transformation be done?

What do we mean by a "post-civilization Christianity"?

How do post-civilization Christians live in the remaining era of civilization?

What do Christians do to assist replacing civilization with post-civilization?

## WHAT IS CIVILIZATION?

I have been an avid, if not exhaustive, student of the archeological evidence for the origins of civilization. Hunter-gatherer societies preceded the practice of agriculture, which was becoming prominent in select places between 10,000 and 8000 BCE. Agriculture required the development of settled villages and their social alliances with other villages. These agricultural societies could be quite large in comparison with the earlier hunter-gather forms of association. Many of these pre-civilization agricultural societies did amazing work with huge monumental stones that required many villages of people to build. These still wondrous social sites for worship and science occurred long before royalty existed or cities were established that enabled a political centralization of rulership over other classes of people—merchants, soldiers, peasants, herders, and sometimes slaves.

We see the first of these civilized city states in about 4500 BCE with the hierarchically organized city of Uruk—a one-city civilization in the northern river valley of the Euphrates River in what is now Iraq. I believe that we can count Uruk as the first civilization, if we define "civilization" as a distinct mode of social organization structured as a social pyramid. With this definition of "civilization," "pre-civilization" includes both simple hunter-gatherer associations as well as the larger, more complex agricultural associations that had not yet discovered or adopted the mathematics of hierarchy for their overall social organization. Pre-civilization can also include certain types of herding societies, often organized as chieftain-headed groups of roving bands.

By 3200 BCE there were many city-states, and there were several multi-city civilizational empires, such as the strong centralized rule along the Nile River Valley in Egypt. By 2500 BCE we find a somewhat less-centralized civilizational group of cities along the Indus River Valley in what is contemporary Pakistan. The pattern of civilization spread rather slowly into Africa and Europe as well as into China and the Americas.

Civilization came to England as late as 800 BCE. The famous Stonehenge religious center created near Wilshire, England was still being completed in 2000 BCE by a pre-civilization type of agricultural society. Though these dates may be approximate, the general picture of this slow migration of both pre-civilization agricultural societies and civilizational forms of society is the true story.

Pre-civilization modes of society have existed alongside civilizations until the present day. If we were able to build a time chart of this, we would find less than 1 percent of humanity was "civilized" in 4500 BCE. Perhaps it was 1000 BCE before half of the human population lived in a civilization. In 2019 CE less than 1 percent of the human population is still living alongside civilizations in hunter-gatherer and early-agricultural modes of society. Most of these groups have fled from the civilizations that gobbled up the more fertile locations.

Our modern "return to the land" communal experiments are civilized groups attempting to recover some of the values of pre-civilization societies. Some of these groups reject the overall mode of civilization, but we cannot count them as pre-civilization societies. These are civilized people trying to be pre-civilized.

Genuine pre-civilization societies were experienced by the early civilized Europeans who came to North America. These Native American societies had existed alongside civilizations, but they had never taken on the idea of having a royalty. When European settlers asked members of these societies to "take us to your king," they were met with the surprising discovery that there was no king. Yes, there were leaders of a different sort—persons called "war chiefs," persons called "peace chiefs," circles of elders including women that had various decisional powers, and other leadership arrangements—but no king, no royalty, no class structure.

So, I underline once again that one basic criterion for defining a society as a "civilization" is the social pyramid—the hierarchical means of organizing society that we often call "classist." A second closely related criterion for defining "civilization" is having a strong centralized state organization staffed by the wealthiest members of society and their employees. Many forms of civilization have existed from small city-states to large empires, and from simple agricultural civilizations to our very complex industrial civilizations. All of these societies have these two qualities: a ruling elite and a centralization of governing power. Democracy has moderated this pattern somewhat, but at this point in time, democracy has not yet overcome the ancient hierarchical mode of social ordering.

We might view our current democratic civilizations as part of a long-range trend toward ending classism—abolishing slavery, letting women vote, etc. These ever-more democratic trends can be viewed as dismantling hierarchy—a beginning on *abolishing civilization!* We have commonly thought of democracy as a reform of civilization, but the achievement of a full democracy and the building of a post-civilization can now be seen as the same basic transformation!

Another key current force that is dismantling civilization and replacing it with something better is the growth of ecological movements that are based on the truth that the Earth comes first, and that the social order (economy, polity, and culture) comes second to ecology in our basic human priorities. Preserving a viable planet for human life is a recent, but very powerful awareness and social trend. We now know that all our social organizing efforts depend on a viable planet that supports human life and all other forms of life that make life on Earth an optimal ecosystem. We also know that the human species has become so numerous and so technologically powerful that we humans are forced into a level responsibility for this planet not experienced in earlier eras.

So our social movements for democracy and our social movements for an optimal ecology join together against any sort of authoritarian class rule by those vast economic and political forces that are producing huge inequities among humans and are decimating the functionalities of the natural planet. We now see fresh forms of authoritarian rule rising across the planet in reaction against further democracy and further ecological transformation. By thinking only of economic growth that pampers the super rich and neglects the rest of us, this new reactionary thinking is a gravely destructive trend. Even with huge economic growth, the economic trickle-down is slight, and the power inequity is being increased.

What actually trickles down from this reactionary style of politics are permanent poverty, an extremely angry underclass, social chaos, and a planet hostile to the well-being of the human species. Some things, like accessing sunshine, need to grow, and other things, like oil burning, needs to be phased out. We need a fully democracy-empowered government that can set the rules for the economic game, enforce those rules powerfully, and thereby put free enterprise in its appropriate secondary place to democratic government. A wealth-ruled government is a covenant with ruin—a fostering of all the downsides of what we call "civilization."

In order to retain our commitment to realism, we must not view these reactionary tends as a viable option for those nations that think they want such a future. We must view these anti-democratic trends as a violation of realism—that is, as a rebellion against obedience to the always-encountering Profound Reality that is the God-devotion of the essential Christian revelation. Democracy, equity, and ecological sanity flesh out the huge opposite of these reactionary trends. Any opposition to these three positive directions is something more than a different political opinion. Such reactionary opposition to post-civilization defines the enemy of humankind as surely as Adolf Hitler's totalitarian racism defined the enemy of humankind in the last century.

## A VISION OF POST-CIVILIZATION

As a further effort to define "civilization," I am suggesting that our vision of post-civilization can be held with the name "eco-democracy." This name picks up the ecological, economic, and political aspects of the transformation we need. An eco-democratic society will also be characterized by many fresh cultural underpinnings—such as a new cooperation among our reality-loving religious practices, a new status for women and their values and stories about being human, a phasing of out racial and nativist social patterns, a promoting an openness to cultural relativity, the conducting of an all-out educational push that builds skills in all four approaches to truth, and more.

Communism, socialism, capitalism, authoritarianism, feudalism, and fascism are all names for various forms of civilization. They have been useful for defining worse and better forms of civilization. But now we need to redefine better and worse—with respect to what? Here is my answer: better and worse with respect to eco-democracy! We can certainly learn things about what to do and what not to do from all the existing political heritages. We can use those acquired gifts to build something better—where "better" is defined by eco-democracy—a post-civilization mode of social organization.

## WHAT ARE THE GIFTS OF CIVILIZATION?

Though it would be horrific to conserve the entire frame of civilization, our experience in being civilized does have gifts for the future. Pre-civilization societies also have gifts not held well by civilization, but we cannot return to pre-civilization forms of society. Our huge population living on the space of a limited Earth cannot make such a return, even if we wanted that type of life. Nevertheless, many of the values held by these ancient societies have been neglected by civilization, and need to be restored. One of these values is a deep sensitivity to the natural world. Earth sensibility includes sensitivity to our own human nature and to our natural relations with one another and with the other species of life. Other gifts of pre-civilization societies include an emphasis on organic leadership, consensus decision-making, cooperation in excess of competition, and more enduring, workable interpersonal relationships. Basically, our pre-civilization recoveries can teach us that being civilized isn't everything we need, and never was.

Here are some of the values of the civilization era of experience that we can and need to retain: (1) a planetary outlook, including the cosmic and evolutionary view of nature that goes with that outlook; (2) wisdom about recreating our common social structures; (3) depth psychology and interpersonal wisdom; and (4) widely known religious practices that civilization members have explored and recorded for our benefit. (5) Scientific wisdom as a whole is a huge gift, even though many of the technologies our sciences have enabled now need to be phased out or used differently. This complex topic of sorting out what to save of civilization and what to drop from our civilized experience deserves a much longer effort of thoughtfulness. Such sorting is one of the key challenges involved in envisioning post-civilization and bringing this new order into being. This transition is a long emergency, not merely a next-decade task. Yet, we are also tardy getting up to speed on this necessary transition.

# WHAT HAVE BEEN THE
# DOWNSIDES OF CIVILIZATION?

We can do without social hierarchy and the oppressions that hierarchy holds in being. In addition, each social hierarchy is constrained to fight the other social hierarchies for their piece of ground. The extent that such ongoing warfare is built into the pattern of civilization has seldom been fully stated. Today with our horrific means of modern warfare, warfare itself has become a problematical means of conflict resolution. Furthermore, migrating somewhere else from an oppressive civilization and its warfare horrors has become limited by the amount of the planet already fully occupied by civilized people. And this situation includes a reluctance to deal with increasing numbers of refugees due to inequities, wars, and climate change. We can only solve these core issues by solving them in a planet-wide manner. Our need for planet-wide ecological solutions also dramatizes the need for post-civilization social forms. Any nationalism that opposes planet-wide cooperation will lead to a cesspool of bad outcomes.

In building our post-civilization future, both our necessities of "common defense" and "domestic tranquility" are advised to use violence as a very last resort. There will always be a few urgent, stubborn dangers faced by both continental militaries and local police forces, and these challenges will require violent restraints. Nevertheless, we will need to define "last resort" in a strict post-civilization manner. Our issues today will require more negotiation, more tolerance, more counseling, and more patience than is suggested by the gun-slinger styles of restraint that are still viewed as heroic.

Another core problem with civilization is that it tends to make a few persons excessively wealthy economic winners in the overall competition for society's wealth and power, while a large portion of the population is confined to situations of borderline survival that make hunter-gatherer social life seem wealthy. More and more wealth for a few with just enough trickle-down to keep the peace among the poorest is a losing game on this finite twenty-first-century planet. The lack of a reasonable equity will only get worse if we keep moving toward a human population of perhaps twelve billion. The costs of moving toward "Eco-Democracy" are minuscule compared with the costs of not doing so. Already the costs of cleaning up the damages of the already present and impending climate crisis are growing astronomical.

Finally, we have to look more deeply at the ecological crises to see the dangerous results of continuing with the social pattern we call "civilization." I will look again and in a more specific manner at these crises in a later chapter. For now, I want to simply note that loving Profound Reality includes loving nature in all of its gifts and challenges. Ecological responsibility has joined the most urgent social justice topics. Ecological topics do not conflict with economic equity topics. These two realms of responsibility depend upon one another for a solution to either.

## WHY MUST CIVILIZATION BE PHASED OUT AND REPLACED WITH SOMETHING BETTER?

We have entered what is being called the "Anthropocene"—a time in history when the impacts of the human species on the planet are so immense that humans are thrust into responsibilities for the planet that no previous era of human history has had to face. Such a unique set of demands results in the necessity to stretch our imaginations beyond the pattern called "civilization" to something very much better.

Our situation is like a fast train heading toward a cliff. We have to slow down and then stop this train before we reach the cliff. There does not appear to be another inhabitable planet to which even a few us could be provided the Earth resources to reach. It is understandable why our science fiction is picturing such a trip, but the reality is that this planet is our human home, and our best hope is reforming the *here* rather than hoping for a viable *there*. Also, some of these new-planet dreamers do not take into consideration that we would be taking all our civilizational flaws with us. We might as well deal with those flaws here at home.

What is hardest for civilized people to grasp is that both our standard capitalism and our standard socialism are forms of civilization that must be radically transformed. We have lessons that we can retain from both our capitalist experience and our socialist experiences. Governments can encourage innovation and refrain from micro-managing the intricate decision-making that each free-enterprise company needs to handle. We can retain from our socialist experience that many services are best handled by government and by government strongly refereeing the economic playing field from the perspective of the populous rather than the perspective of the super-wealthy few.

The battle between socialism and capitalism has been a vigorous recent drama and conversation, but now both of these words have lost their power to represent whole answers to our current challenges. Most people who call themselves "socialists" now incorporate a great deal of wisdom from free-enterprise thought. And most of those who call themselves "capitalists" now incorporate a great deal of wisdom from socialist thought about the needed role of government. And since both of these traditions are forms of civilization, we must now look upon both of them with a critical eye. I, for one, do not pay much attention to whether candidates call themselves "socialists" or "capitalists." I only pay attention to the specific policies they promote and how those policies move the current situation or don't move the current situation toward Eco-Democracy.

All our experience has taught us that the broad rules for any economy are made by government and that this government rule-making needs to be independent of the power of the economic players. If the biggest players on the economic playing field control the governmental referees, that is anti-democratic, and always unfair. People who are clear about that for a football game still go blind when fair rule-making and enforcement is applied to the role of government.

A democratic government in an eco-democracy sets the rules for the economic playing field in accord with the values of the demos, rather than that of the individual players that are competing in the economic game. Without such an arrangement, there is no solution to the ecological crisis, nor are there optimal solutions for values like: equity, safety, pure food and drugs, voting fairness, infrastructure repair, structural racism, sexist oppressions, or any other significant challenges that face the whole society.

## HOW CAN THIS VAST TRANSFORMATION BE DONE?

Both capitalists and socialists have implied or stated that we begin by reforming the economic structures first, assuming that the political and cultural structures will follow. In actual history, however, the rise of both capitalist and socialist societies came about by first making big changes in our basic social ideas—only then could they build the political power to put the new economic systems in place. In other words, our vast social revolutions typically begin with a few people, who then become more and more people experiencing a full cultural revolution in their sensibilities and practical visions and attitudes. These larger numbers of awakened people then capture enough political power to restructure the economic fabrics.

Certainly it is true that the move from civilizational empires to eco-democracy societies is coming about by a cultural awakening of millions of people all across the planet. The next step, already in process, is for those millions to become hundreds of millions of people who are inspired and organized for the capture of political power from those always-present reverse-gear reactionaries aided by the always-present foot-dragging incrementalist thinkers. Full speed ahead toward an eco-democracy empowerment is now in the offing for those who choose to pursue it. And this is a political pursuit not just a nerd-level discussion.

Capturing political power is always a tough fight against desperate and powerful forces, but realism is on the side of completing these fresh directions of movement. Eco-democracy is a real solution to what ails us. Realism in terms of exposing and solving the real problems has a power of persuasion that exceeds the clever lying of the reverse-gear forces.

Nevertheless, capturing political power requires a persistent activism that asks more than most citizens are used to enacting. Capturing political power means making inroads into the thinking and excuses of the foot-draggers, the misinformed, and the "I don't care" potions of the population. In the opening stages of a big shift, the reactionaries will have to be pushed off the political playing field and allowed time to complain before they can be expected to consent to be part of the new consensus.

Capturing political power also means a very hot battle with outright liars and conspiracy theorists—dangerous forces that are well financed by reactionary camps of wealth. Ethical realists who are loyal to Profound Reality are called not only to sideline these forces from overt political power; we must unravel every message of their lying ideologies—hopefully, leaving these destructive forces a minority of foolishness along with the Flat Earth Society. This sternness is not the same thing as dismissing all conservatives. There are always things that need to be conserved. And a conservative critique of unrealistic futurisms can be part of the fight for realism. I will say more about these complexities in chapter 19, on the love of justice.

When visionary forces have captured political power and kept it for a while, they can use that power to do ecological and economic restructuring. In addition, visionary forces can use their political power to complete the cultural revolution and do the hard work of offering healing to those portions of the citizenry who feel contempt for political power, or who are reluctant to think through and use their power to make social changes.

In the beginning of any big social change, winning hearts and minds for the truth of these necessary shifts in social practice is the top priority, and it remains so after achievements have been won. The scholars, the revolutionaries, the contemplatives, the schools, the media, the news outlets, the courts, the lawyers, and the street protests are all key pressure forces that can reshape the public consciousness and counter the brash lies that support the status quo, as well as the go-slow incrementalism. Our Christian ethics strongly supports the vision that trusting the truth is on the side of prompt progress. Indeed, there can never be a return to some great time that never actually was. For example, do we really think that the U.S. population can or wants to return to a Confederacy of White nationalism combined with an authoritarian government ruled by the super rich? This racist and anti-democratic side of our U.S. national character is a weakness in relation to the sword of truthfulness that we can wield against such corruption.

## WHAT DO WE MEAN BY A "POST-CIVILIZATION CHRISTIANITY"?

Jesus was born in the era of civilization, and the entire history of Christianity has, until now, taken place in the context of the civilization mode of society. Today, with the social mode of civilization being replaced by whatever we will call it, we confront another turning point for Christianity. As we noted about post-patriarchy and about the Earth era I called the Anthropocene, post-civilization also confronts Christianity with challenges to change.

We now have, for the most part, civilization-styled forms of the Christian religion. This is vividly illustrated by the hierarchical ecclesiology of the Roman Catholic Church—pope, cardinals, bishops, clergy, and laity. With the possible exception of the Quakers, Protestants did not abandon the hierarchical mode of organization; at best, they only moderated the hierarchical form with elements of democracy and congregational power. The typical hierarchical church organization may have been useful for serving the Middle Ages and even the Protestant era, but it will be a handicap for the organization of Christian communal life of the post-civilization period to come. In fact, a Christianity that clings to the civilization mode of organization for its own community life will become out of sync with the coming age.

Luther did some meaningful critiques of these hierarchical Christian forms when he called the pope of his day "the anti-Christ," and when he spoke of "the priesthood of all believers." But in Luther's ecclesiological practices, he only made small changes from the old hierarchical models. He gave the communion wine as well as the communion bread to the laity. He preached servanthood over social status for the role of the clergy. Nevertheless, clergy retained their hierarchical status within Luther's religious culture. Perhaps such changes were all we should expect of Luther in his time, but the future practices of Christianity will require a more complete priesthood of all believers if we are to be fit for the task of dismantling civilization and assisting in the replacement of civilization with a post-civilization form of social organization.

H. Richard Niebuhr taught us that repentance on behalf or our society begins with (1) turning our own back on the old patterns, then (2) changing those patterns in our own communities of action, and finally (3) leading in the transformation of the whole society.[2] If our post-civilization formation of Christianity is to follow that wisdom on repentance, we will be required to think through having a thoroughgoing democracy within the community of committed Christians. Our view of leadership within this next community of Christian practice will work to overcome the clergy-laity split in which the clergy stand on some sort of protected pedestal and the laity are viewed as second-class members of the Christian community.

Many groups in our culture have already developed some clarity about having an organic leadership that emerges from within the group, rather than having leaders imposed upon our local expressions by a hierarchy of supposed experts. In other words, each group of active Christians will have roles of leadership that each group has created for itself. Each local group then plays a similar role by sending representatives to the next larger scope of decision-making. Ancient tribal societies accomplished this manner of creating leadership; it is only civilization-enculturated people like us who find this pattern difficult.

---

2. See the last section of H. Richard Niebuhr's essay "The Responsibility of the Church for Society," recently published in *The Responsibility of the Church for Society and Other Essays*.

## HOW DO POST-CIVILIZATION CHRISTIANS LIVE IN THE REMAINING ERA OF CIVILIZATION?

Basically, Christians will be outsiders within these decaying societies of the civilization-mode of social life. Post-civilization Christians, in both their common life and mission, will be prophetic exemplars. Christians will occupy the prophet's outsider role. Many other religious and secular groups will take on this outsider role as well.

This new day of Christian living will take our thinking about the separation of church and state to a whole new level. Never again can we suppose that we live in a Christian nation. Indeed, we can announce publicly and decisively that there is no such thing as a Christian nation—that the concept of a Christian nation is as silly as a Christian toothbrush or a Christian sewage system. A Christian empire may have been appropriate for Christians in the Middle Ages, but that has now become obsolete practice. Indeed, it has become more a cause for warfare than for progressive achievements.

Of course, there are nations that might be called "Christian-majority nations," just as there are "Muslim-majority nations." But Muslims too are going to have to get used to the idea that there are no Muslim nations. Jews will have to get used to the idea that there are no Jewish nations. In order for a nation to be a viable social construct for the twenty-first century, a nation's overall constitution (its covenant of basic social understandings) will need to welcome to its geography the contributions of many different religious practices. Christianity can be one of those many contributors, and Christians can do this anywhere on Earth. But conquering geography for a Christian practice must—I want to say "shall"—cease to be Christian practice.

If we are to create a working and peace-loving order of society, a similar challenge must be addressed to all religious communities. State authority and power must cease to be used to champion any specific religious practice. A state's values of human well-being and justice must become an ongoing consensus built from the interactions of many religious modes of exploration—an interreligious or secular process must be our context for settling civil matters. An eco-democracy depends upon these "musts."

Christians can consider themselves called to make their important contributions to every person, whatever their religious practice. Post-civilization Christians do not serve Christians only. Christians will provide services to everyone, and Christians will expect other religions and secular movements to provide services to them. Whatever our religious practice or lack of one, we all confront the same historic challenges, and can assist each other to face these challenges and make appropriate responses.

Obviously, this shift is a shift in the general society as well as within the various religious groups. Attempts by a politician to rile up a particular religious group to serve as their base of support must be deemed as far more than unseemly. Governments in this imagined future will protect nonviolent religious discussion with legal restraints. Surely our religious tensions and disagreements can be played out as cultural dialogues, rather than political, economic, or military warfare.

Though the above changes make Christians *outsiders* within the social establishment, Christians can also be persons who work diligently *within* the established social worlds as transformers of these social worlds. The role of being a minority who are *not of this world* but who are, nevertheless, *in the world* as a transformative force of this world is not unfamiliar in Christian history.[3]

This relationship with the world means a new day not only for a next Christianity but also for all other Reality-trusting religious bodies. In this imagined new era, Christians and others will be content with awakening real persons to more realistic responses that derive from the freedom, love, and trust of that Profound Reality that includes the profound consciousness essentially present within each of us. Accessing this essence entails becoming patient and skilled with building consensus among many religious and secular perspectives for choosing our common norms, customs, and enforceable laws.

Manifesting such a future will also entail viewing the moralities and laws that govern each continent, nation, or state of people as never more than a consensus of those democratic citizens who choose to occupy that geography. We will, of course, continue various struggles among the world's religions and philosophies over what is true about our human essence. But attempts to force a sectarian morality, belief, or practice upon a whole population will need to be considered illegal. Obviously, these social conditions are still to be established. This shift is another emergency with a long time line.

---

3. See H. Richard Niebuhr's *Christ and Culture* on this topic.

# WHAT DO CHRISTIANS DO TO ASSIST REPLACING CIVILIZATION WITH POST-CIVILIZATION?

This is a tough question with many answers and many points where answers are still lacking; nevertheless, I am going to list six guidelines. These guidelines are more radical than they may sound, for they are to be done in the context of a larger aim than the repair of a civilization—such as a better capitalism or a better socialism. I am assuming the replacement of civilization.

There is nothing wrong with reforming civilization, but if we are seeking to achieve true post-civilization solutions, then we need to make a distinction between two kinds of reforms: (1) reforms that are steps toward achieving a post-civilization more than they are steps toward preserving a civilization, and (2) reforms that are steps toward preserving a civilization more than they are steps toward achieving a post-civilization. Our vision of a long-range future that replaces the civilization mode of social organization with a new mode of social organization affects our choices for the overall strategies and priorities of our specific actions. Here are my six guidelines:

1. It is important to *read the best books* on this massive shift toward an eco-democracy in order to train our minds in real-world facts and possibilities. Anything by Naomi Klein, Charlene Spretnak, David Orr, Martin Luther King Jr., Robert Reich, Bill McKibben, or Jim Hightower is a place to begin. These authors can provide key elements of the vision we need to choose the hundred other books we might consider reading and teaching. Also, I recommend a book that I, along with coauthors Ben Ball, Marsha Buck, Ken Kruetziger, and Alan Richard, spent four years pulling together. We called it *The Road form Empire to Eco-Democracy*.[4] This book is a broad summary from numerous social vision sources. "Empire" is a descriptive word for civilization and "Eco-Democracy" is a descriptive word for post-civilization.

2. It is important to *converse with, share life with, and talk straight with persons outside your or my peer-group.* People tend to live inside their own silos of opinion. How then are the fans of obsolete visions going to change, if no one talks with them other than members in their own silo? Black people, White people, Hispanic people, young people, old people, women people, men people, other genders, other religions—they are all

---

4. *The Road from Empire to Eco-Democracy* is an iUniverse and an Open Book edition of Berrett-Koehler (2011).

people who are bending history and deserve to hear about possibilities for doing their history-bending better. Why is such attention to the whole populous necessary? Let us be bold to claim that Profound Reality is calling all people to build these needed Eco-Democracy societies. And we are all called to help call those who are still awakening to this huge calling.

3. If you are an *educator*, know that your job is a revolutionary post in this transition. If you are not an educator, consider becoming one. Lies are the weapons of choice of the enemies of this transition. Neutralizing lies is half of the job of progressive success. And this neutralizing includes providing a vision of workable progressive alternatives.

4. *Start or join a business* that is doing the right things with regard to some need of an eco-democracy future.

5. *Become a community organizer,* which includes *voting and campaigning* for the most progressive representatives on every ballot. Politics is not primarily about voting for people you like, identify with, or agree with on every topic. Politics is about choosing the best of the given alternatives and getting still better alternatives on the ballot. "Perfection" is not a word that can be used in political activism. Politics is about deep ambiguities and choosing the best among partly good alternatives. And this messiness does not change. There is no use waiting for a less messy time to start voting, organizing, or running for office.

6. *Organize or join various protests* that seek to support what is needed and stop what is corrupt. Protesting is the way we vote between elections. We must not underestimate the effectiveness of protesting—both against the corrupt and for the better. Many people will not read the right books or watch the right TV. Large protests reach into the underbelly of the needed citizen re-education.

Why are these familiar tasks unique for Christians to do? They are not. Any awakening person, whatever their religious practice or lack of one, are called to these tasks. Christians join this larger company of the servants of realism and contribute their specific gifts. Sometimes a fresh prophetic insight will be contributed by a Christian participant in some cause. But fresh realism crops up from a wide variety of sources, places, and people. It will be one of our vital next-Christianity gifts to notice these places and people and support them.

One thing is unique for Christians to do—to transform Christian practice from its medieval and modern dead ends. I will explore this topic more in the next chapter.

# 17

## The Dead End of Christendom

... we Christians must stop trying to have the kind of future that nearly sixteen centuries of official Christianity in the Western world have conditioned us to covet. That coveted future is what I mean when I use the term "Christendom"—which means literally the domination or sovereignty of the Christian religion. Today, so understood, Christendom is in its death throes, and the question we all have to ask ourselves is whether we can get over regarding this as a catastrophe and experience it as a doorway—albeit a narrow one . . .[1]

### WHAT IS CHRISTENDOM?

THE ABOVE QUOTATION IS from the forward of a remarkable sixty-six-page book entitled *The End of Christendom and the Future of Christianity* by Canadian theologian Douglas John Hall. What does Hall mean by the term "Christendom"?

The first three hundred years of Christianity was lived in an environment of intermittent persecutions. This was changed in 313 with an edict made by Constantine the Great that released Christians to raise money, build churches, pay leaders, and thereafter become a powerful cultural institution that settled into a core partnership with the political hierarchy. In time the emperors and kings were pressured into being some sort of Christian, and the Christian churches were pressured into being cultural servants of these worldly powers. The bishops of Christianity made this bargain with open eyes, but the style of Christian life

1. Hall, *End of Christendom*, ix.

together and the Christian mission became significantly different from the first three hundred years.

Along with Hall, I will be using the word "Christendom" to mean the post-Constantine form of Christian communal life and mission. The Christendom social form of the Christian religion flowered with Augustine (354–430). The Christendom form was fully established before and after Thomas Aquinas (1225–1274). Martin Luther (1483–1546) and the Protestant Reformation split Christendom into many fingers of this basic Christendom form of religious fabric. Protestants tend to think of ourselves as something different from medieval Christianity, and indeed it is meaningful to speak of a "Protestant era" in Western Christianity. Nevertheless, wherever a religious community of Christianity takes on the task of making a scope of geography "Christian," we are carrying on the imperial form of church organization that Hall is calling "Christendom." I will also be using that word in this way.

The Christendom view of being a Christian was viewed as being a member of a culture that primarily practiced a Christian religion. The governing powers in Christendom actively promoted and defended some version of the Christian heritage. Wars were fought between various Christian-majority cultures—Roman and Eastern, later French and Italian, and still later Roman Catholic and Protestant. All these combatants thought that their form of Christianity needed to rule the culture of some region of geography. Here is what we have learned from that history: as long as any religion and any governing authority choose to be partners in sustaining a specific religious culture for a specific geographical scope, religious wars continue.

In the twenty-first-century United States, many forms of religion now exist within a secular state—a governance that is thought to be a defender of all religions and a promoter of none. Nevertheless, we still have Christians who call for this nation to be a "Christian nation." We even say Christian prayers at secular meetings attended by practitioners of other religions and persons of no religion. Such thinking and practices are expressions of the Christendom oppression. "The Dead End of Christendom" means that in our still-unwinding future a vital expression of Christian practice will and must renounce, in a thoroughgoing way, any form of Christianity that views itself as a geographical culture that must war with other geographical cultures.

In other words, Christians are called to never again promote a Christian rulership for any geographical scope of humanity. Christians must also be active in denying this privilege to any other religious group. Any politician of whatever practice of religion who suggests or promotes such a rulership needs to be opposed by Christians and by every other religious group. This revised attitude protects the integrity of religion as well as the quality of our religious conflicts and the contributions of religions to one another and to the overall societies in which we dwell.

The New Testament writers challenge Christians to preach the good news to the ends of the Earth, but this does not have to mean making people practitioners of a Christian religion. The good news is not, "You need to become a Christian." The good news is, "You can repent of your estrangements that are killing you with the sickness of your own despair, and thereby be restored to the realism and joy of your authenticity."

Spreading this good news is indeed part of the mission of those who sincerely take on a Christian practice. Those who receive this good news, however, can begin living their lives in a more authentic manner without having to become Baptists, Methodists, Lutherans, Presbyterians, Episcopalians, Roman Catholics, or any other denomination of Christendom. Receivers of the good news can remain Jews, Muslims, Buddhists, Hindus, or any other religious practice, or none or many. Christians, at large, have been confused about this in the now-ending period of Christendom. Consciously or unconsciously, Christians have been imperialists and bigots with regard to the Christian religion. We have supposed that persons can only reclaim their authenticity and live it appropriately if they do so within a culture of so-called Christian beliefs, moralities, and communal life. Even if we agree that there are many forms of good Christian community, we do not have to be a member of one of those communities in order to be a beneficiary of the Jesus Christ revelation.

## CHRISTIAN BIGOTRY

My mentor of many years, Joe Mathews, spoke in one of his talks about his own Christian bigotry. After mentioning his history with Roman Catholic bigotry, Jewish bigotry, prejudice against Blacks, and prejudice against non-Western cultures, he continued with these words:

> The deepest bigotry I have is my Christian bigotry, which has to do with the faceless coming. It is the retention of 2000 years of Christian bigotry that is in the depths of my being. If by God's grace we had not stumbled upon the contentless Christ, it would

have been absolutely impossible for me to see this deepest of all my prejudices. What I mean is, not only have I grasped that Contentless Happening as that without which consciousness or consciousness of consciousness can finally take place in a person; but I have found myself a defender of creeds, a defender of liturgy, of ecclesiology, of theology. Only God can open the eyes of a bigot, and I believe that my eyes are being finally opened, giving me the opportunity to repent of the most fanatical form of prejudice there is.[2]

I take this to mean that Profound Reality is revealing to us in this new era the relativity of all cultures and all religions. Seeing this moves us into a new context where living within the singular silo of Christian thought forms is no longer feasible for a totally honest person.

## CHRISTENDOM AS A CULTURAL TYRANT

Perhaps the most controversial challenge in accepting the end of Christendom is giving up the hope of having a top-level cultural power for the Christian religion. This can seem like a loss of success by those who still cling to the notion that a Christian culture or a Christian nation or a Christian planet is a viable objective. For Christianity to simply be one religious community among other religious communities can seem humiliating to those who still cling to the "good ol' days" of Christendom. But this loss of standing in the overall culture is not a loss of power for the living Body of Christ. This loss of standing can mean a strengthening of the radical gifts of the Christian revelation, not only for Christian practitioners, but also for everyone in each culture where Christians live.

Perceptive theologians have always known that the Body of Christ was not synonymous with a religious denomination of Christendom. A denomination is only a temporal structure that, at best, inspires and houses a number of people who may manifest the spirit quality called the "Body of Christ." A denomination can be replaced with a better "housing" for Christian practice without any loss of power for the true "Body of Christ." Throughout the rest of this book, I am going to show how an appropriate new "housing" for the Christian religion can increase the power of our Christian witness and the power of our social justice impact.

2. Mathews, *Binding History*, 1:248.

## THE POWERFUL WEAKNESS
## OF THE BODY OF CHRIST

Social weakness was a quality of Jesus himself, as well as of his first disciples. Our willingness to risk everything for the truth of our authenticity and the authenticity of our species has been and will always be a weak cultural position that, nevertheless, manifests the power of Profound Reality. Let us contemplate this "weak power" with regard to a future sociological shape for our Christian presence by reflecting on these verses from Matthew 5:10–12 (my very slight rewording of the Revised Standard Version):

> Blessed are those who are persecuted because of their authenticity,
> for their joy is participation in the coming Reign of Realism.
> Blessed are you when people insult you, persecute you. and falsely say all kinds of evil against you because of your participation in this Body of Christ living.
> Rejoice and be glad, because great is your reward in true fulfillment,
> for in the same way they persecuted the prophets who were before you.

Seeing the full truth of these verses is seeing that subverting the norms of a deluded society with truth is always costly, but it is also healing of self and others at the same time. Embracing the courage to be an authentic presence is a social power.

I will conclude this section with another quote from Douglas John Hall, the closing words of his book *The End of Christendom and the Future of Christianity*.

> Our Lord's metaphors for our community of witness were all of them modest ones: a little salt, a little yeast, a little light. Christendom tried to be great, large, magnificent. It thought *itself* the object of God's expansive grace; it forgot the meaning of its election to *worldly* responsibility.
>
> Today we are constrained by the divine Spirit to rediscover the possibilities of littleness. We are to decrease that the Christ may increase. We cannot enter this new phase without pain, for truly we have been glorious in this world's own terms. It seems to many of us a humiliation that we are made to reconsider our destiny as "little flocks." Can such a calling be worthy of the servants of the Sovereign of the Universe?

Yet if that Sovereign be the One who reigns from the cross,
could any *other* calling be thought legitimate?[3]

## THE PEOPLE OF GOD—A MISSION OF LOVE

Rather than think of "the People of God" as a nation or a culture or even a
religion, we can embrace the vision of H. Richard Niebuhr in viewing the
People of God as a response to God—that is, as a response to Profound
Reality with the sort of realism that can be said to lead the whole of humanity in fresh steps of realism. "The People of God" can now point to a
secular dynamic built into the structure of human history—namely, the
fact that small groups of people can and do lead the whole of humanity
into fresh terrains of realism.

This means that "the People of God" refers to a response to Profound Reality as that Reality is met in temporal history. So the People of
God is a movement of humans in time rather than merely belonging to a
religious community. If we belong to a Christian religious practice in
order to access, be, and nurture our lives toward being the People of God,
we do so for the sake of a *movement* or *mission of love*. Here is a diagram
that defines this response, this action, this mission of love:

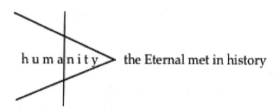

Humanity is divided by the vertical line in this diagram into (1)
those who move to the front of this wedge—symbolizing those who see,
care, and respond to Profound Reality as Profound Reality is actually met
in the ongoing events of social history and in the ongoing events of our
personal lives; and (2) the larger portion of humanity who remain passive
or reactive in the supposed safety of the familiar tenets and behaviors of
the current general culture. This is a sociological line dividing two actual

3. Hall, *End of Christendom*, 66.

social responses of our species, and it is also a decisional line that runs through each human.

Each of us as persons participate on both sides of this line. With some aspects of our being we may respond to Profound Reality, and with other aspects of our being we may not. With some parts of our time we may respond to Profound Reality, and in other parts of our time we many not. Persons who never respond to Profound Reality are a limiting case. And those who always respond to Profound Reality are the other limiting case. By far most of us (perhaps 99 percent) live somewhere in between these two extremes. We actually decide, moment by moment, "yes" or "no," whether to take on the intense action of realism. Also, there are big turning points in the whole of a human life—times when a person's overall approach can switch from one of these two general directions to the other.

In every case, being the People of God is a gift we receive from Reality. Not being the People of God is a rejection of fuller life for some lesser pattern of living that we ourselves have built or copied. This is why being the People of God may be said to be a humble surrender, while not being the People of God can be viewed as an arrogant hubris. Responding to Profound Reality is accepting a gift of realism, while not responding to Profound Reality (withholding, fleeing, fighting) is an achievement for which we can take full credit.

Choosing to not be the people of God is the option being pictured when the mythic Adam and Eve violate their essential innocence by eating from the tree of the knowledge of good and evil. All of us are indeed experienced members of being that fleeing part of humanity who, consciously or unconsciously, have fled from authenticity into our cultural memes along with the human crowd. Each of us has done that retreat in our own way, and we are also full members with the most grievously obvious retreats of humanity in fleeing our birthright of being the People of God.

All these radical sounding statements have to be made in order to make clear that "the People of God" does not point to someone's cultural eliteness, but to a dynamic in the structure of human history that we do not have to create, or change, or do anything to improve. We can simply choose to let the People of God be activated by Profound Reality in the course of our opportunities to abandon our own estranged lives. And this is true for every human, whatever religion they practice or don't practice.

## RECREATING THE CHRISTIAN RELIGION

Religion is a human creation and a temporal social practice on the same level of temporality as fire departments, highways systems, and means of sewage disposal. Good religion does assist humans be more open to accessing the gift of their profound consciousness, but that deep human authenticity must never be called "religion." So, the words "religion," "Christian religion," "Buddhist religion," or any other practice of religion must never be used to point to the everlasting presence of the People of God. Religion is a temporal practice invented by humans, perverted by humans, restored by humans, improved by humans, misused by humans, just like every other social process. A religion is never perfect, and never everlasting. The People of God, however, is perfect—no improvement is needed, no reform is ever required.

The People of God is a dynamic of history built into the structure of the cosmos; it is sheer holiness, sheer enlightenment, sheer Holy Spirit. The People of God is, however, a sociological manifestation of response-able human living. Those humans who are responding to Profound Reality being met in history are "the People of God" and "the Body of Christ," when those powerful symbols are properly used. Such a fresh and radical view gives these biblical symbols a wider meaning than commonly supposed.

In this wider view, the People of God is not a culture or a cultus of people. The People of God are those humans who hear and follow the prophetic voices. They are those who see the revelations of Profound Reality and obey them. They are those who create responses on behalf of their own authenticity and on behalf of the alienated human species is which we all share.

Members of a Christian denomination or a specific congregation are, at best, "sinners saved by grace"—that is, people who are open and responsive to becoming ever more expressive of our human essence—our People-of-God potential, our Body-of-Christ humanity. What Christian theologians have called "sanctification" is forever present and an endless process. We "move on to perfection," as John Wesley insisted, and yet we never arrive, as Martin Luther and others were also quite clear. The temporal person can manifest the People-of-God dynamic, but his or her refusal to do so is also always present in temptation, if not in actualization.

Nevertheless, our essential humanness can be awakened, accessed, nurtured, and sustained through the practices of a good Christian religion, or any other good religion or any good secular practice that genuinely prepares us to access our essential humanity. Any practice, whether it be categorized as secular or religious, that can move our awareness to the starting gate of Profound Reality's gift to us, is good religion. In such thinking, we are developing a new definition of what is "religious." Any practice whatsoever that assists us to be more likely to experience Profound Reality and live from that awareness is religious by this new definition of being religious.

The "true church" or "spirit church" or "invisible church" are phrases used to point to the ever-present response to Profound Reality—the mission of love to God and neighbor, the trusting response to Profound Reality and to every temporal reality that neighbors us. This primal response is always being made by some members of the human species. This response is natural to us. This response is our essential humanity. All of these august names point to this essential humanity: the People of God, the Kingdom of God, the resurrected Body of Christ, the Lord of Lords, the Son of God, and the expected Messiah who has already come.

So, if we understand that these wild symbols of the Christian revelation point to something much deeper than practicing a Christian religion, what does it then mean to practice a Christian religion? Why would we want to do so? Especially, why would we participate in taking on the difficult task of reinventing a relevant, vital Christian practice for our time in history?

Part of the answer to such questions is that any good religion is a practice that assists us to open ourselves to the advent of our essential humanity, our People-of-Profound-Reality participation. A Hindu practice is a good practice if it assists us to enact our authentic humanity. If that happens, that Hindu practitioner joins "the People of God," joins "the Resurrected Body of Christ," even though such phrases are not used in traditional Hindu practice.

A Christian practice can have gifts that a Hindu practice neglects and a Hindu practice can have gifts that a Christian practice neglects. And in both cases these gifts can be about provoking participation in the mission of love, the Body of Christ, the human essence, etc.

I am going to underline two important assumptions: First, *revitalizing Christianity will be a gift* to the overall role of religion on planet Earth to make human-essence participation more likely for humans in any culture, place, and time. Secondly, *the Christian gift is the already being given*, however fragmented or contorted. For the rest of this chapter, I am going to describe a series of sociological shifts from Christendom to a next sociological mode of Christianity—shifts that are appropriate to giving a viable and vital next Christianity its needed impact. Here are my titles for these five shifts:

Ending the Clergy/Laity Split

Renouncing the Edifice Complex

Exiting Christian Culture

Building a Communal Cultus

Theologizing in a Post-Christendom Manner

## ENDING THE CLERGY/LAITY SPLIT

Not only does a future post-Christendom Christian community need a strong focus on twenty-first-century Christian theologizing, but this new Christianity also will require extensive communal, sociological, and ecclesiological transformations. I mentioned in the last chapter how overcoming the clergy/laity split is needed in relating to the post-civilization, post-hierarchical leadership trends. For the last seventeen centuries, Christendom has organized itself hierarchically—with leadership fabrics operating from the top down, rather than the grassroots out into the larger scopes of order and responsibility. (There have been a few exceptions, like the traditional Quakers, that prove the rule.)

To imagine a Christianity without clergy is difficult for many people. Overcoming the clergy/laity split means a radicalization of Luther's priesthood of all believers. This means never again speaking of "lay theologians" or "lay leadership" or "lay orders," or "lay" anything. Every Christian becomes a pastor of Christianity. Baptism and ordination become the same ritual. And this ritual, however we choose to celebrate it, will then be about an adult choice for both women and men who grasp themselves as called to the Christian life and ministry. I don't know how that ritual is to be conducted; nevertheless, it has become increasingly clear to me that the future members of a vital next Christian communal practice must not be divided into two layers of people—clergy and laity, pros and amateurs, fully educated and pablum fed.

This deep shift means no more bishops, cardinals, popes, district superintendents, and other power players that are not fully accountable to local circle of co-pastors. A full-blown post-Christendom community will have meetings that cover various geographical scopes, but the wider-scope meetings will be democratically representative of the smaller scopes of decision-making. Such power dynamics will work in both directions—grassroots to planet and planet to grassroots. While working out the detailed democratic structures of a next Christianity will be accomplished by future generations, we can begin now inventing that full democracy for the Christian community.

Such a democracy is also applicable for the entire societies of planetary humanity. Christians are called to be the part of every society that is sensitive and responsive to the needs of future human societies across the planet. This Christian calling includes being among the first, rather than among the last, on democratization. Therefore, the sort of democracy that a next Christian practice develops now for its own community life needs to be an exploration and demonstration of the sort of democracy needed by the world in general.

For now, this new Christian polity can begin in local circles of twelve or less people, no one of whom is a clergy. All members are co-pastors to one another, and co-pastors in joint mission to their geographical "parish of responsibility." I will say more about the notion of "parish" in later chapters, but for now I want to focus on a new polity for the internal life a local twelve-or-less-person circle of co-pastors.

"Everyone a leader" and "everyone a follower" is a vision that cuts deeply into the lives of both ex-clergy and ex-laity. These ex-clergy will come to view themselves as mere servants, not commanders or privileged in any way. They will be among the nurtured as well as being a nurturer. They will be among the led and well a being a leader. All the old subtle entitlements will be gone. This more humble role will also eliminate any need for pretense—to believe something that he or she does not believe or to be something that he or she cannot yet be. If an ex-clergy person has an extensive theological education or is skilled with some important methodology, such gifts need to be respected by the whole circle of co-pastors. At the same time, similar respect needs to be paid to the gifts that every person brings to the co-pastors circle. For example, a circle member who may not be a theological innovator or a historical scholar of Christianity may bring methodological skills for intimate interpersonal relations that are deeply needed for the optimal functioning of this new Christian practice.

The challenge of this new polity to the ex-laity is also huge. The old role of subordinate laity will also need to be thoroughly renounced.

This will include ex-laity taking responsibility for becoming competent in Christian understanding, methodological skills, and the fabrics of nurture and mission of the Christian community. Being a co-pastor to every other co-pastor is exactly as challenging as it sounds. For the ex-laity this entails the elimination of pretenses having to do with submission to authority. For both laity and clergy, the style of the co-pastorate means being open to specific next steps in spirit journey, skill learning, and leadership calling. In other words, a style of here-and-now realism will pertain to every member of the co-pastorate.

I believe that this fresh sociological and interpersonal style for a next Christian community has equal importance with theological excellence. In chapter 21 I will offer a further description of the internal life of these co-pastors circles, how they function, and the overall importance of honest, intimate relationships among these co-pastors.

## RENOUNCING THE EDIFICE COMPLEX

In addition to excellent theologizing, and overcoming the clergy/laity split, I see another big change in the overall relationship between the next Christian communal life and the general culture. The current institutions of Christendom are weighed down with money-raising for huge buildings and the salaries of those who staff and raise the funds for these buildings. The financial load of those buildings has become a heavy anchor on Christians who want to conduct a fully Christian mission to the planet and have a fully Christian sort of nurture to assist them to do that profound mission. "Do we need those buildings?" This has become a reasonable question. Christians got along without church buildings for the first three years of Christian practice.

After the Constantine edict of 311 CE, it became possible to replace pagan temples with Christian ones. Elite sources of wealth were redirected to build wonderful architecture and pay for the staff needed to maintain and use those buildings for a wide range of cultural purposes. Mediaeval church buildings were not merely worship places for the Christian community; they were cultural centers, education institutions, art museums, spirit therapy, entertainment places, and even political power centers for bringing depth intelligence to the rulers of those times. However effective that practice was for those centuries, today our having ten or more Christian denominations each financing a building in almost every neighborhood is not the same game that Augustine and others were playing.

The strategy of Augustine (having wealthy Christians finance clergy, monks, nuns, and buildings in neighborhoods throughout Europe) was a successful means of evangelism. This placed a sociological presence of Christian action in almost every city and village. This was how people in those centuries came to hear the good news, and how we today came to hear of Christianity. Nevertheless, our thanks to those medieval warriors of the faith does not imply a necessity to mimic them. We live in a different time. Christendom is now an obsolete model for Christian organization. This is a primary axiom assumed in all the proposals in this book.

Today a set of steeples in each neighborhood is simply not needed for the mission of the emerging Christian community. A local co-pastors circle can meet in a living room. When larger meetings are needed, circle members can use hotel meeting rooms or even stadiums. Our liturgical icons can be moveable setups, instead of architectural wonders. That change would save a lot of money, which could be diverted to more controversial and revolutionary types of activities and accomplishments. It boggles the mind to think about what the tithes of a million people could do without the cost of church buildings.

We will continue to have economic issues. We will need to spend money on staffed offices, theological school buildings and their faculty, as well as continent-wide projects of organization and action. We will need good supervision of those tithes, serious financial responsibility, and accountability to a locally based democratic organization. I will say more about regional and continental polity and financing in chapters 22 and 23.

Often our imagination for Christian revitalization has gone no further than giving better sermons and doing better theologizing in those forty-five-minute Sunday morning adult classes tucked in before the choir members leave for the main event. This limitation of our imagination within the existing congregational framework will not do. Such minimal modifications will not be enough to build the enthusiasm needed to continue financing the "edifice complex" of this now-out-of-date Christendom. Also, the introduction of better contemporary theology will soon reveal how unneeded these buildings are for carrying out the true mission of a twenty-first-century Christian practice.

So what happens to those beautiful Christian temples across Europe and across the planet? The "best" of them have or can become museums of religion, like Stonehenge, Angkor Wat, and other religious buildings of the human cultural past. Many of these Christian buildings have little lasting value as religious art; therefore, they may be transformed for other uses.

## EXITING CHRISTIAN CULTURE

We often use the word "culture" to mean those processes of a human society that are not economic processes or political processes. We sometimes use the word "culture" to mean a whole society—like Texas culture or a culture of microbes. "Subculture" usually means part of some larger cultural whole—such as, the United States being a subculture of the English-speaking group of nations. Within the United States we can distinguish subcultures like the Deep South, New England, West Coast, Rust Belt, etc. We also speak of religious subcultures like Catholics, Jews, Muslims, etc. But in my redefinition of religious practice, I find it misleading to view a religious practice as a subculture or a culture.

I feel very strongly that a next Christianity need not aspire to be a culture or a dominant religious culture of some geographical region. Christian practice can take place within any culture. And culture can come to mean something general and secular, not modified by religious terms like "Muslim culture" or "Jewish culture" or "Christian culture." Christians need to begin thinking of culture like toothbrushes and automobiles. There need not be a Christian toothbrush or a Christian automobile. Why should there ever be a Christian culture? Every culture can contain many religions, and many versions within each family of a given religion. A religion is just a practice that a community of people do. These practitioners can of course influence the overall culture within which they are living.

Within each religious community there will be an internal culture of symbols, myths, icons, rituals, thoughtfulness, communal organization, historical roots, perhaps scriptures, key practices, ground rules, ethics, key themes, and more. But this internal common culture need not be imposed upon the general culture. It can simply be a contribution to the general culture for those interested in making use of it. Perhaps the word "cultus," rather than "culture," is the word to use to distinguish the common life of a religious community from the common meaning of a human "culture." I am avoiding the word "cult," for it tends to mean an escape from Reality or from history. I certainly do not see a next Christian cultus being an escape, but rather a contribution to a whole overall culture, polity, and economy of whatever society a Christian community lives and works among.

Everyone who practices a vital version of Buddhism is a cultus within some or many subcultures and cultures. Similarly, everyone who practices a vital version of Christianity is a cultus within some or many subcultures and cultures. Being a religious practitioner is being a member of a religious cultus. Even if a particular person emphasizes solitary practices, those practices likely derive from this or that cultus.

The next Christianity that I am envisioning will feature a strong emphasis on being a cultus, and on being loyal to that cultus, its history, and its future. Group religious practices have an importance in Christian heritage that a number of other religions do not emphasize. A disciplined communal life with regular group nurture and a common mission to the world is central to this vision of a viable and vital next Christian practice that is promoted as a replacement for the many fingers of Christendom.

## BUILDING A CHRISTIAN COMMUNAL CULTUS

I envision the members of a next Christian cultus meeting weekly for the nurture and study they need to serve their local place as well as the relations of that place with the history of the planet. All the persons attending these meetings need not be scholars of the topics being introduced in this book. Each member will, however, be open to the ever-deepening calling with regard to his or her own specific journey toward awareness and competence in the topics being summarized in this book.

For example, all members of a viable and vital next Christian cultus will need to be interested in religion as a disciplined practice that assists humans to access their authenticity. Awakening Buddhists may speak of this deepening as "enlightenment." Awakening Christians will surely use symbols like "healing from despair" and "resurrection" in their understanding of this ever-deepening authenticity. This difference in symbols indicates the presence of a different cultus, even though the awakening experienced is extremely similar. Christians may be studying Buddhist writings and adapting them to their cultus's symbolism. Buddhists may be studying Christian writing and adapting them to their cultus's symbolism.

The next Christian cultus I am imagining will focus most on the study of a relevant sort of twenty-first-century Christian theologizing.

I envision an ongoing study of both Old and New Testaments moving toward a deep familiarity with these texts and finding personal inspiration though a relevant use of this old poetry for illuminating their lives in today's world. I see a need for familiarity with Christian history and a contemporary use of that history. I also see an ongoing study of the future of Christianity—its symbols, its rituals, its communal life, and its mission to this ever-changing set of societies.

Each of these topics is a boundless source of wisdom compared to what each of us now have, ever will have, or even want to have. I am not implying for every Christian a graduate-school knowledge of all these topics. At the same time, I am implying the development of basic sensibilities that are even more profound than the typical graduate-school knowledge of these topics. Persons with a graduate-school grasp of these topics can still be without the core awarenesses to which all members of a vital next Christian cultus need to aspire.

This study vision also implies clarity and commitment to the Christian viewpoint on Profound Reality's friendliness as revealed in the cross-resurrection revelation. This includes a commitment to a life of utmost realism in what is good for me personally and good for every other human being. This faith (or trust in the trustworthiness of Profound Reality) implies a personal passion for ongoing study and an endless openness to ever-deeper experiences within our own spirit journey toward an ever-greater authenticity in the light of these Christianly viewed topics.

For this next Christian cultus, I also envision developing the skills needed for living our true being within the historical context of our times. This means an ongoing study of the historical times in which we are proposing to shape our Christian presence, formulate our witness to the Christian revelation, and construct our contributions to social justice.

Furthermore, these next Christian co-pastors will need interpersonal skills for communicating our authenticity in our words, deeds, and presence. Many secondary skills will also come into play: how to do depth study rather than simply scan written material, how to lead an existentially grounded group study, how to provide leadership to a Christian group as well as to our roles in the world at large. We will need skills in consensus building, skills in ethical thinking, and skills in social action based on our profound consciousness viewpoint.

If we are to be an effective Christian cultus, we will need skills in theological method and skills in biblical interpretation. We will need skills in holding our Christian bearings as we also open ourselves to a personal appropriation of other-than-Christian religions, as well as to the wide field of Christian expressions.

All this can seem overwhelming to any one person, but the cultus I am imagining does this ongoing learning together. It is the whole disciplined group that becomes skilled. Each person participates in these skills within a weekly-meeting community of others—each of whom become skilled in some or most of these ways. And I am envisioning each local group being associated with larger groups that meet quarterly, supported by annual events that nurture a continent of local groups.

Each individual is on his or her own spirit journey and skill journey, and that person can be joyous within his or her own current place in their journey. The members of this next Christianity need one another's assistance for the ever-fuller participation in their ongoing journey. Christianity is a communal religious practice. Even our solitary practices are done within this strong communal context. This communal emphasis is not optional; the resurrected Body of Christ is a communal reality—manifesting in history as a specific temporal form of life together plus a specific temporal form of being a presence within the societies of the world.

## THEOLOGIZING IN A
## POST-CHRISTENDOM MANNER

I credit Søren Kierkegaard (1813–1855) with initiating what has become my method of Christian theologizing. The Eternal and the temporal are not, for him, two competing realms. Rather, the Eternal and the temporal are two aspects of each fully experienced experience. A full experience of the temporal is also an experience of the Eternal. And an experience of the Eternal takes place only within the temporal flow.

In the wide-ranging thought of Paul Tillich (1886–1965), the Kierkegaardian stream of theological thoughtfulness was expanded in a myriad of ways. Dietrich Bonhoeffer primarily distinguished himself from Karl Barth by a somewhat greater love for Kierkegaard. H. Richard Niebuhr criticized Kierkegaard for his lack of communal and sociological focus; nevertheless, Richard and his brother Reinhold were debtors to Kierkegaard in spite of also being powerful continuations of Walter Rauschenbusch's social gospel. Martin Luther King Jr., a student of Reinhold Niebuhr, was another theological and political source for me. Rudolf Bultmann, also a philosophical and theological child of Kierkegaard, was surely one of the most innovative New Testament scholars who has ever lived. His method of yoking the New Testament revelation with contemporary post-Kierkegaardian philosophy is a gift that may keep on giving for the next thousand years.

The wonders of Kierkegaard were first introduced to me by Joseph Wesley Mathews, my teacher, mentor, friend, and co-worker for twenty-three years. His enrichments of this flow of theologizing have also kept on given to me in spite of many other enrichments since his death in 1977.[4]

The absence of women's names in the above characterization of mid-twentieth-century Christian theologizing does not mean that women were absent in that period. It does mean that their lives and thought were kept somewhat invisible by the enduring hangover of the patriarchal climate that dominated that period of Western culture. I will illustrate the presence of women in that theological period with these two names: Simone Weil and Suzanne de Diétrich.

Simone Weil was a prominent writer and activist of Jewish background who become deeply inspired by the New Testament and certain elements of Catholic heritage. She never joined the Catholic Church because she could not tolerate its severe patriarchy, but we can count her as one of the Christian revolutionaries of that period.

Suzanne de Diétrich was more a teacher than a writer, but she excelled in taking the neo-orthodox Protestantism of Karl Barth and Emil Brunner into the French universities, giving students of that period a Bible-centered and Word-of-God witnessing that provided a viable alternative to both crass fundamentalism and weak literalism, as well as to the popular Marxism that appealed to the youth of that time and place.

In the late twentieth and early twenty-first century, increasing numbers of women have picked up important aspects of the ongoing theologizing task. For example, Dorothee Soelle (1929–2003),[5] a personal student of Rudolf Bultmann, expanded upon the sociological, and especially the political, implications of Bultmann's more personal "true deed" of existential faith. Her thoughtfulness deals directly with a sociological interpretation of the New Testament and the faith implications

---

4. My special thanks to John Epps and others for pulling together Mathews's talks with these two books: (1) *Bending History: Selected Talks of Joseph W. Mathews* (provocative talks from a radical churchman in the later half of the twentieth century) and (2) *Bending History: Selected Talks of Joseph W. Mathews Volume II* (societal reformation toward a new social vehicle).

5. Soelle, *Political Theology.*

for opposing totalitarianism. These considerations still have implications for our revolution in the sociology of Christian mission and life together.

Also, the still-living Sabine Dramm (1943–) wrote a book entitled *Dietrich Bonhoeffer: An Introduction to His Thought*.[6] This book is not only a remarkable text for correcting many misunderstandings of Bonhoeffer, but it is also a creative theological work on the part of Dramm herself. I highly recommend this book and this Christian theologian. I count her as another enricher of the Kierkegaardian stream of theologizing.

I have also benefited greatly from the spirit feminism so powerfully presented by Charlene Spretnak.[7] She provides needed emphasis on interpersonal relationships and on integrating into our spirit practices the gifts of Buddhism, Native American spirituality, Jewish and Catholic liberation theology, as well as her historical work on the Great Goddess contributions from our human antiquity. Along these lines, I also owe a debt to Mary Daly for her powerful critique of patriarchal Christianity. And there are many other spirit feminists we might cite.

I want to mention, along with Martin Luther King Jr., the Black liberation theologian James H. Cone and especially his book *Risks of Faith: The Emergence of a Black Theology of Liberation 1968–1998*. In the larger picture of liberation theology, I want to mention the Latin American Gustavo Gutierrez and his book *A Theology of Liberation*.

On ecological Christian ethics I owe a huge debt to Thomas Berry. I enjoyed a personal friendship with him as well as being an avid reader of his many books. My ecological ethics has been further filled out by David W. Orr, in his remarkable book *Dangerous Years: Climate Change, the Long Emergency, and the Way Forward*. He does not present this book as a theological book, but it breathes his religious sensibilities. To this list I want to add Naomi Klein, especially her *This Changes Everything: Capitalism vs. the Climate* and *No Is Not Enough: Trump's Shock Politics and Winning the World We Need*. Her view of social justice is deeply biblical.

In addition, I want to add to this stream of theologizing Thomas Merton and his vast contributions to the contemplative aspects of Christianity. And finally, I want to add my many Buddhist teachers, especially Eugene Cash and Joseph Goldstein. A. H. Almaas and his group of teachers have also opened the wonders of the East to my Western roots. And I could mention a couple dozen other persons who have been crucial

6. Dramm, *Dietrich Bonhoeffer: An Introduction to His Thought*.

7. Spretnak, *States of Grace* is a classic book. For an even deeper dive see *Relational Reality*.

to my theologizing projects of thoughtfulness, teaching, and writing. All these persons and others have added energy to this Kierkegaardian stream of Christian theologizing.

I mention these specific sources to illustrate how Christian theologizing is an ongoing project for each of us who joins this next Christian cultus that I am attempting to describe. I do not consider my own theologizing as done. I do not promote myself or anyone else's thinking as the last word in Christian theologizing. Indeed, "having a theology" sounds like a misunderstanding to me. I have perhaps settled in on a method of theologizing, yet even that method is open to improvements. Nevertheless, in order to create a vital next Christian practice, we must, in my view, join this Kierkegaardian stream of Christian theologizing that is so basic to the vision I am laying out in this book.

In my own written contributions to this stream of theologizing, I have focused on simplifying these more scholarly writings for the ordinary member of a next Christian cultus. My books are written to be useful study books for weekly-meeting Christians. I have also focused on incorporating into this stream of theologizing the ever-new social, ethical, and spirit-level challenges of our fast-moving times.

This chapter is but a sketch of the topics that pertain to moving beyond Christendom to a viable and vital next Christian practice. In the remaining five chapters, I spell out in more detail my description of the qualities I see needed for best conducting an outgoing mission and intimate life together of a post-Christendom Christian practice.

# 18

---

# Witnessing Love and the Echo of Eternity

WITNESSING LOVE HAS TO do with being a means of grace. Grace itself is given by Profound Reality, not manipulated by human beings. Grace is a happening that turns Profound Reality into God the Merciful. This is not a change in Profound Reality, but a change in the person receiving the grace. A grace happening is an awakening to the love of Profound Reality for us, and a discovery of our capacity for a dedicated love toward Profound Reality and all the neighbors with which Profound Reality is neighboring us.

The Christian theologian who has been most helpful to me in describing the grace happening is Paul Tillich. In order to discuss what it means to be a means of grace, I am going to review Paul Tillich's description of the grace happening in his remarkable sermon "You Are Accepted." Here is the moment, according to Tillich, when he says that we can hear that enigmatic voice of the Ground of Being saying to us personally, "You are accepted."

> Grace strikes us when we are in great pain and restlessness. It strikes us when we walk through the dark valley of a meaningless and empty life. It strikes us when we feel that our separation is deeper than usual, because we have violated another life, a life which we loved, or from which we were estranged. It strikes us when our disgust for our own being, our indifference, our weakness, our hostility, and our lack of direction and composure have become intolerable to us. It strikes us when, year after year, the longed-for perfection of life does not appear, when the

old compulsions reign within us as they have for decades, when despair destroys all joy and courage.[1]

It is at moments such as these that we can hear, "You are accepted." We can hear Profound Reality because these are Profound Reality–experiencing moments—moments when our estrangement from Profound Reality is becoming conscious to us, when our falseness is being revealed by the truth, when escape into illusory comforts have been undermined, when the worst of our unrealism appears to haunt us. At such moments Profound Reality speaks to us, "You are accepted." And by "you" is meant the you that has been awakened to your estrangement from Reality. There is no other you than the estranged you—the you who in this moment is aware of your estrangement. So, who or what is communicating this healing message to us? Here is Tillich's text on that:

> Sometimes at that moment a wave of light breaks through our darkness, and it is as though a voice were saying: "you are accepted." *You are accepted* by that which is greater than you, and the name of which you do not know.[2]

Tillich is saying that "you are accepted" is a *far-more-than-words* message that is being said to us by Profound Reality. And what does "Profound Reality" mean? It means, according to Tillich, "that which is greater than you, and the name of which you do not know." So, what do we do now? Tillich gives us this answer:

> Do not try to do anything now; perhaps later you will do much. Do not seek for anything; do not perform anything; do not intend anything. *Simply accept the fact that you are accepted.*[3]

First of all, Tillich is making clear that we do not have to do anything to make ourselves worthy of this enigmatic acceptance. This acceptance is a gift, a 100-percent gift. Nothing is required, other than simply accepting the gift. Tillich is implying that we can refuse or ignore the gift. For example, we can insist on earning what we get, or we can take our gifts for granted, or we can simply space out on this whole topic.

Tillich clarifies that this acceptance of our acceptance is a deed done by the person being healed. This deed of accepting acceptance completes the grace happening. We must not assume that Tillich's list of "do not's"

1. Tillich, *Shaking of the Foundations*, 161, 162.
2. Tillich, *Shaking of the Foundations*, 162.
3. Tillich, *Shaking of the Foundations*, 162.

excludes the "do" of accepting our acceptance. Grace does not become a happening in our lives without our participation. This is a very important point: the entire activist nature of the Christian life depends on viewing the grace dynamic in this complete way. Otherwise, the essential human is viewed as a robot of determining forces in which we have no share. I have heard it said that John Wesley spoke of grace as 100 percent a gift of God and 100 percent a deed of faith. Rudolf Bultmann also clarified that this faith (trusting our acceptance) is "a true deed" enacted by our own essential freedom.

It is of utmost importance that our understanding and description of the grace happening includes the intentional participation of the healing person. Christian theologizing must insist upon the importance of our human decision of surrender to God's forgiveness. This is a full surrender to making a fresh start, based on that commitment to being forgiven of our estrangements. The decision to accept our acceptance is not a minor part of the grace happening. Without our choice to accept forgiveness, grace has simply not yet happened to us. This does not mean that Reality has ceased being merciful; it means that we are not accepting that mercy. The grace happening is a fundamental transformation in our entire relationship with the whole of living—a shift from seeing Reality as despair producing to seeing Reality as love of us. This shift requires our full participation and results is a new life—a more realistic life, a life that presses on to the full perfection of Christ Jesus.

Letting Reality be love for us is a *choice* on our part. It is the biggest choosing or doing that a human being can do. It is the opposite of most of the doings that humans do much of the time. The ubiquitous not doing of such trust among all human beings is called "sin" in the classical Christian language. In the grace happening, sin is healed—that is, we let Profound Reality be instead of creating our own invention of reality that we like better than Profound Reality.

The grace happening that heals despair includes letting be what *Is*. We let our profound consciousness be. We let our wonder be. We let our estrangements from wonder be. We are able to let our estrangements be because we are also surrendering to the acceptance of our estrangements by Profound Reality. We can let our estrangement be because we are letting our forgiveness be, which includes a fresh start in realistic living.

Starting with what *Is* means facing up to our estrangements from Profound Reality and thereby being closer to our in the Ocean of Wonder. Being in wonder means being closer to our true self, which is a

wonder-dwelling being. Building this forgiveness bridge across our estrangements to our essential *holiness of wonder* requires only this simple
deed: *accepting the fact that we are accepted.* This means trusting that the
wondrous Profound Reality holds no grudges against us for our years of
fighting with and ignoring the Profound Reality in which we dwell.

Using New Testament metaphors, we can say that in facing Profound Reality, we are facing an always-loving "Parent" who has run down
the road to meet us as we are coming home to Reality. "You are welcome.
You are accepted. A feast is being prepared for you." Herein is the meaning of Jesus' Prodigal Son parable.

Tillich calls the entire happening he has described an illumination
of the Christian word "grace." This happening is the healing of humanity
that is rooted in the Jesus Christ revelatory event. We Christians need
to not only recover this Christian heritage of grace, but also learn that
this healing process does not happen only to practitioners of a Christian
religion. The grace happening has nothing whatsoever to do with forcing
ourselves to believe unbelievable or believable Christian doctrines. Grace
is simply a deeply human event applicable to all humans in all cultures,
at all times, and in all places. Our authentic Christian God-talk, our
sermons, our theologies, and our Christian doctrines came into being
to share with one another (and with whomever else was ready to listen)
how it is that we are healed from the most important disease that ails
all human beings—namely, our estrangement from Profound Reality, the
sickness that is despair and that leads to our open experiences of despair.

Tillich is clear that life after grace is an ongoing surrender to God's
forgiveness. The life after grace is not a life of imposing our ideals or morals upon the real situations we face. Here are two more Tillich paragraphs
from the "You Are Accepted" sermon that provide the flavor of life after
an event of grace:

> In the light of this grace we perceive the power of grace in our
> relation to others and to ourselves. We experience the grace of
> being able to look frankly into the eyes of another, the miracu-
> lous grace of reunion of life with life. We experience the grace
> of understanding each other's words. We understand not merely
> the literal meaning of the words, but also that which lies be-
> hind them, even when they are harsh or angry. For even then
> there is a longing to break through the walls of separation. We
> experience the grace of being able to accept the life of another,
> even if it be hostile and harmful to us, for, through grace, we

know that it belongs to the same Ground to which we belong, and by which we have been accepted. We experience the grace which is able to overcome the tragic separation of the sexes, of the generations, of the nations, of the races, and even the utter strangeness between man and nature. Sometimes grace appears in all these separations to reunite us with those to whom we belong. For life belongs to life.

And in the light of this grace we perceive the power of grace in our reunion to ourselves. We experience moments in which we accept ourselves, because we feel that we have been accepted by that which is greater than we. If only more such moments were given to us! For it is such moments that make us love our life, that make us accept ourselves, not in our goodness and self complacency, but in our certainty of the eternal meaning of our life. We cannot force ourselves to accept ourselves. We cannot compel anyone to accept himself. But sometimes it happens that we receive the power to say "Yes" to ourselves, that peace enters into us and makes us whole, that self-hate and self-contempt disappear, and that our self is reunited with itself. Then we can say that grace has come upon us.[4]

If we accept such forgiveness for ourselves, we accept it for the whole of humankind. To accept forgiveness for ourselves means accepting forgiveness for our worst enemies, our unfaithful friends, our stupid advisors, everyone. And forgiveness means a fresh start. Everyone on Earth is called to face this possibility of a fresh start. Reality accepts us for a fresh start in realism.

## BEING A MEANS OF GRACE

Being a means of grace means being the Word of God to our neighbors, but it does not mean being Profound Reality. God (that is, Profound Reality) alone provides the grace. We provide nothing but the proclamation that Profound Reality (that Ocean of Wonder or Land of Mystery) is trustworthy—trustworthy to forgive us humans, who are not trustworthy in being realistic.

We can proclaim this trust with our being and with our doing, as well as with our words. We can, in that sense, be the Word of God, for if we trust Profound Reality to be our God, we are the Body of Christ.

4. Tillich, *Shaking of the Foundations*, 162–63.

But even if we are articulating well a Word of God to some well-known neighbor, we do not control the grace dynamic. Profound Reality, our God, is in control of the grace dynamic. The grace dynamic is built into the structure of the cosmos. In our witnessing love to other humans, we are merely obedient to the grace dynamic. Whether or not grace happens to those persons is entirely out of our control. What is out of our control is both (1) Profound Reality being encountered by these persons and (2) the freedom of those to whom we are witnessing to say "yes" or "no" to the trustworthiness of Profound Reality.

So what does it mean to be a means of grace to another person or persons? This can be described in relation to the three aspects of grace that Tillich outlines:

| Grace Happening | Means of Grace |
|---|---|
| Aware of despair | Exposing despair |
| Dawning of acceptance | Proclaiming acceptance |
| Accepting acceptance | Beckoning trust |

## Stage 1: Exposing Despair

This is the first aspect of being a means of grace. It may be the case that the person to whom we are bearing witness is already aware of their despair. If so, we can move on to aspects 2 and 3 of witnessing love. But if not, we will need to take on the task of aiding in the exposure of despair in the consciousness of the person or persons to whom we are witnessing. This does not mean telling someone they are in despair. It means assisting them to discover for themselves the despair in which they are, in fact, dwelling. This is not a matter of argument or opinion. It is a matter of discovery or, we might say, "revelation." No healing of the despair disease can take place unless the disease is consciously experienced as despair, whatever name they might have for it. Experiencing despair is not a bad thing; it is a doorway to realism. Experiencing, rather that fleeing despair, is part of the healing process that witnessing love is out to assist.

In doing witnessing love we may talk about thoughts and behaviors, but we are not out to change minds or change behaviors. We are spirit doctors out to heal lives of their despair sickness. We speak to despair and its reign over human lives not to condemn despair as if it were a moral failing, but to heal despair as a sickness that blocks realism. *Each person has to experience his or her own despair sickness and view his or her own specific walk through the doorway indicated by that despair.*

We who witness can speak with authority, but the authority does not reside in our own specific words or presence. Our authority is occasioned by an *echo from Eternity* that enhances our meager words. We are out to reveal or point out that Eternity is "speaking" to the life of the person to whom we are witnessing. It is not our words that are the healing agent, but the echo of Eternity heard by the despairing person. For example, when the prophet Amos says, "Let justice roll on like a river," he is assisting the king and the rich aristocracy to hear something like this from Eternity: "You are complicit in your neglect of the poor and your excuses are bogus."

The witnesser may have stern words to say, but the witnesser is also standing by the listener as a healing servant of Eternity. The witnesser knows that the realization of one's actual despair is part of the grace process. Despair is the doorway to health. Despair is part of Profound Reality's trustworthiness in opposing life-killing illusions. The witnesser counts on Profound Reality (God) to tell the listener about the specific despair sickness that is afflicting the listener.

The witnesser, in order to be most effective, needs to be able to distinguish between (1) assisting Eternity to heal and (2) taking out moral outrage on the behavior of others. A despairing state will usually be accompanied by destructive behaviors, most of them immoral (some of them moral in a destructive fashion). Witnessing to the Word of God is about healing lives, not condemning bad behavior, even though bad behavior may play some role in the discussion.

If you are a writer, politician, or voter who is out to create social justice, you will often be called upon to condemn bad behavior as a means of arguing for laws that restrain that behavior. The Christian mission of creating social justice has different rules of operation than witnessing love. Justice must be established in laws, principles, and norms that restrain selected human behaviors. Witnessing love is not about law or restraint; it is about healing the sickness of despair. A good understanding of the writings of Paul's New Testament letters clarifies this topic. Paul is clear that healing (grace) is not about obeying laws, however useful the laws may be. Healing is about dying to despair sickness in order to be resurrected to the life of Christ Jesus, our authentic humanity.

Justice is not something that Eternity gives. Justice is invented and accomplished by human beings. Healing despair is accomplished by Eternity. A Christian witnesser is out to assist the despair sick person to allow Eternity to heal their sickness.

I want to underline once more that *healing begins with a person seeing his or her own despair*. This seeing is not a mere intellectual insight. This seeing is seeing with our own profound consciousness a specific disrelationship with Eternity. Therefore, a witnesser may first need to assist a witnessee toward an awareness of his or her despair sickness in order to assist Eternity in healing of that sickness.

We are not doing witnessing love if we are helping people escape from experiencing their despair. As witnessers, we do not join in the lies that are making the despairing person despairing. Such collusion can make the sickness worse. We assist the sick to consciously notice their despair, and perhaps feel that despair more intensely.

Yet, consciousness of despair is only the first stage of our cooperation with Profound Reality. The second stage of healing can follow immediately. If the person to whom we are witnessing is already aware of his or her despair, the witnesser can move immediately to stage 2 of witnessing love. For example, if a despairing person is prepared to jump out of a high window, the witnesser has no need to increase despair awareness. The witnesser can move straight to stage 2.

## Stage 2: Proclaiming Acceptance

The second aspect of our cooperation with Profound Reality in being a means of grace is pointing out the truth that Profound Reality is accepting each of us for a fresh start, no matter how unsatisfying or downright horrific our living has become. Proclaiming the word of Reality's forgiveness or acceptance is actually saying that this despair sickness is a doorway to authenticity—to an absolutely fresh start in human living. Your despair-ridden past can be over, gone, done with, and a new and more realistic life can commence now without further ado. Truly living in the present moment already contains a fresh start. That fresh start is being indicated by the despair being experienced. And the despair is overcome by walking through it.

Our despair may be over a past that is now gone, or our despair may be over an impending future that seems too much to bear. A fresh start means that realistic living is knocking on the door. Right now, a healed self can step forth into that realism.

We must not suppose that this message will be easy for everyone to accept. The hearer of this cosmic word of acceptance may experience a collection of excuses that he or she has been clinging to for decades. For example, a person may be hearing voices in his or her head that say, "There is no fresh start for me, with my limitations, my rotten karma, my misshapen personality, my rotting culture, my lousy family. My case is hopeless." Or, "Anyone who claims my life is now received for glory must be crazy." Or, "People like me need more time to work this out." Or, "I don't believe that such healing is possible for anyone; we are all stuck in our crap."

The persistent witnesser is not taken in by such ways of *taking offense* at the proclamation of forgiveness. "Now is the time of healing," proclaims the acceptance proclaimer. "Now is the arrival of the Reign of Reality. Only now! Not tomorrow! Not yesterday! Now and only now!" The witnesser is simply asking the despair-afflicted person to look and see that *true humanity is not gone—that an entry into the glory of realism is at hand.*

## Stage 3: Beckoning Trust

However difficult it may be to assist people to let go of their despair over their despair and accept their acceptance, the third role of witnessing love beckons people to take this leap. The essence of this third aspect of witnessing love is well told in Luke's story about Peter walking on the water. This is a parable about walking on the wild and windy waters of our real lives. Here is how this story goes. The disciples are in a relatively safe boat sailing on frighteningly wild water with the wind set against them. Jesus comes to them walking on this wind-swept water. At first they think this cannot be a human being—a ghost perhaps. But Jesus assures them that it is just he, himself; humans can do this sort of thing—that is, walk on the wild waters of their wind-swept lives. "Well then," said the ever-bold Peter, "ask me to come to you on the water." "Come on then," said Jesus. In those three words, "Come on then," we have a perfect description of what I am pointing to with the phrase "beckoning trust."

The power of this *beckoning-trust* witness is increased if the witness-er is, like Jesus, walking on the wild water of his or her own life. This trust quality in you or in me makes our words, however fragmentary, more powerful in beckoning a despairing person to hear Eternity communicating with this human being to trust walking out on his or her realism. I have used the metaphor "echo" to suggest this experience. In the case of witnessing love, the *echo of Eternity* is much stronger than the witnesser's witness. The witnesser, even Jesus, vanishes as the source of the beckon, and the trusting human is leaning independently on Profound Reality, not on the witnesser. This means that even a deeply estranged witnesser can nevertheless be Eternity's occasion for echoing the beckon.

Such a healing event is never the end of healing events. The depth of complexity of our despair can be greater than any one healing event restores. And our human capacity for creating ever-new estrangements of despair-destined foolishness is almost boundless. Nevertheless, even a small healing in an otherwise deeply estranged person is a big victory for realism and an event worthy of the name "Christ event." The beauty of the Christian heritage is that it has named such events as revelatory of the essence of Profound Reality and, thereby, of what "sin" is and what "righteousness" is. Sin is unrealism in attitude, thought, and action. Righteousness is realism in attitude, thought, and action. And godliness is nothing more amazing than a devotion to Profound Reality and all its temporal manifestations.

## COMMON-LANGUAGE WITNESSING

The implications of Paul Tillich's theologizing about the grace happening is seldom spelled out fully with regard to the universal application of this threefold happening called "grace." We are describing a healing event that not only shows up in Christian heritage, but in Buddhist, Hindu, Jewish, Islamic, and other heritages. This truth means something very important for interreligious dialogue. In the light of the widespread appearance of the grace happening, we can enrich our conversations among these long-standing religions.

Also, this universal view of the healing event expands our view of Christian witnessing. We can do witnessing love without using the Christian language. We may do 90 percent of our witnessing love using whatever language is being used by those to whom we witness. A plumber comes to your house in a grim state of despair over his whole profession, or with having to do this grimy job today in this house with you. Let's say you see his state, and you say something to him that might provoke some healing. Perhaps you say something about how much you appreciate him doing this. "What would we do without people who know how to fix things? This is something I can't do; thank you for so much for coming." In such a moment when we are seeking to be helpful, we will find ourselves guessing what might work to provoke this universal dynamic to take effect. We don't actually know the Word of God for this person at this time; we simply risk some well-chosen words. Being an effective witness requires creative freedom applied to the living moment. And we count on Eternity's echo to our feeble words.

Whatever we say, we can be sharing with this plumber that his life is significant in spite of the fact that he is telling himself something to the contrary. If he breaks down and tells you about his wife's illness or his children's jail time, you just listen. You just let him experience his despair and his despair over his despair. After listening a while, after identifying the humanity of this authentic despair, you might say something simple about how his honesty about these topics is a doorway to a realism and the happiness that honesty fosters. You say whatever works for that person at that time.

You don't have to know if it works, or for how long it works. You just have to know that this plumber is a child of God with whom you are having a relationship, and that you possess a familiarity with God's Word that can be articulated in a billion ways—one of which might get an echo from Eternity on this particular occasion for this particular person in this particular moment in his or her life journey.

Simply not despising people and not ignoring them may function as a sort of witnessing love for them. Perhaps your empathy as a fellow human being in this moment may open in some future moment the possibility of saying something that has more potential for healing. Or maybe not. In witnessing love, we can never be certain about the results.

Perhaps you are a teacher of some sort. You can do witnessing love in any classroom working with whatever topic you find yourself scheduled to teach. Perhaps you have prepared a curriculum of some sort for such occasions that has witnessing love built into it. Witnessing love, using language other than the language of Christianity, can be built into any curriculum. Lives can be healed without using your treasured Christian vocabulary. You can use other language to point to the experiences that Christian language has illuminated for you.

In a conversation with friends about a movie you have just seen together, you may have a wonderful opportunity for providing an informative witnessing love about the lives of each of you stirred by that movie. No Christian language is needed for this conversation. Or it may be useful on some occasions with some people to use and interpret Christian language. Nevertheless, the number of witnessing opportunities that are possible for using an other-than-Christian language is vast.

## CHRISTIAN-LANGUAGE WITNESSING

Why do we need Christian-language witnessing as part of our responsibility as Christians? Here are four reasons that have impressed me:

1. *If we are Christian practitioners, we need an effective use of the Christian language to complete our own nurture.* A competent use of this language is needed to root out of ourselves inappropriate misuses of this heritage. We need to grasp the deep meanings and power of the Christian symbols if we are to effectively conduct any of our ongoing witnessing love. The Christian language can serve us in an ordered and useful way to undergird our living, including our witnessing love.

2. *Billions of people misuse the Christian language.* This grim fact confronts those of us who are awakening Christian practitioners to the following truth: *no one else is going to clean up this mess.* Someone needs to take on this task of assisting billions of people find relief from the despair-causing misuse of the Christian language. This includes also taking on the task of learning and teaching an appropriate use of the Christian language as a means of healing estrangement in the deep life of humanity.

For example, the way that the best of contemporary Christian theologizing understands the word "sin" as despair sickness assists us in a conversation with someone who uses the Christian word "sin" in a moralistic manner. Morals are, of course, an important part of every society, so Christians will need to deal with the moral life of societies and of individual persons. But the word "sin" as developed by the apostle Paul, Luther, Kierkegaard, Tillich and others has a different meaning than moral violations. From these sources, sin is viewed as a deep sickness that can warp the lives of individuals and whole societies like a plague. To say that sin can be "forgiven" means that this dread sickness can be healed—that your and my and everyone's whole life can have a fresh start in realism. This can be quite liberating for people trapped in a moralistic theologizing that results in harsh contempt for self and others.

Similarly, Christian-language witnessing can direct attention not only to healing despair-producing, moralistic misunderstandings of sin, but also to many other grimly misunderstood words in the Christian vocabulary—"grace," "love," "God," and so on.

3. *Building a viable and vital next Christianity requires a valid recovery of the Christian language.* The Christian language is our only route to the original revelation of Christianity. Though I can talk about the essence of that revelation in other languages, this revelation has been placed into human history using a specific language of enduring symbols. To continue this heritage as a healing resource, the original symbols need to be freshly broken open to the depth of Profound Reality that originally called forth these symbols. To do this ongoing refreshment, transformation, and updating, we need to read and understand the New Testament. That set of historical writings can again breathe the Word of Eternity called "Jesus Christ," which is not merely a historical personage but an event in history that reveals something critical about the Abyss of Mystery we also call "God." The event of Jesus, seen as the Messiah, is about a revelation in the human relationship with this incomprehensible Eternity. So understood, Jesus Christ is an ongoing eventfulness of revelation that keeps on revealing the essence of that always-mysterious Profound Reality. We need the New Testament witnesses using their specific language to continually test our own understanding of this enduring revelation.

4. *The Christian language holds a contribution to interreligious dialogue.* As Christian practitioners who have learned witnessing love at the feet of Jesus, we are responsible to keep the Christian-language understanding of witnessing love in being in order to take our seat at the table of interreligious dialogue and cooperation. This will not be easy, but with the freedom being bestowed upon us through the healing of Profound Reality, all such things are possible. We can build a relevant and vital next Christianity that can converse with other Profound Reality-revealing practices.

We must not minimize the healing power that the ministry of Christian heritage has occasioned in so many rare times and places. That healing power can still be contributed to human life. We will need to take pains to correct the horror created by the many Christian perversions and misapplications that have done so much damage. But abandoning Christianity because of those perversions is not necessary. We can take responsibility to correct those flaws and assist this heritage to rise again and sit at the table of realism.

In chapter 9, on the meaning of revelation, I outlined how the Jesus Christ event is not the only revelatory event that peers into the Eternal Abyss of Mystery and sees a friendly face. The exodus from Egypt is an event of revelation that has never lost its power to speak to us of the unimaginable possibilities of realism. The Islamic writings that fill the Qur'an also comprise a revelatory event of great magnitude in this "Western" set of lasting monotheistic religions. As Christians, we have some identity with all these religions, and some responsibility for this entire scope of monotheistic offerings.

If we want to take the journey of consciousness to the core of our human reality, we cannot avoid choosing specific religious practices for our own personal nurture. But these practices are not our spirit destination; they are just our own preferred rowboats to the universal shore of our profound consciousness of Profound Reality. Paul Tillich calls this "directed toward the Unconditional."[5] Each religion at its best deserves the title "religion" only if it is a member of this fleet of rowboats that assist us on this universal journey to our true home. Our true home is a polarity of the Unconditional and the conditional, the Infinite and the finite, the Eternal and the temporal, Heaven and Earth. Witnessing love, appearing within in whatever set of religious practices, is a means of grace intent on opening us to echos of healing grace coming to us from our true home.

## A FINAL WORD ON WITNESSING LOVE

It will require of us a bit of skill to do Christian-language witnessing. Just reading the Bible in a new way can be challenging. But there is nothing magical about it. And no one needs a Master of Divinity degree to do witnessing love. We have learned hard things before—chipping flint for arrowheads, working a computer, figuring out our taxes, giving birth to a baby, living within our budget, keeping a job, making a marriage work. One of my gym companions appears to know the story of almost every football player in the NFL. Surely learning to do Christian witnessing is no harder than that, provided that we are already taking the leap of Christian faith ourselves. If we are dying to our ego loyalties and being raised to our Body of Christ liberty, then we are ready for the task of

---

5. Tillich, *What Is Religion?*, 76.

witnessing love—namely, witnessing to our own living companions concerning our own trust in radical realism.

Finally, let us keep firmly in mind that we are only a means of grace, and that the *Eternity of Profound Reality* stands ready to *echo* our feeble witnesses.

# 19

## The Mind of Commonality
## and the Love of Justice

> What is ethics then? Certainly not a morality, nor more
> complexly, a hierarchical system of values. Ethics instead is a
> form of thought that breaks open and through the totality of
> thought. Ethics appears as the immediate and urgent call for
> justice from the call of the Other. Ethics is the taking on the
> infinite responsibility, which precedes and exceeds the self's
> limited and finite capabilities.[1]

THIS CHAPTER HAS TO do with how our trust of Profound Reality works
out in our thinking and acting in matters of ethics and social justice. This
chapter may be helpful to those who love justice but have no sense of
how or why the Christian life includes social justice commitments. This
chapter may also be helpful to those who seek to live a Christian life, but
do not see how this includes a sense of justice and a lifetime of participation in matters of social action.

The term "justice" has many different meanings, some of which I
will not be using. The meaning of "justice" that I will be developing will
not be limited to how existing laws are enforced. I will be concerned
with a deeper view of justice that includes a means of judging existing
laws as just or unjust. Such justice is not a mere matter of opinion; it is
a matter of truth—the kind of truth developed in chapter 3 under the
heading: "The Commonality Approach to Truth." I will provide a brief
review of that topic.

---

1. Robbins, *In Search for a Non-Dogmatic Theology*, 137.

## THE COMMONALITY APPROACH TO TRUTH

Justice is a topic that arises in the commonality approach to truth. Justice considerations are affected by the scientific approach to truth, the contemplative approach to truth, and the intimacy approach to truth, but "justice," as I am using this term, also includes and primarily uses the commonality approach to truth.

Justice has to do with social processes—with the manifest forms of cultural processes, political processes, and economic processes—as well as with the ecological processes that sustain our social processes. The question of justice is the question of what manifestation of social and ecological processes works best for all the humans who comprise a given society at a given time in its history. Since our quest for commonality truth is always a work in process, justice is also always a work in process. The fight for justice is never complete. Our definition of justice is never complete. Creating appropriate justice for this time and place in human history is an unending quest.

No view of justice drops down from a heavenly space or from a mental universe of ethical absolutes. Justice is created by humans in accord with a human obedience to Profound Reality within a specific historical time and place.

So, the Bible, the Qur'an, the writings of Plato and Aristotle, or any other source does not settle our current specifications for what is just. Nor do these famous referenced texts even complete our overall definition of what justice is. These sources do deal with topics of justice, and they may stimulate our minds to do better thinking for our time and place—no more no less.

In other words "justice," as I am defining that word, is not laws, principles, or moral norms imposed by human thought upon our current challenges. Justice results from a truth quest by a body of humans discerning what is workable for a given society. In Christian ethics this includes thinking through values grounded in obedience to Profound Reality and thus to what results in creative realistic living within a given social situation and its neighboring forces.

## Love, Power, and Justice

Paul Tillich wrote a whole book entitled *Love, Power, and Justice*.[2] In this book he showed that without various forms of social power that enforce justice, there is no justice. "Social power" can mean many things: popular opinion, cultural norms, economic opportunity, but most fundamentally, social power means politically built laws and their enforcement. "Governing power" is essential in our understanding of justice as a real-world factor. In other words, justice is not mere ideas in someone's head. Justice is an operational social actuality.

Our current culture is flawed with so much individualistic overemphasis that the importance of governing power tends to drop from view for many people. The study of justice means opening our minds to the raw fact that we live and can only live in a society with other humans who must create ongoing formations of social power. Further, social power is always ambiguous. At best, it is restraining the worst impulses of a human population. Unfortunately, the existing social power arrangement may be holding in place laws and law enforcement that express the worst impulses of the human species: classism, racism, sexism, authoritarianism, etc.

It will be the social ethicist's job to define what justice is for some here-and-now situation with justice definitions that are based on love, rather than unlove, neglect, foolishness, and hate. "Love" enters into Tillich's discussion as the third essential dynamic in his trilogy of *Love, Power, and Justice*. "Love" means for him the same dynamic pointed to with the Greek word "*agape*" as used by the apostle Paul. This *agape*, as it appears in the New Testament, is not only an idea in the vocabulary of Christians. It is a Christian attempt to describe a dynamic of *primal care* that is present in that profound consciousness that is given with our essential being as humans. This absolutely crucial understanding of "care" or "love" has already been elaborated in earlier chapters.

This *agape* dynamic of love is present in all human beings, however deeply this essential care has been buried beneath human-created estrangements. Tillich explains how both "just power" and "empowered justice" can only be appropriately manifest in companionship with this dynamic of essential care/love/*agape*. Love of this sort includes a love of social power as a means of enforced justice. To say that we can love our neighbor without

2. Tillich, *Love, Power, and Justice*. See pages 11–17 for his introduction to this topic.

loving with our social power is to misunderstand the nature of that essential human dynamic called "love" in the Tillich discussion.

So, this *agape*/care as it applies to social life is not merely listening with empathy and responding helpfully to individual persons, nor is it simply the manifesting of a Christian presence of acceptance and tolerance. *Agape*/love, when applied to social life, includes some hard-headed power plays of effective strategy and tactics that get results in actual social situations. If we are allergic to possessing power and wielding social influence, we are allergic to the love that Tillich is discussing in *Love, Power, and Justice*.

The meaning of "witnessing love" for others was summarized in chapter 17. This chapter expands the scope of that same love for others in relation to the task of creating justice for a specific historical human society. Such loving use of social power has been neglected by many, perhaps because we are so aware of its misuse. We have also been miseducated into an individualistic overemphasis. There is only one counter to the misuse of social power, and that is using social power to extend love for humanity—that is, using social power to create and establish appropriate justice in the course of social history.

## CONTEXTUAL ETHICS

H. Richard Niebuhr suggested that there have been three basic ways that human beings (at least in Western societies) have done ethical thinking.[3] The first deals with *rights and wrongs* and with *principles and laws* that define what is right and what is wrong. We teach our children right and wrong. We set up laws in our society to define right and wrong for all of us. In our religious instruction, we talk about "universal laws"—the "laws of God" or the "laws of nature." Perhaps we are told that there is a "supernatural law" that has been revealed to us and is contained in our holy book. Perhaps we are told that there must be such a universal order of law for us to use in deciding which of our other principles and laws are right and therefore trustworthy to define what is right and what is wrong in our daily lives. Most of us are familiar with this way of doing ethical thinking. It is the mode of ethical thinking that is predominate in the Bible.

A second mode of ethical thinking is inherited from Greek philosophy. It works with the concepts of *good and evil aims*. This way of thinking

---

3. Niebuhr, *Responsible Self*, 47–68.

is concerned with goals or ends toward which our behavior should move. If we are pursuing a good end, then our behavior is good. We evaluate our laws and principles to be good or bad according to whether or not they are consistent with good ends—safety in our neighborhoods, justice for all races, etc. We are using this type of ethical thinking when we argue about whether a good end justifies an ambiguous means to that end. More often we talk about values: about what values are worth pursuing and about what values are sacrificed by using a given means. When we are asked whether something is good or evil, we may respond with this important question: "Good or evil with respect to what end, or with respect to what center of value?" If we place our nation in the center of value, then "good" is what is good for our nation and "evil" is what is bad for our nation. If we make pleasure our center of value, then "good" is what is pleasurable to us and "evil" is what is boring or painful to us. If such centers of value seem shallow to us, we might ask if there is an absolute center of value that clarifies the relative values of all other centers of value. Theologians like Thomas Aquinas distinguished between our natural ends (survival, food, sex, shelter, companionship) and our supernatural end (our final blessedness). This was a way of answering the question about *absolute values.*

However, for most of us today, the idea of absolute values causes our minds to boggle. Both absolute values and universal laws tend to be problematic for most thinking people today. Why? Because such ideas are part of that two-story metaphysics that has, as we noted earlier, passed away as a meaningful religious metaphor for many, if not most, people. Of course, we still have people who attempt to use two-story ideas like absolute values and universal laws. But such thinking robs us of the clear understandings needed for our best-case ethical thinking today.

In recent centuries we have seen the birth of a third type of ethical thinking. Instead of working (in the first instance) with legal principles of right and wrong or with good and evil ends, this more recent way of doing ethical thinking works with the concepts of *responsible and irresponsible.* The basic question now goes something like this: "Given the *situation* in which we are living, what is the *befitting* response?" A good response is the one that is *appropriate* to the situation. A good law or a good principle is one that fits the situation in which we are now living. Similarly, good ends and good means are those that make a realistic approach to the real situation. This mode of ethical thinking many people are finding more fruitful than the kind of thinking that begins with absolute values or universal laws.

However, this third mode of ethical thinking is most often used in connection with a limited perspective on an ethical situation. For example, the board of directors of a chemical factory might weigh up its situation relative to the cost of materials, the cost of disposal of wastes, the price at which the manufactured product will sell, and the profits for the shareholders, but never weigh up the dangers to human beings and animals in the area, the long-range damage being done to the environment, or the costs to governments and taxpayers for cleaning up the messes. These decision makers may come up with an appropriate response relative to their limited view of the situation. But if this same response were viewed within the larger context of what is going on in the whole community or the whole planet, those chemical factory responses would appear inappropriate.

This example illuminates the need for master contexts of understanding within which our smaller contexts of understanding can be appropriately created. The commitment to realistic living described in previous chapters means commitment to the Wholeness of Reality. Hence, the ethical thinking appropriate to such a profound religious commitment keeps in mind the importance of the largest picture of what is taking place. Treating a small part of Reality as if it were the whole is another way to define idolatry. If we think nationally before we think about the well-being of the whole planet, we are idolizing the nation. If we think about the well-being of our generation before we think about the well-being of all the generations to come, we are idolizing this little narrow piece of life called "our generation." Our commitment to the Wholeness of Reality provides responsibility ethics with an overall reference. The earlier ethical thinkers in our Western heritage were trying to achieve such overall reference with their concepts of absolute values or universal laws. If Christian thinkers are to avoid confusion and build a strong base of ethical consensus among people today, we will need to flesh out our *inclusive God-and-neighbor context* for our thinking through the smaller contexts for actions within our specific life situations.

While our ethical thinking begins with the largest perspective, our action begins locally. We must act where we are located. We cannot act globally. We cannot act in some future generation. We act here and now. But how we act here and now is shaped by how we think through the ethical contexts in which our local action is to be illuminated and our responses chosen. So we first need to begin our Christian ethical thinking with our ongoing planet-wide considerations. Within that planetary context we can then do more specific thinking for our continental scope of issues. Thirdly, within those two contexts we can do our still more specific local scope of thinking and acting. Each of these three scopes of thinking has ramifications for the other two. We are creatures of planet Earth, we reside in a local place, and we are citizens of scopes of geography between the planetary and the local.

Keeping in mind these views of Niebuhr about contextual ethics and with Tillich's views about "Love, Power, and Justice," I move to specific thinking about these three contexts: (I) planet-wide imperatives for century twenty-one, (II) governing the United States of America in 2020 and following, and in the next chapter, (III) considering some guidelines for a social mission of justice in a local parish of responsibility.

## I. PLANET-WIDE IMPERATIVES FOR CENTURY TWENTY-ONE

I will discuss the following four core concerns that I see arising for all humans on planet Earth in this century:

1. The Role of Humans in the Anthropocene Era

2. The Long-March toward Economic Equity

3. The Dream of Democracy

4. Informed Citizens

## 1. The Role of Humans in the Anthropocene Era

The onrushing Anthropocene has been created by the responses of human beings, but it is now a life-and-death challenge to all human beings. In the pre-Anthropocene era, human beings could count on this huge planet taking care of itself in spite of whatever use was made of it by humans, or whatever wastes produced by human action were thrown into the oceans, rivers, land fills, and skies. The wonders of the Industrial Revolution have been real and many aspects of that innovation we will surely want to keep; however, this gift has come to us along with huge downsides.

Humans are now required to correct something that we humans caused. To say that these horrors are too vast to do anything about is an untruth. This will be a huge feat of courage and action, but we have done other huge feats that were thought impossible at the time: the abolition of slavery, winning World War II against fascism, leaving the planet to land on the moon, and even the Industrial Revolution itself has been a huge feat. For us to insist that we are not able to clean up our ecological messes is gross excuse-making, sloth, and cowardice to fight those huge powers that cling to the status quo of endless destruction.

The climate crisis is the core emergency among the many other ecological crises. We have polluted the atmosphere with such huge amounts of $CO_2$ and other greenhouse gasses that we must now phase out our massive fossil fuel burning or suffer untenable consequences. This shift will require a total mobilization. Not doing this shift will result in losses of life we can barely imagine.

This ethical challenge is based on physics and social workability, not on sentiment or idealism. Lack of obedience to the truth of this grim historical necessity is now globally criminal, and needs to be treated as such. A valid Christian social ethics is founded on loyalty to realism in the context of obedience to Profound Reality. This radical realism supports the call to immediate activism in overhauling our energy system. Climate responsibility has become a permanent element in the ecological style of living appropriately within this Anthropocene Era.

## 2. The Long March toward Economic Equity

"Equity" does not mean "equality." Human beings are not equal with regard to any temporal matter. We do not need to expect an exactly equal level of wealth and power in our social allocations. "Equality before the law" can have a workable meaning. And "equal before God" simply means that all differences fade to zero before the Infinite Source of everything. This ultimate equality before Profound Reality provides those of us loyal to Profound Reality support for creating a workable equity among humans and a critique of the "divine right of kings" and other such hierarchical arrangements. Equity can include a high degree of respect for each person, as well as protection, opportunity, and care for every member of a society. The present state of planet-wide social practice is far removed from such equity.

Here are some numbers about the real situation on our planet: the top 1 percent own more wealth than the bottom 99 percent, and a handful of billionaires own more than the bottom half of people around the world—that means 3.7 billion people. This is not equity. Authoritarians around the world promote even further extension of this horrific inequity. Clearly, the main economic issue on planet Earth in 2020 is the inadequate distribution of wealth and power.

## 3. The Dream of Democracy

The underlying political issue all across this planet is building a more complete democracy. If the people who are currently oppressed (economically, politically, and culturally) by existing economic inequities were represented fully, we would see very different policies and overall results in the course of human affairs on this planet. Democracy has become a widespread dream, but the realization of this dream is strongly resisted by very powerful forces. Political polices to correct both the lack of democracy and the lack of economic equity would include reducing the huge influence of the biggest pools of wealth over our political power centers.

In other words, the key change needed is: *building truly democratic governments at every scope of government—thereby making governments the rulemakers of the economic playing field, rather than allowing the largest economic players to make the rules with which these players then plan to win still more wealth and power.*

Our current political practices would be considered corrupt in a football game in which one team owned the referees. Competition among the economic players is not itself the problem. The problem is that the rules of the game are designed to favor the biggest most influential wealth pools of political power. So, there has to be strong restraints of all the economic players; otherwise we have something like the board game Monopoly, in which the object of the game is to drive all the other players into bankruptcy. Such an economic game does not work for a real-world economy.

Nevertheless, we now have almost everywhere this "winners take all" economic arrangement in which key decisions are being made by economic oligarchs operating from biased perspectives that are grossly uninformed by the experience of the whole body politic.

There are still economists who think that the main conflict in world affairs is between capitalists and socialists. But the truth is that today the key conflict is between the lovers of democracy and both capitalist and socialist authoritarians. The democratic socialists and the democratic capitalists are on the same side in a joint fight against these authoritarian destroyers of democracy and the further developments of authoritarian rule.

The realistic ethicist can learn useful lessons from the dozen or so types of social thought that call themselves "capitalist." And the realistic ethicist can learn useful lessons from the dozen or so types of social thought that call themselves "socialist." But as we look to the future instead of the past, the words "capitalism" and "socialism" become blurry, neither of which can now define what is required for the future. What is required now is a fresh approach to both economics and politics, and to the relations between these two aspects of social process that appear in every society.

Competition goes on in a wolf pack, a ball team, or a human society, but cooperation and teamwork also go on in wolf pack, a ball team, and a human society. To argue for an unregulated competitive market as the solution to all our economic ills is a destructive illusion. A competition-exaggerating viewpoint destroys free enterprise, competition, and the markets—as well as democracy and common sense. Cooperation within a democratic government can create the *rules* for the market—for its *fair competition* and for its needed *freedom of innovation*—doing both of these things within the context of a pursuit for economic equity, ecological sanity, and a fully functional democracy.

In other words, ideological name-calling and sloganeering are quite beside the point with regard to the sort of polices that will actually work for a program of justice that supports economic equity, ecological values, and the basic workability of a democratic society.

The nature of human beings necessitates a form of human society that is somewhere between an ant-den collectivism and a bear-like individualism. In an ant den most of the members are neutered females who build the den, bring in the food, carry out the trash, and die for the den whenever needed. The drones do basically nothing other than fertilize the queen. The so-called queen is not a ruler in the human sense, but simply a living womb that replenishes the den members and contributes her genes, along with those of the drones to the evolution of ants.

Many human queens have done little else than be a womb for the ongoing life of their royalty, but some human queens have found ways to participate significantly in the rulership of their society. Meanwhile, most human kings, in order to maintain their spot in the hierarchy, have needed to be more than drones. In the best-case instances, kings have provided a measure of service to the whole human order.

The hunter-gather society of humans (with no kings or queens) was highly successful for at least fifty thousand years of human life before there was an agricultural village or a hierarchical civilization. The hunter-gatherer society was more like a sports team in which the coaches and rule-makers were among the players. Different roles were played by persons with different gifts and skill levels, but a type of political and economic equity existed throughout this social order of a hunter-gatherer society.

Civilization can be viewed as an aberration of hunter-gather democracy. Civilization was a move in the direction of the ant den. Of course, it was not quite that extreme. Civilization had to use strong restraints to keep most people compliant with their assigned class and range of opportunities. Also, limited forms of the hunter-gather mode of democratic teamship kept arising within the overall canapé of civilization.

It was not until the eighteenth-century democratic revolutions that a full assault on the overall hierarchy of civilization began to take place. In spite of the fact that the U.S. Revolutionary War was fought for a limited democracy for White male property owners, it set in motion an evolving process that eventually did away with African American slavery, gave women the right to vote, and several new deals for the working classes. Such movement toward a full democracy is still far from complete. Human rights protections and an equity of opportunities for all members of the society are not finished anywhere on Earth. Such progress has barely begun, if at all, in many places.

In established democracies such as the United States, the wealthy elite still buy for themselves most of the political power to make the big decisions that keep society favorable to themselves. This anti-democratic attitude has become desperate enough to take over education, religion, and the media in order to lie and cheat their way to an ever-fuller control over our authentic democratic impulses.

Since all humans are estranged in some measure from their authentic humanness, we will always need to restrain dehumanizing impulses with the power invested in governments to enforce justice on planet Earth. We have seen political rallies that encourage people to leave their conscience at home and indulge in an orgy of hate, bigotry, and lies. With effective law and order designed by justice-loving citizenries and administered by representative leadership, society can be prevented from descending into rule by its meanest members and most avid liars.

A court system is a peace-creating and justice-building branch of government, because it provides a space for the detailed pursuit of facts in relation to relevant laws and guidelines. Police departments that are law-abiding investigative agencies are part of good government. Also necessary for a functioning democracy are intelligence organizations that are pristinely scientific, public media sources that are honest, as well as schools and universities that are truth loving. Authoritarian ant-den type oligarchs hold these institutions in contempt or seek to control them for their own uses. This sort of behavior can only be restrained by a power-wielding democratic government.

## 4. Informed Citizens

In a workable democracy, the voters will need to be educated on all the above issues and be provoked to become highly motivated to play their part in the democratic process. For democracy to work in an optimal fashion societies will need strong democratic norms, styles of life, and well-financed and skilled education from preschool to graduate school. In order to have equity, democracy, and ecological sanity we need to assist entire populations to become informed and able to think for themselves in the pursuit of all forms of truth, including justice for our social commonalities.

For an unfortunately large sector of the U.S. population, we have allowed "truth" to mean "what I believe" or "what I would like to believe" or "what I would like other people to believe about me." This is 180 degrees away from the view of "truth" presented in chapter 3. Truth is about finding rational order that is supported by Reality—truth that can make useful predictions and build useful guidelines for action. The fact that our rational order is never complete or that our cultural patterns are always temporal and changing is no excuse for believing whatever we want to believe. Obeying Reality creates true freedom. There is no freedom in fleeing from Reality: that is a pathway to the slavery of despair.

Hope for a viable future includes having informed citizens in a workable democracy who can challenge the "winners take all" monopoly game and bring into play a government that promotes justice. An informed citizenry is creatively detrimental to the goals of the dictatorial "winners take all" forces. Herein is a difficult-to-face truth: we confront forces that are hell-bent on selling us lies, twisting the facts, hiding the truth, rousing our fears, fanning our bigotries, encouraging our sloth, and otherwise distracting us from what is truly challenging and what we can do about those challenges. Underfunding public schools and over-pricing college and graduate levels of education are examples of these democracy-destructive patterns.

## Christianity and the Love of Justice

We can talk about the importance of democracy without using Christian language, but if we are to understand the meaning of *"justing love"* for the mission of a vital next Christian community, we need to know that "God-and-neighbor" is a hyphenated word. God is the overall Profound Reality that is meeting us in the neighbors that are neighboring us. We are neighbored by the trees and the frogs, as well as the humans. We face the Anthropocene era in which we are responsible for this planet. We are also neighbored by strongly negative social forces, and by huge possibilities for greater social justice. Whatever is neighboring us is a gift from the Profound Reality that Christians, in our faith-devotion, meet as God-and-Neighbor. We respond to this confrontation in either escape, sloth, and rebellion, or in trust, care, and freedom. Herein is our Christian social ethics for planet Earth—an ethics that can be respected by all humans. Christian social ethics is a form of secular thinking that persons of all religious heritages or none can embrace.

## II. NEXT STEPS IN UNITED STATES POLITICS IN 2020

There are many next steps in U.S. politics. In order to further illustrate doing social justice ministries by a viable and vital next Christianity, I am going to discuss five specific steps that I put at the top of my list for 2020 in the United States.

1. Ousting Authoritarians

2. Opposing Confederate Racist Backlash

3. Promoting Post-Patriarchal Uprising

4. Providing Medicare for All

5. Enacting the Green New Deal

## 1. Ousting Authoritarians

*Ousting authoritarians* has become a top issue in the U.S., because in 2016 authoritarians took over our federal government. An open fight with the institutions, norms, values, and spirit of democracy has shaken this nation to the core and damaged domestic and foreign polices in ways not easily corrected. A surprisingly large number of various types of authoritarians have gone along with this disaster. The full truth of this development is clouded in a host of often-told and well-financed lies. The truth is that above-the-law king-like pretenders to democracy have joined other authoritarians across the planet—Putin, Erdoğan, Orbán, Xi Jinping, Bolsonaro, and Mohammad bin Salman, to list a few.

Removing the anti-democratic authoritarians from the U.S. Oval Office and both houses of Congress may take a while, but doing so is what must be done by those citizens of this nation who are even minimally interested in realistic governing of a democratic sort. This truth cannot be said too strongly. Even the slightest love of democracy recommends a clean sweep of these anti-democracy forces from every powerful office.

Meanwhile, the lovers of democracy are split between (1) bipartisan cooperation for minor improvements and (2) fighting hard for long-term solutions in healthcare, the climate emergency, assault rifles off the street, and other pressing issues that require taking on the big-money oligarchy that has been gaining excessive strength for decades.

The big-money oligarchs of the United States apparently prefer an authoritarian like Vladimir Putin, but are willing to settle for a far less competent dictator for this country.

Realism in this historical situation requires removing the scourge of reverse-gear politics from every office, from local school boards to the U.S. Congress and the presidency. Nothing less than this qualifies as realism. Realism, let us recall, is the key quality of any viable and vital next Christian ethics, and realism is the essential ingredient in all programs of justice conducted by our U.S. institutions of democracy and in our outgoing national presence on the world scene.

## 2. Opposing Confederate Racist Backlash

*Opposing Confederate racist backlash* remains a prominent issue. A large percentage of the U.S. population of European descent unconsciously, or even consciously, embody a backlash of Southern Confederacy lifestyles.

The Civil War is not yet won. The civil rights movement is not yet complete. Institutionalized forms of racism remain to be done away with promptly.

The racism woven into our personality formations may take several more generations to heal. Such healing, however, will happen only if our institutions strongly support further progress in our personal lives. It is true that Martin Luther King Jr. and Malcolm X led civil rights revolutions that made remarkable institutional progress and enabled personal transformations among millions of people. But let us not suppose this revolution is complete.

This "we are done" view must be treated as a form of racism, which it is. Having our first Black president must not be interpreted as a sign of final victory. The Obamas were severely hated by a significant portion of the population, and the recent administration has reversed almost every change the Obama Administration made toward greater justice.

The current U.S. social justice emergency with regard to institutionalized racism centers in severe flaws in our criminal justice system—arrest biases, police overreaches, court corruptions, improper convictions, excessive incarceration, and unjustified executions. "Black Lives Matter" is a significant symbol for this far-reaching malady. The entire experience for a black, brown, or tan man or woman is different than it is for those who can pass for white. Conservatives who rant the obvious truth that "police lives matter" are actually implying that protecting White lives does matter but protecting Black lives does not matter.

## 3. Promoting Post-Patriarchal Uprising

*Promoting post-patriarchal uprising* means joining women of the U.S. who are moving against every instance of rape, abuse, disrespect, unequal treatment, and control of women's bodies. This oppression is still ignored or dismissed by millions of men and also numerous women. For example, there are women who now have jobs that only men used to hold who still say publicly that they could never vote for a woman president.

A far greater number of women and men now acknowledge that it is not fair that women are paid 80 percent or even 50 percent of what men are paid for the same work. What we face here is another hangover from the past, one that has at least five thousand years of momentum.

Like racism, sexism is still in us. A few more generations will likely pass before our sexist personality patterns lose their hold on us.

Nevertheless, our institutionalized sexism can and must be corrected promptly. Failure to do so slows or prevents the needed changes in the personality qualities of male entitlement and female disempowerment. Religious bigotry as well as racism overlap with promoting this second-place standing for women, robbing women of control of even their own bodies. Liberating women is not an extreme political opinion; it is a realistic priority for our basic Christian ethics.

## 4. Providing Medicare for All

*Providing Medicare for all* is a real solution to the problem of denying affordable healthcare to millions of people within the U.S. geography. By saying this I am not speaking about doable politics. I am speaking about ethical truth, the challenge of Reality.

Medicare, like Social Security and the Post Office, is one of the most successful programs in the history of this nation. The vast majority of seniors love it. To limit Medicare to old folk is plain wasteful. Medicare works fine—not perfect, but fine. No other healthcare system in the U.S. works fine. And like everything else, Medicare can be improved.

A well-written Medicare-for-all bill is already on the floors of both House and Senate. This bill includes improvements to what Medicare is already providing our seniors. A restored Obamacare plus a public option is not affordable healthcare. "Public option" means the opportunity to buy into Medicare. Neither the choices offered by the current health insurance companies nor the choice to buy into Medicare results in affordable healthcare for most people. The pubic option is a step hated by the healthcare establishment, but it is not affordable healthcare. This is simply the truth.

The worry some people have that Medicare for all will raise taxes is a huge misunderstanding. Medicare for all lowers healthcare costs for everyone but the super rich. For the middle-income majority, Medicare for all means approximately this: for every $1,000 you give the government through the tax system for Medicare for all, you would have had to pay $2,000 for similar coverage from the current broken system of health insurance provision. So it is misleading to call this a tax increase. It is at least a $1,000 savings on the average cost of health insurance.

And for those too poor to pay taxes at all, health insurance is simply free under Medicare for all. No other system accomplishes this. Those who are in the largest income tax brackets will pay a bit more than they may pay now for their health insurance. But this "bit more" goes for the people who are dying from a lack of healthcare for the mere reason of being poor.

Billionaires, who don't need health insurance at all, are given the most opportunity to help finance a system that provides affordable healthcare to every person. In other words, Medicare for all is a justice system—providing justice that is not provided by even the best of Obamacare-plus-public-option plans.

Any plan that continues using the current privately administered healthcare system is unstable. Even if you are getting a good deal from some employer, you can lose it if you are fired, move to something else, or that company goes into bankruptcy, changes CEOs, or just decides to change plans. The Medicare-for-all system relieves the pressures on employers and employees both. This is one of the reasons why 70 percent of the voting population favors Medicare for all. The federal government could indeed give those 70 percent what they want.

Consciously or unconsciously rejecting the Medicare-for-all goal is working for the current healthcare insurance establishment's continued profiteering.

The United States is a come-lately nation for this commonsense government-administered way of doing healthcare insurance. This is not at all an extreme way of doing health insurance. Something similar is already being done in Canada, England, France, Sweden, Norway, Cuba, etc.

*Money-making over citizen care corrupts the healthcare system.* Some things are best administered by government; health insurance is one of them. Highways, fire stations, police departments, and the Post Office are other examples where government, especially democratic government, is the best way to administer such services.

### 5. Enacting the Green New Deal

Even more than healthcare insurance, the climate crisis is a challenge that calls for a full leap forward—no halfway measures will do. The Green New Deal is a resolution on the floor in both the U.S. Senate and House of Representatives. This resolution is waiting for a vote. Its passage is even more controversial than Medicare for all. Oil companies and their politicians are willing to say that global warming is a hoax and give up democracy in favor an authoritarian government rather than phase out their product.

So, what does the Green New Deal mean? It is a huge jobs program that promotes millions of good-paying jobs for our under-employed, mis-employed, and non-employed workers. It will offer coal miners and oil-field workers better jobs, as well as good jobs for millions of others.

Enacting the Green New Deal also means building the infrastructure and needed institutions for moderating the number and extent of the hurricanes, the tornadoes, the forest fires, the floods, the mud slides, the ocean rising, the loss of food sources, increased poverty, social chaos, and the extinction of species. The Green New Deal can help us avoid the increasingly unmanageable social chaos that will result if we continue to postpone making the basic energy system changes that we so desperately need.

Many are expressing their terror over the very idea of raising Franklin D. Roosevelt's New Deal from its sleep with this new, relevant, workable, and exciting new New Deal. Some left-of-center thinkers are likewise frightened of the Green New Deal. "Too big," they say. It does indeed violate what many have come to treasure as normal politics.

"How can we pay for it?" is a question raised by moderates, as well as a loud scream being uttered by the wealthy recipients of big tax cuts and preposterous CEO salaries. Most of these screamers have had no qualms about paying many trillions to a military-industrial complex that has channeled money to the rich while wasting trillions on useless wars, needless weaponry, sheer corruption, and astonishing administrative snarls.

Yes, the Green New Deal will redirect trillions of dollars of the wealth of this wealthy nation to solving real problems, and it will significantly moderate the climate crisis without dumping the cost of revising the energy system on workers and other middle-class taxpayers. The Green New Deal is indeed a significant leap for both economic justice and ecological sanity.

The Green New Deal is not nearly as extreme as its opponents claim. It is as modest, in its own way, as the Postal Service and Social Security. And it will take a while to phase out fossil fuels and build a next energy system. The actual doing of the Green New Deal will be a step-by-step, get-things-done sort of doable activism. We have done hard things like this before. We can do this one now.

We do not have to scale back to ineffective programing in order to get things done. The Green New Deal is often opposed by a do-it-someday style of thinking. These go-slow excuses cloud our wisdom about starting now with long-range, emergency-solving, large-enough policy adventures. With the climate crisis, only big leaps forward are realistic action.

Perhaps compromising with oil companies was the best we could do in recent decades. Even that is debatable. Nevertheless, I am willing to thank those diligent persons who did succeed in getting some progress made. But times have changed. We now need to demand that our moderate politicians lean progressive, rather than asking our progressives to continue leaning moderate.

Beginning now with some Green New Deal enthusiasm could end the current authoritarian side trip with true alternatives, rather than simply returning to the politics of 2015 and before. Yes, the Green New Deal will entail pushing some powerful forces to the sidelines of political power. Nevertheless, it is surely high time to enjoy the excitement, as well as the pain, of phasing out oil company wealth-kings, big-bank corruption, and greedy oligarchs not fit for any age.

The Green New Deal is a perfect example of how there are no moderate solutions to the climate crisis. The climate crisis requires full speed ahead for the rest of our lives. We are already grossly tardy.

## U.S. Justice in 2020

More than the above could be said about U.S. challenges for social justice in 2020. But as examples of the call of Profound Reality for justice in this place and time, I stand by these five guidelines for action.

1. Ousting Authoritarians

2. Opposing Confederate Racist Backlash

3. Promoting Post-Patriarchal Uprising

4. Providing Medicare for All

5. Enacting the Green New Deal.

If these challenges seem utopian, it is because they are. In her book *No Is Not Enough*, Naomi Klein quotes Oscar Wilde's 1891 comment, "A map of the world that does not include Utopia is not worth even glancing at, for it leaves out the one country at which humanity is always landing. And when humanity lands there, it looks out, and, seeing a better country, sets sail."[4]

4. Klein, *No Is Not Enough*, 221.

## LAST WORDS ON JUSTING LOVE

I confess to putting my views in a passionate form that may hide my own commitment to an ongoing perpetual change of my views.

Also missing are the specific actions that a local citizen or group of citizens might do—getting out votes, educating citizens, organizing voters, running for office, and much more. The whole picture of *justing love* is far more vast than one essay can cover. Always it remains true that our overall ethical thoughtfulness, as well as our specific strategies and tactics, will be constantly changing. Nevertheless, the illustrations I have spelled out above indicate how awakening Christians are called to think boldly about justing love for human life on planet Earth today.

I have not yet spoken about the dynamics of justing love and witnessing love in the context of a local group of Christians ministering to their local parish of immediate responsibility. I turn to that topic in the next chapter.

# 20

The Bioregional Parish of Responsibility

SOMETIME IN THE EARLY 1970s, I and two others were assigned to teach a theology course for a group in Phoenix, Arizona. We were housed with a couple whose names I cannot recall. But I do recall the wife entering my room and grabbing my big toe at about 6:00 in the morning and announcing to me that it was time for breakfast. She took the three of us out into that cool early-morning desert for a picnic. I remember the spectacular beauty of the big cacti and other desert plants and flowers all illuminated in that early light under such a clear blue sky. She was smiling such a big smile—happy to have impressed us.

My Chicago lakeside or my Oklahoma hills were nothing like this Arizona desert. Wherever we live, we live somewhere on planet Earth—on some grasslands, in some forest, on some mountainside, in some valley, along some seashore, next to some river. We each dwell in some region of the planet with unique flora and fauna, weather and seasons, landscapes and people. Some local place is our home of responsibility. A circle of next Christians will do most of their witnessing and justing love in some local scope of geography.

## PARISH

In the Middle Ages of European society, the term "parish" did not mean the members of the Catholic Church. "Parish" meant the buildings, the bricks, the roads, the animals, the trees, the farmlands, the faithful and unfaithful Christians, those other than Christian—everybody and everything in that local vicinity of Earth. The clergy, monks, and nuns who were assigned to that place viewed that piece of geography as their parish of responsibility. They felt called to nurture people, befriend people, care for people, bring justice to people, and seek wholesome life for these people, for their social institutions, and for the natural order of their entire surroundings.

Of course there were great priests and lousy ones, but the frame for their being love for their neighbors was defined by this geographical parish of responsibility. While the state of Louisiana still calls "parishes" what Texas calls "counties," the term "parish" in the Protestant era has come to mean "the members of my Christian congregation."

With the term "bioregional parish of responsibility," I am recommending a revolution in thought for a local circle of Christians with regard to the place, scope, and quality of their local witnessing and justing love.

## BIOREGIONAL

The term "bioregional" is the name of a movement that began growing in prominence in 1984 when David Haenke and others of the Ozark Area Community Congress (OACC) and Ken Lasman, Caryn Goldberg, and others of Kansas Area Watershed (KAW) put out a call to ecological writers and activists to convene the first North American Bioregional Congress in northern Missouri. "Congressing," according to Haenke, meant creating a decision-making body that did legitimate decision-making because, he said, such decision-making took into account the well-being of the Earth.

Also prominent in the origin of the bioregional movement was the activism and writings of Peter Berg of Planet Drum, who created a radical form of environmentalism featuring the idea of "reinhabitation" of your local place. This means viewing where you live as a natural region of the planet, rather than as a county or city whose boundaries were created by human beings.

Over many years, I have given talks on this topic using the image of the bioregional leap. Here is the idea of this leap: joining the bioregional movement is like jumping up in the air—out of Fannin County, Texas—and then coming back to the ground on planet Earth, now living in the "Red River Flats" bioregion. In someone else's case, that may be the "Trinity River Watershed" or the "Texoma High Plains." Such names evoke an ecologically described region of the planet rather than districts like zip codes, city limits, counties, states, or some other human way of indicating where you live. Of course our human districting may be useful for some specific purposes, but coming home to a practical sense of your planetary home place is key to the environmental reinhabitation called "bioregionalism."

Another inspiring writer who attended this first continental bioregion congregating of the Northern Americas was Kirkpatrick Sale, whose book *Human Scale* had deeply impressed my wife Joyce and I before we read about this first bioregional congress in the *In-Context* magazine. "Human scale" is another key topic of the bioregional movement, attacking globalism in the bad sense of an international monetary bigness that rules the whole world without appropriate attention being paid to human beings living in local places. Human scale asks us to look at specific humans living in specific communal associations with one another as a baseline beginning for all social thought.

Joyce and I decided to go to that first North American Bioregional Congress. Though the group was secular, interreligious, and culturally diverse, it had a spirit quality in which we felt at home. After a year of brooding about it, we became organizers in Texas, and then helped organize the continental bioregional movement for the next couple of decades.

At that first congress, we met a number of prominent persons, including those already mentioned. Among those persons were: Charlene Spretnak, Thomas Berry, his brother Jim Berry, and a Quaker facilitator, Carolyn Estes. In later years, Canadian publishers and feminists Judith and Chris Plant, Hispanic leader and artist Alberto Ruz, consensus innovator Bea Briggs, and scores of others—Native Americans, Blacks, Central and South Americans, Canadians, and even a few Europeans—came to celebrate with us.

The vision, strategies, and detailed actions of this movement have now been written up in books and essays too numerous to list here. I will only cite a few more general themes that I want to emphasize. This movement retains its deep commitment to localism in spite of also realizing that all the big environmental challenges are global in scope. Nevertheless, this movement sees a huge part of the overall transformation as taking place through small groups in local places—local humans taking responsibility for every blade of grass, every tree, every animal, and each and every human no matter what their current associations or backgrounds may be. Such localism also includes buildings and roads and institutions, all of which need to be transformed to fit beneficially within these home regions, as well as become healthy contributors to this one and only home planet.

This bioregional perspective includes a critique of any form of anthropocentrism in which the center of value is humans only. Our so-called humanism often means a few rich humans at the expense of other humans living in some form of squalor. In the bioregional perspective the center of value for ethics is moved to the entire natural planet upon which all meaningful human values actually depend. The bioregional movement's Earth-first valuing of the natural planet is, in my sort of theologizing, consistent with a devotion to Profound Reality.

It turns out that the bioregional movement is a type of spirit movement in which the word "spirit" means being in touch with some key aspects of profound consciousness. The bioregional spirit fosters a culture for this movement that undergirds the bioregional movement's political, economic, and environmental concerns. Joyce and I found bioregionalism a movement within which we, as participants in radical Christianity, felt fully at home in spite of the vast variety of religious representatives that showed up at these bioregional gatherings. The bioregional congresses were interreligious gatherings that struggled openly with what "spirit" could mean as a basically secular quality for a movement of this nature.

## THE BIOREGIONAL PARISH

So what does bioregionalism have to do with a next Christian practice and its local forms of witnessing and justing love? If, as I believe, the birth of a next Christianity begins as circles of weekly-meeting radical Christians, then bioregionalism can help those circles define their local mission of witnessing and justing love. I am imagining these circles to be something more than support groups, nurture groups, or study groups. Their members will be co-pastors to one another, as well as a group pastorate to a local geographical vicinity of planet Earth—that is, to a local bioregion. I will be referring to these circles of radical Christians as "co-pastors circles." And by the term "bioregional parish" I mean a local geographical vicinity of planet Earth that defines the local parish of responsibility for a co-pastors circle—or for a network of co-pastors circles if there is more than one co-pastors circle in that bioregional parish.

In the next chapter (chapter 21) I will be describing my recommendations for the interior life of a co-pastors circle with recommendations
for organizing one of these circles. In chapter 22 I will be describing
recommendations for organizing a network of co-pastors circles. This
network will begin at the local bioregional level of organization with
a meeting I am calling a "regional assembly." I am imagining that the
members of all the co-pastors circles in one bioregion meet quarterly
to inspire one another, organize more circles, and plan the mission of
those circles to that bioregion. In this chapter I am going to focus on
the mission of a single circle or a single network of circles to their bioregional parish of responsibility.

If you are the only person in your local bioregion who is interested
in being part of a co-pastors circle in your bioregion, then you are the
co-pastors circle until you get others to join you. And if your circle is the
only circle in your bioregion, then your circle is also the regional assembly until you have organized a second co-pastors circle in that bioregion.
I am imagining a movement in process of being built—a movement in
which each of us is the whole movement, as well as a small part of this
movement for a viable and vital next Christianity.

Next, I will clarify a bit more what a "local bioregion" means. A bioregion does not have precise borders like a county or a state. A bioregion
blurs into the bioregions that surround it. Bioregions come in many sizes.
There is a bioregion described as the "Great Grassland Prairie," which extends all the way from lower-mid Texas north to lower-mid Canada. This
is much too large a geographical scope to qualify as a local bioregional
parish of responsibility. So let us imagine that we can find meaningful
ways to break down that vast stretch into a dozen or more bioregionally
described segments.

For example, I live in Fannin County, Texas. My bioregion is a scope
of geography larger than my county. County boundaries do not define
a bioregion, but here is an image of the size of my bioregion that I call
the "Red River Flats." My bioregion includes at least the adjacent Texas
county to the west and two adjacent counties across the Red River into
Oklahoma. These four counties, plus and minus bits of land, are a segment of the Great Grassland Prairie. Farther north in the Great Grassland
Prairie there is an already-organized local bioregion called the "Kansas
Area Watershed." Between my local bioregion and the KAW bioregion,
we might have three more local bioregions.

## THE CHRISTIAN PARISH MISSION OF LOVE

In relation to these bioregional contexts, I will review the four types of Christian mission suggested in chapters 18 and 19: (1) common-language witnessing love, (2) Christian-language witnessing love, (3) justing love for non-Christian institutions, and (4) justing love for Christian institutions.

### Common-Language Witnessing Love

I will not comment further than I did in chapter 18 on the thousands of witnessing actions that each radical Christian makes within his or her personal relationships using whatever language those acquaintances understand. I am going to share in this paragraph a few suggestions for group actions by radical Christians that can be done for the local culture of their bioregion. For example, I envision a spirit-level workshop for women and men on "Overcoming Patriarchy," such as the one designed and facilitated by Joyce Marshall and Pat Webb. We surely need to design and facilitate a spirit-level workshop on moderating the climate crisis and on doing the persistent work that needs to be done by all of us to promote the transition from our fossil-fuel energy system to an energy system powered by sunshine and wind power. We also need clarity on establishing an infrastructure that delivers this energy through electricity and hydrogen fuels to all our needed uses. People need to understand clearly how such a system will work, and how it will work better than the system we have.

We also need a workshop on how to care for people being affected by the climate crisis tragedies already taking place. There are many other programs that can be invented, conducted, improved, and expanded over time. Doing such common language witnessing with an ever-wider inventiveness and persistence is part of the revolutionary love of being radical Christians in a local bioregion parish of planet Earth.

This sort of programing can be done in a secular manner. This is not merely Christian ethics; this is an ethics to which many religious and secular traditions can contribute. The key point here is that such pro-graming is done not to recruit people to a Cristian practice, but simply to serve a local geographical parish of this planet with some witnessing love on topics deemed needed by that co-pastors circle for that population of people. Such programing can be love that is a means of grace happenings to individual lives without using words like "grace" or "sin."

## Christian-Language Witnessing Love

Programs, workshops, and courses that use the Christian language in the fresh ways introduced in Part Two of this book are also a crucial part of the work of the radical Christians I see as the ministries of these co-pastors circles. Restoring the healing message of Christianity is a sort of love that only Christians can do. A few years ago, I made friends with a rather liberal pastor of a Presbyterian church in this quite conservative county where I live. I suggested that I could offer on Wednesday nights for his congregation an eight-session course on the book of Genesis. I showed him a booklet I had assembled for that topic. About ten people enrolled in that course, which I led for eight Wednesday nights. The enrollees attended most of the sessions. Most of them had never heard before that the story of Joseph was a novelette, or that these old myths and legends could mean something profound in their own lives. I would say we had at least a 50-percent wake-up result. That pastor moved on, and I got busy with other things. Nevertheless, this experience illustrates how a co-pastors circle member can do this new form of Christian witnessing love within some congregations. These same Christian language courses can be conducted in secular or interreligious settings. I can imagine teams of teachers organized from among a group of co-pastors circles of a given bioregional parish doing year in and year out an ongoing schedule of this kind of witnessing love.

It is important to note that doing Christian-language witnessing will be needed to awaken persons to the radical nature of Christianity. Some of these awakening persons will feel called to join the co-pastorate ministry—perhaps become members of your or of my co-pastors circle, or perhaps organize another circle in another part of your or my bioregion. This result is a consequence that we will want to encourage, but the first order of business for doing Christian-language witnessing is simply healing lives.

Persons experiencing the call to a co-pastor role will be an added benefit that may or may not result from any particular course. Patience will be required and much work done before we have a dozen people in your circle or a dozen co-pastors circles in your bioregion. How this can come about, I will discuss in chapter 22.

## Justing Love for Secular Institutions

Social injustice and ecological insanity take on specific forms in each bioregion. Committees composed of co-pastors and other activists will need to identify the "pressure points" in their bioregion and launch actions or join actions along with whomever in that bioregion is similarly concerned. In these complex and uncertain times, all of us have a reluctance to be activists in this ongoing fashion and in our own local places. Our calling to be Christian co-pastors includes overcoming our reluctance and leading other citizens to overcome their reluctance.

Moving on prominent injustices will always be controversial, and will sometimes be risky or even dangerous. Our personal safety is a key value, but not the only value. We will want to carefully think through the risk-results relationship as we choose what to take on, and in what order. Caution needs to be taken to not act from either fear or moralistic rage. Calm, thoughtful, long-range plans and actions will result in wins for social justice and ecological sanity. If this entails sacrifices, let them be worth it. We need an optimism that is not sentimentality. And we need a pessimism that is not sloth.

A regional assembly of co-pastors circles can take on the task of organizing, maintaining, and giving active participation in a bioregional congress in their home bioregion. This congress would be composed of people from a variety of religious and cultural backgrounds. They would need to be willing to take on bioregional community building, nurture of bioregionalism's eco-sane membership, ecological and social education for all the humans in that bioregion, and social actions appropriate for progress in all the processes, natural and human, in that bioregion.

This bioregional congress might meet once a year for several days. Perhaps some or even all of its members might meet on a single Saturday four times a year near the time of an equinox or solstice. Whatever meeting patterns are appropriate for your bioregion, they need to promote both spirit-level values and decision-making values for ecological actions and social justice actions (cultural, political, and economic) that are called for in that bioregion. Most co-pastors in a given bioregion will be members of such a bioregional congress as one of their means of doing justing love for that bioregion.

Co-pastors may participate in organizing and maintaining the bioregional congress, but they need not be the leadership, or the only leadership, of that body of people. The bioregional congress is not a

Christian organization; it is a secular organization open to every resident of that region who wants to advance the bioregional perspective on planetary responsibility.

In numbers of active members, we need to imagine a bioregional congress attended by many times as many members as their are co-pastors who share in its life and work. This public quality of the bioregional congress distinguishes it from the regional assembly of co-pastors. The regional assembly is open only to Christian co-pastors and perhaps their invited guests. The regional assembly of co-pastors has a different mission and set of tasks than the bioregional congress. The regional assembly promotes circle organizing and the witnessing love and the justing love that arise from an explicitly Christian perspective. The Christian co-pastors are members of the bioregional congress as one aspect of their justing love for that bioregion. A co-pastor may do a secular form of witnessing love within their bioregional congress participation, but Christian-language witnessing should not be imposed on persons who have not enrolled in courses or consented to talk about such matters in the more personal settings Christians have with friends and inquirers.

## Justing Love for Christian Institutions

Many persons of radical Christian awareness feel alienated from the inherited Christian institutions. And it also may be true that very few of these institutions have any hope of becoming adequate expressions of a fully radical Christianity. Nevertheless, Christian congregations can be as good as most other institutions for doing some of the right things in a typical bioregion. In fact, many congregation members will be more open to ecological and social justice projects than to a contemporary theology course. It will almost always be appropriate to ask some of the members of typical liberal and conservative congregations to be supporters of some controversial topics or even to become active members in the bioregional congress.

One of the ancient qualities of reform-minded church members has been playing the role of prophets of justice who shape the conscience of nominal Christians on such elemental matters as poverty, ill treatment, racism, sexism, authoritarianism, healthcare, perhaps the climate catastrophe, and so on. The co-pastors of these radical circles are called to such prophetic ministries. And the co-pastors circle is called to pastor the entire bioregional parish, including the religious institutions that serve that geography. It is in that basic context that the co-pastors circle takes responsibility for Christian institutions, however flawed those bodies may be from a radical Christian perspective.

## CARING FOR THE CO-PASTORS MOVEMENT ITSELF

Imagine having a dozen circles in one bioregional parish, with five to twelve members in each circle (that means, 60 to 144 co-pastors). A network of this size implies the need for internal structures of care for one another—for our common spirit life, our courage to act, our safety, our needs for quality witnessing and justice work, for our ongoing skill improvements and our effective organizations, our useful methods, our inspiration, our shared stories, and whatever else. In the light of such ideas I am proposing the building of an ongoing presence of Christian love serving an entire parish of responsibility. Such love is more than a set of ideas or even a set of actions; this love means the promotion of an ongoing *presence* of an organized, interactive community of persistent persons who become over time an effective social force in that bioregion. Caring for the ongoing quality of this force of people will be an important part of the mission of all the members of the co-pastors circle network.

# 21

---

# The Mind of Intimacy
## and the Co-Pastors Circle

IN CHAPTER 3, I introduced the importance of the interpersonal approach to truth. Each of us has in our makeup this "mind of intimacy" along with our "mind of commonality," our "mind of scientific knowledge," and our "mind of contemplative wisdom." Our awareness of interpersonal intimacy and our skills for conducting interpersonal relations are of utmost importance for discerning and describing the quality of life needed for conducting a viable and vital next Christian practice.

### My Journey into Deeper Intimacy

I was fifty years old before I became relatively clear about the critical importance of the interpersonal quest for truth for living a realistic life. I grew up with a father, mother, and sister who were competent and responsible people, and who were kindly enough, but who never became skilled in the intimacy dimensions of living. Their own feelings and the feelings of others were unconsciously suppressed. I found the First Methodist Church of Stillwater, Oklahoma a place where I first learned a bit more about the truth of intimacy. The first memories I have of this gift was my Sunday school class of fifth-grade boys that was being led by a college professor of remarkable willingness to attentively listen to boys of that age. Later, I was an active member of the Methodist Youth Fellowship of teenage boys and girls conducted by leaders who let us share honestly with one another about our life experiences, including sex and dating. I am sure that some of that was a bit sentimental and even moralistic, but I was involved with others in ways that revealed that my scientific bent was not the whole quest for truth in matters of successful living.

In college I joined the Wesley Foundation, led by a couple who were quite innovative in their intimate honesty. Under their leadership, I participated in open discussions, sometimes gave presentations and led discussions, did folk dancing with Black students from a Black college, (the first African Americans I had ever touched), participated in ways to strengthen a community of poverty-stricken Native Americans, attended Methodist Student Movement events in Oklahoma, and as president of the Oklahoma MSM was a delegate to United Christian Student Movement meetings. Some decent theology showed up in some of these events, but mostly what I was learning was a taste of interpersonal life at a spirit level of personal meetings.

At Perkins School of Theology in Dallas, Texas, three of my professors became close friends and encouraged deep friendships among a band of fellow students. Later, my first wife Ruth and I, plus three young children, joined one of those professors, his family, and seven other families in starting a Christian religious order of families that grew to about 1,200 adults and their children. But even my vigorous participation and leadership in that group were only a beginning in my further grasp of the importance of the interpersonal or intimacy approach to truth.

After leaving that order, creating a second marriage with Joyce, a talented woman of interpersonal openness, attending with her a number of therapies, retreats, and workshops on interpersonal skills, I began to discover the fathomless depth of what I am attempting to indicate with these words: *interpersonal/intimacy skills as a mode of truth.*

Before I began these post-1977 experiments in intimacy, I had read and even taught portions of the writings of Sigmund Freud, Karl Jung, Karen Horney, Victor Frankl, Rollo May, and others. These psychological authors were helpful to me in understanding intimacy, what intimacy I had with other people, as well as my lack of competence in this dimension of being human. Nevertheless, I had yet to discover that reading psychology books was not enough. Reading is no substitute for intimate therapy with skilled therapists.

In the late 1970s, my wife Joyce and I ventured into a long series of therapies and therapy-like workshops and retreats. We spent over a year with a community of feeling-centered therapists. When that community collapsed, we began therapy with some very competent neo-Reichian and Gestalt therapists. Along the way we did a number of workshops and private therapy sessions with trained therapists and workshop leaders of the A. H. Almaas tradition.

These personally intimate experiences with skilled psychological innovators were still further enriched in sessions with some inspiring Buddhist teachers. It may have taken this much personal push to bring me to my current appreciation of the intimacy approach to truth. It is clear to me now that intimacy is an approach to truth that is as important as the scientific approach to truth, the contemplative approach to truth, and the commonality approach to truth.

## Intimacy and a Next Christianity

It is now abundantly clear to me that intimacy skills are of critical importance for building a vital next Christian practice. Intimacy skills have also played an important role for me in married life, offspring relations, friendships, teaching, learning from other teachers, leading a team of persons, being on a team of persons, and other contexts, including our small circles of Christian life together.

Intimacy has many layers. There is intimacy on the level of touch, sensory awareness, and sexual contacts. There is intimacy on the emotional level of awareness. There is intimacy on the intellectual level of sharing meaningful thoughts. And there are times among and between other human beings that we access an interpersonal meeting with other humans in which we are mutually present to our profound consciousness.

These spirit-to-spirit meetings may seem to be a rare thing, but such meetings are not as rare as we might think. Simply attending a music program and being carried away by a particular artist or composer may be a form of such intimacy. Singing together, dancing together, and playing together may occasion meetings of this deep sort. Sometimes even encountering a complete stranger who somehow sees you and sees you seeing him or her can touch these mysterious depths for which we have no ready name.

In our Christian life together, personally relevant study, silent meditation, group ritual, social actions, and other practices may be excellent nurture, but none of these activities is a substitute for a frequently meeting group of Christian colleagues practicing intimate spirit care for one another. Two or three persons who view us personally and who care for the deep qualities of our living can do for our spirit journey what we clearly cannot do for ourselves. Many well-read, lucid people do not see the full importance of intimacy, or at least they find excuses for not putting intimate religious practices into their regular schedule of living.

Here is my well-considered conclusion about this matter: *Intimate life together is as important to a vital Christian practice as meditation is to a vital Buddhist practice.* I have explored small-group, intimate, weekly-meeting Christian practices for over three decades. My conclusions include the conviction that the honest sharing of our lives within the proclamation of forgiveness is a healing practice that is essential for a viable and vital next Christian practice.

I want to elaborate on the weekly nature of the practice I am recommending. Monks and others have met daily, but this is too often for the practical schedules of most ordinary people today. Monthly or even biweekly is not often enough. Weekly works for this practice in that it is frequent enough to be spiritually effective and it can fit into the schedules of most people in a workable way. For these reasons, I strongly recommend weekly meetings for the core local group practice of a viable and vital next Christianity.

## THE ESSENTIAL DYNAMICS
## OF A CO-PASTORS CIRCLE

This weekly meeting of life together I am calling a "co-pastors circle." "Circle" describes the seating arrangement. "Co-pastors" describes a nurture function toward one another and a mission function toward the surrounding society and natural world. I view this co-pastors circle as a local *atom* in the planetary *cosmos* of a viable and vital next Christianity. The following chart spells out the inclusive dynamics of this local *atom*. This diagram also applies to the inclusive dynamics of the planetary *cosmos* of this projected next Christianity. I am going to spell out the meaning of each of the words on this chart, but first let these relations of meaning be sealed in the mind of the reader with a few moments of meditation on this chart. Notice the polarity of "nurture" and "mission." Notice the breakdown of the activities of nurture and the activities of mission. And notice the enclosed circle of disciplined self-consciously Christianity-practicing persons who do all these nurturing and missional activities:

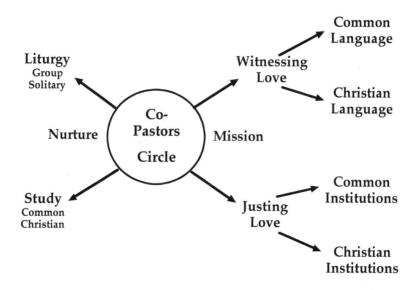

This chart has a long evolution. In about 1963, this chart was given the affectionate name the "Bug Model." It was first used in a course taught in the mid 1960s by the faculty of the Ecumenical Institute on renewing a local congregation of Christendom. At that time, the body of the bug represented a Christian congregation and most especially, the forces of renewal within that congregation. This bug dynamic has four legs; the two hind legs are about the *nurture* we need on behalf of doing the *mission* of love for our neighbors in the general world. *Liturgy* and *study* are the basic aspects of *nurture*. *Witnessing love* and *justing love* are the basic aspects of *mission*.

I have given this old chart two fingers on each of its four legs. I have also given a new name for the core body—the co-pastors circle. That new name indicates that renewing the congregations of Christendom, though needed and still ongoing, is no longer the center of attention for launching a vital next Christianity. In this new bug model, the congregation is viewed as a passing institution of Christendom. The congregations of Christendom appear on the justing love leg of this new bug model as a mission field for the co-pastors circle body of the bug. This does not mean a denial that congregations can and often do well a number these activities, but the co-pastors circle does these activities in a basically fresh organizational manner.

In this new bug model the missional actors within the body of the bug are ex-clergy and ex-laity who are called to be a co-pastors ministry of a *next* Christian practice. The circular skin or membrane around the body of this new bug symbolizes the call to a new Christian practice and to a new Christian ministry. The skin around the bug body now symbolizes a spirit passage—previously ritualized by both baptism and ordination. In this next Christianity, I view baptism and ordination as the same passage, for in this new model there are no laity or clergy—only co-pastors.

## An Intimate Christian Circle

So how does spirit-level intimacy shape the structuring of a new and effective next Christian practice? After considerable exploration on this topic, I have concluded that a new or experienced co-pastor needs to structure time with other co-pastor members who are committed to practicing Christianity as their means of nurturing their lives. These regular meetings undergird us, as well as organize us into a radical Christian mission to a bioregional parish of responsibility.

My wife Joyce and I began weekly meetings with several other awakening Christians in 1984. In 2020, a somewhat different nine of us are still meeting every week, with very few exceptions. Many changes in what we do have been made over that long evolution. Even the name has changed. At first we called these meetings a "house church." Later, we adopted the name "Christian resurgence circles" (CRCs). We invited other persons in other places to experiment with us in doing similar weekly meetings. Most recently we began using the name "co-pastors circle," emphasizing the dynamic that the members are co-pastors to each other as well as a team *pastorate* to a local *parish* of responsibility.

Our parish task includes witnessing to the truth of the Christian revelation in both secular and Christian languages. "Witnessing," "parish," and "revelation" are all Christian language, but our witnessing will often be done in ways that are invisible to its Christian practice groundings. Our parish task includes working with all persons of good will for social justice and ecological improvements within all the institutions of a local bioregion of planet Earth. From this local place of engagement in both witness and justice actions, the co-pastorate also serves whole states, nations, continents, and the natural planet and all its human institutions and persons.

In our circle experimentation, we have viewed ourselves to be in a covenant that includes the discipline of attending the circle meeting each week, or notifying the group when we have to miss. This includes coming on time and coming prepared for our study and for our leadership roles.

Nevertheless, our covenant of discipline is relatively moderate. We are not a religious order. We do not include a sharing of our finances or live in commonly owned space. I have done such practices with other families in my past, but I am now convinced that a current renewal of Christian practice does not require monastic living in this post-Christendom period. Within our rather simple co-pastors covenant, we attempt to keep in balance: (1) each person's individual journey and vocation, (2) the existing covenants of marriage and other pairings, and (3) our covenants with other groups of people—jobs, professions, social organizations, political bodies, and so on.

Our religious covenant is, however, demanding in an inward sense: it requires an intense openness to each other on the spirit level and a joint commitment to serious mission to the local parish and to planet Earth. The covenant also requires a physical presence—sitting in a circle together, doing appropriate ritual, serious study, and doing activist activities together. Most important, this intimacy includes an honest sharing of our real lives—both in the study and discussion methods and in the ritual of confession and absolution.

## DISCIPLINED PRESENCE

The inner life of the co-pastors circle can also be called a "disciplined presence." Discipline is what holds together in one body the four legs and eight fingers of this new bug model. In this co-pastors circle, everyone is called to the ministry of Jesus Christ—a discipline of lifelong realism. And it includes an ongoing quest for further wisdom in all four approaches to truth. And most of all, it includes living out the viewpoint of the cross/resurrection, ever-widening Christian "revelation." These rules for living together are fairly simple, but the spirit commitment for this life together in mission is very deep.

## MISSION

The mission of the co-pastors circle includes both witnessing love and justing love, topics we have already discussed at length in chapters 18, 19, and 20. Taken together, witnessing love and justing love are a presence of love that is the sociological importance of the co-pastors circle. Witnessing love and justing love are two legs on the same bug—two aspects of the same body of love for every human, every society, and the planet itself. The discipline and the nurture aspects of the co-pastors circle are for the sake of this mission of love.

*Witnessing love* concentrates on the spirit life of individual persons—assisting persons to access their higher angels, so to speak. Witnessing love is important for *justing love*, for it requires despair-healed individuals to carry out justing love for the societies of the planet, and for the well-being of the planet.

Insofar as justing love has accomplished justice, it supports witnessing love. It does so by protecting realistic witnessers. It does so by restraining the reign of unrealism that is leading people astray with false stories and non-inclusive policies that justify injustice. Nevertheless, these two modes of love are quite different in the doing of them. The distinction between them is important, even though they are complementary, rather than conflictual enterprises.

The mission of love is not a hobby or an avocation. This mission is the underlying vocational meaning of all the temporal vocations of the co-pastor. Being a co-pastor and being a Christian practitioner are now the same thing.

Nurture of the co-pastors for one another is part of the mission of love. This mission defines what nurture needs to be. Nurture needs to be a preparation for the mission as well as for the healing of each co-pastor to be more effective in doing that mission.

The drive to survive is built into our biology, but the meaning of a co-pastor's survival is to do this mission. This mission does not exclude taking care of myself, but I now take care of myself in order to do this mission. This mission does not exclude taking care of my health, but I now take care of my health in order to do this mission. This mission does not exclude educating myself, but I now educate myself in order to do this mission. This mission does not exclude having fun, or rest, or joy, but I am now having fun, or rest, or joy in order to do this mission. Everything in the life of a Christian co-pastor is swept up into this mission of love. Even the death of the co-pastor is for the sake of this mission.

## NURTURE

The nurture of the co-pastors circle is a crucial part of the overall loving presence and mission of this co-pastorate. The nurture that is needed is the nurture that enables the mission of love. The above bug model has two nurture legs—study and liturgy. The study leg has two parts—*common-language study* and *Christian-language study*. The liturgy leg also has two parts—*solitary liturgy/exercises* and *group liturgy/processes*.

## Study

Ongoing study is a hugely important preparation for a vital next Christian ministry to this complex planet of cultural developments, political power struggles, economic systems changes, ecological emergencies, and the presence of deep human estrangements from realism.

We need many types of study experience. Here are three: (1) We need study content and group processes that help us get *out of our minds* and *into our profound consciousness*. (2) We need to learn skills in using our minds to become more competent in each of the four approaches to truth spelled out in chapter 3. And (3) we need spirit, intellectual, and group methods for doing the contextual planning and the relevant work of witnessing and justing love in our local parish of responsibility. The study I have in mind is not just ideas, but thoughtfulness for the sake of practical living. And this study, though focused on local responsibility, also builds a planetary context for our local action.

Having spent decades doing weekly small Christian group studies, I have developed some specific guidelines about what to study. Let me emphasize that these are guidelines, not dogma. In our Bonham, Texas circle, we plan four quarters of study with at least ten sessions each quarter. At each of these weekly two-hour meetings, we have a fifty-minute session of study on previously read text or topic preparation. Some quarters of study might use a series of relevant workshop processes, and other quarters might view a series of forty-five-minute videos each followed by discussion. Every person comes to the meeting prepared for that session. The study leadership role can be passed around among the co-pastors—each circle deciding how to do that with the members they have. We have three leadership roles each session: (1) the guide (or liturgist), (2) the scripture or religious poetry discussion leader, and (3) the study leader.

We also find helpful a rotation of types of study content. First of all, we need a balance between (1) Christian heritage content and (2) other-than-Christian language content. Our Christian-language studies ground us in the primal symbols that hold the vision of underlying good news and life calling. Our other-than-Christian-language studies join us with other people and movements of good will in appropriately changing the world we are all called to serve.

The Christian-language study in our Bonham circle includes (1) contemporary theologizing, (2) a study of scriptures, and (3) a study of church history. Our common-language studies includes: (1) other-than-Christian religious sources, (2) general spirit methods, (3) planet-wide social ethics content, and (4) social action materials that might be useful for meeting specific challenges of the times in our parish and/or for our planet.

The specific study materials that I cite in the paragraphs below are meant to be suggestive, rather than prescriptive. Nevertheless, I count these suggestions relevant, for they indicate the type of study I am viewing as needed for a nurturing life together of a viable and vital Christian co-pastors circle. These sources suggest basic methods of truth-seeking, as well as honesty and faithfulness to the core Christian revelation. Alternative ways of saying things and disagreements will always be present, but I see these circles seeking a commonality of profound awareness, a Christian heritage competence, and the skills, methods, and insights necessary for our preparation for carrying out a vital co-pastors circle ministry to one another and to the parish in which we live.

## Some Christian-Language Study Suggestions

1. *Contemporary theologizing* within the Søren Kierkegaard stream, as outlined in chapter 17, is of first importance as nurture for the co-pastors circles that we are promoting. I recommend setting aside one quarter every year to study Christian theologizing from this huge treasure chest of resources from the post-Kierkegaardian stream. Such contemporary theologizing provides an overall context for choosing other study content. There are many theological texts that are both accessible and profound. We especially need texts that are appropriate for people who have done little theological reading or who cannot easily absorb super-scholarly works.

Those of us who do read major theological works need to write essays and books and prepare useful study guides that make these core theological insights accessible to a more general population. In 2018 I published an updated version of a 1985 book entitled *A Primer on Radical Theology*. Its new title is *Radical Gifts: Living the Full Christian Life in Troubled Times*. This easily readable book with discussion exercises is an example of how to introduce new people to this type of contemporary Christian theologizing. Paul Tillich's three books of sermons provide an accessible way to dialogue with a recognized theological pioneer. I would start with *The Shaking of the Foundations* and move on to *The New Being* and *The Eternal Now*.

2. *New and Old Testament studies* are also key to the basic nurture of the co-pastors circle members. We cannot call ourselves Christians without accessing in our minds, emotions, and gut responses the basic Christian symbols contained in these texts. Skillfully understood in a twenty-first-century fashion, these old texts illuminate the core revelatory event that makes the Christian religion viable for our practice. We need to learn good methods for doing this. These are ancient sources, easy to misunderstand. They are mostly poetry, story, and metaphorical material from a surprisingly different cultural time. Some of these texts are intentionally cryptic parables that require life changes in ourselves in order to understand them.

The Old Testament is not lesser content than the New Testament. "Old" here does not mean lesser. And "Old" does not mean un-Christian. We Christians are viewing these older texts through the eyes of the New Testament revelation. So viewed, we are seeing these older texts as Christian foundations for newer, more obviously Christian revelation texts. This Christian perspective on these ancient texts need not entail any sort of disrespect for the use made of these same texts by Jewish and Muslim practitioners.

Biblical study (Old and New Testament) is so important for the life together of the co-pastorate that I recommend that one whole quarter every year be devoted to relative mastery of these texts. For a first biblical study, I recommend my own commentary on the gospel of Mark. I have entitled it *The Creator of Christianity*; it spells out the perspective summarized in chapter 12. Every verse is quoted with comments on every set of verses. I have also written study manuals on selected verses from the book of Genesis, the Psalms, the gospel of John, and the writings of Paul. My aim in all these study resources is to provide a contemporary route to opening the relevance of these very old writings. Walter Brueggemann has done similar work on the Old Testament, especially the Prophets. I suggest his *Hopeful Imagination: Prophetic Voices in Exile* as a place to begin.

3. *Church history* has many of the same characteristics and difficulties as Scripture. We can even consider many key texts as an extension of Scripture. I do not consider it needful to allocate a whole quarter for church history study every year. But such a study can be a substitute for a scripture quarter or a contemporary theologizing quarter, whenever that seems appropriate. Paul Tillich's *A History of Christian Thought* is a profound and fairly accessible source. I recommend starting with Augustine's controversy with Pelagius, on page 122. Herein are many old clarifications still needed today. Another useful introduction to church history can be found in Part Two of my book *The Love of History and the Future of Christianity*.

## Some Common-Language Study Suggestions

We must not, however, limit our four quarters of co-pastor group study to Christian-language studies. We also need to read other-than-Christian materials every year. Resurgent Buddhism and Hinduism are both important. The best of the East is important to our understanding of the general topic of profound consciousness and religion. Jewish and Islamic theologizing are also important, for these heritages are members in the same family of Arabic-originated religions as Christianity. This proximity leads Christians to believe that they understand more than they do about these two sister religions.

We also need to expose ourselves to contemporary spirit methods that may apply to any religion. I am recommending that a co-pastors circle spent one quarter every year studying some other religion or some general spirit method like meditation, prayer, or internalizing devotional poetry.

I also recommend spending one quarter each year on *social ethics and/or action plans* for our circle. This can include secular topics like basic contextual ethics, contemporary social justice, ecological responsibility, overcoming patriarchy, bioregionalism, as well as workshops on planning the co-pastors circle's action within its parish of responsibility.

## Other Religions and/or Spirit Methods

I suggest circles begin with taking in the wisdom of the East. I strongly recommend Jon Bernie's *The Unbelievable Happiness of What Is.* Consider also Joan Tollison's *Bare-Bones Meditation: Waking Up from the Story of My Life. Emptiness Dancing* by Adyashanti is also an excellent study book on Eastern wisdom. Among the hundreds of good books on Eastern gifts, these three are both accessible and profound.

On Islam, our circle found helpful Reza Aslan's *No God but God: The Origins, Evolution, and Future of Islam.* This book provides a strong historical overview and a devotional exposition that illumines some universal insights of this overall heritage. Charlene Spretnak's *States of Grace* provide a good introduction to Buddhism, Native American spirituality, Goddess spirituality, and the Semitic traditions. This is a splendidly contemporary affirmation of all of these very different practices.

Here is a surprisingly useful spirit-methods workshop: viewing each week a forty-five-minute session from a spirit-sensitive video series like *From Lark Rise to Candleford* or *Friday Night Lights* and following each viewing with a fifteen-minute conversation, using an art-form method of conversation that follows the sequence of these four types of questions, asking for responses to (1) objective memories of the viewing, (2) emotional reflections about the impact of this drama, (3) interpretive comments of a general nature, and then ending with (4) theological questions like: "Where in this video did you see a state of estrangement in some character?" And then, "In what scene did you see in the ongoing life of some character the healing of an estrangement?" Then, "What do you mean by 'healing'?" And, "Which character and when in his or her story did that character encounter what you point to with the word 'God'?" Then, "What do you mean by 'God'?" See Appendix A for a fuller explanation of this art-form discussion method.

## Social Ethics and Action Plans

Here is an example of the kind of social ethics studies that a co-pastors circle needs to share: David Orr's *Dangerous Years: Climate Change, the Long Emergency, and the Way Forward.* We studied this well-written, visionary book in our circle with great effect for both planetary clarification and our local activism. A study guide for it is posted on our website: https://realisticliving.org/blog/study-outlines/. Our circle also studied the forward-looking fourth part of Naomi Klein's *No Is Not Enough: Resisting Trump's Shock Politics and Winning the World We Need*. Part 4 on "How Things Could Get Better" speaks strongly to the lack of hopefulness that clouds our thought and work. Another key study is Naomi Klein's *This Changes Everything: Capitalism vs the Climate*. This is Klein's most complete analysis of our most urgent topic.

An older but still primary ecological context book is Thomas Berry's *The Great Work: Our Way into the Future*. Also included in this list of recommendations is a broad primary book pulled together from many sources by me and four co-authors—Ben Ball, Marsha Buck, Ken Kruetziger, and Alan Richard: *The Road from Empire to Eco-Democracy*. On the crucial topic of "Overcoming Patriarchy," I recommend a three-part video series entitled *Women and Spirituality: The Goddess Trilogy*. Part 1 is entitled *Goddess Remembered*. Part 2 is entitled *The Burning Times*. And part 3 is entitled *Full Circle*. These three one-hour videos provide an emotional wallop that can then be followed up with selections from the abundant prose articles and workshops being written on this topic. For example, Joyce Marshall and Pat Webb, two committed spirit feminists, created a one-day workshop, "Beyond Patriarchy," on assisting women and men to move beyond their patriarchal entanglements.

Co-pastors circles also need to study bioregionalism and thereby learn how to live in place, reinhabit the Earth, and build ecological action plans for their geographical home places. A ten-session course could be constructed out of selections taken from these two rather massive volumes: *The Biosphere and the Bioregion: Essential Writings of Peter Berg*, edited by Cheryll Glotfelty and Eve Quesnel, and Mike Carr's *Bioregionalism and Civil Society: Democratic Challenges to Corporate Globalism*. Berg is a founder of this movement, and Carr is a long-term member of this work.

In spite of these many study suggestions, I have only skirted the surface of the sorts of imaginative studies that may be best for a particular co-pastors circle. Each co-pastors circle will live in a different bioregional parish, a different sector of the planet, and work with different people. Even more than the specific study content, I am underlining my conviction that serious study of the above type, continued over years together, is essential for the mission of a vital next Christian group to this increasingly complex and problematic societies in which we live. Study also plays an important role in the nurture of the individual spirit journey of each co-pastor.

## LITURGY

By "liturgy," I mean something very general—any order of nurture, perhaps containing many types of rituals, such as singing, dancing, iconic, and thought-filled elements. "Worship" is another commonly used word for this mode of activity. We may want a word with less attachment to a hierarchical mode of discourse. Perhaps the word "liturgy" can be detached from its associations with its more static, stayed, and stuffy forms.

On the above chart, I indicate a need for both solitary liturgy (or exercises) and group liturgy (or nurture formats). I will begin with a few words about the importance of solitary exercises, plus some suggestions for creating your own. Then I will provide some illustrations of group liturgical practices that have applications to local regular-meeting groups.

### Solitary Liturgy

Because the solitary spirit life needs nurturing and stretching, each co-pastor, in my view, needs at least twenty minutes per day in solitary time that supports an ongoing awakening to profound consciousness. This time alone, done in a scheduled and disciplined fashion, must be tailored by each co-pastor for that person's own perception of his or her current spirit journey. We can learn to let our solitary time emerge from our lives, and yet still find many resources useful to us. These practices may be drawn from Buddhism and other non-Christian sources, as well as from Christian sources.

Here is a threefold typology of solitary practices found in many religions (1) profound dialogue, (2) foundational meditation, and (3) persistent intentions. These three types of solitary practices are spelled out in chapter 5.

1. *Profound dialogue* means reading books, talks, essays, scripture, devotional poetry, profound stories, myths, theology, music, paintings, dance etc. Such time spent with "spirit greats" includes internal dialogue with these authors, artists, or personal acquaintances. We all have an inner council of human voices who can help us access next steps in our spirit journey. And we are each in charge of this process.

2. *Foundational meditation* means a contemplative inquiry that looks within and looks beyond the symbol-using mind toward a conscious *mindfulness* of consciousness itself in quest for our profound consciousness or

authenticity. Time spent in a Buddhist type of meditation is becoming increasingly popular among Christians, Jews, and many others.

3. *Persistent intentions* means employing our essential freedom to initiate requests, often called "prayers," addressed to the onrushing force of Profound Realty. As a solitary practice, such intentions are rehearsals for real choices in the bending of events in the outward responses of our whole lives—toward the lives of others and the course of history.

## Group Liturgy

With regard to illustrating an overall direction for creating an adequate *order of nurture* for a weekly meeting co-pastors circle, I will share in detail the weekly group practice now being used by the Bonham, Texas co-pastors circle of which I am a member. This order of nurture is the result of three decades of practice and many improvements. It illustrates a direction for small group nurture, not a prescription for all groups. It can, however, be a place to begin for newly organized co-pastors circles. Some important elements are illustrated here, and the style of simplicity, yet richness, is demonstrated.

### *The Order of Nurture of the Bonham, Texas Co-Pastors Circle*

The pattern of our two-hour meetings is a three-act drama of: (1) knowing the forgiveness of our lives before the awesome Mystery, (2) hearing the Word of the awed ones who assist us to celebrate a life in awe, and (3) doing the lives of the awed ones—that is, lives of trust, love, and freedom.

This three-act ritual can be described as three rehearsal activities: (1) confession, (2) celebration, and (3) dedication. And these three acts can be described as three qualities of "spirit holiness": (1) humility, (2) gratitude, and (3) compassion.

### Act 1: Confession/Humility

The act of *confession/humility* concludes with a confession and absolution ritual. Before the confession ritual we do some activities that move us into the place of standing before Profound Reality. After hellos and hugs, we gather around a coffee table upon which are three unlit candles. These candles are lit by the guide for this meeting while the whole group sings these words to the tune of "Ghost Riders in the Sky."

> In the name of the Infinite,
> the Silent Mystery,
> In the name of those who lived
> in truth and equanimity,
> In the name of the wind of freedom,
> as it blows through me.
> Amen, Amen.
> Hallelujah! Hallelujah!
> In the name of the Silence,
> the Word and Liberty

During the "amens" and "hallelujahs" we raise our arms. We hold hands during the last two lines. After this general opening, we move to some secular dance music, the rhythm of which we can feel in our body, as well as our emotions. The aim in this part of the ritual is to move out of our ordinary minds and habits and into a confrontation with the Mystery that confronts us in this well-selected music, and by analogy in the temporal flow of Reality.

Following that, we do a five-minute period of silent meditation, focusing on our enigmatic inner being, rather than on mental content. The aim in this part of the ritual is tasting the inner discipline of the contemplative quest that we may do for longer periods in our solitary practices. Here is our introduction to that ritual of silence.

> "Set aside any need to be doing or thinking. Rest in seeing, hearing, touching, tasting, smelling. Let the happening of the moment reveal itself."

A bell is rung to end the silence period. Then we sing a song from our songbook as a transition to the confession and absolution ritual. The confession ritual entails a go-round in which each person shares an answer to a question like, "When this week were you challenged to accept something in your life?" After each person has spoken from the heart with everyone else only listening from the heart, the person serving as guide for that meeting voices a pronouncement of absolution like, "Whatever your relation to your challenge, you are accepted by that Inescapable Mystery in which we dwell."

## Act 2: Celebration/Gratitude

After the absolution, we share *celebrations*—holding up events that have happened to ourselves or others. We hold up anything from a simple happening to the death of a celebrity or a friend. We also celebrate birthdays and anniversaries. We have simple intimate means for doing these celebrations.

Next, an assigned leader reads aloud a bit of Scripture or a bit of religious poetry, and follows the oral reading with these three questions: (1) "What word of phrase do you recall from the reading?" Everyone is asked to answer in sequence around the circle. We call this a "go-round." (2) Then the leader takes three or four responses to this question: "How would you put the meaning of this reading in your own words?" We call this discussion method "popcorn." (3) The leader conducts another go-round, everyone answering this question: "How does this reading address you personally?" The aim of this conversation method is to allow each person (and the group as a whole) to probe our lives with a bit of tradition that is likely to be inspiring to our journey of spirit.

Then, we take a short break for bathroom and refreshment. We reconvene with a song and then do the fifty-minute study or workshop assigned for that evening. The purpose of the study is to *take in* insight that assists us in our spirit journey and/or in our preparation for our mission to our local region and our planet. We allocate this amount of time for study because it has become our view that establishing an adequate practice of Christianity in this hour of history requires a surprisingly deep level of thoroughgoing thoughtfulness. Recovering the essence of Christianity in its *contentless* depth is challenging. The times in which we live and to which we design our mission is complex. The spirit struggle of our age, according to Paul Tillich, specializes in the "anxiety of meaninglessness."[1]

## Act 3: Dedication/Compassion

The transition to act three is made with the singing of these words:

> Come now and pray in us.
> Holy Spirit, come and pray in us.
> Come now and pray in us.
> Holy Spirit, come and pray in us.

1. Tillich, *Courage to Be*.

Then time is allotted for persons to raise their concerns for other persons or for public concerns and causes in the world. A bell is rung ending this time of praying. The meeting is then ended with another singing of the opening song, this time extinguishing the three candles.

In terms of time spent in this order of nurture, Act 3 is relatively short, but the Act 3 theme of dedication to compassionate action has characterized the whole drama. Many of our study sessions are contexts we need in order to serve our parish better. Some of our workshops are explicitly on planning what we will do together in our local place. The prayers we now offer in Act 3 are an exercise of our freedom in order to freely act to bend history in the whole round of our living. And the time given to this prayer service could be extended and elaborated.

Some of our weekly sessions have a different format than the one just outlined. We typically use the last study session each quarter for planning the next quarter. We typically have one whole meeting for celebration with food and some sort of play. Sometimes we show a full-length movie and discuss it.

## Other Group Liturgies

In addition to the weekly *order of nurture* exemplified above, other group liturgies are being explored and developed over time. For example, the Christian bread-and-wine love feast came into being during that first year after the crucifixion. This ritual is thoroughly entangled with the primal symbols of the cross/resurrection revelation. A fresh practice of Christianity need not, perhaps cannot, proceed without a fresh form of this celebration.

We do not do a Eucharist ritual every week in the co-pastors circle meeting. At least one sister group has done so. We have explored experimenting with doing a Eucharist ritual at quarterly celebrations and at some of our training programs. See Appendix B for the most recent version of that experimentation.

In addition to this central ritual, we need to develop new rituals to celebrate various passages in human life: deaths, births, adulthood, marriage, divorce. When a new person joins a co-pastorate, we may want to develop a ritual that includes the meaning of both baptism and ordination. That ritual might use a combination of a water-washing from our estranged era as well as an oil anointment to Christian ministry. We feel in no hurry about putting such rituals into practice, but we want to keep these topics in mind for the long-range reformulation of a viable and vital next Christian practice.

## CONCLUDING OBSERVATIONS

This above description of the co-pastors circle is more than a mere sketch, but less than a completed story. This whole story is yet to be lived. Each co-pastors circle is only an *atom* in the *cosmos* of a viable and vital next Christian practice. Or, each circle is seeking to manifest a *cell* in a next life-phase of the *Body of Christ*.

In the next chapter, I will describe further what I imagine it might look like for two or more co-pastors circles in one bioregion to meet together and act together in ways that are helpful to the life of each circle and to the common mission of two, or perhaps twelve, circles to their home bioregion and to their home planet.

# 22

---

# Building a Network of Co-Pastors Circles

SO WHERE ARE WE now in picturing a viable and vital next Christian practice? In chapter 14, "The Friendliness of Trees," I made the point that a Christian community will be living in the Anthropocene Era, in which humanity is responsible for the ecology of this planet. Christians will take their place in ecological responsibility. In chapter 15, "His-Story, Her-Story, and a New Story," I emphasized that Christianity will share in building a post-patriarchal world—a radical revolution undoing over three thousand years of male rule, entitlements, and put-downs of women—all prominent in our own biblical and church heritages. In chapter 16, "Post-Civilization Christianity," I focused on Christians sharing in building an *eco-democracy* alternative to the top-down organization of our human economies, polities, and cultures. In Christian communal life, this will include overcoming the clergy/laity split. In chapter 17, "The Dead End of Christendom," I noted that we are going to be living in a post-Christendom form of church life that no longer assists kings and queens and other aristocrats to rule an entire human culture. Going forward, Christians will be composed of small groups alongside other small groups of other religious practitioners who are also influencing the overall society. In chapter 18, "Witnessing Love and the Echo of Eternity," I defined the mission of *witnessing love* and what that looks like in the work of a vital and viable next Christianity. In chapter 19, "The Mind of Commonality and the Love of Justice," I defined the mission of *justing love* and what that looks like in the work of a vital and viable next Christianity. In chapter 20, "The Bioregional Parish of Responsibility," I spelled out how both witnessing love and justing love can operate in the

Christian pastoring of a local bioregional parish of responsibility. Finally, in chapter 21, "The Mind of Intimacy and the Co-Pastors Circle," I introduced the deep need for intimate group practices and spelled out a model for a disciplined weekly-meeting Christian life together of nurture and mission—that is, the co-pastors circle.

In all the above chapters, I have been thinking on the basis of decades of practical experiences with these topics. But now, in chapter 22, I am turning toward a vision of the future of Christianity in which I will be sharing images and extrapolations from experiences that I have had in other movements—the civil rights movement, a Christian congregational renewal movement, the bioregional movement, and my more recent experiences with Christians anticipating a next movement in Christian practice. With regard to a movement of co-pastors circles that I am proposing to describe, I have not yet lived to see what I will be envisioning in this chapter.

## THE NEED FOR NETWORKING INSTITUTIONS

The co-pastors circle that I am imagining needs companionship with other co-pastors circles. Each circle will surely have its unique struggles with this new mode of theologizing and with these new modes of religious practice. Being in intimate communal life together and being a group pastor to a bioregional parish are radical commitments that do not cease to be challenging. So each circle can benefit from a network of circles with which it is actively connected. Such networking can be a means of improving the life and work of each co-pastors circle, as well as a means of sharing with other co-pastors circles the innovations taking place in those other circles.

The form of networking that I am imagining will create ties that are quite different from the hierarchical patterns that have been used by most of the Christian organizations we have known. Hierarchical structuring is at most six and a half thousand years old, and in most places much younger than that. Networking among hunter-gather tribes in a cultural vicinity is a very old practice. These small-group, non-hierarchical relations worked well for millions of years. This basic pattern of association can also work well today.

The word "institutions" as used in this networking discussion does not mean hierarchical institutions. I use the word "institution" to mean any relatively stable form of human association practiced by humans in order to get something done that could not have been done without this social device. A mob is not an institution. Social Security is an institution. The English language is an institution. An institution gives order to some part of human life together—it provides modes of association, rules, customs, mindsets, methods, regularities, and a great deal of widely understood common sense.

The co-pastors circle is an institutional form. I am going to describe two more institutional forms that I believe are absolutely necessary for a workable communal life carried on by this projected movement toward a viable and vital next Christianity: the *regional assembly* and the *servant office*.

## The Regional Assembly

The first networking social form or institution that I am imagining is a quarterly meeting of all the co-pastors circle members working in a bioregional parish of responsibility. I am imaging a piece of geography small enough to be within a two-hour drive of each co-pastors circle. Why is such an institution needed? As I have mentioned, each circle needs a wider association with other members of this movement both to receive help from the broader movement and to make contributions to that movement. These contacts need to take place at least quarterly for each co-pastor and every co-pastors circle.

This can be structured by having one of the weekly meetings of each circle commonly scheduled on a day that everyone can attend. For example, each co-pastors circle in a given local bioregion might schedule each quarter a Saturday celebration with the other co-pastors circles in that region. This needs to be a substantial, well-planned event worth attending. Let us suppose it begins at 10:00 a.m. to allow for travel time to get there, and is over at 4:00 p.m. to allow travel time home for supper. The meeting might begin with a spirit-intense song or two and an inspirational spirit talk by a member co-pastor of this regional assembly. The talk might be followed with some well-facilitated spirit discussions in smaller groups (nine or less), each group containing members from several different circles. The noon meal might begin with a simple bread-and-wine ritual. A sack lunch, potluck, or catered meal is then enjoyed by all, perhaps eaten at round tables with representatives from several

different circles. The afternoon (1–4 p.m.) could then be devoted to committee meetings of various sorts—dealing with assigned topics of nurture
or mission. All these committees might come together at 3:00 p.m. for
reports and discussion. A day-ending ritual finishes the regional assembly day at about 4:00 p.m.

These details will differ from place to place and time to time, but
such a well-planned and useful meeting is what meets the need I am imaging. I envision all the details for this meeting being worked out by a
committee of talented people chosen at the previous regional assembly.

When the number of co-pastors circles in a region become numerous enough, it may be possible for a more permanent arrangement to
be financed, with a paid staff of about three people from among the co-
pastors in that region. These three people—at least one man and at least
one woman—do much of the organizing work for that regional assembly,
such as: outreach programs of witnessing love or justing love, assisting
new circles to form, problem-solving throughout the region, and training events for both the older and newer co-pastors of that region. The
financial support for this more evolved and larger arrangement would be
the responsibility of these scores of co-pastors. And if a board of directors were desired for holding these finances accountable to the body of
co-pastors, these board members would all be chosen from among the
members of that regional network of co-pastors. The autonomy of each
region and the protection of its culture of nurture and mission depend
upon such an arrangement of financing and polity.

Such a regional operation might create a small office arrangement,
perhaps located in a home. Steps made in these directions would need to
be carefully done in a manner that prevents any anti-democratic policy-
making or outside economic influence. Each region of co-pastors circles
does what it can afford with personnel and money derived from the co-
pastors circle members who live in that region. I am imagining a regional
assembly being a fully local manifestation, starting simply and becoming
more complex in a careful, step-by-step manner.

A paid office of three persons will manifest a certain power of influence regarding the local circles, but that power needs to be strictly accountable to the circles so that a balance of influence exists both ways—from
circles to regional assembly and from regional assembly to circles. We
have all been conditioned to use organizational methods different from
these. Such non-hierarchical patterns may occasion a rocky learning curve
in many instances. Nevertheless, it is important to avoid any return to a

subtle form of the clergy/laity split. We want to have only democratically selected leaders who are servants of the whole body of co-pastors. These servant leaders need to be in trios who check each other's individualism and habitual waywardness. The temptation to become singular chieftains pretending to be servant leaders will never go away. Consensus processes can be difficult at first, but get easier. Consensus among leadership trios does not exclude vigorous discussion. Vigorous discussions may be had throughout all aspects of this political arrangement. In order to maintain the good order of this alternative form of Christian life together, a practical ordering of a consensus-formulated democratic polity is essential and enduring, never optional or of trivial importance.

## The Servant Office

These local, bioregional-oriented regional assemblies across each continent of the planet can be served by a continent-oriented and planetary-oriented institution I am calling a "servant office." This institution serves and yokes this entire movement of regional assemblies and co-pastors circles with one another throughout the planet.

The mission of the servant office I have in mind offers inspiration, publications, useful study materials, training programs, and ongoing research conducted specifically for the co-pastors network. A servant office also acts on behalf of the co-pastors network doing programming for the general population, as well as coordinated dialogues and coordinated actions of an interreligious scope. In chapter 23 I will discuss the specifics of the public programming of a servant office and how it might be organized and financed.

At the present time, the Realistic Living organization is an experiment in the direction of exemplifying the type of programming I am imagining for dozens of these servant offices in the long-range future of this movement. For now the priority is organizing co-pastors circles and their regional assemblies.

## MOVEMENTAL CHRISTIANITY
## AND THE TASK OF ESTABLISHMENT

The entire co-pastors network needs to be viewed as a movement within Christianity, rather than a new establishment of Christianity.

"Movemental Christianity" is a term that points to a long history in the life of Christianity. Most Roman Catholic and Eastern Orthodox religious orders can be viewed as examples of movemental Christianity. Like religious orders, many Protestant denominations in their early history can be considered movemental expressions on behalf of reforms for the overall Christian establishment.

The various movemental forms of Christianity have commonly had serious tensions with the established expressions of this religion. Tensions with established Christianity will also be inevitable for the movemental form of Christianity being described in this book. The tensions between this emerging co-pastors movement and the current establishments of Christianity may be severe. The Protestant Reformation was a reform of Christendom—something less than a replacement of Christendom. This co-pastors circle network, however, will be an alternative mode of social organization from Christendom, with a basically alternative style of theologizing, innovative life together, and quality of missional work. The co-pastors movement I am describing is a replacement for Christendom, rather than a reform of Christendom—a replacement of congregational life, of denominational structures, of the entire public face of existing Christianity across the world.

The type of theologizing I outlined in Part Two of this book necessitates a sociological break with Christendom and the construction of a viable and vital next Christian practice. This is somewhat like the first-century Christ-Way Jews coming to see that their new wine of spirit required new sociological wineskins. It is my long-considered view that such a circumstance has become true again. We need a thoroughgoing sociological break from the currently existing establishments of Christian practice.

Of course, there will be continuity with the basic faith and spirit discoveries within the entire history of Christianity. In that sense, I am not talking about a different religion, but I am talking about a clear turning point in the history of the entire set of existing Christian religions. Nevertheless, for the time being this movement for a next Christianity can be said to be taking place within the Christianities of Christendom, even though the aim of this movement is a type of starting over alongside congregational life, rather than a reform within congregational life.

Practically, what this means now is that a co-pastors circle is not a program within an existing congregation. It is done alongside, not within, the congregational canopy. This practice will be of benefit both to the congregation and to the co-pastors circle. Any attempt to have a co-pastors circle within a congregation will challenge the congregation in ways that are not helpful for the congregation to do the job it can still do. Also, trying to do co-pastors circles within a congregation will limit the vitality and realism of a co-pastors circle. With these last two sentences, I am describing experiences that most of us have had.

This organizational tension does not mean, however, that the co-pastors circle movement must hold the congregations of Christendom as irrelevant. The co-pastors movement can retain respect for the existing formations of Christendom while also radically departing from them. Here are values some congregations maintain: (1) memory banks of the deep history of the Christian heritage, (2) people who are still open to giving Christian practice a try, (3) people who somehow hear the basic address of the gospel and are making some measure of response to the Christian revelation in spite of inadequate theologizing and restricted responses to twenty-first-century ethical challenges, (4) some Christian congregations make positive contributions to their neighborhoods, and do so in excess of the service clubs, neighborhood organizations, and other concerned groups.

The co-pastors circle movement can elicit cooperation and assistance from Christendom, as appropriate. This cooperation may be more lively with regard to the social mission than to realistic theologizing and Christian nurture. We are experiencing a formidable tension between the co-pastors theologizing and Christendom's heavenly God-talk.

It is important for co-pastor members to understand that the two-story symbol system was not always a destructive force. In the past, this symbol system was used helpfully, as well as unhelpfully, for thousands of years. We must watch out for our own historical blind spots. Our best-case theologizing is about finding twenty-first-century ways of translating the practices of the past into relevance for our present and future cultures.

The above considerations bring many difficulties into the co-pastors circle movement's relations with the congregations of Christendom. We cooperate where we can, and yet over the long haul we will struggle with these congregations for both people and money. We will be letting these congregations die their natural death. Herein is the destiny we are choosing: the congregational model will decrease and the co-pastors model will increase. This huge shift will be taking place, however, over a period of decades, not years. Patience will be required, along with the urgency to make these necessary changes as quickly as we can. The enduring context for this whole transition will require the benefit of forgiveness.

During the long-range dismantlement of Christendom, there can also be reforms of Christendom. There is no need for these congregations to be sexist, racist, anti-evolution, anti–global warming, anti-intellectual, and so on. Such improvements in these passing organizations can be viewed as a positive development from the perspective of the co-pastors circle movement. In spite of the fact that reforms will allow these congregations to last longer, reforms can be viewed as steps toward the co-pastors network vision of the future.

## NEXT STEPS IN THE EMERGENCE OF THE CO-PASTORS CIRCLE MOVEMENT

Let us assume that you are one person, or one couple, or perhaps three people, and you want to begin a co-pastors circle—as well as help build the co-pastors circle movement. What do you do first, second, third, and so on?

### Step 1

Conduct courses for interested people in your parish of responsibility. You can start with secular courses on any topic that you find people will attend. At some point (perhaps right away), you will need to conduct a course on contemporary Christian theologizing. I have written the following accessible books for this exact purpose. I am listing them in order of their accessibility to people relatively new to such theologizing.

*Radical Gifts: Living the Full Christian Life in Troubled Times*

*The Creator of Christianity: A Commentary on the gospel of Mark*

*Great Paragraphs of Protestant Theology*

*The Call of the Awe: Rediscovering Christian Profundity in an Inter-Religious Era*

*The Love of History and the Future of Christianity.*

*Jacob's Dream: A Christian Inquiry into Spirit Realization*

*The Thinking Christian: 23 Pathways of Awareness*

The Søren Kierkegaard thread of theologizing has been followed up best, in my view, by these four mid-twentieth-century theologians: Paul Tillich, Dietrich Bonhoeffer, H. Richard Niebuhr, and Rudolf Bultmann. There have been many other men and women before, during, and after these four luminaries—persons who have fleshed out the mid-twentieth-century theological ferment. These four, however, have been the center of the swirl for me, and I think that studying them in the co-pastors circles is needed for a successful movement to establish a viable and vital next Christianity.

My own writings mentioned above have attempted to synthesize and simplify the essence of these four luminaries into a more accessible form. I have also worked at adapting these breakthroughs for the late-twentieth- and early-twenty-first-century flow of cultural events. Many other writers have done similar writing, often in a somewhat different direction than mine. I maintain, however, that the co-pastors of a viable and vital next Christianity need to study these four renowned theologians and give them prominent places on their meditative councils.

Here are a few of the more accessible books of these five stalwarts of Christian theologizing:

Paul Tillich's sermons: *The Shaking of the Foundations*, *The New Being*, and *The Eternal Now*

Dietrich Bonhoeffer's *The Cost of Discipleship* and *Life Together*

H. Richard Niebuhr's *Radical Monotheism and Western Culture*

Rudolf Bultmann's *Primitive Christianity in Its Contemporary Setting*

Søren Kierkegaard's *Training in Christianity*

I consider these books good places to begin. I mention in the bibliography several other books by these authors that I consider basic, but many of them (such as Tillich's *The Courage to Be*) are more challenging than those just listed.

I am fostering a basic familiarity with these four theologians over the many other good works written later, because I consider these four writers playing a similar role in the history of contemporary Christian theology as Mark, Matthew, Luke, and John played in the first-century definition of Christian thoughtfulness about the cross/resurrection event of revelation. In both cases, four theologians have written four quite different theologies, but all four operate from a similar inspiration. This is not easy to see, for we confuse thought with spirit (that is, with the profound consciousness that transcends thought). We have to look through thought to spirit in order to see what I am attempting to indicate with the unity of this quartet of theological luminaries.

Some of the theological thinkers who have been enamored with liberation theology in its many forms have been critical of the above four theologians for not pursuing these social ethics matters far enough. Liberation theology was indeed a move beyond these four earlier theologians, but I do not believe that liberation theology was as radical a move as these four were a move beyond liberal theology. The liberation theologians have been more like spelling out supportive additions to these four mid-twentieth-century revolutionaries in theological thoughtfulness.

I believe that all four of above theologians were liberations theologians. Indeed, Tillich left Europe mostly due to his Christian-rooted political thinking. H. Richard Niebuhr, like his brother Reinhold and Reinhold's student Martin Luther King Jr., were strongly sociological Christian thinkers, still followers of the Social gospel of Walter Rauschenbusch. Bonhoeffer's book *Ethics* is a fight with the lack of good politics in both liberalism and Nazi perverseness. Bonhoeffer died in his social activism. And while Bultmann focused almost entirely on the outer reaches of biblical interpretation, he was also a critic of the German state-church ethics, as well as a risk-taking Christian who assisted Jewish scholars to escape Germany. Also, Bultmann's understanding of *faith as a true deed* has sociological implications, some of which were spelled out well by his student and critic Dorothee Soelle.

Liberation theology first emerged as an interpretation of and liberation for the poor. Such thinking then moved into Black liberation from ongoing racism and liberation for women from the still strong hangovers of patriarchy. These remain crucial topics in Christian theology and ethics. Books on these themes can be important studies in our co-pastors circles. For example, in our circle in Bonham, Texas, we spent a fruitful quarter studying Howard Thurman's *Jesus and the Disinherited*. Many other books of this quality and accessibility can be found.

Also crucial is the late-twentieth- and early-twenty-first-century advent in ecological theologizing, which can also be viewed as an important vision moving beyond these four mid-twentieth-century revolutionaries. Thomas Berry's *The Dream of the Earth* makes a convincing case for a Christian theology of ecology. But again, I see no revolutionary contradiction between Berry's work and the social implications of the above four theological players.

The same applies to the extensive expansion of Christian dialogue with other religions. In his last years, Paul Tillich wrote an essay on Buddhism, and he most likely would have done more if he had lived longer. In this book I have included many reflections on the ongoing Christian dialogue with Buddhism, Hinduism, Taoism, and other Eastern spirit probes. I count this an enrichment of the Kierkegaardian thread of Christian theologizing and recommend a once-a-year study of these topics in co-pastors circles.

The "death of God" thread in post-mid-twentieth-century Christian theologizing has included some needed further critique of the heavenly-God-talk mode of theologizing. Here again, I count the above four mid-twentieth-century Christian theologians as doing an early form of "death of God" theologizing. At the same time, they were introducing a new use the words "God," "theology," "sacred," and other such words. They were giving these words a *devotional*, rather than a *rational content* meaning. This topic has not been expanded upon adequately, in my view, by most of these contemporary "death of God" theologians. My mentor Joe Mathews pushed this *contentless* topic toward ever further clarity until his death in 1977. I have continued this emphasis, which I consider vital to a next Christian theologizing and for maintaining an adequate devotional contact with both Old and New Testaments, as well as with the classical Christian theologians. So, while reading late-twentieth- and twenty-first-century "death of God" theologizing can be useful, provocative, and even needed, the tendency in these works to do without the word "God" altogether make doubtful the claim that this is "theology" of any sort. I also maintain that any recovery of a communal and liturgical practice of the Christian religion cannot be adequately brought to be without a use of the word "God." And we do not need to wait for such a "God" to come. A new use of the word "God" has already come in the mid-twentieth-century vision. Here it is: this word "God" has no *content* except *devotion* to all the content of our own lives. These insights recommend having a strong background of familiarity with the four theological giants I have chosen as my key gospel writers for contemporary theologizing.

So, whatever later theological works a typical co-pastors circle may choose to study, I recommend a basic familiarity with the unity of spirit thoughtfulness that characterizes these earlier four theologians cited above, as well as their core spirit ancestor, Søren Kierkegaard. We have in these five key theologians a firm foundation for discerning what is poor theologizing and what is best-case theologizing among all the later decades of liberation, ecological, interreligious, and "death of God" theologizing. Please notice that I am recommending for our co-pastors theological study life an openness to the trends in contemporary theological writing, yet also developing a critical core loyalty to the spirit essence of the cross/resurrection revelation. This need not be characterized as either orthodoxy or "anything goes" thinking. I am recommending a spirit-driven form of thoughtfulness rooted in the core Christian symbols.

## Step 2

If study is step 1, step 2 is starting to meet weekly with at least three people, preferably five to twelve, who are open to a new and serious means of practicing a next Christian religion. In the beginning such weekly meetings will surely include further study together and then begin to include some discussion about this very discipline of weekly nurture meetings, perhaps soon employing a simple liturgy as suggested in chapter 21.

Once decisions have been made to begin meeting together, the nurture and mission of a disciplined co-pastors practice can be further clarified and a more complete ritual of nurture put in place. Much of the learning needed for doing step 2 is best done by be doing step 2. Step 2 includes patiently learning the various practices that nurture your group over a period of time.

And we will need to become and remain aware that taking on this co-pastors calling is a major adventure for ourselves—for anyone. Organizing a workable co-pastors circle will require growing into this task—including a great deal of forgiveness, a certain amount of patience with one another, and some steady work clarifying the contexts that make for ongoing encouragement and boldness. Though this book is based on decades of group experiences, it is still only suggestive to other groups. Life is unique for each person and for each group. I am calling for every co-pastors circle to follow your own "spirit lights," rather than personality propensities. This is not only possible, but necessary for a spirit-focused next Christianity.

## Step 3

Step 3 includes assisting one another, in this now-active meeting co-pastors circle, to understand and accept the calling to be a new kind of ministry to a local bioregional parish of responsibility. This can begin by learning the rough boundaries of that geographical parish and what goes on in that region. Your specific parish designation needs to be large enough to have bioregional meaning for a dozen co-pastors circles, and small enough to be less than an hour's driving distance from any part to any other part of that bioregion.

We will want each member of a co-pastors circle to be clear that our Christian mission is to every person in that region, whether they practice a Christian religion or not. In doing our ministry of justing love, our Christian practice can usually go unmentioned. This invisibility can also characterize our common-language type of witnessing love. Only in our Christian-language witnessing does our own Christian practice become overt and clarified. Our Christian-language witnessing is precisely healing the Christian language. We let that language carry its own healing power as it does when existentially understood by specific individuals.

We do not need to point out how our "good work" is rooted in our Christian faith. At the same time, we are not hiding our Christian commitment. When appropriate, we are willing to share our Christian understanding and practice in a confessional rather than an oppressive way. We will be arranging occasions when such Christian language understandings are shared with interested persons or in courses and other public programs that we have organized people to attend or have been invited to conduct.

## Step 4

If you are the only co-pastors circle in your region of the planet, your circle will also function as the regional assembly for that bioregion. Each circle begins and remains responsible for conducting courses and circle organizing for that entire region. If there is to be a movement for a next Christianity of this quality, we must build and continue to build from the grassroots out to whatever larger scopes can come into being. These larger-scope organizations will then help the entire effort, but each member of each local circle remains responsible for the whole movement. We never arrive at an organization in which each and every-co-pastor ceases to be responsible for the whole.

Such a view of responsibility increases the agency for each and every member of this emerging co-pastors Network. We each do what we are able to do, but we do it in the context of organizing and maintaining this entire movement toward a viable and vital next Christian practice. There is no such thing as my tiny part. My tiny spoon lifts the whole mountain. Each of us remains responsible for the entire enterprise our whole life long. In that context we make our specific choices. Guilt for what we do not do for this large scope of responsibility will always be present. This does not crush us, because all is forever forgiven. This forgiveness is also our freedom to expend our lives here or there or somewhere else. This freedom is our only righteousness. We have no intelligible laws by which to confirm our specific deeds as righteous.

## Step 5

When there are two or more circles in your region, you can begin meeting quarterly as a multi-circle regional assembly. This will include expanding the mission for that region of witnessing and justing love as outlined in the above chapters. This also includes expanding the inspiration of more co-pastors circles and regional assembles across the planet. These images of responsibility are overwhelming to the extent that we will always be finding ourselves guilty of omissions. Here again, we live in trust that we are being forgiven for the inevitable smallness of our responses toward the emergence of this huge project of establishing a movement toward a viable and vital next Christian practice. We can, however, each grasp our small corner of the load and walk our path.

## WHAT IS MOVEMENT-BUILDING?

We won't fully know how to build a movement like the one I am describing until such a movement has been built. Movement-building is especially mysterious when we are building a movement that has not yet happened anywhere in a full sense. Furthermore, movements don't just happen. In the beginning a small group of persons work to inspire a larger movement of humans to move. This same sort of sociology of ongoing communal practice provides structures of nurture and mission that sustain the movement through times of resistance, as well as through times of temptation among the movers to quit moving.

These dynamics I saw firsthand when in the early 1960s I joined two movements simultaneously—the civil rights movement that was already moving, and a religious order of Christian families whose teaching and organizing called into being what we called a "spirit movement" to "re-new Christianity for the sake of renewing the world." Many members of this "spirit movement" participated strongly in the civil rights movement and in other justice and ecological movements. This twentieth-century movement to renew Christianity swirled around the leadership of the Order:Ecumenical and its incorporations: the Ecumenical Institute and the Institute of Cultural Affairs. These actions touched tens of thousands of people with regard to their relevant theologizing, religious practices, and justice participations.[1]

Later in 1984, Joyce and I joined the bioregional movement. After a year of getting acquainted with this new and important movement, we took on organizing roles in this movement for over two decades. Our experiences of successes and difficulties with sustaining that movement also enriched our sensibilities about movements in general.

Also beginning in 1984, Joyce and I began sharing, in a fresh version of a "spirit movement," to put in place on this planet a viable and vital next Christian practice along the lines I am now outlining in this book. I am pulling together reflections that paint an overview of this movement. I am seeking to provide more clarity about the realistic possibilities for creating a successful result toward establishing in history a viable and vital next Christian practice.[2]

## Blocks to the Moving of This Movement

By "blocks" I mean what is resisting movement in our world situation and in ourselves as awakening Christians. Blocks to a social movement are always both within the culture at large and within the change actors themselves.

For example, the main block I am addressing in Part One of this book is the loss within our culture and within ourselves of a clear grasp of what healthy religion is all about. This includes a sense of what religion

1. See Mathews, *Bending History*, vols. 1 and 2.

2. For further information see the Realistic Living website: RealisticLiving.org.

has always been about at its best, and what religions can be about and need to be about in the societies of our human future. In order to do the hard work of creating a next Christian practice of religion, we need clarity about religion in general—what religion is for, the importance of religion, and what a reworked Christianity for our time needs to be in relation to this whole spectrum of religious renewal taking place on planet Earth.

In Part Two of this book, the main block I am addressing is the conscious and unconscious hatred of Christianity as currently experienced by millions of people. One quite strong hatred is the mostly unconscious habit of burying the Christian revelation in syrupy sentimentality and hypocritical moralism. There is also an eclipse of true Christianity beneath our culture's conscious and unconscious rationalism, individualism, and collectivism. The holders of these widespread partial truths wish not to be disturbed by the more forceful realism that a Christian recovery uncovers.

A justified hatred of current forms of Christianity is found among progressive humanists, who are clear how current Christian practices are indeed complicit with some of the worst impulses of our humanity. A fourth form of hatred of Christianity is a form of cynical sloth that views the deep challenge of a fully active Christian faith to be too severe or too overwhelming for mere human beings to consider. This last hatred is as excuse-making about living in general that all of us, if we are honest, find in ourselves quite often.

In Part Three of this book, the main block I am addressing is a paralysis of action among those of us who are genuinely seeking to live our Christian faith. It can seem overwhelming to confront the enormous challenge of being a co-pastor to other co-pastors who then together assume responsibility for a whole region of humanity. Taking up such a calling to make such a contribution to human history can stun even the most dedicated Christian. Indeed, it is a challenge simply to work with ourselves and our Christian colleagues, for all of us are prone to backsliding into distractions, trivialities, self-glorifications, blaming others, and ingrown complaints about almost everything.

Being "crucified with Jesus" takes on fresh detail when we notice the power of the above blocks to building and sustaining a next Christianity. It will take hearts devoid of egoism to see clearly and feel deeply the hope and joy in this activist approach to Christian living. Fortunately, the sustaining of our joy, love, and passion is out of our hands. The Christian life is sustained by Profound Reality. Nothing is required of us, except our surrender to our real possibilities.

## CONCLUDING CONSIDERATIONS

Beginning to actually do the above five steps will undoubtedly improve our vision of this whole project. As our successes and failures are manifest, this vision will surely lead to further opportunities to clarify this vision. The purpose of composing such a vast vision is not to discourage, but to give encouragement. Our vision is not about perfection or probabilities; our vision is about clarifying what we are choosing to do. Our hope and joy reside in this choosing and in the support we feel for it from Reality.

We certainly want realism in our vision, but Reality in the profound sense is a huge unexplored Mystery. We have to prove that our vision can or cannot be done by moving toward doing our vision. We can remain open to that still-better vision that will surely emerge in the process of action toward the vision we now hold.

The vision I am exploring in this chapter is a limited vision. I say this not to discourage, but to encourage. I am making extrapolations from previous experiences in doing movement-building. From those past experiences, I find evidence for the truthfulness of this vision. Nevertheless, what is true for any vision is well said in this old saying: "The proof of the pudding is in the eating."

# 23

## A New Public Face for Christianity

THE FIRST PUBLIC FACE of the movement that became Christianity was a sect of Judaism. Through most of the first century, Christians presented themselves publicly as what we might call "Christ-Way Jews."

### PUBLIC FACE 2

Sometime after 70 CE, Christianity began to emerge as a separate religious practice, a people who understood themselves to be *called out* of Judaism and also *called out* of the Roman Empire to be a new humanity ritually washed of that corrupt era and *called to* the task of *calling* others to join this ritual washing.

Being "in Christ" came to mean a new peoplehood—a new covenant, continuous in some ways with the older exodus covenant, yet also quite new. Leaving Egypt was still part of the Christian story, but a new story was being used now to interpret the old story. This development amounted to a new public role in the history of human affairs.

### PUBLIC FACE 3

In 311 CE, Constantine the Great made being Christian legal. He may have done this for his own imperial purposes, but Constantine clearly joined forces with this now-significant social force—most strong among the middle and lower classes of the Mediterranean world. Constantine called a council and facilitated it, hoping to initiate some unity among the widely differing expressions of this wildly expanding and quite diverse movement. He was perhaps distressed by the need to take sides in some serious fights among Christians to define the "orthodox" Christianity.

Within this new situation of opportunity for safety and further expansion, most of the leaders and luminaries among the Christian forces opted to create a new public face for themselves within this now-friendlier imperial world. They became partners with the imperial government. This had downsides as well as upsides. Many opposed it in theological ways. Others revolted from this "dilution of faith" with ascetic practices. But the overall pattern of being Christian was chosen by most of this movement to become *a*, and eventually *the*, center of cultural influence—a new overview of religion and consciousness for all the classes of the Roman and Eastern hierarchies.

Church-state Christendom was born—a very different public face for this movement of spirit than existed in the first three centuries. Within this stable public form the original wildly creative quality still moved. Both contemplative and activist religious orders gave new energies to the overall. There were ongoing theological fights and reforms. Several forms of Christendom arose, sometimes seriously warring with each other for prominence. Yet the main notion driving these warring segments was the drive to be a unified religion for a whole society. This public face for Christianity persisted until the breakup that has been called the Protestant Reformation and the Catholic Counter-Reformation. These developments opened up the possibility for another basic form for the public face of Christianity.

## PUBLIC FACE 4

During the Protestant era, a new public face came to characterize the Christian religion in most places. This new face was rather slow in emerging; early Protestant churches were simply an alternative form of the state-church arrangement. But by the eighteenth century we see a new public face emerging—self-supporting Christian denominations with competing congregations in most neighborhoods. Hangovers of church-state financing and organizing continued in some places, but the overall planet-wide picture was becoming a "separation of church and state," as we sometimes speak of it. This refers to the predominance of self-supporting denominations that present to the public a wide range of options for their Christian practices and do not depend upon state financing, but only state protection and state privilege of pursuing their influence upon social affairs. We might understand tax exemptions as a hangover of state support, but it can also be understood as a form state protection.

This Protestant-era public face of Christianity was also grounded in an array of buildings, from simple frame boxes with steeples to magnificent cathedrals hundreds of years old. There were also monasteries where people lived, and offices, gymnasiums, preschools, universities, and centers for almost every purpose.

All of these buildings were staffed with people, some in special garb, most of whom lived at home and came to work at these properties. Crosses, crucifixes, and Bibles were visible in these buildings, in homes, and scattered widely throughout the society. Every mode of art, from architecture to sculpture, to painting, to music, to dance, to drama, developed its Christian forms. Almost every library had its books. Billions of people attended its events. Various Christian pageants appeared on secular calendars.

In chapter 16, I joined with Douglas John Hall in viewing this Protestant-era public face as another form of Christendom. I am envisioning a future public face for Christianity that is beyond both the medieval and the Protestant-era forms of Christendom. I am describing the emergence of an already-present movement of Christians who will be, in my view, putting into history a fifth public face for Christianity.

## THE PUBLIC FACE OF A VIABLE
## AND VITAL NEXT CHRISTIANITY

I am envisioning the next public face for Christianity as more like the first three centuries than like the Middle Ages or the Protestant era. I am also viewing this post-Christendom public face as significantly different from the pre-Christendom period as well. In both its nurture and its mission, it will have a fresh local quality, planetary quality, democratic quality, and interreligious-dialogue quality we have not seen in these earlier eras. Also new will be the post-Kierkegaardian mode of theologizing. These new awarenesses will generate new types of religious practices and new modes of social mission.

The next public face of Christianity that I am envisioning will forgo bishops and other singular potentates. Everyone is a leader to the extent that he or she is able. And all paid leaders of this movement will be structured as members of leadership teams of at least three persons. Each leadership team will feature both women and men, and such gender equity will be counted as an enormous improvement in the quality of Christianity.

My reasons for these patterns of operation have to do with protecting a spirit democracy from the singular charismatic, hiding within us all, who wants to build community around a single personality of whatever spirit maturity. Rather than charismatic persons, we will be building community around the leadership of the Jesus Christ revelation of realism to which we will all share a devotional surrender and commitment. In addition, our common style of thinking and action will be based on experiencing Eternity in every temporal event that is happening to us.

Like pre-Christendom, our mission will emphasize calling humanity out of this world. And like Christendom, our mission will call humanity into this world as perpetual revolutionaries of justice. We are in this world—body, mind, consciousness—and in a specific society. We are also in the Eternal Now, which allows our spirit life to dwell with Abraham, Moses, Jesus, and Paul, as well as to travel in time to imagine the tomorrows we are building.

A major feature of this new public face for Christianity includes a broad set of awakenment speeches, training courses, workshops, inter-religious conversations, books, essays, and social media that reach the general public in ways that communicate, "This is what Christianity can look like today and tomorrow." We see similar patterns of programming in many current Buddhist movements throughout North America with five-day, ten-day, and thirty-day retreats and other programs, websites, books, and media—all handled by various offices and programming centers that are well staffed and organized.

The co-pastors circles and their regional assemblies will not be like secret societies that hide the fact of their existence. Yet, the regular meetings of these two institutions will be less obvious to the general public. There will be no steeples on our meeting places, no signs on the door of the homes that house the weekly meeting circles. The regional assemblies may take place in ordinary motel and hotel meeting rooms. The co-pastors circle and the regional assembly are meetings for co-pastors and, occasionally, a few guests who are seriously exploring becoming co-pastors in this network of nurture and mission.

The introduction of new people to the thinking, action, and communal life of this next Christianity does not take place in the co-pastors circles or regional assemblies. This takes place in programing designed and conducted for the express purpose of presenting this new vision of Christian understanding along with some experience of these new religious practices. The introductions to this next Christianity may take place in small private conversations or in Christian language courses and workshops conducted by teams of co-pastors from one or more circles. These courses and workshops are public-face events in the sense that they are publicly advertised through various media, church bulletin boards, mailings, and publications. And these public events will fit within the questions and concerns of the existing world. Theology courses will cover the same edges introduced in this book, and ethics courses may tackle the most controversial issues.

The servant offices introduced in the last chapter are focused on producing this sort of visible programming and assisting the regional assemblies and co-pastors circles in creating and producing their local programming. The servant offices, unlike the circles and assemblies, will be publicly known institutions, publicly known by each co-pastor and publicly known by the surrounding culture at large. These servant offices make strong efforts to be publicly known, both for the sake of their mission and for the sake of their human constituencies and their financial support.

The social justice work of each co-pastors circle and network of circles will be done along with other persons of good will, thereby making Christian visibility in that work unimportant. Only the Christian-language programming of these local circles, assemblies, and servant offices will qualify as a publicly visible face of Christianity. Courses and workshops on Christian-language topics will be among the main tasks of these three organizations of co-pastors. Such programs will be publicly advertised and open to persons who have little or no interest in being Christian circle members. This programming will seek to interest people in knowing and using the radical gifts of Christianity for any religious or secular purpose (being better Buddhists, or whatever). As stated before, healing lives is a prior emphasis to calling people to participation in a co-pastors circle.

It is true, however, that doing the Christian-language programming is building a pool of people from whom new persons can and may feel called to the co-pastors ministry and take up membership in a co-pastors circle. Publicly, these programs will not in the first instance encourage people to become co-pastors—not until they have themselves signaled being called to this work.

Some sort of simple covenanting with a baptismal/ordinational ritual will help mark the entry into one of these circles. However extreme this suggestion may sound, the simple purpose would be to make clear to each circle member that we are taking on a serious commitment to be the living Body of Christ and its mission to all the spirit-level suffering and lack of social justice on planet Earth.

## The Servant Office Programming

The Christian-language programming of the servant offices provides many of the strongest aspects of the public face of this next Christianity. Following are some of the programming that I am imagining being done by one of these servant offices. These programs not only serve the needs of co-pastors circle members, but also reach out into the general society on behalf of the co-pastors circle network. Here are some of the ways that this might be done.

## Books, Booklets, Methods Manuals,
## and Essay Publishing

With books and booklets I am not thinking only of my own half-shelf of books; I am thinking of all the books written and being written that are especially focused on giving form to a next Christian practice. A large number of books exist already—many of which were written by friends. Many of these books cover criteria for supporting the sort of next Christian practice that I am advocating. And I am sure that many more such books will be written and have already been written unbeknown to me. We might even envision a book-publishing company growing out of this co-pastors network movement when our numbers and/or wealth are strong enough to support such an enterprise.

Any co-pastor member anywhere may do this sort of writing, but each servant office has, as one of its key tasks, the producing and distributing to the co-pastors circles and to the general culture useful materials about the quality and practice of a next Christianity. This function is already taking place; one such organization, Realistic Living, is being conducted by a three-person team: Joyce Marshall, Alan Richard, and myself. Realistic Living can be viewed as a precursor of the sort of servant office I am proposing for the long-range future of this co-pastors network.

Realistic living has already published many study courses, study guides, solitary exercise manuals, group life manuals, seventy-two issues of a twice-annual *Realistic Living Journal*, and now a monthly emailing called *Realistic Living Pointers*. In years to come these tasks will, in my imagination, take place in numerous servant offices, financed by the co-pastors circle network. Realistic Living has been a small experiment in developing many of these suggestions. But in the long-range promise of a next Christianity, these experiments have been a bare beginning on the creativity that I am anticipating.

## Web Presence

I envision websites and other means of web presence being created by members of the co-pastors circle network. Each servant office will surely be a focus of some sort of web presence—part of the public face of this next Christianity I am imagining. A well-kept website or blog site can direct spirit seekers to all kinds of resources, Christian and otherwise, that might be helpful to anyone, as well as to assisting members of the co-pastors circle network. The Realistic Living website (RealisticLiving. org) is an example of the kind of services I envision these servant offices doing. A servant office will surely, over time, develop a well-constructed website to mark its presence to the public. A strongly developed regional assembly might also find a website useful. A single co-pastors circle will rarely feel any need for a website, for its tasks can be handled quite well with emails and the Post Office. But a website might be useful for the personal work of an individual co-pastor member. A website might also become useful for various long-running social justice or ecological projects of a bioregional parish.

Other social media that reaches out to selected audiences can also be useful. Web presence is still a fast-changing means of being a public presence. The best norms for its various uses may still be emerging.

## Talks, Courses, and Workshops

Christian-language talks given by co-pastors in various settings are an important part of this ministry. These presentations are what can become of preaching as it morphs into spirit talks, talk-discussions, contexts for workshops, and more. We must in these contemporary times emphasize evoking responsive participation from others, rather than delivering content that is unanswered or crassly manipulated. Content can be important, but personal appropriation is even more important.

Christian-language courses and workshops taught and facilitated by co-pastors will also be a prominent part of the public face for this next Christianity. These activities will also be participatory events. Even if the occasion includes a study of written material, the time involved is used to engage every person personally. Each person is encouraged to respond to the content and share their relationships with it. Christianity is an active faith, not a passive absorption.

Christian-language programming conducted by the staff of a servant office will be an especially big part of the public face of the next Christianity that I am imagining. These programs might be a 9 a.m.–to–4 p.m. part of a Saturday including a noon meal together. Another familiar format is the five-session weekend (Friday evening to Sunday noon).

Ten weeknights of two-hour sessions is also a useful format where teachers and attendees live close to a common location. These events can take place in hotel meeting rooms, campsites, homes, and even churches. Every co-pastors circle and servant office can conduct such events and do so frequently. This is hard work and it entails skills, but these personally helpful events are the key to a meaningful public face for this next Christianity. All co-pastors live in a continual state of learning these skills.

These programs will build constituencies, who can be followed up with other events for those who want to explore these matters further. It will be from a widening community of those who are being healed in this Christian-language programming that some will feel the call to join a circle of co-pastor healers and help with their mission. When people are ready to discuss such engagement (and not before), we will need to be ready with our vision of a co-pastors network of healing and justice mission.

## Four-Day Seminars

This format is for those persons who are already-on-their-way with regard to a spirit awakening. I am thinking here of groups of about thirty people living and meeting in a motel, hotel, or camping facility using such sleeping rooms, meeting rooms, and food services that allow for an uninterrupted four days together (for example, all day Saturday, Sunday, Monday, Tuesday, with travel time on Friday and Wednesday). I am imagining a team of five or six experienced faculty from servant offices and/or the co-pastors circles, who prepare publicity for these seminars, their recruitment, set-ups, talks, workshops, and the detailed care that such an event requires.

I envision eight intensive three-hour training sessions conducted on the four mornings and four afternoons. Each three-hour block might contain an hour talk and fifteen minutes of discussion, followed by a break and then a ninety-minute workshop. The evenings are devoted to various art, spirit life, sensory awareness exercises, a model co-pastors circle meeting, dancing, singing, and other celebrations of life. These are not come and go meetings, but mini-schools for full participation of already awakening men and women who wish to become better leaders of this movement.

## Six-Day Sojourns

A sojourn is another type of leadership training event. The six-day sojourn can be led by two or three trained faculty at the location of one of the servant offices. Such sojourns have been conducted by Joyce Marshall, Alan Richard, and me at our Realistic Living location. One or two people (maybe three) come to live in our guest rooms from Sunday through Friday with travel days on the bookending Saturdays. Each person or couple spends an hour a day with each of the three of us. This hour is tailored for that person or couple. The topics of these hour sessions are related to several of the following: a person's current spirit journey, vocational directions, interpersonal snarls, theological topics, skills with spirit methods, profound consciousness probing, handling one's own personality type, and/or relating to the personality types of persons who are their primary relationships or coworkers. In addition to these uniquely personal matters, a sojourner also participates in the whole round of ongoing common life at this location, a co-pastors circle meeting, art experiences and their discussions, meditation, Tai Chi, dancing, singing, cooking, eating, exercise, solitary practices, and serious rest. Each six-day sojourn is a tailored retreat focused on a person's or a couple's next steps in appropriation of profound consciousness and activism.

## The Eight-Week Training School

If we are going to develop theologically and methodologically trained members in every co-pastors circle, we will need arrangements for thorough training to be done. This can begin with eight-week-long educational modules that might be done in four-week segments. This has been done before with considerable success with the Ecumenical Institute, where I was dean of twelve of these eight-week academies over a period of six years. Each of these academies had eight to twelve faculty with ninety to one hundred eighty participants from a number of locations across the planet. Training events similar to this, using an updated design, can be done in the future when this movement has assembled the human and economic resources to make such events possible.

The need for this level of next-Christianity training is a result of the huge and rapid changes that are taking place in the general culture, as well as in Christian practice. I envision these eight-week schools sharing edge cultural and theological content, methods of truth-seeking, using depth-discussion methodologies that involve each participant personally, plus using art, drama, music, dance, and ritual practices of high quality.

Such innovations may overlap with innovations already happening in the best of Christian seminaries, but rather than using the traditional academic style, I imagine these eight-week schools being an intimate life together in the style of the seminars and sojourns described above.

## Interreligious Convocations

I can imagine groups of Christian co-pastors joining with awakening groups of contemporary Buddhists, Hindus, Taoists, or combinations of these and other Eastern practices to share deep awarenesses and build cooperative action. Other such programs for similar purposes can be held with awakening groups of Muslims or Jews or combinations of these three Western practices. Christian co-pastors might also join in similar dialogues with pagan, Goddess, Native American, and Native African, and other long-practiced traditions. I envision co-pastors initiating convocations that build mutually enhancing and cooperative contributions made to our times.

## Other Programming

I do not claim that the above is an inclusive list of the Christian-language programing that may emerge from the needs and outreach of this movement. Part of the job of the servant office is to invent programming that meets the needs of the times for wide learning and wide sharing of what has been learned. Some programming will be directed toward training the co-pastors of this movement. Other programming will be an outreach to the general culture—both sharing with that culture and learning from that culture how to make this co-pastors movement more pertinent to that culture.

# SERVANT OFFICE ORGANIZATION

Organizing a servant office waits on the organization of co-pastors circles and their regional assemblies to support these offices with financing for a hired staff of capable members from the co-pastors network. Meanwhile, some of the programs that a servant office will do later are needed now to organize the co-pastors network. So we can imagine using organizations we have or can create to provide now the currently needed services. In the paragraphs below, I am going to describe how I imagine a fully supported network of servant offices might look and operate.

I imagine a servant office having at least three staff or faculty members who are also movement organizers—men and women who meet these three qualifications: (1) they are members of a co-pastors circle and its regional assembly, (2) they are capable of working at least forty hours a week for the servant office, and (3) they possess the training and skills required to provide the services needed by the co-pastors circle network. So how are these persons chosen? How are they paid? And how is their ongoing work financed?

Let us suppose that three regional assemblies chose to support a servant office. If each regional assembly selects one woman and one man from among their, say, sixty co-pastors to be board members for a servant office, that creates a board of at least six people to set up a servant office. These six hire three persons comprised of at least one man and at least one woman from among the, say, 180 co-pastors that comprise those three regional assemblies.

The salaries for those three persons are raised from those 180 co-pastors. Each co-pastor contributes an average of $1,000 a year ($20 a week) to that cause. Perhaps, in order to foster broad support and avoid dependence on a very few persons, there should be a cap on the amount any one person contributes to this salary fund.

Whatever other money is needed for the office costs and program costs of the servant office is raised by these three staff as part of their ongoing work. That money can be raised from whomever the servant office serves or from those who simply wish to see that service done. This includes both individual donors and organizations that would provide money for this specific work. The three staff members for the servant office annually account to the six-member board of directors—reporting to them the money raised and the expenditures of that money. The board of directors uses a separate monetary account to keep the books on the salary fund and on raising and paying the salaries of these three paid staff. One of those board members will need to be the bookkeeper and two of them sign the monthly salary checks.

The staff of a servant office are accountable to the regional assembles of co-pastors circles served by that office. These three staff do the planning and management of all the detailed expenses for the servant office programming. The staff have responsibility for raising and spending the money needed to research, produce, conduct or distribute these services. The staff do not, however, have to raise their own salaries, but they do have the responsibility to create, conduct, and finance services for the co-pastors circles and services for the general population that these circles support putting into play.

These arrangements can, I believe, maintain the key values we need to keep in place. I am not concerned to standardize the programming or the financial details of any of the above, but I am very concerned to describe the sort of guiding principles that make the financing of these servant offices feasible and appropriate with respect to a set of critical values. Perhaps my deepest concern is to guard against the rise of personality cults within any and all aspects of the political, economic, or cultural life of this co-pastor circle movement. By "personality cult" I mean the sort of polity and economics that characterize the typical independent megachurch—a polity that is similar to the polity of a typical secular dictatorship, mob organization, or any other single-person-centered body of people. A deep value within the best of Christian heritage is the view that our one and only core leader is no one else than Jesus Christ, seen as the human exemplar, whose Holy Spirit can fill any one of us with the leadership qualities needed for our time and place.

The earliest "bishops" of the first-century communities of Christians functioned more like bouncers, whose main task was to throw out of the community any self-appointed charismatic or moralist who was disturbing the primacy of the Jesus Christ revelation. Later "bishops" typically became theoretical and liturgical dogmatists, as well as power brokers. This was a quite different function from those earliest attempts at unity-building leadership roles.

The temptation to drift into a personality-cult type of organization is very strong. And we are still learning what it means to live in surrender to no one other than the Jesus Christ revelation, which calls each of us to be a *servant leader*. I am convinced that we must find ways to move beyond the leadership style of a singular individual of supposed charismatic, theoretical, or moral superiority. Such a group leadership style will be a struggle because charisma, clarity, and moral quality are important gifts to the community and its leadership roles. The key value here is promoting a servant leadership community of spirit-savvy human beings.

We can notice how obedience to a single person can enslave us, while obedience to the Jesus Christ revelation opens us to our *perfect freedom* from self, from others, from law/morality/norms, from doctrine, and from all the other temporal factors in our lives. Any social arrangements of the co-pastors circle network that erodes this *obedient freedom* to the Christ revelation on the part of each and every co-pastor is a pattern I want to see avoided.

## GETTING FROM HERE TO THERE

The above arrangements for organizing and financing servant offices assume an already-well-organized co-pastors network. Between our meager now and that future state of organization, we will need servant-office-type functions to be done by volunteers who are financed differently. For example, the not-for-profit organization Realistic Living has had for decades two or three volunteer staff securing their own self-support, independent of the Realistic Living budget. This organization has raised from a six-hundred-member constituency a set of about two hundred active contributors providing an average of approximately $30,000 a year for the programming expenses of Realistic Living. Such organizational financing is not a sustainable model for the long-range development of the co-pastors-circle movement that I am projecting. In the future, volunteers cannot perform all servant office work. Nevertheless, servant organizations are needed now to assist in movement toward a next Christian expression that, when established, can supply the financial backing needed for a further expansion of these offices.

The immediate need of this movement is organizing co-pastors circles. Five steps for doing that were summarized in the previous chapter. This servant office vision entails an additional scope for the responsibilities involved in taking on the co-pastors calling. Not only does the prospective co-pastor anticipate launching for himself or herself a weekly-meeting nurture practice and a bioregional parish mission, but also planning that longer-range future of regional assemblies and servant offices.

In my own long-range vision for the Northern Americas (that is, Panama to Alaska), I am imagining that by the year 2040, or sooner, there might be fully functional servant offices in the vicinity of at least a dozen urban locations: Mexico City, Dallas/Fort Worth, Denver, Winnipeg, Los Angeles, San Francisco, Portland and Vancouver, Atlanta, New York City, Boston, and Toronto. Each of these offices would serve regional assemblies and co-pastors circles in the vicinity of their continental scope.

From the perspective of our current small beginnings, this vision can seem close to preposterous. But this is precisely what it means to contemplate building a movement of co-pastors circles that is out to foster the establishment of a viable and vital next Christian practice that has a meaningful public face in the cultures of this planet.

If you are a single person who feels called to join or start a co-pastor circle, I am asking you to consider yourself to be that co-pastor circle and begin doing in your bioregion the mission that a co-pastors circle would be doing if it were larger than one person. If you and others are the only circle in your bioregion, you can also consider yourselves the regional assembly for that bioregion. When there exists a second circle in your bioregion who will join you in quarterly meetings, you can then flesh out a full regional assembly. Finally, even more demanding is considering yourself an embryo servant office for your part of the continent until there are enough regional assemblies and co-pastors circles to sustain such an office in its fully fleshed out form.

Strange as this may sound, this entire movement toward a viable and vital next Christian practice begins with any three persons who want to bend history in these general directions. Like biological evolution, this movement begins as tiny cells and moves steadily, and sometimes in leaps, toward larger organisms.

Obviously, all these matters do not have to be solved immediately, but they do need to be anticipated. Those of us who read books like this one and sense ourselves called to organize a movement for a viable and vital next Christianity are volunteering to be concerned about all the following and more: (1) hard-headed financing, (2) maintaining a democratic polity, (3) fostering an open yet stable theological culture, (4) thoroughly realistic ecological and social justice missions of love, (5) effective spirit-healing methods and programs, and (6) embodying an ongoing loving presence that is worthy of our exemplar, Christ Jesus—who is present as a community that presents the presence of Profound Reality and Profound Reality's enduring love for everybody.

# Closing Comments

I REALIZE THAT I have laid out an overwhelming project for which the workers are far too few. And that is not even the most challenging part. Our most challenging issue is that all the Christian colleagues with whom we will work are sinners—"sinners, saved by grace" perhaps, but still sinners.

Everyone of us, including me of course, has his or her own disappointing qualities—places in our lives where particular personality formations have not yet given up their tyranny—including some difficult-to-live-with aspects. At times, we may experience the glory of seeing ourselves and others dying to our most personal estrangements and exposing the true joy of our authentic being; nevertheless, when particular "dying to" topics arise, we are all prone to cop out into distractions, bitterness, cynicisms, postponements, stupidities, and downright meannesses. And this will be true of all the colleagues who are called to this work.

Fortunately, a maturity of spirit does tend to emerge from coming together week after week, honestly confessing our lives and hearing again and again and again the proclamation of our forgiveness—especially as that forgiveness is specifically applied to our next steps toward true humanness. In such intimate relations with one another, we find ourselves required to be more forgiving than we at first wish to be, more patient than the norm with other people's strange lives, and willing to be more truthful than we had so far dreamed of being.

But as Paul, facing these same circumstances, once said, "We press on to the full stature of Christ Jesus." I love that teaching. It helps me realize that perfection is not required right now or ever, yet at the same time, perfection is present right now at the roots of our own lives, and that perfection is calling us to our own meaningful next steps. The joy of the Christian life is in its perpetual arriving, not in you or me or someone else having arrived at perfection. Like high school basketball players, we practice our Christian game every week, in order to play this game better in the real game of our ongoing, ever-changing lives.

The Christian life calls us to a paradoxical sort of glory: complete disengagement into the ever-present Eternal Now and complete engagement in the ever-persistent temporal flow of events. There is no perfection in our disengagement alone, and there is no perfection in our engagement alone. Yet, as we find ourselves simultaneously disengaged in the freedom of the Eternal Now and engaged in the freedom of choices and action within the temporal flow, we are touching that perfection whose Christian name is "Jesus Christ."

The traditional "grace and peace" salutation means wishing our companions transformative happenings and boundless equanimity. From such a root awareness comes our deeds of loving everybody—whoever they are and wherever they are in their own bumpy journeys toward the authenticity in which we can all share.

# Appendix A

## An Art-Form Conversation Method

AFTER SEEING A MOVIE, viewing a painting, or experiencing some other form of art in a group setting, an effective conversation can be held using a method that probes the depth of that experience. Rather than going directly to interpretation or general comments of meaning with regard to that art experience, a more useful approach is to postpone the interpretive aspect of the discussion until the group has done some objective questions about the experience and then some reflective questions that probe the emotional or personal responses to this art form.

So picture yourself leading this conversation with a group of twenty-five or fewer people who have seen a movie together. Seat them in a circle or a set of concentric circles, so that you can easily conduct a "go-round" sequence of questions in which each person, one after the other, is asked a question about this art form experience.

This art-form discussion method uses three types of questions: *objective*, *reflective*, and *interpretive*—used in that order:

An *objective* question is about something we actually saw, or heard.

A *reflective* question is about emotional or feeling responses.

An *interpretive* question is about rational meanings or understandings.

Following are examples of questions that you might ask in a typical movie conversation:

# OBJECTIVE QUESTIONS

*In a go-round order ask each of a number of persons:*
Name a scene that you remember?
*Ask a few more continuing in go-round order:*
What objects do you recall?
*Continue for a few more persons in go-round order:*
What sounds did you hear?
*Continue for a few more in go-round order:*
What lines of speech can you recall?
It is important to ask these questions in rather quick succession—taking quick answers and moving on. The point is to create a group memory of what "all of us" have actually seen and heard.

# REFLECTIVE QUESTIONS

*Continue a few more in go-round order:*
Where did you notice strong feeling expressed in the movie?
*Then ask that person the following:*
What was being felt there?
*Continue a few more in go-round order:*
Where did you have strong feeling?
*Then ask that same person:*
What feeling did you have?
*Continue a few more in go-round order:*
Which character did you dislike the most?
*Ask a few more in go round order:*
Which character did you identify with most?

## INTERPRETIVE QUESTIONS

Ask *a few more in go-round order:*

In what scene did a transformation happen to a character?

*Then ask that person:*

Describe how the transformation happened.

Ask *a few more in go-round order:*

What was this movie about for you?

*Shift to popcorn participation and take three or four answers:*

What name would you give to this story?

## THEOLOGICAL QUESTIONS

*If you want to do theological interpretation, here are some useful questions to use after the general interpretive discussion has been concluded. Save time of this, for you will want at least ten minutes to do this part of the discussion. Use these questions with three or four volunteers:*

Where in this movie did you see a character manifesting Sin?

*After a specific scene has been identified, ask:*

And what do you mean by Sin?

*Use these questions with three or four volunteers:*

Where in this movie did you see a character having a Grace Happening?

*After a specific scene has been identified, ask:*

And what do you mean by a Grace Happening?


More questions and different questions may fit your group, or your movie, or perhaps some other type of art form than a movie. The above questions are only examples of the overall method. Every application of this method can be unique to the occasion. This art form method is an illustration of how conversation methods, well led, can be effective means of grace.

# Appendix B

## A Communion Meal Ritual

**Leader:** We are gathered here to remember our true humanity, which was manifest in Jesus, the Christ, who lived life as a gift, who gave himself as a servant of all, who served the Truth and the Truth alone.

**All: We pray to the One to whom all hearts are open, all desires known, and from whom no secrets are hid: Cleanse our hearts that our words may flow in truth and our deeds in love and freedom. Amen.**

**Leader:** Let us humbly confess our falling away from our true essence.

**All: We have forgotten that our lives are a gift; instead we have lived from closed and resentful hearts.**
**We have ignored our call to be servants of all; instead we have sought honor and status.**
**We have suppressed the Truth; instead we have sought power and control.**

**Leader:** Nevertheless, mercy is extended to us this day. Jesus the Christ proclaims to us that our entire lives are forgiven. No matter what our failings have been or still are, we are welcome home today to a new beginning in being who we are. Amen.

**Witness:** (*A member of the group shares a meditation on the meaning for him or her on this particular day of eating the broken body and drinking the spilled blood of those who have lived their lives that*

*our spirits may be healed, and who have called us to offer our
own bodies and blood for the healing of humankind.)*

**Leader:** Jesus said, "I am the bread of life. She who comes to me shall
never hunger; he who believes in me shall never thirst."

**All: Amen.**

**Leader:** *(Breaks the bread)* The broken body of Jesus, the Christ.
*(Passes half the loaf to the person on the leader's left who breaks
a piece for the leader and passes it to the next person who breaks
it for him or her, etc.)*

**Leader:** *(Pours some wine)* The spilt blood of Jesus, the Christ.
*(Passes the bottle to the person on the left who pours a small
portion for the leader and then passes it to the next person who
pours for him or her, etc.)*

**Leader:** As the bread and wine are passed, let us offer our prayers of
petition and intercession.

**Leader:** *(After all have been served and prayers ceased)* Let us pray.

**All: Oh Ground of our being, we give thanks for your eternal
love and healing presence in our celebration of bread and
wine. Bless this Body of Christ that we may attend faithfully
to our call to be your servants for each other, for humanity
throughout the world, and for the planet that you have given
us. Amen.**

**Leader:** Let us feast.

# About the Author

GENE WESLEY MARSHALL BEGAN his education at Oklahoma State University as a mathematician and physicist. In 1953 he decided to leave a mathematics career and attend seminary at Perkins School of Theology in Dallas, Texas. He served as a local church pastor, a chaplain in the army, and in 1962 joined a religious order of families (the order:Ecumenical). For six years he served as dean of the Ecumenical Institute's eight-week residential Academy that trained leadership for religious and social engagement work with participants from many parts of the world. In the early 1960s he was an active participant in the civil rights revolution, serving for one year as the Protestant executive of the National Conference on Religion and Race. As a faculty member of the Ecumenical Institute, he also traveled the United States, Latin America, Europe, India, Hong Kong, and Australia as a teacher and lecturer of religious and social ethics topics. These trips included an in-depth study of world cultures and a view of the social conditions of the world's peoples. In the mid 1980s he was one of the organizers of the bioregional movement. Beginning in 1983 Gene and Joyce Marshall organized a nonprofit educational organization, Realistic Living, and began co-teaching innovative programs and workshops plus publishing journals, books, and essays. This book is Gene's ninth book-length project. Joyce and Gene live in Bonham, Texas in a straw-bale house.

# Bibliography

Adyashanti. *Emptiness Dancing*. Boulder, CO: Sounds True, 2006.

Almaas, A. H. *Essence; with The Elixir of Enlightenment*. York Beach, ME: Samuel Weiser, 1984.

———. *Void: Inner Spaciousness and Ego Structure*. Berkley, CA: Diamond, 1986.

Aslan, Reza. *No God but God: The Origins, Evolution, and Future of Islam*. New York: Random House, 2011.

Berg, Peter. *The Biosphere and the Bioregion: Essential Writings of Peter Berg*. Edited by Cheryll Glotfelty and Eve Quesnet. New York: Routledge, 2015.

Bernie, Jon. *The Unbelievable Happiness of What Is*. Oakland, CA: Non-Duality, 2017.

Berry, Thomas. *The Dream of the Earth*. San Francisco: Sierra Club Books, 1988.

———. *The Great Work: Our Way into the Future*. New York: Bell Tower, 1999.

Berry, Wendell. *Life Is a Miracle: An Essay against Modern Superstition*. Washington, DC: Counterpoint, 2000.

———. *The Unsettling of America: Culture and Agriculture*. New York: Avon, 1977.

Bonhoeffer, Dietrich. *Ethics*. New York: Macmillan, 1955

———. *Life Together*. New York: Harper and Row, 1954.

Boulding, Kenneth E. *The Meaning of the 20th Century: The Great Transition*. New York: Harper and Row, 1965.

Brueggemann, Walter. *Hopeful Imagination: Prophetic Voices in Exile*. Philadelphia: Fortress, 1988.

Bultmann, Rudolf. *Jesus and the Word*. New York: Scribner, 1958.

———. *Kerygma and Myth*. New York: Harper, 1961.

———. *Primitive Christianity: In Its Contemporary Setting*. New York: Meridian, 1956.

Carr, Mike. *Bioregionalism and Civil Society: Democratic Challenges to Corporate Globalism*. Toronto: UBC Press, 2004.

Cone, James H. *Risks of Faith: The Emergence of a Black Theology of Liberation, 1968–1998*. Boston: Beacon, 1999.

Dramm, Sabrine. *Dietrich Bonhoeffer: An Introduction to His Thought*. Peabody, MA: Hendrickson, 2007. English translation from original German, 2001.

Feynmann, Richard. *The Character of Physical Law*. Chambridge, MA: MIT Press, 1995.

Gutieerrez, Gustovo. *A Theology of Liberation: History, Politics, and Salvation*. New York: Orbis, 1985.

Hall, Douglas John. *The End of Christendom and the Future of Christianity*. Valley Forge, PA: Trinity, 1997.

Hammann, Konrad. *Rudolf Bultmann: A Biography*. Salem, OR: Polbridge, 2013.

Kazantzakis, Nikos. *The Saviors of God*. New York: Simon and Schuster, 1960.

Kierkegaard, Søren. *Fear and Trembling and The Sickness unto Death*. Princeton, NJ: Princeton University Press, 1954.

———. *Training in Christianity*. Princeton, NJ: Princeton University Press, 1944.

Klein, Naomi. *No Is Not Enough: Resisting Trump's Shock Politics and Winning the World We Need*. Chicago, IL: Haymarket, 2017.

———. *This Changes Everything: Capitalism vs. the Climate*. New York: Simon and Schuster, 2014.

Langer, Susanne K. *Philosophy in a New Key*. New York: Mentor, 1942.

Marshall, Gene W. *The Call of Awe: Rediscovering Christian Profundity in an Inter-Religious Era*. New York: iUniverse, 2003.

———. *The Creator of Christianity: A Commentary on the Gospel of Mark*. Bonham, TX: Realistic Living, 2018.

———. *Great Paragraphs of Protestant Theology*. Bonham, TX: Realistic Living, 2005.

———. *Jacob's Dream: A Christian Inquiry into Spirit Realization*. New York: iUniverse, 2003.

———. *The Love of History and the Future of Christianity*. Lutz, FL: Resurgence, 2011.

———. *Radical Gifts: Living the Full Christian Life in Troubled Times*. Kelowna, BC: WoodLake, 2018.

Marshall, Gene W., Ben Ball, Marsha Buck, Ken Kruetziger, and Alan Richard. *The Road from Empire to Eco-Democracy*. New York: iUniverse and Open Book edition of Berrett-Koehler, 2011.

Mathews, Joseph W. *Bending History: Talks of Joseph Wesley Mathews*. Edited by John L. Epps. Lutz, FL: Resurgence, 2005.

———. *Bending History: Talks of Joseph Wesley Mathews, Volume II*. Edited by John L. Epps. Lutz, FL: Resurgence, 2011.

Merton, Thomas. *The Way of Chuang Tzu*. New York: New Directions, 1969.

Niebuhr, H. Richard. *Christ and Culture*. New York: Harper and Row, 1951.

———. *The Meaning of Revelation*. New York: Macmillan, 1941.

———. *The Responsible Self*. New York: Harper and Row, 1963.

———. *Radical Monotheism and Western Culture*. New York: Harper and Row, 1960.

Orr, David W. *Dangerous Years: Climate Change, the Long Emergency, and the Way Forward*. New Haven, CT: Yale University Press, 2016

Powers, Richard. *The Overstory: A Novel*. New York: Norton, 2018.

Robbins, Jeffrey. *In Search for a Non-Dogmatic Theology*. Aurora, CO: Davis Group, 2003.

Roszak, Theodore. *Person/Planet: The Creative Disintegration of Industrial Society*. Garden City, NY: Anchor, 1978.

Rubinstein, Mary Jane. *Strange Wonder: The Closure of Metaphysics and the Opening of Awe*. New York: Columbia University Press, 2008.

Scott, David Sanborn. *Smelling Land: The Hydrogen Defense against Climate Catastrophe*. Canadian Hydrogen Association, 2007.

Soelle, Dorothee. *Political Theology*. Minneapolis: Fortress, 1974.

Spretnak, Charlene. *Lost Goddesses of Early Greece: A Collection of Pre-Hellenic Myths*. Boston: Beacon, 1978.

———. *States of Grace*. New York: Harper Collins, 1991.

———. *Relational Reality: New Discoveries of Interrelatedness That Are Transforming the Modern World*. Topsham, ME: Green Horizon, 2011.

Thurman, Howard. *Jesus and the Disinherited*. Boston: Beacon, 1976.

Tillich, Paul. *The Courage to Be*. New Haven, CT: Yale University Press, 1952.

———. *A History of Christian Thought*. New York: Harper and Row, 1968.

———. *The Irrelevance and Relevance of the Christian Message*. Edited by Durwood Foster. Eugene, OR: Wipf and Stock, 2007.

———. *Love, Power, and Justice*. New York: Oxford University Press, 1960.

———. *The Shaking of the Foundations*. New York: Scribner, 1948.

———. *What Is Religion?* New York: Harper, 1973.

Tollison, Joan. *Bare-Bones Meditation: Waking Up from the Story of My Life*. New York: Bell Tower, 1992.

Watts, Alan. *Out of Your Mind*. Bolder, CO: Sounds True, 2017.

Wilber, Ken. *A Brief History of Everything*. Boston: Shambhala, 1996.